AF896793

Economic Planning for the Peace

Economic Planning for the Peace

BY E. F. PENROSE

PRINCETON, NEW JERSEY
PRINCETON UNIVERSITY PRESS
1953

London: Geoffrey Cumberlege, Oxford University Press
L.C. Card 52-8776

Printed in the United States of America
by Princeton University Press at Princeton, New Jersey

IN MEMORIAM

John Gilbert Winant

PREFACE

THIS work is a blend of analysis with a record of experience. It follows, therefore, that I am indebted to many persons, both in the realm of thought and in the realm of action, and there is no hope that all my debts can be acknowledged individually.

The greatest of them is to the late Ambassador John Gilbert Winant, whom I served as economic adviser in nearly nine years of international work. The dedication of this book conveys but imperfectly my sense of the magnitude of this debt. Although I shared his ideals and worked in close harmony with him, it should not, of course, be assumed that he would necessarily have agreed with all the views expressed in the following pages. It will be understood, also, that the references to him are related only to the particular theme of this book and cover only a small part of his astonishingly diversified activities in public life.

To the Institute of Advanced Study, Princeton, where the first draft plan of this study was made, I am indebted for appointing me as a member in 1947, and to Professors Winfield Riefler and Walter Stewart and the late Professor Robert Warren for profitable discussions during my stay in the Institute.

The subsequent development of the study took place after my appointment as B. Howell Griswold Jr. Professor of Geography and International Relations at the Johns Hopkins University. But for the time and facilities for research and writing which, on the initiative of the late Dr. Isaiah Bowman, were made available to me by this appointment, this book could not have been produced. Dr. Bowman, with whom I had already discussed postwar plans in 1944 in London, showed a keen interest in the progress of the manuscript up to the time of his death and was particularly helpful on questions relating to the attitude at "top levels" towards the dismemberment of Germany. I am indebted also to a number of postgraduate students in economic geography and economics for the stimulus of many discussions on postwar economic events.

In recent years my outlook on international trade and finance has been influenced by the writings of, and by conversations (which began in my prewar Geneva days) with Mr. Folke Hilgerdt, formerly of the League of Nations, now of the United Nations Secretariat. In his *Network of World Trade* he opened up, to my mind, one of the most promising approaches yet made to international economics. My debt to him is particularly apparent in a chapter included in an earlier draft dealing with the period beyond that to which later it was decided to limit this book; nevertheless the outlook in parts of this study has been influenced by his approach to international trade.

For the laborious work of typing a succession of draft manuscripts I am indebted to Dorothy Elliott, Mary Jane Langrall, Gladys Parker, and Frances Young.

To my wife, Edith Tilton Penrose, I am indebted for reading and criticizing the successive drafts, notwithstanding her preoccupation at the same time with a manuscript of her own—which, however, absolves me from the obligation to add the customary apology for many hours of silence.

E.F.P.

August 1952

Contents

Economic Planning
for the Peace

INTRODUCTION

THE Second World War lasted six years and the end, when it came, was not, like the end of the First World War, unexpected. There was time to plan for the peace, and planning began early. Some of the plans were completed before the war ended and were quickly put into effect, saving Europe from starvation in some areas and economic breakdown in others. But the plans and preparations as a whole fell far short of what was needed to restore the world to economic health.

This study seeks to determine how it was that, notwithstanding the warnings that might have been taken from the First World War, and the time, the energy, and the resources that were given to postwar planning, economic disaster came early in Germany and was narrowly averted in 1947 and 1948 in the rest of Europe. It is not an "academic" study. It uses no technical terms and trespasses freely outside economic boundaries, assuming that it is better to fall into error in the pursuit of a trail wherever it leads than to remain impeccable by staying within narrow and conventional limits. The minds and the emotions of men and the affairs of nations are not to be subdivided into compartments corresponding to the "subjects" or "social sciences" into which it is now fashionable to divide academic studies. These pages are addressed, therefore, not only to those whose special interests lie in international economics but also to general readers who are concerned above all with the means of avoiding in the second half of the twentieth century the worldwide disorders of the first half. Economic measures are only one part of a comprehensive remedy, but in an interdependent world international economic harmony is one of the conditions of international political harmony.

The present work has its origin in two memoranda. The first, which is reproduced in Chapter VII, was written in April 1944 in the United States Embassy in London, at the suggestion of members of a visiting State Department mission on postwar questions. It described the position then reached in postwar international economic planning, pointed out the gaps that remained, and suggested means by which they might be filled. The second was written at the Institute for Advanced Study, Princeton, in the summer of 1947, just after I had left Government service. It was an extension of the first in the light of events between 1944 and 1947 and was intended as a basis for a short book to be completed within the year.

The death of Ambassador Winant in November 1947 led to a change in these plans. Finding that the Ambassador had scarcely begun the second book which he had planned to write, and which presumably would have discussed at least part of the economic as well as the political planning in London after 1941, I decided to enlarge the scope of my study, to trace the development of postwar international economic plans from their origins and to account as nearly as I could for what, since the opening of 1944, had seemed to me to be serious errors of omission and a faulty sense of proportion in the planning.

Any writer who attempts such a study will be inescapably influenced by the position and circumstances in which he was placed during the war and immediate postwar years. This both sets limits to and at the same time largely determines the positive contribution of the study. Since I was economic adviser to Ambassador Winant during the war and early postwar years, this work inevitably reflects for most of the period a more detailed knowledge of persons and events in London than of those in Washington and Ottawa, which also played leading roles in the planning. At a number of critical points, however, I have had to reconstruct the course of events in Washington from records of personal discussions there during visits on consultation, from information derived from Ambassador Winant, from later conversations with former colleagues in government service and from the memoirs and records which have been published since the war. Nevertheless it has been impracticable to attempt as intimate an account of the personal aspects of the development of postwar plans in Washington and Ottawa as of those in London. The gaps should be put down to limited experience and not to lack of appreciation or of goodwill. Much of the inside history of Washington can be written only by those who were there during the whole of the war.

The historian of the future will be able to put together from a variety of contemporary accounts and interpretations of events a far more complete picture than any contemporary observer can hope to produce. But the stage is not yet fully set for him. Meanwhile his task will be lightened and in the end his account will come closer to reality if some of those who observed events directly from various points of view will set down their versions while their memory of the events is still clear. Notwithstanding all that has been written there is still room for further studies of the detailed circumstances in which the important decisions on postwar questions were made. The present work offers some new evidence and interpretations based largely on experiences in London at a point through which most of the exchanges between Washington and London passed.

Since my central thesis is that the economic errors of the peace were the outcome of omissions and a faulty sense of proportion in planning for different aspects of postwar international economic activities, it is necessary, for purposes of exposition, to adopt a broad classification of these activities. For convenience I have divided them into three main categories, among which there is much overlapping but each of which embodies a distinct function and type of activity. The first may be called relief, consisting in the provision of consumer goods, some of which are essential to the preservation of life and others to the restoration or maintenance of working capacity. The second is reconstruction, which includes the restoration of stocks of raw materials, the supply of new equipment, the rebuilding of destroyed or damaged areas, and the reconversion and reorganization of such parts of agriculture, industry, transport, and finance as were deranged or retarded during the war. The third consists in permanent or standing measures of international economic organization, designed to meet the continuing needs of international economic life in times of peace.

Another category, of which I have made only slight use, is that of rehabilitation, which may be taken to consist mainly in immediate repairs to damaged or worn equipment, in the supply of spare parts to existing equipment, and in the restoration of essential services as far as practicable and mainly with existing equipment. For many if not most purposes rehabilitation may be subsumed partly under relief and partly under reconstruction. Nevertheless, the distinction is occasionally useful, especially when scarcity of resources limits the scope of reconstruction.

The period to be covered by the study and the form of organization of the material raised serious difficulties from the start. As I wrote, the events of the postwar world seemed to be confirming the criticisms made in the memorandum written in 1944: but at the same time an astonishingly bold and statesmanlike measure was taking shape to meet the gaps in preparations for the postwar period. Absorbed in the unfolding of this great international plan, I extended my study beyond the war period to cover the important events of the first five years of the postwar period during which the wartime plans were tested by experience. But this swelled the manuscript to an inconvenient length for a single book and led to an uneven treatment of the two periods, in the first of which I observed events from inside government and in the second from outside.

The present study, therefore, apart from a few paragraphs in the summing up, closes roughly at the position reached in the early months of 1947, when the full effects of the gaps in postwar planning were showing themselves, when Britain was moving toward an external financial crisis, when Western and Southern and a large part of Central Europe were in sight of general economic collapse, when the European Recovery Program had not yet taken definite shape, and when the international economic outlook was bleaker than at any time since the fighting had ceased in Europe. The turn of the tide began later in the year and is touched on very briefly in a closing chapter. Thus, except for a few paragraphs in the last chapter, the present study is confined to the period in which I was able to follow events from the "inside."

The arrangement of the diverse materials which had to be included was even more difficult than the choice of the period to be covered. The first draft was an attempt at a more or less chronological approach after the manner of most of the political studies of wartime experiences, such as those of Mr. Sherwood, Mr. Stimson, and Mr. Hull. The results were more intelligible to readers already familiar with part of the ground covered than to readers with little or no previous experience of any of it. A chronological approach represents more closely than any other the conditions in which postwar plans were prepared and executed. But it confuses the general reader by frequently switching his attention abruptly from one part of its field to another, thus increasing the difficulties of tracing developments in any single subdivision.

After the study had been rewritten several times, the chapters dealing with events up to the end of the war in Europe were arranged in three broad groups divided roughly according to the classification described earlier. The first deals with long-term measures of international economic organization and is in turn divided into subgroups dealing with international finance and investment, international raw material agreements, and international commerce. The second deals with relief and is divided into subgroups dealing with food relief and with the establishment of an international relief organization. The third deals with reconstruction and is divided into subgroups dealing with reconstruction in liberated Allied countries and reconstruction—positive or negative—in ex-enemy countries. In each of the subdivisions a chronological approach has been followed.

Before the middle of 1943, postwar planning was not so sharply divided into these categories as it became later, but the drift was in that direction and ultimately, except for some overlapping between relief and reconstruction in Allied countries, these groups, and to a large extent the subgroups, correspond roughly to the groups into which the civil servants who took part in postwar international economic planning were divided. The separation of civil servants into those concerned only with long-run questions and those concerned only with short-run questions was a striking feature of the organization of economic postwar planning and itself influenced the course of the planning.

There is one exception to this scheme of organization. Chapter VII, on the Hot Springs Food and Agricultural Conference, analyzes an approach to postwar planning in which questions of the long run and questions of the short run were treated simultaneously, and the reports and resolutions dealing with them were carefully coordinated. This was the only outstanding case of its kind during the period of postwar planning.

The scheme of organization followed in the chapters on postwar planning during the war has been modified in the chapters dealing with the two years after fighting ceased in Europe. In the formulation of postwar plans during the war, political opportunities and the ideas and interests of the leading civil servants went far to determine the direction of the planning and the sequence in which the plans were made. In the application of the plans and the improvisation of new plans after the war, immediate needs and pressing economic events were the predominant influence. This contrast should not be pressed too far. During the war economic necessity influenced the planning at some points, and after the war political obstacles for some time hindered the preparation or application of appropriate economic plans even when the need for them was demonstrated. But with these qualifications the contrast holds good, and the order of treatment and extent of discussion of the different topics has been somewhat modified in the later chapters. Long-run questions, instead of holding first place as they had done in the planning during the war, sank into the background in the face of short-run emergencies, though perhaps not as far as they should have done. Gradually the realization grew after April, 1945, that economic chaos in Germany, Britain's immediate balance-of-payments difficulties, and subsequently the impending economic breakdown in Europe, should take precedence.

Notwithstanding the stress laid in these pages on errors of omission and commission, especially the former, the aim of this study is not destructive nor iconoclastic, and the merits as well as the defects of postwar planning have been discussed. In the present state of political witch hunting in Washington it may be too much to expect that no one will attempt to misuse any statements in this book to serve partisan ends in an unscrupulous pursuit of power. Yet the motives for the criticisms of persons and policies contained in the following pages lie not in political partisanship nor, it may be hoped, in personal likes and dislikes, but partly in economic judgments and partly in beliefs about values.

In tracing the details of postwar planning and its outcome the question will recur again and again to those who wish to penetrate below the surface of events, whether or not the record justifies the hope that human societies will accumulate the knowledge and develop the wisdom, the moral sense, and the capacity to act, through which alone they can profit by past experience and avoid the repetition of old errors and the commission of new errors in the future. Twice within the span of a generation we have been plunged into world conflicts which have brought unimaginable disaster to millions of human lives. Each time the survivors have been given a reprieve and an opportunity to reconstruct the world in a new image. Each time the task of reconstruction in a more densely populated, more specialized and more interdependent world has increased in complexity, requiring greater knowledge and executive capacity, greater integrity and magnanimity. The limitations of human foresight may excuse some of the errors of the peace. But others might have been avoided by a proper interpretation of the past. Unfortunately, it is immensely more difficult for large societies than it is for individuals or small groups to profit from past errors. The interpretation of past experience is difficult enough in itself and may be possible only for trained minds. But even when a small number of individuals agree on a reasonable interpretation, a long and difficult road must be traversed before their interpretation is accepted by the mass of their fellow countrymen, most of whom never study the past, or by the government of their country, preoccupied with day-to-day events. Too often the politician heeds past experience only so far as he can extract from it an interpretation, however spurious, which can be pressed into the support of ulterior aims of his own. The last state may then be worse than the first; it is often better to ignore the past than to misinterpret it. Moreover, an excessive anxiety to avoid a repetition of the disasters of the past may hinder preparations to avoid new disasters of a different kind in the future, as it did among those military general staffs who gave their main energies in the interwar period to preparing for a new war on the same lines as the old.

But these difficulties do not excuse the fatalistic, cynical, and defeatist attitudes which permeate American politics today. They should spur us to greater efforts to determine why the counsels of wiser men are so often discarded by or never reach the ears of those in positions of political authority, and why certain forms of supposedly democratic government are retained which give undue opportunities to selfish and obstructive minorities that place themselves in opposition to international measures. They should lead us also to inquire into the widespread belief that human nature in politics can never be changed, that he who aspires to political office must inevitably pander to the prejudices of the ignorant and the pressures of selfish interests, and that the man of culture, integrity, and intellectual attainments, with rare exceptions, is and always will be out of place in political life.

For the economic successes and failures of the peace were political successes and failures and had their origin not only in the adequacies and inadequacies of economic and political knowledge and judgment but also in the characters of the individuals who made the political decisions and of those who influenced them in their choices among alternative courses of action.

CHAPTER I

Negotiating a Text for Postwar Sermons

THE First World War ended suddenly and unexpectedly and caught the statesmen in Allied countries unprepared with plans either for relief or for reconstruction. Widespread human misery followed, much of which, with foresight, could have been prevented.

During the Second World War, government officials in London and Washington were anxious to prevent a repetition of this error, but in the earlier part of the war great difficulties stood in the way of open and concerted economic preparation for the peace. With the abrupt end of military inactivity on the Western front in the spring of 1940, popular sentiment in Great Britain was directed toward winning the war; and, since the United Kingdom was fighting against heavy odds, it could not be expected that a ready ear would be turned towards proposals for postwar measures. When Pearl Harbor awakened the American people to international realities there was a sharp revulsion in Washington political circles against any discussion of postwar matters, as the magnitude of the task of winning the war came to be realized. By this time Whitehall had begun to study postwar questions, but it was difficult to begin Anglo-American discussions of the difficult and urgent questions that might be expected to arise on a small scale as soon as any of the Allied countries was liberated and on a large scale when the war in any one theater or in all theaters came to an end.

At this stage the supreme objective was to draw a full and united war effort from all sections of people in the British Empire and the United States. It was easier to obtain unity in the war effort than unity in the larger objectives to be pursued after victory. In 1942 it seemed to many that the war position of the Allies was so unfavorable that no risks of disunity among political parties should be run by stirring up public discussion of the social and economic questions of the future peace. It was not, indeed, supposed that controversies on the subject would turn any parties or significant sections of the people against the war effort. But it was feared privately by many political leaders that controversies in the legislatures and among the public on postwar questions would distract attention from the task of bringing the war effort to its highest pitch, and would create in the outside world an appearance of disunity that would encourage the enemy. For some time these fears seemed to dominate the minds of the administration leaders in Washington, particularly since the increasing Republican minority, aided by the conservative section of the Democrats, were prone to identify constructive postwar planning with the spirit of the New Deal which had aroused their ire in domestic affairs.

The appointment of John Gilbert Winant as Ambassador to the United Kingdom in succession to an extreme isolationist, Joseph Kennedy, brought a new spirit into Anglo-American relationships through the Embassy in London and greatly influenced the course of discussions on postwar questions.

Ambassador Winant came to his post with wide interests and experience in international as well as national affairs, and in economic as well as political affairs. To him the outbreak of war was an occasion not for suspending public concern with economic and social questions but rather for reexamining the existing order to determine how far past shortcomings had contributed to present strife. He did not believe that political settlements in themselves could provide an enduring basis for peaceful international relationships, and he knew that economic settlements would require long and arduous preparation if the errors made after the First World War were not to be repeated. Although he was well aware of the political pitfalls in Washington which held back the administration, particularly after the Pearl Harbor disaster, from raising controversial issues on peacetime questions while the Allied arms were suffering reverses at the front, he took every opportunity, from an early stage in the war, to advise the State Department and sometimes the White House to take constructive action on a variety of postwar international economic matters.[1]

In London, Ottawa, and Washington small groups of civil servants played a large part in the initiation as well as in the detailed prepara-

[1] Numerous incoming telegrams in the State Department files will be available to the future historian in confirmation of this.

tion of plans for the postwar period. They were made up of an effective combination of permanent officials and of temporary officials who were drawn into government service for the war period, and some of whom were outstanding economists. The union of these two types of officials in wartime was fruitful in many ways: not only were the newcomers able to fill gaps which could not be filled from the ranks of permanent officials, but the experience and the intellectual equipment of each type supplemented those of the other to the advantage of both of them. No such array of economic talent had ever before been mobilized in the service of government in the three capitals.

The first impetus toward the discussion of postwar economic questions between the U.S. and the U.K. came from the system of Lend-Lease or, as it subsequently became, Mutual Aid. This brilliant conception of President Roosevelt's was one of the greatest achievements of the war. It was designed not only to assist in the war effort but also to avoid such burdensome commitments to repay as were foisted on the United Kingdom during and after the First World War, and which were a source of discord through the interwar period. From the beginning there was not only a desire but also a determination to avoid a repetition of this experience which had contributed to the Second World War by giving a pretext for the passing of the mischievous Johnson Act which banned loans to countries that had not paid the debts contracted in the First World War.

In the summer of 1941, when Keynes visited Washington, the State Department was drafting clauses to complete the text of the agreement to be negotiated with the United Kingdom and subsequently with other Allies, which would specify the obligations arising out of Lend-Lease operations. Although most of the clauses in the agreement were concerned with the forms of mutual aid to be undertaken by the parties, the framework of postwar settlement of the balance of mutual aid had to be dealt with, at least in general terms. The article relating to this happened to be the seventh in the agreement: hence the term "Article VII," which will recur frequently in the following pages and which came into everyday use among the planners who worked on postwar international economic questions in London, Washington, Ottawa, and Canberra.

If commitments to repay or replace the balance of goods received were to be avoided an alternative form of settlement acceptable to the United States Congress had to be devised. This article inevitably raised postwar economic questions and was the subject of long and strenuous discussions in and negotiations between London and Washington. In Washington at the outset some officials wished to demand political concessions from the United Kingdom, particularly the cession of military and air bases, and others wished to demand unilateral economic concessions. But wiser counsels were accepted in the formation of U.S. policy and it was realized that obligations must be common to both sides. The original draft was revised many times in the course of internal discussions and of negotiations with the United Kingdom. Its chief provisions were that in the settlement of obligations arising out of the Lend-Lease Act no conditions should be laid down which would obstruct commerce, but agreement should be reached on measures to reduce trade barriers and to abolish preferential duties.

But the economic position of the United Kingdom was changing and some of the effects of the change were not yet fully realized in Washington. Before the war a proposal to remove preferential duties in the United Kingdom would have led to a division of opinion mainly on political party lines. But a striking new factor had to be taken into account in 1941. The United Kingdom, unable to raise loans in the United States because of discriminatory legislation adopted by Congress, had been obliged to sell the greater part of its marketable liquid foreign assets to obtain dollars. This created a difficult postwar problem even for those British circles which before the war had opposed imperial preferences. It was left to the great British economist, John Maynard Keynes, who had been appointed as adviser to the Chancellor of the Exchequer, to state it forcibly in Washington in the summer of 1941 on a visit arranged by Ambassador Winant. With his customary vigor Mr. Keynes spoke plainly on the implications for postwar policy of the liquidation of the foreign investments of the United Kingdom to pay for orders placed in the United States during the period of the "cash and carry" policy. An appreciable proportion of U.K. imports before the war had been offset by the returns on past investments abroad. The loss of these investments, he pointed out, would force Great Britain to export considerably more after the war if the same level of imports was to be maintained. But he added, "imports do not automatically breed exports," particularly at times when an appreciable proportion of the productive resources of the richer countries are in a state of chronic unemployment or underemployment. Consequently it was probable, said Keynes, that Britain would be obliged for some time after the war to make bilateral commercial arrangements with other countries, providing for the acceptance of British exports by countries supplying Britain with its essential imports. Exchange control would also have to be maintained for a considerable period to limit total imports and to discriminate between essential and unessential imports.

These views were disturbing to official Washington in the summer of 1941. One of the most active and well organized divisions in the State Department was the Division of Commercial Policy and Trade Agreements. The Reciprocal Trade Agreements Act and its applications in a series of commercial treaties were almost the only exceptions to a general advance of trade restrictions during the 1930's. The division was headed by Harry Hawkins, who had worked closely with Secretary Hull on commercial policy for a decade, and who combined an exact and detailed knowledge of trade policy with great ability and long experience in international trade negotiations. The outbreak of war had not dimmed his belief and that of his staff in the desirability of freer trading among nations. They held that trade restrictions and economic warfare in peacetime were a danger to international harmony not less important than political antagonism, and that as much as possible should be done even during the war to clear the way for freer trade in time of peace.

In August I was called to Washington to receive from Dean Acheson, then Assistant Secretary of State, and from Harry Hawkins and convey to Mr. Winant an account of the questions which had arisen during Mr. Keynes's visit and of the attitude of the State Department on them. An impasse appeared to have been reached between Washington and London on what at the time appeared to us to be one of the most important aspects of postwar policy. On the flight to Lisbon I discussed postwar difficulties with Professor Alvin Hansen, the distinguished economist of Harvard University, and Dr. Luther Gulick, who were visiting London for a few days to address a scientific meeting. We agreed that in any discussions with Mr. Keynes it would be wise to accept unreservedly the view that, after postwar reconstruction had been completed the chances of freer trade would be lost unless a high level of employment were maintained. Hansen and Gulick rendered valuable service by showing Keynes that there were Americans who were equally concerned with him about the necessity of placing full employment as high as free trade among the prerequisites for the postwar economic order. However, Keynes remained unconvinced of the adequacy of any measures proposed up to that time to deal with Britain's balance-of-payments difficulties. Nor did Whitehall take an optimistic view of the ability of the United States to maintain full employment in peacetime.

In September Ambassador Winant requested the State Department to postpone discussion of Article VII, in view of urgent war questions that were absorbing all the energies of the government. The postponement enabled officials in London and Washington to reconsider the draft article. In Washington, Redvers Opie, economic adviser to Ambassador Halifax, held "off the record" discussions with Dr. Leo Pasvolsky, Secretary Hull's adviser, and Harry Hawkins. In London I engaged in similar informal conversations, first with a few of the younger economists who were close friends of Mr. Keynes, and later with Mr. Keynes.[2] Such informal and unobtrusive exchanges of personal views on postwar matters continued throughout the war, helping to clear the way for organized, official negotiations, removing misunderstandings, keeping a small and discreet group of officials in each capital in touch with the development of thought among their counterparts in the other and establishing a spirit of cooperation in a common Allied cause.

At the outset Keynes stressed the difficulties that would beset Britain when Lend-Lease ended. It could not be expected, he said, that increased exports sufficient to pay for those imports which had previously been offset by earnings on foreign investments would be "automatically generated by the price system." At the end of the war Britain would be more damaged and would start with a greater reconversion problem than most if not all her industrial competitors who were not ex-enemy countries. His impression was that in spite of his explanations the seriousness of the position was not appreciated in Washington.

[2] Throughout the rest of the war I exchanged personal views frequently with Mr. Keynes: we discussed war and postwar economic issues fully and frankly. When particularly important economic issues arose both the Ambassador and I would spend an evening in discussion with Keynes, free from interruption.

This was a strong case which needed a more comprehensive reply than it had yet received. Unfortunately, there were formidable political difficulties to be faced. The proper remedy, as it appeared to me at the time, would have been to make Lend-Lease retroactive and reimburse Britain for the investments liquidated in the United States to meet war purchases before Lend-Lease began. But I was obliged to add that there was no hope that Congress would consent to that remedy. Two points in the British case, however, had to be acknowledged without reservation: first, the grave balance-of-payments difficulties that would confront Britain at the end of the war, and second, the necessity of maintaining a high level of employment among the leading industrial countries of the world and especially in the United States. Admitting all this, however, it was doubtful whether bilateral negotiations to force suppliers abroad to buy more in Britain than they would otherwise have bought, could ever be an effective remedy. Markets and sources of supply were not always closely matched and could not be forced into correspondence without a general lowering of efficiency. Freer trade was necessary to help Britain to increase its exports after the war. Moreover, a series of exclusive bilateral bargains between the United Kingdom and the countries from which she obtained her imports would provoke retaliation from other countries, with the result that international buyers would be forced more and more to purchase goods from high-cost instead of low-cost producers and total trade would diminish. It would be difficult to solve Britain's problems within such an international economic framework.

Mr. Keynes's attitude in the second half of 1941 was, I believe, primarily a reflection of a temporary mood of despair regarding the chances of getting international agreement on a more enlightened solution than that of bilateral pressure and bargaining. A somewhat analogous situation had arisen in the early 1930's, when for a brief period he advocated tariffs as a remedy for British unemployment, but soon turned away to better plans. Then and later the case for so-called "bilateralism" on its economic merits rather than as a counsel of despair was upheld chiefly by a group of economists who, though living in Britain, were of continental European origin and training.

However, in the Treasury Mr. (later, Sir) Hubert Henderson, who had been a Cambridge economist, editor of the *Nation* and a member of the Economic Advisory Council, continued to argue the case against Article VII on the grounds that some discrimination would be unavoidable in the conditions that would exist after war. This was of course a markedly different point of view from that of the political supporters of imperial preference, since it did not rely on political sentiment and indeed supported discriminations in favor of certain foreign as well as Empire countries when economic circumstances appeared to require them.

At that time and later I did my best to impress on Mr. Keynes and other government economists that the desire for freer and for non-discriminatory trade in the State Department should not be written off as the product of a nineteenth century laissez-faire attitude toward economic affairs, untouched by recent economic thought and experience. It was true that Secretary Hull and Harry Hawkins had a particular concern with trade, but this arose from the Secretary's leading role in that field for many years and Hawkins' position at the head of the division concerned with trade matters. In conversations in Washington both Acheson and Hawkins showed themselves progressive in outlook and under no illusion that freer trade alone was a panacea for all economic ills. However, it soon appeared that the contrary view had been expressed to British officials in Washington by some U.S. officials outside the State Department.

It was Keynes who, notwithstanding his controversial position in Washington earlier in the year, took the lead in the preparation of constructive alternatives to discriminatory bilateral bargaining. Impressed by the reasoned objections to exclusive bilateralism which were expressed to him informally by Mr. Meade and other British economists after his return to London, he set to work energetically on the preparation of an alternative approach to the question. This will be discussed later, but it should be noticed at this stage that Keynes's plan was well advanced by the time negotiations on Article VII were resumed. In his own mind Keynes had dropped, or was on the verge of dropping, the argument that hard bilateral bargaining would have to be resorted to; and he was replacing it by a plan for an international institution to deal with balance-of-payments questions. Thus the powerful influence of Keynes was at last thrown on the side of those within Whitehall who advised that Britain should agree to a revised draft of Article VII which still included the provisions relating to the reduction of tariffs and the elimination of preferences.

In Washington, also, by the end of 1941 the subject was approached more broadly. There was fuller appreciation of the dependence of trade policy on internal employment policy and a clearer recognition of this in revised drafts of Article VII. The revised drafts introduced a clause placing an obligation on the parties to promote the expansion of employment and production. These drafts, regarded as satisfactory in the State Department, can be taken as evidence of the scant foundation for the view held in some parts of Washington and London that the United States position was dominated by an outworn nineteenth century doctrine of free trade as part of a system of general laissez-faire.

In these months political events overshadowed economic events. The war clouds over the Far East darkened and the storm broke on December 7. In the closing weeks of 1941 great political and economic decisions had to be made, and it was not until February that Ambassador Winant told me that he was informing the State Department that in his view the time had come to take up Article VII again. Negotiations were resumed and drafts and redrafts were presented by both sides, but agreement was not easily or immediately reached. The chief difficulty in the final negotiations centered on the proposed "elimination of discriminations," which attracted the attention and aroused the opposition of a section of the Conservatives in the coalition government.

The controversy became more political than economic, a matter of sentiment rather than of calculation. A section of the Conservative Party valued the system of preferential duties on Empire goods as a force making for solidarity within the British Commonwealth of Nations. They pointed with pride to the readiness with which Canada, Australia, New Zealand, and the Union of South Africa had voluntarily entered the war side by side with Great Britain and sent their young manhood across the world to fight in the deserts of Tripoli and the mountains of Greece at a time when the fortunes of war favored the enemy, when the survival of civilized society seemed doubtful, and when other countries lay inactive—conquered, acquiescent, or in a stupor. They recoiled from the suggestion that at this of all times Great Britain should join in a public declaration of policy aimed at the severance of special economic ties uniting the

Commonwealth, and it seemed to them particularly inappropriate that such a declaration should be suggested by a country which, though it had given material help, had persistently refused to enter the war until it was forced involuntarily into it by direct attack.

Those who held these views believed that they were acting directly in the interests of Great Britain and the Commonwealth. They sought no personal gain and were not moved by individual self-interest. Perhaps their most active and uncompromising member was Leopold Amery, who had great energy, high integrity, and keen political insight, but little facility in economic reasoning. The case rested essentially on sentiment and on political rather than economic considerations.

The Prime Minister has often been described as an "imperialist." In fact, however, Mr. Churchill had been brought up as a free trader: he was a minister in the Liberal government which before the First World War successfully withstood the attacks of the Conservative opposition and the protectionist campaigns of Joseph Chamberlain; and though later, when he was in the Conservative Party, he acquiesced in a certain degree of protection as a *fait accompli*, he still thought there was a general presumption on the side of free trade and felt no enthusiasm for the system of Empire preferences adopted at Ottawa. His hesitations and objections on the clause relating to discriminations arose, therefore, not from his personal views on the intrinsic merits of the subject, but from a desire to preserve unity and harmony within the coalition cabinet and to bring undivided energies to bear on the conduct of the war. He saw this as a matter of supreme importance, with all other things of no moment whatever in comparison. He felt that internal controversy on a question relevant only after victory had been won was out of place at a time when victory was as yet no more than a distant goal.

A considerable section of the Conservative Party was by no means wedded strongly to imperial preferences. From the time when Joseph Chamberlain started his campaign for a preferential system, the Conservatives have been and remain divided on the question. The impassable barrier to comprehensive proposals for a preferential system approximating "Empire Free Trade" has always been the desire in each country for domestic protection. In the United States serious misconceptions have prevailed concerning the Ottawa Conference. The records of that conference show Australia and not Great Britain as the driving force behind the movement for an extensive preferential system. Canada temporarily occupied a position somewhat similar to that of Australia. It was Mr. Bruce, the Australian representative, and Mr. Bennett, the Canadian representative, not Mr. Baldwin, who pushed the preferential system as far as it was carried at Ottawa and would have pushed it farther but for the resistance of British Conservatives who were more interested in raising barriers against imports generally than in lowering them on Dominions products.

By 1941 the attitude of the Dominions had changed considerably. Mr. Bennett, Canadian Premier at the time of the Ottawa Conference, had disappeared from Canadian politics, and Mr. MacKenzie King, who had been leader of the opposition in 1932 and had opposed Mr. Bennett's policy at the Ottawa Conference, was Prime Minister. Australia was now particularly interested in obtaining in the postwar period a wider market for its wool in the United States. Mr. Bruce, who had become High Commissioner for Australia in London, was no longer the crusader for imperial preference that he had been in 1932. In the intervening period it had become clear that the preferential system had not borne out the enthusiastic claims that had been made for it. Moreover, Mr. Bruce was convinced of the importance of harmony in the postwar period, as well as in the war years, between the British Commonwealth and the United States. Both during the discussions in Washington on a wheat agreement and during the Article VII discussions in London, Mr. Bruce and Mr. MacDougall, his economic adviser, visited our embassy and discussed the difficulties with Ambassador Winant and me. Though they did not in any way compromise the British position, it was clear that they were extremely anxious to assist in reaching a solution satisfactory to all sides.

In still other ways the situation had changed since 1932. The Ottawa Conference and the measures which were adopted by it were a response to the disastrous Smoot-Hawley tariff which in 1930 had been accepted by President Herbert Hoover, against the emphatic advice of the country's economists. With the fall of Mr. Hoover and the Republicans the position changed. The new Secretary of State, Cordell Hull, from the beginning pursued an unwavering course toward freer trade. The instrument which he chose for reducing barriers was indeed a slow and cumbersome one, involving a long-drawn-out series of bilateral negotiations. But it had the great advantage of not requiring ratification by Congress. For once, American representatives were able to make commitments which they were certain that they could fulfil. Moreover, the political condition of the world after Hitler seized power in 1933 would have given slender chance of success to any enterprise for simultaneous multilateral reduction of trade barriers. The aggressor countries were moving into a war economy. They desired the greatest possible supply of goods useful in war, not the greatest possible volume of production and trade to satisfy human wants. Faced with this threat, it was in the interest of the potential victims of aggression to follow the same course for their own defense. Some of the smaller neighbors or near neighbors of Germany were coerced into bilateral arrangements. Others belatedly began to prepare defensive measures. The scope for the application of the Reciprocal Trade Agreements Act was therefore limited by the political state of the world.

However, it was in the interest of some of the threatened countries to maintain a considerably greater volume of external trade under the protection of powerful naval forces than they would have been able to risk if they had been only land powers. Consequently Britain was able to enter into an important reciprocal trade agreement with the United States as late as 1938. Her policy of relying on her navy and air force instead of seeking agricultural self-sufficiency was wholly justified when war came. A considerable proportion of German labor was tied up in small-scale agriculture, partly in an attempt to approach as nearly as possible to self-sufficiency in food and partly in the belief that the rural population were more reliable supporters of the Nazi regime than the urban population. The result was that Britain's labor mobilization for direct war purposes, especially in the manufacturing industries, was far more complete than that of Germany. At the same time Britain achieved a record increase in domestic food production with the aid of an increase in agricultural machinery.

Thus on the United States side the Smoot-Hawley tariff act had been undermined at some points by Secretary Hull and on the United Kingdom side the war was beginning to demonstrate that even for defense purposes the maintenance of British external trade was sounder than the pursuit of self-sufficiency.

There remained only two economic arguments of substance against the abandonment of imperial preferences. Mr. Keynes mentioned the first in one of the conversations I had with him during these negotiations. He was not, he said, impressed by the views of some of the British ministers who supported preferences for reasons of sentiment and who held that they were an important political link holding the Commonwealth together. The ties among the members of the Commonwealth did not depend on such economic bargains, the negotiation of which sometimes caused friction. But once the system of preferences had been established it did provide a fairly reliable market for several million pounds sterling of U.K. exports. The sudden abolition of this market would not necessarily be followed automatically by the opening of alternative markets of the same value. The proportion of U.K. exports involved was not great, but unless adequate remedies were found the British position at the end of the war would be such that even a small assured market would count.

This argument could be met in one or more of three ways: first, by providing at least equivalent concessions in other markets to offset probable losses in preferential markets; second, by a direct remedy for the U.K. balance-of-payments difficulties arising out of the liquidation of external assets for war purposes; third, by far-reaching constructive international measures to create conditions in which it would be easier to solve the problem of the U.K. balance of payments. As we shall see, the text of Article VII which was adopted opened the way to the application of the first and to some extent of the third but not of the second of these remedies. My impression was that Keynes, while not overlooking the first was mainly concentrating his attention at that time on the third, in which he hoped that his plan for an International Clearing Union would find a leading place.

The second substantial economic argument against the sudden abolition of preferences was that certain colonial territories, particularly in the West Indies, which could balance their payments abroad only by the proceeds of exports admitted at preferential rates on the U.K. market, would be crippled by the removal of the preferences. Sir Hubert Henderson, who had been a member of the Royal Commission on the West Indies, had been greatly impressed by the precarious position of these colonial areas relying chiefly on sugar exports and by the difficulties of finding alternative export crops.

There was much force in this argument but, notwithstanding all the hullabaloo about imperial preferences in Washington, then and later, the United States had for years itself granted preferences, notably to the Philippine Islands and Cuba, and it might be taken for granted that the State Department could not, even if it wished to do so—which was not certain—induce the Filipinos to accept and Congress to endorse the sudden abolition of American preferences.

Keynes, who was adviser to Sir Kingsley Wood, the Chancellor of the Exchequer, was now in favor of signing Article VII, and the opposition in the late stages arose chiefly from political circles. It seemed that all but one of the Chancellor of the Exchequer's advisers in the Treasury were in favor of acceptance. Economists in other parts of Whitehall held similar views. The provisions of the Ottawa Conference had hardly gained more approval in British economic circles than the Smoot-Hawley tariff had gained in United States economic circles, and once the draft recognized that preferences and tariffs had to be dealt with together and that they could be dealt with effectively only if high levels of employment were maintained, British economists supported an accord with the United States.

But the political opponents of Article VII maintained a stiff opposition for some time after civil servants and a number of ministers, including Mr. Eden, the Foreign Secretary, and Richard Law, the Minister of State, were prepared to agree.

Early in February Ambassador Winant spent a week-end at Chequers with the Prime Minister. Returning, he described the ministerial position to me as follows: some three-quarters of the Cabinet were opposed to having any reference to trade preferences in the Lend-Lease agreement. Of these, a few were out-and-out supporters of empire preference on principle but others, including Mr. Churchill, did not believe that preferences served any useful purpose and were ready to begin discussions immediately, outside the scope of the Lend-Lease negotiations, on preferences, tariffs and other postwar questions of economic policy. They objected, however, to carrying on such discussions within the framework of the Lend-Lease negotiations, on the ground that the association of these two subjects gave the impression that Empire ties would be bartered away or sold in exchange for goods which Britain needed to wage the war.

A smaller group, led by the Foreign Secretary, had not read this association of ideas into the United States proposal and was ready to accept a draft, prepared by the Foreign Office, which was in harmony with the U.S. position. But Mr. Amery and Sir Kingsley Wood had led a stiff opposition which prevented the acceptance of this proposal. Sir Kingsley Wood, besides being Chancellor of the Exchequer, was in a position resembling that of a "party manager" of the Conservative party and was concerned with the maintenance of unity within the party.

Thus the signature of the draft agreement was delayed and the Foreign Secretary handed an alternative draft to Ambassador Winant, who, on returning from the Foreign Office, asked me to examine it before he gave Mr. Eden his answer. So far as it went it was unobjectionable; it included an obligation on both sides to seek the reduction of trade barriers. But it made no reference to preferences or discriminations. This issue, therefore, had to be squarely faced, and it appears that there were some in Washington who would have been willing to accept such a draft in principle and who were doubtful whether it was worth while to prolong the controversy on the issue of discrimination. However, my advice to the Ambassador was that the British draft should not be accepted and that consultation with Washington before answering the Foreign Secretary was not necessary. After going over the draft carefully once more, the Ambassador agreed and communicated his answer to the Foreign Secretary, after which he dictated a telegram to the State Department informing them of the action which he had taken.

The question was now wholly at the "ministerial level." Messages passed between the President and Prime Minister and between the Secretary of the Treasury and the Chancellor of the Exchequer. Ambassador Winant talked with Mr. Churchill, Mr. Eden and Sir Kingsley Wood. Lord Halifax cabled from Washington to the Foreign Office arguing vigorously that the latest State Department draft should be accepted.

Finally agreement was reached on the following text of Article VII:

"In the final determination of the benefits to be provided to the United States of America by the Government of the United Kingdom in return for aid furnished under the Act of Congress of March 11, 1941, the terms and conditions thereof shall be such as not to burden commerce between the two countries, but to promote mutually advantageous economic relations between them and the betterment of world-wide economic relations. To that end, they shall include provision for agreed action by the United States of America and the United Kingdom, open to participation by all other countries of like mind, directed to the expansion, by appropriate international and domestic measures, of production, employment, and the exchange and consumption of goods, which are the material foundations of the liberty and welfare of all peoples; to the elimination of all forms of discriminatory treatment in international commerce, and to the reduction of tariffs and other trade barriers; and, in general, to the attainment of all the economic objectives set forth in the Joint Declaration made on August 12, 1941 by the President of the United States of America and the Prime Minister of the United Kingdom.

"At an early convenient date, conversations shall be begun between the two Governments with a view to determining, in the light of governing economic conditions, the best means of attaining the above-stated objectives by their own agreed action and of seeking the agreed action of other like-minded Governments."[8]

The divergences of view which had arisen in the discussions behind closed doors preceding the agreement were to be revived subsequently in public discussions on both sides of the Atlantic. Article VII has been misrepresented by a small minority in Great Britain and misunderstood by a large majority in the United States. Its general purpose was to commit the two countries to international economic cooperation after the war for the attainment of peacetime objectives stated in skeleton form. It set up a series of interdependent obligations. Thus, for example, the obligations in respect to trade barriers and discriminations would no longer be binding on one party if the other party violated the obligations in respect to production and employment. Similarly, if one party failed to take steps toward an appropriate reduction of trade barriers the other party would no longer be obliged to take steps toward the elimination of discriminations. Hence there is no foundation either for the contentions of those who, in Great Britain, have made it appear that the United Kingdom had been forced to agree to unilateral scrapping of preferences and to unconditional abandonment of all defenses against a slump in the United States; or for the ideas of many Americans who have

[8] Mutual-Aid Agreement with Great Britain, Article VII.

seized on the elimination of British imperial preferences as the main object, and who, besides following British critics in ignoring the plain meaning of the language of the article, have greatly overestimated the economic importance of the preferential system within the British Commonwealth and Empire and have conveniently forgotten the preferential system of the United States with the Philippine Islands and Cuba and the inclusion within the U.S. tariff wall of Hawaii, Puerto Rico, the Virgin Islands, and Alaska. Actually, the United States and Great Britain were equally committed to each of the mutual obligations stated in Article VII, regardless of the balance sheet of Mutual Aid at the end of the war. Thus it cannot be said fairly—though in Britain it has sometimes been said unfairly—that the commitments constituted a price to be paid by Great Britain for its net receipts under Mutual Aid.

The clause in Article VII relating to discriminations was then and has remained since the subject of acute controversy. There were and still are differences of opinion in both London and Washington about its importance. The motives of those who advocated its retention in the final draft were not identical. Among leading State Department officials there were those who were sincerely anxious to obtain a general reduction of trade barriers and who believed that the elimination or reduction of imperial preferences would be necessary in order to remove or reduce the opposition of certain domestic interests in the United States, notably the lumber industry, to the whole trade agreements program. Some of them had worked for the historic reversal of the United States attitude toward the most-favored-nation clause which took place in the 1920's and, having taken part in conversions to the true faith at home, naturally wished to follow up with vigorous proselytizing abroad. Other Washington officials were jealous on political grounds of any ties between Canada and Great Britain that were not shared by the United States. Still others were "anti-British" on principle, carrying on from colonial days a tradition which, though archaic, has never died in the United States.

In discussions with Ambassador Winant and in personal talks with British officials I approached the question differently. Close relations between the U.K. and Canada were all to the good, not a matter for suspicion and jealousy. But it was doubtful whether imperial preferences improved the relationships among the members of the Commonwealth. Much hard bargaining and the friction that accompanies it went into the making of the preferential system. However, the central point against preferential systems which was almost completely overlooked was not the effect of British imperial preferences on American trade, but the effect of discriminatory practices in general on the poorer countries, particularly those in Asia and Africa whose natural resources per head of population were much lower than those of the ringleaders of discrimination, and whose only chance of benefiting from the more varied resources of the world as a whole lay in equal trading opportunities with other countries. For example, the American and British preferential systems on sugar have injured cane sugar producing areas outside the favored circles, all of them areas with less domestic economic resources per head of population than the United States and Great Britain possess.[4] No world economic order could be morally defended which weighted the scales against the poorer countries. In planning for the future, steps should be taken ultimately to remove existing discriminatory practices, some of which injured those in greatest need. The United States was not seriously affected by imperial preferences but the small and the poor countries would be placed at a serious disadvantage in world trade if the United States and the British Empire were free to set up or to expand exclusive preferential systems at will. The doctrine, "From him that hath not shall be taken away even that which he hath," would be given a deplorable form of application to world trading opportunities.

A somewhat similar line of reasoning can be applied to tariffs—except in cases where the "infant country" argument is relevant—and to restriction by quotas of the physical volumes of imports of particular goods. Here discrimination is less than it is under preferential systems, but it is not eliminated. Tariffs and physical quotas on any particular goods, even though they are the same for goods from all sources, injure countries which normally produce such goods and do not directly, though they may indirectly, injure others. Most of all, they injure those producing countries which, like Japan, are poorly endowed with natural resources per head of population and which must therefore rely on external trade to obtain a wide range of products. All trade barriers involve a substantial element of dis-

[4] This point seriously limits Sir Hubert Henderson's arguments concerning the West Indies and seems to restrict their legitimate application to the short run.

crimination and no countries stand to gain more than the poorer countries do from their reduction.

Thus freer trade must be an essential part of any plans to establish a more equitable world order in the years to come, and it is a striking example of the confusion of much recent political thought that many of those who profess and call themselves liberals or progressives have belittled the efforts of the State Department to advance the cause of freer trade in the postwar world. Some of them have apparently linked the movement in their minds with laissez-faire and the absence of planning, forgetting that the real issue is whether or not *national* boundary lines shall be made into or shall be allowed to remain as barriers to economic relations, and that it ill becomes liberals or progressives to place themselves on the side of exclusive nationalism. It may be agreed that at times countries are obliged to protect themselves against the "export of depression" from other countries with which they have economic relations. But existing trade barriers are not adapted to this purpose and there are sharp limits to the possibilities of insulating a country from external economic influences. In practice agreed international measures to combat depression whenever it appears will be more effective than unilateral protective measures by single countries.

The link in Article VII between freer trade and full employment placed trade policy in a modern context, clearly differentiating it from the laissez-faire of the nineteenth century. The economic doctrines which Keynes expounded from the middle 1930's and the economic policies which he began to advocate still earlier had borne fruit on both sides of the Atlantic and British and American economists concerned saw eye to eye on the general principles enshrined in Article VII. Some, indeed, were inclined to stress the importance of employment policy rather more than that of trade policy, while others were inclined to tilt the balance the other way. But all of them accepted the view that the maintenance and expansion of trade and production were complementary aims, both of which required concerted action by governments in their domestic and in their international spheres of activity.

One of the most important of the postwar international economic questions, however, was left untouched by Article VII. In the discussions before the article was signed the special difficulties of Great Britain arising out of the sacrifice of a large part of her external investments owing to the neutrality legislation and the Johnson Act were clearly understood as a vital postwar question. It would have been extremely difficult at this stage for the State Department or the White House to enter into any agreement, however tentative, for direct assistance to Great Britain to meet these difficulties after the war. It would also have been difficult to draft a clause covering this subject by a statement of general principles—which is all that Article VII was intended to be. Notwithstanding the great importance of the subject, the lack of reference to it in Article VII may be justified on the ground that the article was intended to cover all Mutual Aid agreements made with the United States, and that Britain's special difficulties could be dealt with separately and directly outside the general framework of the Mutual Aid agreement. Meanwhile, constructive measures to give effect to the general objectives of Article VII might by indirect means reduce the direct obstacles to the solution of Britain's special problem.

Unfortunately, however, nothing was done before the end of the war to deal with Britain's special difficulties. The chances of putting Article VII of the Mutual Aid agreement into effect within a short period were lost. Here, as in other important matters, the sins of omission were greater than the sins of commission.

In retrospect I believe that the arguments which I used in 1941 and 1942 fell short of a full grasp of postwar international trade problems. As I gained experience of short-run problems of relief and, still more, of reconstruction, and as I studied the actual structure of multilateral world trade in the past,[5] I came increasingly to recognize their limitations and to see the reconstruction of world trade, not simply as a problem of reducing trade barriers and maintaining full employment, but rather as an immensely complicated problem in economic geography, calling in the early stages for unorthodox and makeshift devices to restart trade where it had ceased or diminished to a trickle, and, in the longer run, for new and delicate adjustments in the division of labor between and within every continent. These adjustments depend, not only on the establishment of appropriate price relationships between countries, but also on farsighted international cooperation to work out on broad lines an amended pattern of multilateral trade which would enable the lack of

[5] Chiefly in the remarkable work of Folke Hilgerdt, *The Network of World Trade*, League of Nations, Geneva, 1943: reprinted by the United Nations.

balance in the exchange of goods across the North Atlantic to be offset by a reconstructed network of trade between the peoples on each side of that ocean on the one hand and those of Asia and Africa on the other. This longer-run goal cannot easily or quickly be reached: it involves "real" as well as monetary factors and different degrees of economic development as well as different regional endowments of natural resources.

CHAPTER II

A Period of Frustration

THE signing of Article VII of the Mutual Aid Agreement was a landmark in the history of postwar international economic planning. But the commitments which it embodied were in the form of general principles to be followed in planning more detailed measures to govern postwar practice. The success of the agreement depended on the zeal, the ability, and the speed with which each government would plan at home and negotiate abroad.

In plain language Article VII committed the signatories "at an early convenient date" to confer on measures to give effect to it, and both Whitehall and the United States Embassy in London expected that this part of the agreement would be carried out with little delay, particularly in view of the pressure that Washington had exerted on Downing Street to agree to the text that was adopted.

Shortly after the agreement was reached, Ambassador Winant and I spent an evening in discussion with Mr. Keynes on the next steps to take. At dinner Keynes expressed his satisfaction with the agreement on Article VII, adding that he had for some time advised the Chancellor of the Exchequer to agree to the text. The Ambassador, who had held frequent conversations with the Chancellor during the negotiations, replied cordially, "I knew you did."

We then agreed that it was too early to begin formal negotiations to give effect to Article VII. The Ambassador held that the best course would be first to assemble a small group of British and American economic experts to discuss the whole ground covered by Article VII and to prepare tentative plans, embodying what seemed desirable on economic grounds, to serve as a basis for discussion in official negotiations later. It might subsequently be necessary to modify these plans for political reasons, but at least the economic issues would be made clear at the outset. He believed it would be a mistake to throw such complex economic questions directly into formal diplomatic negotiations. His experience in public office had led him wherever possible to obtain the impartial advice of a group of trained experts before throwing an economic question into the political arena. In this way the specialists were able to concentrate on the merits of the question. If they were brought into the discussions only on the eve of formal negotiations they were bound to be diverted frequently by political maneuvers from the work for which they were peculiarly fitted. Moreover, formal negotiations could not be undertaken in practice without the knowledge of the public and consequently without exposing the negotiators to fierce political pressures from all sides.

Keynes said that these views were in harmony with his own and he believed with those of the Treasury. We agreed that it was too early to begin formal negotiations and that preliminary talks should be strictly confidential and designed only to clear the ground without committing either side.

A few days later Nigel Ronald, the Assistant Under-Secretary who throughout the war dealt with postwar economic questions, told me that these views were similar to those of the Foreign Office. The Ambassador then showed me a telegram which he had drafted, proposing that the State Department should send a group of experts to London in a short time to discuss the economic implications of Article VII privately and informally, without commitment, with a group of British economists in Whitehall. He suggested names for the group, including not only economists in full-time government service, but also Professor Jacob Viner.

The United Kingdom had hesitated long and raised many questions before accepting Article VII, but once agreement was reached the British negotiators wished to follow it with early discussions on the way in which the commitment should be fulfilled, starting with informal, exploratory and non-committal talks. In the embassy we all shared this desire and expected that it would be shared in Washington.

But to our dismay the months went by without any action in Washington to carry out the commitment in Article VII to enter into discussions "at an early convenient date." The State Department, the Treasury, and the White House had pressed vigorously for the acceptance of Article VII but, when it had been accepted, to outward appearance they seemed to lose all interest in the matter. A long period was to pass before organized discussions between Washington and London began.

The Ambassador renewed his proposal again and again and varied its form in the hope that if a team could not come at least a few individuals could come singly. A complete explanation of the delay cannot be made by one who, like the present writer, was in London all through the year. It seems likely, however, that the postponement of action was due to Secretary Hull's attitude rather than to that of his aides who were concerned with the subjects covered by Article VII. The Secretary was an able statesman, interested in economic matters. But he was cautious—sometimes overcautious—by nature, and his caution had been deepened by decades of experience in the ways of Congress and the motives and subterfuges of Congressmen. The United States had entered or rather had been thrown into the war only a few months before and was suffering serious reverses in battle. It might have been argued that at such a time Congress would be hostile to any discussions on postwar matters, and that the notorious difficulty of keeping secrets in Washington would make the chances very slender of moving a team of leading economic officials to London without attracting the attention of journalists and congressmen. In the embassy we believed that this difficulty could have been met by sending one or two officials at a time, ostensibly to deal with some of the numerous interallied wartime economic questions that frequently arose.

However, officials in London and Washington, though unable to negotiate abroad, made important progress in planning at home during this period, and in each capital personal and unofficial discussions took place "off the record." At this point it is appropriate to examine briefly the processes of postwar planning in the earlier war period in London and Washington. After the early war crises passed there was a striking development of postwar economic and social planning in London, but it will be discussed in the present study only where it is directly relevant to international measures.

The background against which Whitehall's postwar planning was carried on stood in sharp contrast with that against which the administration and civil servants had to struggle in Washington. Members of Parliament as well as the public constantly agitated for more definite evidence that the government was working on questions of postwar reconstruction. From an early stage Ambassador Winant and I, moving in somewhat different circles in London, came independently to the conclusion that the lethargy of the sorry days of Baldwin and

Neville Chamberlain had ended, that the British people were determined on far-reaching change and that the British government would take the lead in political, social, and economic changes after the war. The public demand was concentrated more on domestic than on international aspects of postwar reform, but in Whitehall the experienced civil servants, both permanent and temporary, were well aware of the inseparable relations between domestic and international affairs and threw their energies into the formation of plans for both parts of the work.

In response to public and Parliamentary agitation for greater government activity in postwar planning, the Minister without Portfolio, Arthur Greenwood, was charged to coordinate the work on reconstruction and was given a small secretariat. This group was sometimes referred to in public discussion as the "Ministry of Reconstruction." In reality it was a clearinghouse of information and not a body which initiated proposals and formulated measures. Particularly, it was a center to which voluntary organizations outside the government could convey their ideas on postwar plans. The public expected more from Mr. Greenwood, but the transfer of these functions from him to the Paymaster General, Sir William Jowitt, provoked derisive comment: in the public mind a Paymaster General had something to do with control of the purse and was more likely to restrict than to hasten costly schemes of reconstruction! In reality, of course, the public critics of both Greenwood and Jowitt misunderstood the structure of their own government and overestimated the results that could reasonably have been expected from these ministers and their secretariat. In the cabinet form of government no minister appointed to deal with postwar reconstruction could stand above and give directions to cabinet ministers in charge of departments. All he could do was attempt to persuade the departments to integrate their work, to reach agreements, and to take up questions on which work had not yet begun.

The direct role of formal organization in Whitehall should not be overestimated. It was more adapted to bring postwar measures to a head than to initiate them. It was a clearinghouse rather than a source from which the original plans came. Some of the plans ultimately adopted had their origins in the initiative of individuals who drafted schemes, persuaded their colleagues in the departments in which they worked to accept them, perhaps with modifications, and discussed them informally with colleagues in other departments. When a plan had been adopted, either by the department of its originator or by another department to whose sphere of work it properly belonged, it was placed before the interdepartmental committee dealing with postwar international questions. There it was critically examined by the leading civil servants in Whitehall. Keynes played a constructive role on this committee, bringing his quick and powerful mind and his charm of manner and persuasiveness to the task of piloting constructive plans, containing innovations disturbing to the able but less original civil servants of high rank, through a group whose members were not prone to accept anything uncritically.

Other economists besides Keynes, who were brought from the universities into Government work during the war, made important contributions both to the establishment of a war economy which was probably the most efficient in the world and to the initiation of postwar economic plans. This development seems to have begun when Lord Stamp, early in the war brought in two economists, Austin Robinson of Cambridge and John Jewkes of Manchester. The results were most successful, and after the formation of the coalition government in the spring of 1940, vigorous measures were taken to strengthen the organization and personnel of Whitehall. A number of economists and others, who were subsequently to distinguish themselves in public life, were brought into the government departments and the War Cabinet secretariat. Professor Lionel Robbins, the well known economist of London University, and James Meade, an Oxford economist whom Ambassador Winant and I had known in Geneva when he was on the staff of the League of Nations before the war, both joined the Economic Section of the War Cabinet secretariat and Professor Robbins became head of the section. While Mr. Keynes and Lord Catto became advisers to the Chancellor of the Exchequer, H. D. Henderson and later D. H. Robertson, two other distinguished Cambridge economists, also entered the Treasury, and Henry Clay joined the Board of Trade. Others from the universities who were not trained as economists achieved distinction in economic administration during the war. For example, Oliver Franks and William Morris, both philosophers, played leading roles in the Ministry of Supply and John Maud, a historian, and Mr. Hollins, an inspector of schools, filled leading positions in the Ministry of Food: all of them played important parts in international negotiations on economic matters.

The union of these leading members of the universities with the experienced and well-trained permanent civil servants in Whitehall produced striking results in economic administration during the war and in economic planning for the postwar period. The strongest part of the whole machinery of government lay in this area, least noticed by the outside world. But postwar plans could not be finally adopted here: they had subsequently to pass the scrutiny of ministers.

When a plan was approved by the interdepartmental committees an opportunity was sought to bring it before the ministerial committee to be examined and passed on and, if acceptable, to be sent to the War Cabinet for final approval, after which it became official government policy to be followed in negotiations with other countries. However, throughout much of the war period it was difficult for civil servants to persuade ministers to give thorough consideration to postwar economic plans which raised complicated issues on which much thought was needed before an intelligent judgment could be reached. When military reverses, or losses on the high seas, or assaults on Britain from the air, or secret planning of air and land attacks on the enemy were occupying ministers, there was little inclination on their part to turn aside to study plans for dealing with postwar conditions. Often the evil was more than sufficient for the day and ministers were left too exhausted to take up good works relating to the time when the tyranny would be overpast.

Fortunately a second procedure was worked out which permitted greater flexibility and made less demand on the time of ministers. It provided for cabinet approval of documents on postwar questions as a basis for discussion in external negotiations. This did not commit the government to subsequent final approval of the proposals as a whole but served as a "green light" to move forward on preliminary discussions with the representatives of other countries.

During this period postwar planning in Washington was carried on under conditions much more difficult than those in London. The members of the legislature, instead of pressing the government to hasten preparations for postwar reconstruction, looked with suspicion on all aspirations for recreating the postwar world in a new image, particularly when they imagined that they could detect resemblances between the aims of postwar reconstruction and the aims of the New Deal, which by then had lost its earlier momentum. The form of government in the United States provided reactionary groups and vested interests with opportunities unequalled in other democratic countries to hinder or wreck reforms at home and co-operation abroad. In May 1942, Secretary Hull, in a private meeting of the Advisory Committee on Postwar Foreign Policy, "expressed anxiety over the interest groups and opposing ideological influences that would inevitably bring their strength to bear against the constructive views on peace settlement and world improvement to be developed by the Committee. Such interest groups and influences constituted perhaps the greatest threat that the work would face; he anticipated that the best document that could be devised would be attacked. He was convinced of the necessity of making better preparation for world peace than had been made in the course of the First World War. The chances nevertheless were about one to two or three whether a soundly conceived peace could be carried to fruition."[1]

These long-standing difficulties were intensified in 1942 by the abrupt transition from peace to war organization in the United States. Jolted suddenly out of two decades of isolationist illusions, the American people were forced to adjust themselves abruptly to a new role in the world, and many of them were not yet prepared to look further ahead still and to consider the form which a more distant readjustment should take. The British people, having lost their illusions earlier and having passed their darkest hour, were looking with more eagerness and determination to the dawn, distant though it might yet be.

But, as usual, the Roosevelt administration had been more far-sighted than Congress and the Advisory Committee on Postwar Foreign Policy was set up in February, 1942, with sub-committees on economic reconstruction and economic policy. The first of these was expected to deal mainly with the short-run postwar questions and the second with the long-run topics that would come up mainly under Article VII of the Mutual Aid Agreement. But in 1942, as we have already seen, political caution prevented these committees from initiating or from accepting invitations to Anglo-American discussions on Article VII matters. The organization itself was modified

[1] U.S. Department of State, *Postwar Foreign Policy Preparation*, 1939-1945, Washington, 1949, p. 92.

during the year and was replaced in the spring of the following year by the Committee on Postwar Foreign Economic Policy—a large body composed of a mixture of cabinet officers, heads of departments and divisions, and a few prominent persons from outside government.

More important than the work of the committees was the work of civil servants, who were organized and distributed among the departments on different lines from those followed in Whitehall. The Foreign Office never set up an economic staff and, as we have seen, the economic preparations in London were conducted by a small number of highly qualified economists spread over a number of departments. The State Department, from an early stage, began to build up an economic staff. In 1941 and 1942 Dr. Leo Pasvolsky, Secretary Hull's trusted adviser, who had unusually wide qualifications in both economic and political matters, headed a Division of Special Research which was divided into economic and political sections. In addition Harry Hawkins, notwithstanding his large operational responsibilities, always provided for the conduct of research in his division of Commercial Policy and Trade Agreements. Thus the State Department was the chief agency of government to engage in postwar planning. Next came the Treasury, where Dr. Harry White, with a capable group of assistants, set to work early on postwar monetary plans. Secretary Morgenthau and Dr. White were never excessively cordial toward Secretary Hull and the State Department, and the lines became rather sharply drawn between international financial reconstruction, which Morgenthau claimed as his more or less exclusive province, and other aspects of international economic reconstruction. Next to the Treasury in importance came the Department of Agriculture, which showed a keen interest in commodity agreements and in trade policy where it affected the movement of agricultural products. Here again there was always danger of clashes of jurisdiction.[2]

The signing of Article VII of the Mutual Aid Agreement led

[2] The influence of personal factors on the work of the committees and research staff were at times important but could better be evaluated by those who were in Washington during 1942. They are naturally ignored in the official publication of the State Department, *Postwar Policy Preparation 1939-1945*, Washington, 1950, which came out after most of the present study was written. Such publications are valuable records of the facts concerning formal organizations, meetings and other activities but they necessarily leave out the complex interplay of human personalities which in the last resort is the very core of history.

to increased activity in Whitehall on the international aspects of postwar economic reconstruction. At the same time Ambassador Winant was anxious that an outline should be drawn of the international economic measures necessary to fulfill the obligations undertaken in Article VII, and asked me to work on the subject, and, after discussing it with a leading economist in Whitehall, to bring him a draft outline.

This discussion took place on a purely personal and unofficial basis. In brief summary, it led to the conclusion that postwar economic plans should provide for the following: (1) an international organization with enough resources to preserve exchange stability and tide over balance-of-payments difficulties among member countries; (2) an international organization to foster long-term international capital movements, avoiding the abuses in international investment of the 1920's, advancing the development of poorer areas and meeting needs which are important in the long run but which might be passed over by private investors in favor of openings likely to yield profits earlier; (3) an international supervision of commodity agreements to ensure that they would be used constructively to reduce useless price fluctuations, that they would give proper representation to consumer countries, and that they would refrain from restricting low-cost production to bolster up high-cost production indefinitely; (4) international measures to reduce trade barriers drastically, and ultimately to remove discriminations; (5) international organization of relief and reconstruction; (6) measures to maintain full employment.[3]

We considered all of these measures except relief and reconstruction as arising directly out of Article VII and indispensable to its

[3] Some if not most of these suggestions had been in the air for several months. It would be impossible for any single individual to trace them all to their origins. In the quiescent period of the war I worked with a group of League and ILO officials in Geneva who threw out a number of ideas. I recollect also some later personal discussions in Washington with Professor Alvin Hansen and in Montreal with members of a group of the Canadian Institute of International Affairs. My notes also indicate that early in 1941, as economic adviser to the International Labor Office I suggested that postwar reconstruction measures should include a joint U.S.-U.K. exchange stabilization fund through which, in the early postwar period, British balance-of-payments difficulties would be met; international supervision of raw material agreements; international investment machinery to assist countries which urgently needed capital and technical knowledge but which had difficulty in competing for them through private channels; concerted reduction of trade barriers; and continuation and extension of the international food and nutrition work of the League and ILO. Subsequently the ILO published studies on two of these subjects.

fulfillment. But it was clear that each of them would have to be prepared and negotiated in detail, probably in separate plans, and that no time should be lost in making a start.

Keynes had already made great progress on his postwar financial proposals. He had not remained long in the mood of pessimism that had seemed to dominate him in Washington in the summer of 1941 and for a time after he had returned to London. In the autumn of 1941 he had set to work on the substance of his future plan for an international clearing union. When several months had passed without any response from the State Department to the Ambassador's proposals for informal British-American talks, Mr. Ronald and Mr. Keynes informed me that to reduce loss of time and to prevent separate crystallization of the ideas of London and those of Washington economists into hard and fast positions which later might prove to be difficult to harmonize, they were prepared to exchange papers with us in order that each side might learn the general lines on which the other was working.

Unfortunately, political caution in Washington at that time delayed the exchange of papers as well as the conversations.[4] When an informal response came from Washington it came from the United States Treasury. Meantime the British plan for an international clearing union was handed to us.

This came to be known as the "Keynes Plan," though it should be remembered that the plan had been studied and worked over by other able officials, analyzed and debated in committee, and approved as a basis for discussion with other governments. The document carries many evidences of the hand of Keynes. It is unusual among government papers in the distinction of its style, in the form of its presentation, in the breadth of its vision, and in its underlying moral earnestness. Keynes felt that humanity must be spared the economic disorders which had brought so much individual human suffering in the interwar period.

The document made a modest disclaimer of originality for the proposals, which were described as "an attempt to reduce to practical shape certain general ideas belonging to the contemporary climate of

[4] It should be mentioned that a valuable paper on postwar economic planning was prepared about this time by Dr. Leo Pasvolsky, adviser to Secretary Hull, who headed the postwar planning groups in the Department of State. This paper, however, could only be circulated to a few individuals at this time; it was not "cleared at the political level."

economic opinion, which have been given publicity in recent months by writers of several different nationalities." The general ideas "are born of the spirit of the age" and the details of the plan "are offered in no dogmatic spirit, as the basis of discussion for criticism or improvement. For we cannot make progress without embodying the general underlying idea in a frame of actual working, which will bring out the practical and political difficulties to be faced and met if the breath of life is to inform it."[5]

The aims of the plan were comprehensive—far more so than those of the plan ultimately adopted at Bretton Woods. However, its central provisions were simple. The typically British device of the overdraft seems to have influenced their form. The facilities for overdrafts could be used particularly to deal with any temporary adverse balance of payments which under laissez-faire conditions would disrupt world trade as well as the economy of the country primarily concerned. The limits of the overdraft facilities were to be related to the average annual value of the imports and exports of the member country in a selected previous period—a value designated as the quota of the country. Thus the financial resources of the international clearing union were to be equal to the average annual value of the imports and exports of the member countries in a previous period. These were to be expressed in units of an international money named bancor, fixed in value in gold and in member's currency.

Overdrafts up to one-quarter of the value of a member country's quota were to be drawn on unconditionally if desired; above one-quarter the permission of the governing board of the Union was to be required; and above one-half increasingly stringent conditions were to be laid down by the board, leading to a declaration of default if the overdraft exceeded three-quarters for more than two years. On the other hand a member country with credit balances exceeding one-half of its quota was to consult with the board on measures to reduce its balance.

Such, in brief and rough outline, was Keynes's proposal for dealing with temporary balance of payments difficulties. A permanent international organization, operating or ready to operate long after

[5] Quotations taken from paragraph 2. In view of the different forms in which the document was printed, page references are not appropriate. Among previous writings I believe Keynes was influenced to some extent by a paper by Mr. E. Schumacher which I have read only in typewritten form.

postwar difficulties had passed away, was to be established. If it had existed in 1931, when Britain's assets abroad, though adequate over a longer period to cover her debts, could not be mobilized quickly enough to meet the sudden call on her short-term liabilities, the crisis could have been avoided without abandonment of the gold standard and the international consequences—political and economic—that followed. Not all the international economic ills of the day would have been cured, but there would have been more time to find remedies for the deep-seated maladjustments that lay below the economic surface.

But the Keynes Plan in its original form was more than a measure for dealing with temporary balance-of-payments difficulties. Its additional features, which have been largely forgotten in later discussions, carried it far beyond a mere plan for dealing with long-run conditions which would be established only after reconstruction had been completed. From the beginning, Mr. Keynes was acutely conscious of the problems of the immediate postwar period.[6] He was willing to use the proposed International Clearing Union for short-term as well as long-term purposes:

"The Union might set up a clearing account in favour of international bodies charged with post-war relief, rehabilitation and reconstruction. But it could go much further than this. For it might supplement contributions received from other sources by granting overdraft facilities in favour of these bodies, the overdraft being discharged over a period of years out of the Reserve Fund of the Union, or, if necessary, out of a levy on surplus credit balances. By this means it is possible to avoid asking any country to assume a burdensome commitment for relief and reconstruction, since the resources would be provided in the first instance by those countries having credit clearing accounts for which they have no immediate use and are voluntarily leaving idle, and in the long run by those countries which have a chronic international surplus for which they have no beneficial employment."

The last sentence of this quotation seems to be oversimplified, but the proposal to give short-term functions to the Union must be ex-

[6] From time to time I discussed with Mr. Keynes various proposals for dealing with relief and reconstruction with which we were concerned in the Embassy. He was as keenly interested in them as in proposals for long-run measures and was fertile in constructive ideas, though at times he did not wholly appreciate political difficulties in Washington.

amined in the light of Keynes' early conception of the nature of the problems of the immediate postwar transition. The Clearing Union plan has been attacked on the ground that it would be inflationary. Keynes did say categorically that, "The plan aims at the substitution of an expansionist, in place of a contractionist, pressure on world trade."[7] But this statement is clearly intended to refer only to long-run conditions following the reconstruction period. Nowhere in the documents on postwar planning can a clearer apprehension be found of the dangers of immediate postwar inflation than in the Clearing Union plan. In one of the most penetrating sections of the document Keynes pointed out the advantage of launching the plan quickly after the war "in the first energy of victory and whilst the active spirit of united action lasts."[8]

But, he continued, "Such a proposal presents, however, something of a dilemma. On the one hand, many countries will be in particular need of reserves of overseas resources in the period immediately after the war. On the other hand, goods will be in short supply and the prevention of inflationary international conditions of much more importance for the time being than the opposite. The expansionist tendency of the plan, which is a leading recommendation of it as soon as peace-time output is restored and the productive capacity of the world is in running order, might be a danger in the early days of a sellers' market and an excess of demand over supply."

Keynes proposed to resolve this dilemma by adjusting the overdraft facilities of the Clearing Union to whatever financial provisions might be made for relief and reconstruction. If the Union were to make overdrafts for the latter purposes, it would restrict if necessary its normal overdraft facilities to the amount of gold paid in by members. In other words the Union would fulfill short-term emergency functions for the transition period in place of the long-term functions which would be its normal concern after reconstruction were completed. If relief and reconstruction were to be financed wholly outside the Clearing Union, the overdraft facilities of the Union might be suspended during a relief period of perhaps two years.

Since 1942 this part of the original Keynes Plan has been given less attention than it deserved. However impracticable it may have been from a political point of view it showed accurate foresight, even at this early stage in the war, of the nature of immediate postwar

[7] Par. 8.

[8] Par. 41.

economic conditions.[9] Thus the Keynes Plan was drawn on comprehensive lines and was not conceived of purely as a long-term measure to come into force after the transition period. If more of its provisions had been accepted the economic chaos into which the world lapsed soon after the end of the war might have been largely avoided.

The Keynes Plan was not long to hold the field alone. During the late spring of 1942 the Ambassador was informed through Treasury channels of a postwar international monetary plan drafted by Dr. Harry D. White at Secretary Morgenthau's request. This plan, a copy of which was sent to the embassy, was modified several times before it was later made public. It aimed at the creation of an international stabilization fund and a bank for reconstruction and development. In form it seemed trite and pedestrian by comparison with the Keynes Plan, but in content it was ahead of its time and showed a reasonably clear vision of postwar difficulties. It resembled the Keynes Plan in many of its aims but differed in its methods. It provided for advances to tide over temporary balance-of-payments difficulties but the advances were to come, not from overdrafts but from a fund subscribed by members in accordance with an elaborate formula in which arbitrary weights were assigned to gold stocks, gold production, national income, foreign trade, population, foreign investments, and external debts. This formula, the pseudo-scientific trappings of which covered political motives, would have required the United States to contribute an amount five times as great as that of the next largest contributor and at the same time, since votes were to be proportionate to contributions, would have weighted the United States vote in the same proportion. This scheme contrasted with that of Keynes, whose overdraft facilities were to be proportionate to the volume of foreign trade and thus were larger for the United Kingdom than for other countries. Presumably, however, both these positions were taken partly for bargaining purposes, and there was much argument, not to say wrangling, over them in the negotiations that followed later.

The White Plan laid great stress on stability of exchange rates and would have given the Fund authority to fix exchange rates in its own currency dealings. These rates were to be changed only with the

[9] Keynes also had grasped the magnitude of the immediate postwar difficulties to be expected. He expected that, even if the resources of the Clearing Union were used for relief and reconstruction, it would be necessary in addition to continue Lend Lease "or other aid from outside the Clearing Union." (Par. 43).

consent of four-fifths of the members. In the controversies on devaluation in early 1949, Washington pressed for, while London for some time opposed, changes in exchange rates, but in the early drafts of the monetary plans and throughout the earlier negotiations Washington had argued for drastic restrictions on the right of any country to change its exchange rate unilaterally, while London had insisted on considerable flexibility.

The White Plan was cast in more conventional commercial forms than those of the Keynes Plan. The general conceptions in it were familiar to bankers and businessmen whose support would be needed in the United States to obtain the consent of Congress for the U.S. to join the proposed new organization. The more original scheme of Keynes would have gained acceptance in London but hardly in Washington political circles. Unfortunately, a measure which is, as it were, ahead of its time has little chance of political acceptance under the form of government in the United States, which gives so many opportunities for irresponsible obstruction and consistently weights the scales in favor of conservatism.

As it was with the Keynes Plan, so it was with the White Plan; the first draft contained bold proposals ranging much wider than the plan ultimately adopted. Just as the failure to adopt the bolder proposals of Keynes necessitated new emergency measures in 1947 and 1948, so the failure to adopt the bolder proposals in the White Plan led to new emergency proposals for 1949 and 1950. For a prominent place was given in the earlier version of the White Plan to a scheme for liquidating the blocked sterling balances which had accumulated during the war as a result of Britain's costly activities in the front line of resistance to the enemy. In 1942 White estimated that these balances would exceed $5,000 million, and that Britain's liquid foreign exchange holdings would be far less. His scheme would have enabled a government to sell to the International Monetary Fund blocked balances accumulated during the war, on condition that both the creditor and the debtor country after a three-year interval would begin to repurchase 40 per cent of them at the rate of 2 per cent annually. The balance held by the Fund would not be sold without permission from the debtor country. No restrictions on convertibility would be placed on the amounts repurchased by the creditor country. The danger that the Fund would be encumbered with too much blocked currency was to be met, (1) by permitting the Fund to buy the Government bonds of the debtor country and use them as security for loans in any country except the debtor country, and (2) by giving to the Fund authority to limit the proportion of the blocked balances which it would be obliged to purchase in a stated period of time.

The war continued nearly three and a half years after Dr. White's plan was prepared and blocked sterling balances increased to about $15,000 million—far beyond White's estimate. It is questionable whether the Fund would have been able to deal with balances of such a size. But if the Fund could have undertaken to deal with the whole amount then Britain would have been free of its burden of war debt until 1948 and afterwards would have had to release about $300 million a year, which is less than she has actually freed in some postwar years. The Fund, however, would have carried the exhange risk on about $3,000 million and it would have been difficult to get agreement among its members that it should deal in such large balances. None the less, the proposal was a serious attempt to grapple with a problem that would become urgent and immediate as soon as the last shot was fired. If adopted it would have made the Fund an important international agency of the transition period and not—as it actually became—merely an organization whose work was designed only for the long-run conditions which were expected to follow the period of postwar reconstruction. Moreover the proposal was based on the enlightened doctrine that the burden of the war debts, incurred by Britain for the common good, should be shared among those who had received the benefits of the expenditures.

When the two plans had been confidentially exchanged and studied in Whitehall and Washington by groups of officials, Ambassador Winant became increasingly anxious to bring their authors into preliminary discussions to clear the ground and avoid the risk of each becoming attached to his own plan so closely as to endanger the success of future negotiations. The opportunity came when Mr. Morgenthau and Dr. White arrived in London in the late summer of 1942 to discuss with the U.K. Treasury currency questions concerning future operations in the Mediterranean theater.

Mr. Winant obtained Mr. Morgenthau's agreement to a private discussion between Dr. White and Mr. Keynes and instructed me to arrange it. A private conference of economic representatives of the Dominions, India, and the U.K. was taking place that day and Keynes was to speak to it in the afternoon. Mr. Morgenthau and Dr.

White were leaving for the Mediterranean in the evening. When I mentioned Keynes's engagement in the afternoon, Dr. White, who was as much of a prima donna in his way as Keynes, said abruptly, "I don't want to talk with anyone except Keynes." Fortunately, when I represented the matter urgently to the leading Treasury official, Sir Wilfred Eady, the meeting of the Dominions in the afternoon was cancelled and a private meeting was held in the Ambassador's room attended by the Ambassador, Dr. White, Lauren W. Casaday, the Treasury attaché to the Embassy, Lord Keynes, Mr. Phillips, U.K. Treasury representative at the British Embassy in Washington, and the present writer. It is a melancholy reflection of the toll taken by the war that by 1949 Mr. Casaday[10] and the present writer were the only survivors of this group.

The exchange of views was left almost wholly to Keynes and White. It was lively and at times somewhat acrimonious but exceedingly fruitful. There was a substantial area of agreement but there were also sharp differences. Keynes thought the fund proposed by White would not be large enough. White considered it would be impossible to get more, if as much, out of Congress for the U.S. share. This led to some controversy over the question whether the capital should be subscribed or created as a new issue, as Keynes proposed. Keynes vigorously attacked the idea of subscribed capital but White held to it as the only approach that Congress would accept. He also attacked as politically impossible the proposal of Keynes to use the Clearing Union to finance relief and reconstruction or any part of it. Keynes made it clear that the proposal that a four-fifths majority vote should be required before a change in a country's exchange rate could be made would not be acceptable to London. Britain, because of its precarious financial position, must retain considerable freedom to act unilaterally in such matters if necessary, he maintained. Differences arose on the voting system and other points. Finally Keynes argued for direct negotiations between the U.S. and U.K. alone or possibly with the Dominions and the Soviet Union added, while White maintained that this would create suspicion of an Anglo-Saxon financial "gang-up." Keynes heatedly argued that, the subject matter being complicated, it was essential that the U.S. and U.K. should work out a plan themselves, invite the Russians, in order to allay suspicion, and perhaps the Dominions

[10] Now Dean of the Business School at the University of Arizona.

and French, to join, and then set it up and invite the rest of the world to join. To throw open to a meeting of over fifty nations so complicated a matter, involving the opening of new paths, would be to throw it into a "monkey house," he said. White argued that a beginning might be made in two or three separate small groups, for example, the U.K. and European Allies and the U.S. and a Latin American group.

It seems unnecessary to record the points of agreement in detail, since it was the act of bringing differences into the open that had the greatest effect on subsequent preparations in Whitehall and Washington. At the close of the meeting, which was presided over by Ambassador Winant with his usual charm and skill in introducing a humorous touch when undue heat was shown by the principals, both White and Keynes agreed that as a result of the exchange of views they would return to their colleagues with proposals for modifications on a number of points.

No official record was made by us of the meeting. The State Department had not yet given us permission to engage in any form of discussion on postwar matters and this meeting was held on the personal initiative of Ambassador Winant. It was the first of many meetings between the two able, conscientious and indefatigable men who, more than any others, were responsible for the establishment of the International Monetary Fund and the International Bank for Reconstruction and Development, and who in the process sacrificed their physical health and lived to see only a fragment of the results of their labors.

CHAPTER III

Progress in Financial Planning for the Long Run

IN 1943 Mr. Keynes continued to give first place among postwar plans to the proposals for an international clearing union. In the latter part of 1942 and the early part of 1943 he frequently asked me impatiently when Washington would be willing to hold discussions on the plan.[1] The exchange of documents on the Keynes and White plans had been valuable in acquainting Washington and London officials with each other's ideas. But Whitehall, which had started the exchange, was not wholly pleased with the results and decided to withhold for a time its document on raw material questions, apparently fearing that if it were given to Washington it might draw forth rival plans, as the proposal for the International Clearing Union had done. There was a danger that vested interests and personal prestige would grow up around each plan and increase the difficulties of producing a common plan. This danger was increased when "leakages" to the public occurred during 1943. On different occasions there were leakages both in Washington and London, which eventually led to the publication of both plans and a third plan prepared by Ottawa. The whole truth is often less embarrassing to negotiators than half-truths are, though it is usually still better to withhold all information in the early stages of negotiations.

After the private meeting between Mr. Keynes and Dr. White in the autumn of 1942, the next discussions took place in Washington. They were informal exchanges of view between Dr. White and Sir Frederick Phillips, British Treasury representative in Washington, and Dr. Redvers Opie, economic adviser to the British Ambassador. Although they committed neither side to anything they were valuable in checking undue crystallization of views and in enabling each side to study how far it could go to meet the other. In postwar matters

[1] For an account of his dismay when President Roosevelt chose food instead of finance as the subject of the first international conference on postwar matters, see pp. 119-20.

civil servants in London, Washington, and Ottawa did all they could to keep the ball rolling, even if it only rolled slowly. But it was in international finance that the ball rolled fastest and was least often at a standstill. Secretary Morgenthau was more forceful and independent than other members of the cabinet, and through his close friendship with President Roosevelt and frequent opportunities of meeting him was not always obliged to obtain the consent of his colleagues to his own moves. Moreover the monetary plans were not clearly understood by the public, and hostile congressmen ready to seize any opportunity to attack the administration were less likely to venture into the mysteries of finance than they were to oppose the reduction of trade barriers.

The conversations on the monetary plans were not long confined to Britain and the United States. A meeting was arranged in London with the Finance Ministers of the European Allies in exile, and in Washington with a group of Latin American countries. The U.S. was represented by observers at the London meeting and the U.K. at the Washington meeting. The London meeting was the last occasion when our Embassy, represented by the Treasury attaché and the present writer, took part in the monetary discussions, which were thereafter conducted entirely on the other side of the Atlantic except for discussions from time to time between the United Kingdom and the representatives of the Dominions and India. The Canadians went to Washington for discussions and in June added another plan to the Keynes and White plans.

From time to time differences arose among the U.S., U.K., and Canadian representatives on a number of points in the monetary plans. These had first arisen in the conversation between Keynes and White in our embassy. White held tenaciously that the capital fund should be subscribed by governments in the orthodox manner. In March 1943, Keynes, who had resisted this for some months, expressed to me the opinion that the principle of subscribed capital was "academically discreditable but not practically important." He and his colleagues in the Treasury were seriously disturbed, however, by what they considered to be the inadequate size of the fund proposed in the U.S. plan. But White was inclined to reduce rather than to increase the fund, especially after he and Mr. Morgenthau began to take soundings in congressional circles.

The acceptance of the principle of subscribed capital placed the

United Kingdom in a less favorable voting position than she would have had under the Clearing Union Plan. Each of the proposals for an international monetary organization was based on "weighted" voting—a far-reaching divergence from the principle, "one country, one vote," which had been accepted in all important international bodies, whether political or economic, up to then. The divergence went in different directions in the Keynes and White Plans. In the White Plan it leaned toward the principle, "He who pays the piper calls the tune," and thus would have tended to set up an aristocracy of wealth. In the Keynes Plan it would have set up an aristocracy of commerce, favoring the nations of shopkeepers. When the nations were arrayed in order of their wealth the United States came off best; when they were arrayed according to their prewar commercial importance Britain took a leading position.

It is perhaps an oversimplification to say that the White Plan would have adjusted voting to comparative wealth or income. As we have seen, the voting formula proposed was made up of a hodgepodge of criteria arbitrarily lumped together, with a superficial appearance of "objectivity" masking the real aim of political expediency. In the first edition of the White Plan it would have given the United States such sweeping power in the organization that it could not be taken seriously: obviously White was using it as a position from which to bargain. Keynes opposed it vigorously but by the spring of 1943 was less concerned about the precise voting formula. He said to me in March: "I now consider the success of the plan depends on the will to cooperate; without that will no manipulation of voting powers will help; with it the details of voting are of secondary importance."

Both Keynes and the other leading Treasury officers doubted whether the organization could serve any large purpose in the postwar period unless it could draw on more resources. They seem never to have modified this view. Reluctantly, they came gradually to acquiesce in the argument based on political necessity in Washington, but it went against the economic grain. At this time the British hoped for an organization much more immediately useful in the postwar period than the monetary fund ultimately became.

The sponsors of the monetary plan had to contend with domestic political difficulties in London as well as in Washington. But there was a sharp contrast between the kinds of obstacles in the two capitals. London's difficulties were to some extent shared by the Allied governments in exile. Writing to the State Department and Dr. White shortly before the informal discussions which took place in the early autumn of 1943 I called attention to one of these difficulties as follows:

"On certain points British opinion differs considerably from many sections of American opinion. The strong opposition in Britain to anything that smacks of laissez-faire or old-fashioned orthodoxy has been reinforced by inter-war economic developments to create a suspicion of the gold standard and of unregulated exchanges. This is readily explicable in terms of Britain's unfortunate experiences after 1926, and its quicker recovery after 1931 than was made by a number of other leading countries.

"It is my understanding that the recent movement in Washington in favor of requiring that a large proportion of the contributions to the international fund of countries possessing substantial amounts of gold should be made in gold, arises out of a desire to reduce the great inequalities between the reserve positions of different countries. This may be on sound lines but the case for it needs to be formulated with special care in relation to opinion outside the United States. It is doubtful whether it is yet appreciated sufficiently here. First, there is some fear that the public may interpret it as giving undue prominence to gold. Second, it may tend to be viewed less favorably in smaller countries whose gold reserves, though substantial in proportion to their reserve needs, are small in an absolute sense and in relation to world stocks or American stocks. Some feel that such countries might hesitate to hand over a large proportion of their gold at the outset to a new institution."

A section of British public opinion misconceived the relation of the White Plan to the gold standard and even up to the time of ratification of the Bretton Woods agreement looked with fear and suspicion on the plans for an international monetary fund. Whitehall did not share these fears and wisely strove to avoid words and phrases that might intensify them.

Already there were indications of hostility in some Washington departments to the "dollar pool" of the sterling area[2] and even to the continuance of exchange controls for more than a brief period after the war. A few academic economists in the United States actually

[2] This will be discussed later.

held that the United Kingdom should abandon exchange controls at the end of the war and rely on exchange depreciation to adjust the balance of payments! In the following passage in the communication just referred to I attempted to represent the position as it appeared on the spot.

"In practice it may not be easy to control exchanges and regulate capital movements without in any way causing hindrances or delays to bona fide current transactions and capital movements that lead to increased total productivity. But experience not only with the British but also with the European Allied governments in London leads to the conclusion that these difficulties will have to be faced and overcome and it will not, at least for several years after the war, be practicable in Britain or on the European continent to retreat into a position in which there is no control over exchanges except that which is exercised by an exchange stabilization or 'equalization' fund, the manipulation of money rates and open market operations."

In June 1943 informal discussions took place in Washington between the British Treasury and Embassy representatives and U.S. Treasury officials. They were designed to prepare the ground for fuller discussions between a U.S. and U.K. group in Washington later in the summer. The sudden death in London of Sir Frederick Phillips, the able British Treasury representative who had taken a prominent part in these talks, set back British preparations for a time, but the conversations began in September and made great progress. They were part of the first full-fledged talks provided for in the text of Article VII of the Mutual Aid Agreement.

Throughout the winter, conversations took place among experts of some thirty of the United and Associated Nations and the result was embodied in a "Joint Statement by Experts on the Establishment of an International Monetary Fund of the United and Associated Nations." This document was published in the capitals of the leading Allies. The experts had worked on the three separate plans of the U.K., U.S. and Canada. The new draft resembled the White Plan in many respects. The capital was to be subscribed and this time a definite amount was inserted, equal to $8,000 million, if all the United and Associated nations joined, as compared with the earlier White proposal of "at least" $5,000 million. The gold subscription proposed in the revised White Plan of July 1943 had been scaled down sharply in response to the wishes of Britain and a number of smaller countries. A different schedule of borrowing powers had been laid down. The powers of member countries to change their exchange rates were increased: changes of 10 per cent might be made unilaterally and an application for a further 10 per cent was to be passed on by the Fund within two days. In practice a member country could thus change its rates by 20 per cent without much difficulty. Thus British insistence on greater flexibility of exchange rates had been met. The provision for rationing of scarce currencies was maintained, but the exclusive jurisdiction of each member country to apportion the limited supplies among its nationals was affirmed. The proposal to establish an international unit of currency was dropped.

But the most important change, as it seemed to me at the time and appears even more strongly in retrospect, was to be found in the abandonment of the provisions in all versions of the White Plan and in the Canadian plan to deal with wartime-blocked balances. In a new section headed "Transitional Arrangements" it was stated that "... the Fund is not intended to provide facilities for relief or reconstruction or to deal with international indebtedness arising out of the war. . . ."[3]

Thus disappeared the last vestiges of the bold attempts of Keynes and White to shape the international monetary body into an effective instrument for dealing with short-run as well as long-run questions and in particular for grappling with the immediate difficulties of the transition period, which seemed likely, even at that time, to transcend all other questions in importance as soon as the war ended. A leading British Treasury official, however, had informed me earlier that he hoped for a "scaling down" of the war debts incurred by Britain in helping to defend Egypt, India, and other areas, and feared that the inclusion of the clauses in the White Plan or the Canadian plan which dealt with blocked balances would encourage Britain's creditors to hold out for a larger measure of repayment, in the belief that they could get it from the Fund if they could not get it from Britain. It was difficult to determine how widely this view was held in Whitehall. No doubt something might be said on these grounds for postponing the adoption of international measures for dealing with blocked balances until preliminary negotiations for the reduction of

[3] U.S. Department of State, International Organization and Conference Series: Pub. 3031. *Proceedings and Documents of the United Nations Monetary and Financial Conference*, Washington, Government Printing Office, 1948, p. 1635.

the debts had taken place. But there was a serious defect in such reasoning. First, there was no assurance that the creditors would voluntarily agree to a substantial reduction of the debts in direct negotiation. Second, the opportunity to commit the member countries of the Fund to a plan for dealing with blocked balances would be lost if it were not taken at the outset and incorporated into the terms of reference of the organization. The categorical statement that the Fund was not intended to deal with war debts removed all hope that the clauses dealing with blocked balances could be revived at a more appropriate time. Third, if the Fund were not to be used to deal with war debts, what prospect was there that any other international body would be found more appropriate for the purpose? If this function were not to be given to any international organization it would have to be left to ad hoc action in which the debtor would be at a grave disadvantage.

In those days the plans for an international monetary fund to deal with balance-of-payments difficulties overshadowed those for an international organization to lend capital for reconstruction and development. The experts of the thirty countries who issued the "Joint Statement" in April 1944 confined themselves to the former. There were some wider informal exchanges of views between London and Washington. Dr. White and his colleagues particularly wished to obtain British views on the terms of reference of the proposed international bank: they pointed to the long experience of London in lending abroad. Some memoranda were exchanged in 1943, and in November the U.S. Treasury published a draft scheme for the first time. In many points it resembled the proposals in the original unpublished White Plan. But the emphasis had shifted. There was no longer any suggestion that the resources of the bank might be used to finance relief shipments, or postwar reconstruction loans at "nominal" rates of interest. "Development" now took an equal place with "reconstruction" in the objectives of the proposed organization. In short, when this and the earlier plan prepared in 1942 are compared a trend may be detected away from immediate short-run postwar functions toward greater concentration on long-run functions to be discharged after the postwar transition had ended. This trend resembled but did not go so far as the trend running through the successive versions of the plans for the international monetary fund or union. Short-term functions were not eliminated from the Bank as they had been from the Fund. But they were losing ground and were not destined to regain it.

Whitehall, under the influence of Mr. Keynes and his Treasury colleagues and of Nigel Ronald of the Foreign Office, and Washington, under the influence of Dr. Harry White and Mr. Morgenthau, pressed steadily on with preparations for setting up the Fund and the Bank. As we shall see in another chapter, progress on other Article VII matters was held up in 1944 by internal controversies in Westminster. But this did not affect the monetary and investment plans, and the final conference to clinch them was held at Bretton Woods in the middle of 1944. Shortly before that conference a meeting of experts was held in Atlantic City. Hence the Bretton Woods agreement was the culmination of much labor, discussion, argument and compromise. If all other general conferences on postwar matters had been preceded by preparations as thorough as those which preceded the Bretton Woods conference, much international friction would have been avoided.

Nevertheless, it was a strenuous conference at Bretton Woods and the delegates were on the verge of exhaustion at the close. Many alternative drafts of the Articles of Agreement of the Fund were debated, and much work remained to be done on the Bank. Since the documents on the conference have been published it is not necessary here to summarize the discussions,[4] and attention will be directed mainly to those points which are most relevant to the main thesis of the present study.

The earlier inclusion in all versions of the White Plan of proposals for dealing with war debts, and its later abandonment in the "Joint Statement" of the experts, had been noticed by countries not represented in preceding discussions. A new clause was proposed which would have included among the purposes of the Fund "the multilateral settlement of foreign credit balances accumulated during the war."[5] An alternative draft proposed that the Fund should "promote and facilitate settlement of abnormal indebtedness arising out of war."[6] These drafts were offered by Egypt and India, the two largest wartime sterling creditors of the United Kingdom. They were pushed vigorously for a time but spokesmen for other countries argued that it would be difficult and dangerous to place on the Fund the

[4] See preceding footnote.

[5] *Proceedings and Documents, op.cit.*, 122.

[6] *ibid.*, 123.

responsibility for arranging the settlement of such large indebtedness. The sponsors of the proposals persisted in their efforts and endeavored to meet objections by a new draft, offered by India, as follows: "To facilitate the multilateral settlement of a reasonable portion of the foreign credit balances accumulated among the member countries during the war so as to promote the purposes referred to . . . without placing undue strain on the resources of the Fund."[7]

But the U.S., U.K., and France firmly opposed the inclusion of any of these statements. The U.S. spokesman expressed confidence that "the problem can best be settled directly by the countries concerned,"[8] and argued that, "The Fund can contribute most effectively to the solution of international monetary problems if it confines its work to the specialized tasks for which it is designed."[9] He added the vague and unjustifiably optimistic forecast that, "While the International Monetary Fund cannot deal directly with indebtedness arising out of the war . . . its operations will facilitate the development of an environment of orderly and stable exchanges free from restrictions that hamper world trade—an environment in which the problem of wartime indebtedness can be amicably settled by the countries directly concerned."[10]

The British view was stated by Lord Keynes, who argued that the Fund was not intended to deal with war debts, and stated as the "clear and settled judgment" of the United Kingdom that "the settlement of these debts must be . . . a matter between those directly concerned."[11] In the eloquent language with which he so often adorned what would otherwise have been purely formal statements he lifted the subject to a higher plane: "The various members of this alliance have suffered in mind, body and estate from the effort and exhaustion of war in ways differing in kind and in degree. These sacrifices cannot be weighed one against the other. Those of us who were most directly threatened and were nevertheless able to remain in the fight, such as the U.S.S.R. and the United Kingdom, have fought this war on the principle of unlimited liability and with a more reckless disregard of economic consequences than others who were more fortunately placed. We do not plead guilty of imprudence; for in the

[7] *ibid.*, 278. For the able and moderate arguments of the Indian delegate for this clause see *ibid.*, 1171-73.

[8] *ibid.*, 1168.

[9] *ibid.*, 1169.

[10] *ibid.*

[11] *ibid.*, 1170.

larger field of human affairs nothing could have been less prudent than hesitation or a careful counting of the cost."[12]

Thus passed without result the only organized effort made during the war to deal with the war debts by international action. Not only was the new international monetary organization to stand aside when questions of war debts arose but no prospect was held out that any other international body would step in to fill the gap. The question was to be left to bilateral negotiations. It may, and to me it still does, appear strange that a debtor country should have come out for a procedure which placed it at a disadvantage in bargaining. Apparently the government of the United Kingdom believed that its creditors would accept the overwhelming moral case for writing off a large part of the debts. This is a tribute to the integrity of British officials but not to their insight into political conditions in the creditor countries.

The clause which stated that the Fund was "not intended to provide facilities for relief or reconstruction . . ." was accepted with little controversy. UNRRA had been established about six months earlier but its funds were not to be used to pay for relief imports into Western Europe. No financial provision had been made to finance reconstruction in any country, but the Bank and not the Fund was considered to be the appropriate body for that purpose. The Netherlands delegation interpreted the relevant clause in the articles of agreement as permitting "the use of the resources of the Fund for the financing of the imported commodities which might be considered as relief goods," but excluding "the use of the resources of the Fund in a quasi-permanent way for the financing of relief or any other imports."[13] This interpretation should be read in the light of the conditions of the time. "Relief" goods were widely understood to consist largely of food and other goods for final consumption, while most producer goods were to be supplied as a part of reconstruction and "development." This was not a rigid line and there was a danger of confusion. The Western European countries were to pay for their imports of consumer as well as producer goods and therefore did not wish the former to be classified as "relief." Actually, distinctions among relief, rehabilitation, and reconstruction do not correspond precisely to distinctions between different types of goods.

Some of the critics of the proposed articles of agreement of the

[12] *ibid.*

[13] *ibid.*, 607.

Fund had argued earlier that the needs of countries in the immediate postwar period might cause a dangerous drain on the Fund unless safeguards were devised. However, once the principle of subscribed capital had been adopted it was difficult to prohibit access to the Fund by countries which kept within the limits of their drawing rights. In practice these limits were themselves a sharp check on the use of the funds for financing relief or reconstruction. In addition a new clause was introduced at Bretton Woods (Article 5, section 5) giving the Fund power to limit or cut off access to it by a member country which has used "the resources of the Fund in a manner contrary to the purposes of the Fund. . . ."

Thus it remains substantially accurate to say that the International Monetary Fund was suited to deal with short-period fluctuations affecting international balances of payments, but not with long-continued and deep-seated economic maladjustments resulting from drastic wartime changes in the economic positions of countries, nor with the disruption of the network of multilateral world trade. The Fund was adapted to help a country to tide over a temporary shortage of foreign exchange without disrupting its own monetary system and perhaps injuring those of other countries. But the shortage had to be temporary and the advances repayable within a few years. These conditions existed in Britain in 1931, but already in 1944 it was clear to a few, and ought to have been clear to the many, that they did not exist then and would not exist for some years after the war. Circumscribed by the perverse politics of Washington, the representatives at Bretton Woods, like the experts who laid the ground for them, in adopting the Articles of Agreement for the Fund, prepared to deal with a recurrence of the last great depression. Their work might bear fruit in a more distant future; for the early postwar period it was of little value. Starting on ambitious lines conceived by men of insight and imagination, it was whittled down in successive stages to pass the scrutiny of little men of conventional views and partisan political motives.

Before the meeting at Bretton Woods much less attention had been given to the plans for the International Bank for Reconstruction and Development than to those for the Monetary Fund. Yet within the limits imposed by political obstacles the Bretton Woods plan for the structure and functions of the Bank was more clear cut and held out more promise for the early postwar period than its plan for the

Fund. In the public discussion that followed the conference the plans for the Bank drew more widespread support than those for the Fund.

The White Plan for the Bank had given more prominence to reconstruction than to development, but the presence of representatives from the underdeveloped countries led to increased emphasis on development in the Articles of Agreement accepted at Bretton Woods. The articles gave roughly equal prominence to both functions. Some of the underdeveloped countries proposed a rule that reconstruction and development loans should be made in equal amounts. Fortunately, this proposal was rejected; its acceptance would have either restricted reconstruction loans unduly or extended development loans beyond the scope of well-conceived plans for using them.

The conditions under which the International Bank was to lend were discussed at length during the conference. Lord Keynes, in my talks with him in London, had frequently spoken of the danger that if governments or an intergovernmental organization were to conduct or guide international lending the flow of capital for risky ventures would be reduced. It was his opinion that one of the most important factors in world development had been the willingness of investors abroad to run risks and embark on what by conventional standards would be considered unsound enterprises. He sometimes spoke scornfully of "sound" and "prudent" lending, and on some days when I met him he seemed pessimistic about the possibilities of establishing a vigorous and enterprising international organization to lend for purposes of development. A trace of Keynes's viewpoint seems to have crept into one of the draft clauses put forward at Bretton Woods as follows:

"In making or guaranteeing a loan the Bank shall pay due regard to the prospects of the borrowing country being in a position to service the loan; and in determining the destination, the character and the volume of its loans it shall act prudently in the interests both of the borrowing member country and also of the guaranteeing members. At the same time it shall not seek to avoid the incurring of some measure of reasonable risk (taking account of the commission chargeable—see below) where the loan is in the general interests of reconstructing or developing the world's resources or expanding international trade along mutually advantageous lines; and shall seek to conduct its operations taken as a whole in such manner as to avoid, so far as possible, the calling up of the capital reserved for guarantees, rather than seek full security from risk in each transaction taken separately. These considerations shall govern the lending policy of the Bank especially in approving reconstruction loans to countries which have suffered from the war."

CHAPTER IV

International Control of Raw Materials

BEFORE the war a series of measures variously described as "raw material controls," "commodity agreements," "commodity arrangements" were applied to a number of agricultural and mineral raw materials that entered widely into international trade. The controls, agreements, and arrangements differed widely in scope. Some were wholly governmental, some were partly governmental, and some were made between groups of producers in different countries. The form and scope of representation on the control bodies differed widely from one to another; consumers of most of the products had little voice in the agreements that were reached. The control bodies acted independently of one another and the principles followed were widely divergent. Rarely could any of them be reconciled with the principle of equal access to markets and raw materials. There was no supervisory body and no court of appeal. In these circumstances it was not surprising that international commodity controls were frequently a source of international friction and that sharp diplomatic exchanges took place between a number of the countries which later became allies in a common cause during the war.

Prewar commodity agreements ceased to be of immediate practical importance under wartime conditions, when the idea of "surplus" had given way to the reality of scarcity. But many of them were merely held in abeyance and in the absence of a new approach would come into force again at the end of the war. The renewal of some of them after the war was already being considered in 1943.

A choice had therefore to be made among (a) forming no policy and taking no action at all; (b) adopting a negative policy aimed at suppressing all raw material agreements; or (c) planning international measures to avoid excessive fluctuations in raw material prices, to provide a way out of serious maladjustments in the conditions of supply of some important raw materials, and to ensure that such agreements as might be made were consistent with the other postwar economic aims of the Allies.

A refusal to make plans for concerted international action on raw material questions would have left the way open for the restoration of the prewar hodge-podge of uncoordinated raw material controls, most of which were inconsistent with the principles accepted in Article VII of the Lend Lease Agreement. The expansion of high-cost production during the war would leave many raw material producers in a difficult position when wartime demand declined, and it seemed likely that if the international organizations to be set up in the postwar period took no action on commodity agreements the chief producing interests would seek to maintain unduly high prices by restrictive agreements sheltering high-cost production. This would place a severe burden on consuming countries not fortunate enough to possess domestic sources of supply. Hence an attitude of laissez-faire and a hands-off policy not only would fail to solve old difficulties but might create new difficulties, especially in the later part of the transition from wartime to peacetime conditions of supply and demand.

An attempt at organized suppression of all controls gave no better prospect of a satisfactory solution. There were indeed extreme supporters of anti-monopoly measures who, besides striking at private international monopolies, would have dissolved all raw material controls and agreements—whether wholly governmental, partly governmental, or between private producers—and would have prohibited the formation of new ones. But to attempt to solve raw material problems simply by police measures would be to assume that apart from monopolistic practices there would be no raw material problems, and the supply of and demand for all raw materials would be adjusted "automatically" at satisfactory levels. It may indeed be readily agreed that some of the prewar raw material controls at times aggravated instead of relieving maladjustments. But it does not follow that when maladjustments exist—even if they came into existence solely through unsound measures of control—they are best corrected by a policy of non-interference. Nor can it be safely assumed that, when no appreciable maladjustments exist, none will be likely to arise so long as there is no organized interference with "the free play of supply and demand." The textbooks of academic economics, notwithstanding a superficial appearance of sublety, give an extraordinarily oversimplified impression of the complex conditions of supply and demand in the real world. If adjustments of supply are more difficult in agriculture generally than in industry they are even more strikingly difficult in tree-crop agriculture which now supplies both food and industrial raw materials. And although output may sometimes be changed more easily in mining than in agriculture the fluctuations in the conditions of supply go far beyond those in manufacturing industry.

Finally, the violent fluctuations in raw material prices, short-period as well as long-period, seasonal as well as "cyclical" or "secular," are often disproportionate to the changes in the conditions of supply and demand which touch them off, and instead of serving as a corrective or making for readjustment, in themselves create new dislocations.

Such, in brief outline, was the case which, early in the war, presented itself to the postwar planners—the case for seeking international cooperation in the preparation of measures for dealing with postwar raw material problems.[1]

Although the subject arose during unofficial discussions in the quiescent opening months of the war, it entered prominently into government negotiations only when, in the summer of 1941, discussions commenced between the United Kingdom and the four leading wheat-exporting countries (the United States, Canada, Australia and Argentina) on a postwar international wheat agreement. A small committee drafted a "Provisional Wheat Agreement" providing for export quotas, enforced by the importing countries, and for the regulation of wheat prices in accordance with an average of the wholesale price indexes in the four exporting countries.

For a time the work of the committee, which sat in Washington, attracted little attention: Whitehall was occupied with urgent war matters. The British member of the drafting committee, who had assented to the proposed plan, had not been as closely in touch with opinion in the United Kingdom as British representatives usually are. When Whitehall awakened to the significance of the proposals the British delegation that went to Washington to take up negotiations in full conference was instructed to oppose them. The United States delegation, however, was dominated by the Department of

[1] The preceding statement follows the lines of a memorandum which I submitted in Washington during my visit in the spring of 1943.

Agriculture, which strongly supported the draft proposals. The negotiations soon reached a deadlock, and in the embassy in London we were drawn into the controversy in the autumn of 1941 just at the time when we were endeavoring to obtain British agreement to the principle of freer, nondiscriminating trade in the postwar period.

It was not long before I found, and reported to Ambassador Winant, that the proposed wheat agreement was prejudicing the chances of agreement on the text of the postwar clause in the draft Lend-Lease Agreement. Whitehall doubted the sincerity of our advocacy of freer, nondiscriminating postwar trade when we were at the same time demanding that the British, instead of buying in the cheapest market, should buy in fixed proportions from four markets and should be responsible for preventing any attempts by merchants to exceed the quota from any of the markets. This would have raised the average price of the most important and irreplaceable item in British imports. Since the principal question that worried officials in Whitehall at the time was how to pay for future imports after the loss of external assets, they were dismayed by a proposal to make their chief import dearer and to deprive them of the right of buyer's choice between markets with divergent costs.

The all too frequent inconsistencies in the United States position, which were hardly noticed in the highly specialized departments and divisions in Washington, placed Ambassador Winant in a difficult position. Information and instructions converged on our embassy from different parts of Washington, and the inconsistencies and incompatibilities of piecemeal policies were thrown into clear light. During the war Washington sometimes appeared at a distance to contain not one government but three or four governments engaged in a competitive struggle in which one dominated on one issue and another on another issue. Since the principles underlying the issues often overlapped, it was not surprising that when external affairs were handled in that way confusion arose at home and bewilderment abroad.

When I reported my conversations in Whitehall to Ambassador Winant he quickly appreciated the danger to the Article VII negotiations and, though occupied with urgent war problems, turned his attention to the wheat question for some hours, inquired into every aspect of the economic issues involved, scrutinized a critical draft message which I had prepared for Washington, and added some sharp sentences to it.

The Wheat Conference ended in agreement on a very different draft from that with which it started. A draft convention was drawn up for submission to an international wheat conference to be held "at a propitious time." In the intervening period, however, a provision to set up a relief pool of wheat for future use in liberated areas was to take effect if conditions permitted. The price provisions in the original draft were replaced by a sensible provision for an annual agreement on maximum and minimum prices for the year. Consumer countries were to be fully represented. Quotas for the exporting countries were to be expressed as percentages of the total volume of international trade in wheat, and stocks in the exporting countries were to be held within agreed upper and lower limits. The draft convention was to remain a draft until a truly international conference could be called; thus were removed the fears of countries not represented at the Washington meeting that agreements affecting them would be made without consulting them. In short, the draft convention, though open to criticism on some points, was a marked advance on earlier schemes. Whitehall, like Washington, had its internal differences on raw material agreements, and some officials disapproved of certain provisions, particularly those providing for export quotas. But there would be an opportunity to reconsider such provisions at a full international conference in the future.

Following this controversy, though not necessarily because of it, Whitehall studied postwar raw material questions, and during 1942 and the first half of 1943 the attention given to the subject in postwar planning was perhaps second only to that given to international monetary questions. However, the approach to it was not the same in all parts of Whitehall and there was much debate over the recommendations to be made. Keynes took the initiative vigorously on a plan for "buffer stocks" to reduce industrial fluctuations, while a group of Board of Trade officials under Sir Frederick Leith Ross were concerned chiefly with plans for improving the position of raw material producers. Thus the point of view of Keynes differed from that of the Board of Trade raw material specialists both on the purpose and on the means of international commodity control. Keynes was not experimenting with a subject new to him; he was following up and trying to apply in practice ideas which he had formed in more than a decade. These ideas were a side product of his concern with trade cycles. As far back as the 1920's he initiated with J. W. F. Rowe some studies in commodity stocks and their relations to economic fluctuations, which were published in the bulletins of the London and Cambridge Economic Service. In the later 1930's, when war was near, he turned his attention to commodity stockpiling for national defense. In August 1938, he stated his views in a brilliantly written paper at the annual British Association meeting.[2]

In characteristic manner, Keynes looked beyond the immediate difficulties of producers and consumers of particular raw materials to the origin of those difficulties in a fundamental weakness of the competitive system of individual enterprise. "The competitive system," he said, "abhors the existence of stocks, with as strong a reflex as nature abhors a vacuum, because stocks yield a *negative* return in terms of themselves. It is ready without remorse to tear the structure of output to pieces rather than admit them, and in the effort to rid itself of them. . . . If demand fluctuates, a divergence immediately ensues between the general interest and the course of action in respect of stocks which is most advantageous for each competitive enterprise acting independently."[3]

This disharmony arose, in Keynes's view, from the cost of storage, from the tendency of speculative buyers on a declining market to await further decline before buying, from the disinclination of the trader and manufacturer to run speculative risks by buying materials well in advance of the need to use them, and from the limited ability of the outside speculator to maintain stocks without rapid turnover. The result was that on the one hand the prices of raw materials subject to unrestricted competition fluctuated widely, and on the other the prices of raw materials brought under private control were much more stable, but this stability had been achieved by private monopoly.

Keynes then discussed the powers given to the government by the Essential Commodities Reserve Act which Parliament had just passed into law. The immediate object of the act was to assist in building stocks for war needs. Keynes agreed that this should remain the dominant object until "the arrival of happier days." But he

[2] J. M. Keynes, "The Policy of Government Storage of Foodstuffs and Raw Materials," *The Economic Journal*, September, 1938, pp. 449-60.

[3] *ibid.*, p. 449.

argued that in peacetime the powers of the act should be used to carry a fluctuating volume of raw material stocks "so as to damp down the trade cycle." He proposed "that the Government should offer storage to all Empire producers of specified raw materials, either free of warehouse charges and interest or for a nominal charge, provided they ship their surplus produce to approved warehouses in this country."[4] The stocks "would remain in the ownership of the depositors." Their presence in the U.K. would be invaluable if war broke out, but in addition the procedure could be financed in such a way as to diminish price fluctuations in peacetime. Even the Exchange Stabilization Fund might hold liquid stocks of raw materials as well as stocks of gold and devisen.

In the postwar planning in Whitehall in 1942, Keynes returned to this subject. This time he was faced with a somewhat different problem. In 1938, partly for war purposes and partly for stabilization purposes, he had urged the government to store in the U.K. large stocks of raw materials produced in the British Empire. In 1942, he urged that the Allied governments should take international measures to store raw materials in suitable places for stabilization purposes. He expressed himself with as much brilliance and feeling as he had shown four years earlier. His object was a plan for primary products which the U.K. and the U.S.A. could both accept and jointly sponsor, and which would not be open to the charge that it was designed to serve restrictive and selfish ends. In conversations which I had with him at the time, Keynes deprecated schemes that would tend to keep raw materials trade in fixed channels. There must, he said, be provision for peaceful evolutionary change to meet technical advances, improvements in transport between particular areas, changes in taste, and the introduction of substitutes. Over a long period there must be room for gradual changes in prices in harmony with changes in the fundamental conditions under which raw materials are produced and consumed.

But the violent short-term price fluctuation in the prewar period was one of the greatest evils in international trade, and its reduction was Keynes's chief aim. Keynes distinguished between "true de-

[4] P. 455. The reason for specifying Empire countries was economic, not political. Keynes feared a strain on the exchanges and pointed out that in the case of Empire products "the proceeds of additional financing are more likely to remain here as an accretion to the banking reserves of the sterling area." (p. 457)

mand" and "apparent demand." The first was demand for current use together with "normal" and necessary stocks. The second was actual demand, which fluctuated much more widely than true demand because it was influenced by the operations of merchants dealing in stocks and speculators entering the market when prospects for speculative profits were favorable and leaving it when they were unfavorable.

The central point in Keynes's plan was the establishment of buffer stocks for important raw materials entering into international trade. These were to be regulated and administered by an international body, composed of a General Council for Commodity Controls and a group of individual Commodity Controls each dealing with a particular product. The General Council would pass on proposed plans for particular commodities, in accordance with the principles of policy accepted by the countries taking part, and would from time to time review the operations of the Commodity Controls and, when desirable, approve changes in the basic prices and the size of the stocks. Its functions were first, by buying and selling operations, to stabilize, within a range of 20 per cent, the prices of that part of raw material production which entered into international trade, and second, to hold stocks sufficient to offset short-period fluctuations in demand and supply. With these limitations competitive international markets would continue. The location of stocks would be widely distributed. Keynes assumed that some form of international security and police organization would be set up and that the commodity controls would cooperate with it in deciding how to distribute its stocks of raw materials particularly important in war.

In preparing the Clearing Union Plan, Keynes had suggested that it should be used to finance buffer stocks. In preparing a commodity control plan, he developed this idea in more detail. The difference between the buying and selling prices of the Commodity Controls might cover costs of storage, he said without optimism, but the total resources needed to finance holdings might be large. First he advocated that over-drafts should be provided by the Clearing Union, but when calculations were made of the costs of carrying even "normal" stocks of some of the chief commodities he suggested that in addition public loans guaranteed by the Clearing Union might be raised to lessen the strain on the funds of the Union.

Thus Keynes was chiefly if not wholly interested in Commodity

Controls for purposes of reducing economic instability generally and not for purposes of aiding high-cost producers in distress. He felt no enthusiasm for and much suspicion towards most of the prewar types of commodity control, with their production restrictions and their export quotas, their one-sided representation of vested interests and their failure to touch the roots of maladjustments.

His view did not pass unchallenged in Whitehall. The Board of Trade at that time contained a section under Sir Frederick Leith-Ross working on raw material questions. Within this section were a number of specialists with experience in the working of some of the prewar commodity controls. They were critical of Keynes's early drafts on the ground that buffer stocks without quantitative regulation of output would break down in practice because of the slowness in the response of output to price changes. In personal conversations they said that Keynes, however brilliant an economist he might be, had no "practical" experience of commodity controls. But a number of other Whitehall officials, including economists in the War Cabinet secretariat, were more ready to support Keynes than to support the officials who favored quantitative controls.

However, provision was made in the version of the paper accepted later to permit the use of export quotas in special cases approved by the General Council. It was agreed that export quotas might be useful if they were applied only to ease the pains of transition when old sources of supply or old products had to give way to new and cheaper ones. The differences arose on the question whether the abuses would outweigh the proper uses of what should be a temporary device but in the past had too often come to stay. Consequently, the opening left in the U.K. plan for quantitative restrictions was carefully hedged around with qualifications and limitations to prevent its use until alternative remedies had been considered and to close it as soon as the need for it had passed.

It is a tribute to the initiative, the originality and the energy of Keynes that the proposals for buffer stocks and commodity controls should have come from the Treasury. The British Treasury has a wide concern with economic affairs, but under ordinary conditions it would be less likely than several other departments to lead the way in questions relating to particular raw materials. As it was, Keynes's first paper stirred up a wide interest in a number of other departments in plans for dealing with international raw material questions after the war, including the Colonial Office, which before the war had struggled with the difficulties of colonial raw material producers. Officials of the Board of Trade, the Colonial Office, and the India Office took an active part in the discussions in the Inter-departmental Committee on Keynes's paper. They held that quantitative regulation of some raw materials would at times be necessary for the success of the general plan. Some of them, I believe, remained privately unconvinced that the paper which was agreed on went far enough in this direction.

However, there were strong restraining influences in Great Britain on those who were inclined to favor restriction of raw material production and quota regulation of exports. The Colonial Office had to concern itself with the interests of territories one of whose chief means of livelihood lay in the exports of primary products. But most other departments, and notably the Treasury, were occupied with the needs of the United Kingdom as the world's largest importer of food and raw materials. The regulation by quotas of exports from the food and raw material exporting countries tends to restrict the power of an importing country to buy in the cheapest markets, to bolster up high-cost production among overseas suppliers, and thus to raise the cost of the largest items among the indispensable imports of a country that cannot possibly supply all of its own needs of commodities essential to life. Unless export prices rise this in turn tends to increase the physical quantity of exports needed to offset a given physical quantity of imports. At a time when the loss of overseas investments had already increased the quantity of exports needed to offset the large irreducible amount of indispensable imports, the civil servants of the Treasury, the Department of Overseas Trade, the Cabinet secretariat, and the Foreign Office looked askance at any schemes that might add to a burden which Lend-Lease had postponed but which would fall with a great shock on the British public at the end of the war.

Nevertheless, British officials took a reasonable view of the difficulties of overseas food and raw material producers. With characteristic moderation they held that it was not in the long-run interests of Great Britain to take the fullest advantage of these difficulties when they arose. Though the wide fluctuations under laissez-faire conditions brought abnormal cheapness in some years, in others they sometimes led to high prices, resulting either from spontaneous contraction of supplies by individual producers or from organized restriction schemes designed to remove or prevent the accumulation of surpluses. Even more important, perhaps, was the relation between the overseas demand for British manufactured goods and the prices of food and raw materials in world markets. The collapse of food and raw material prices on the world market in depressions sharply reduced the ability of the overseas producing countries to buy manufactures abroad and to remit payments on interest and amortization due on previous loans. Whitehall was therefore willing to pay somewhat higher prices for overseas food and raw materials than might otherwise have to be paid in depression, if, by so doing, fluctuations in the markets for primary products could be reduced, the goodwill of overseas producers could be retained and their ability to purchase United Kingdom exports could be sustained.

Finally, the point of view of the domestic agricultural producer was represented in the government. It could not be given free rein in a country so dependent as Great Britain was on imports of agricultural products. But during the war British farmers were achieving extraordinary increases in domestic production in spite of a wide mobilization of agricultural workers for the army. The supplies of agricultural machinery were increasing, the efficiency of land utilization was rising, partly through the organized spread of knowledge and partly through the work of the local agricultural committees which held the power to supplant inefficient farmers. These developments increased the influence of British agricultural interests. The grain producers among them were attracted by any scheme to prevent grain prices from falling to low levels. It was not, therefore, an accident or a mere matter of personal idiosyncrasy that in 1941 and 1942 R. S. Hudson, Minister of Agriculture in the coalition government—a minister who took unusual pains to master the details of his work—had been the chief supporter of the Wheat Agreement among British ministers. In a conversation with me, he expressed approval of the quota regulation of trade and of the Wheat Agreement and sharply criticized Article VII of the Mutual Aid agreement. He appeared to have no faith in comparative cost as a regulator of trade between nations and favored stiff international bargaining—usually between governments acting partly on behalf of private producers—which would lead to agreements to exchange specified amounts of different classes of goods. His aim appeared to be, not bilateral balancing of trade but a sort of managed multilateral trade.

These views were not widely shared in the Conservative Party. But before the war the Conservative ministries had imposed "quota" restrictions on imports of the more perishable agricultural products. Major Walter Elliott, a distinguished administrator who, as Minister of Agriculture for some years in the 1930's had led the move to impose these restrictions, appeared in a conversation which I had with him to find difficulty in appreciating, even in principle, the benefits of regional specialization. At times he seemed full of an emotional dislike of international trade!

But changes of government and the establishment of the Ministry of Food brought a policy which ensured that the consumer's interest would not in the future be subordinated to the extent to which it had been in the 1930's.

The outcome of these varied and on some points conflicting currents of opinion was a document more restrained than some groups wished it to be but free of doctrinaire tendencies and flexible enough to be adapted to the incompletely foreseeable conditions that might arise in the working of the controls. It was hoped in Whitehall that the document might be used in 1942 as a basis for informal Anglo-American discussions. But these hopes were not to be fulfilled for some time to come.

When, after an absence of eighteen months, I arrived in Washington to take part in the preparatory work for the Hot Springs Food Conference I was unable to discover any organized interdepartmental planning on postwar raw material questions. But the agricultural aspects of these questions were certain to be raised during the conference, and in the United States secretariat (drawn from the Departments of Agriculture and State) which prepared the agenda and papers for the conference efforts were made to reach agreement on the position which the United States delegation should be recommended to take.

However, the differences within Washington were even more serious than those which existed within Whitehall at the time when Keynes put forward his paper on buffer stocks. The Department of Agriculture had pressed for a Wheat Agreement and was interested in securing a Cotton Agreement. In the prewar period the United

States had been losing ground as an exporter of wheat and cotton. The growth of population and of nonagricultural production and the rise in wages and land values were reducing the competitive power of the United States in agricultural raw material markets abroad. The increased domestic demand, arising mainly from the growth of population, was insufficient to take off the "surplus" production. International raw material agreements, which would fix export quotas based on a past period and modified by subsequent hard bargaining, would benefit a large and politically influential country whose exports of the raw products in question would otherwise decline. Other members of the Department of Agriculture were genuinely seeking remedies for the violent fluctuations in the fortunes of raw material producers the world over. The attitudes in the Department of State and in other departments differed from that in the Department of Agriculture, particularly in looking with suspicion on "producer interests." But there did not appear to be any settled and generally agreed position in the early spring of 1943, even within the State Department.

These differences were discussed in the United States secretariat which prepared papers for the United States delegates and eventually for the whole conference.[5] Those whose experience had been mainly in agricultural production matters argued that control of the amounts produced in, and of the proportions exported from, the chief producing countries were necessary in peacetime to carry out agreements effectively. Those whose experience was in marketing and consumption matters replied that such rigid controls would bolster up high-cost production indefinitely and play into the hands of vested interests. A compromise was reached between these conflicting views. It was agreed that control of production and exports should be accepted only on condition that measures to divert productive factors away from high-cost production would be put into force. Thus production quotas and export quotas would be temporary devices to ease the pains of transition, and would help to accomplish in an orderly manner what otherwise would be accomplished by bankruptcy and competitive reduction of wages or would be avoided by private

[5] Since the Hot Springs Conference was an ad hoc conference there was no standing international secretariat to prepare for it. Hence the working group formed by Mr. Acheson, with Dr. Howard Tolley as chairman, was in effect turned into a temporary international secretariat for the conference.

restrictive agreements or by hastily formed governmental schemes ignoring the interests of consuming countries.

Lively discussions of raw material agreements took place at Hot Springs. Some though not all of the fundamental issues were debated at length. The United Kingdom spokesmen expounded orally the substance of their paper on the subject but decided to withhold the paper until informal conversations began on Article VII of the Lend-Lease agreement. They stressed chiefly the stabilizing value of buffer stocks. But from personal conversations outside the meetings I gathered that there were differences of opinion within the British delegation. Although the secretariat had drawn up papers embodying general policy, the United States delegates held somewhat divergent views. In personal discussions outside the meetings at least three different policies were supported within the delegation and its advisers. Those from the Department of Agriculture advocated a number of agricultural raw material agreements with export quotas and if possible measures to regulate output. Some of those from other departments were skeptical both of buffer stocks and of quantitative regulation and preferred to rely mainly on measures to maintain full employment, which, they hoped, would prevent the accumulation of surpluses. Others were willing to experiment with buffer stocks and to control production and exports only as a temporary device during adjustments to lower average costs of production. Among the American delegates, Mr. Appleby represented a position more favorable and William Clayton one less favorable to commodity agreements, while both appeared to be skeptical of the practicability of buffer stocks without control of production.

These differences of opinion within national delegations, even when they were expressed openly and in conference meetings, should not, I think, be condemned. The Hot Springs Conference was a preliminary and exploratory conference and not a conference to draw up hard-and-fast operating plans for immediate and permanent adoption. At such a stage it may be all to the good that differences should cut across national lines: this makes for greater individual sincerity and for a clearer concentration on principles.

The resolution adopted at Hot Springs on raw material agreements was partly a combination of and partly a compromise between these different points of view. The preamble stressed first what may be called the buffer stock approach designed to bring a more even flow of products on the market and thus contribute to the reduction of agricultural and industrial fluctuations. But both the latter part of the preamble and the recommendations went further and cautiously suggested that regulation of production might be needed to prevent serious dislocation during periods of readjustment and to dispose of surpluses. The most positive part of the resolution recommended the early creation of an organization to study raw material agreements covering particular agricultural products and to work out principles governing such agreements.

A conflict of opinion on future international organization of raw material agreements began also during the preparations for the conference and continued in the hotel lobbies during the conference. It was assumed that one of the acts of the conference would be to establish a permanent international agency to deal with food and agricultural matters, displacing and surpassing in scope the International Institute of Agriculture which, to its detriment, had maintained its headquarters in Mussolini's Italy. Within most delegations the representatives of departments of agriculture advocated that the new organization should include among its functions the international discussion of agricultural raw material questions. But the representatives of foreign offices and of the U.S. State Department argued that all raw material questions—agricultural and mineral—should be dealt with by a single body which might be a specialized agency dealing only with such questions or might be a wider body dealing with international trade in all its forms. This controversy continued long after the conference and became increasingly acrimonious in Washington. In retrospect it appears somewhat barren.

The discussions at Hot Springs and the decision that informal British-American talks on Article VII matters would begin in the later summer of 1943 led to increased activities on raw material questions in Washington. During the summer of 1943 an interdepartmental committee undertook a more systematic examination of these questions than had yet been made. Differences between the Department of Agriculture and the Department of State, foreshadowed at Hot Springs, showed up again in the committee. At this stage, however, it was unnecessary to reach a rigid position and draw up a formal and detailed government policy, either in Washington or in Whitehall. The subject was a complicated one, most of the economists in government had little knowledge of it, and the lessons of experience were not wholly clear, particularly for a future in which conditions might be expected to differ considerably from those in the past. Conflicts of opinion did not run according to nationality but were all represented in each of the governments and among the public of the United States, the United Kingdom, and Canada. It was far better at the outset that persons with special knowledge of the subject in all three countries should exchange views freely on the merits of the proposals that were being made than that they should be mouthpieces for fixed national positions.

This was the practice followed during the discussions on raw material policy at the informal meetings on Article VII matters in Washington in September and October 1943. In the general discussions of the subcommittee which was set up to deal with "commodity policy" no attempt was made to secure uniformity of opinion within each delegation. Such freedom of expression of individual opinion was an ideal method of commencing the discussions between the experts. It brought out a far greater diversity of analysis and of experience than would have been possible if each group had followed a "party line."

During the meetings the British group distributed copies of their paper on raw material questions to the United States group. But, they said, the paper was not a statement of official policy: already there had been some change in the direction of British thought on the subject. American officials distributed copies of a report made by the interdepartmental committee on commodity agreements: they, likewise, pointed out that the conclusions in it did not represent an official United States point of view. The work of the committee continued after the Anglo-American discussions had ended. When the British experts returned to London I learned their views on the discussions and kept in touch with further developments in their ideas. Hence it will be convenient here to examine the position reached about the end of 1943.

Differences remained not only between the British and the United States groups but within each group, particularly within the United States group. The chief difference was still on the need for regulation of production and trade in certain raw materials. No one denied that such regulation might be necessary. The conflict of opinion was on the question whether it should be regarded as a normal and permanent feature of commodity agreements or an exceptional and temporary expedient to tide over special difficulties and to be discarded as soon as possible. The United States spokesmen for agriculture leaned toward the former view, the British spokesmen and the United States nonagricultural spokesmen toward the latter. But the British and United States officials who opposed quantitative regulation as a normal and permanent characteristic of commodity controls differed among themselves on the practicability of permanent raw material agreements without provision for quantitative regulation. The British advocated buffer stock schemes in which quantitative regulation would be the exception, while the Americans, who frowned on permanent quantitative regulation, were at the same time skeptical of the practicability of buffer stock schemes. Thus the United States viewpoints stood at opposite extremes and the British in an intermediate position.

But during the winter the position in Whitehall changed. I discovered that the reason for the greater disagreements on this subject in the United States group than in the United Kingdom group in the Washington discussions was that the former had included while the latter had omitted agricultural representatives. When the papers on the Washington discussions were read in Whitehall after the return of the British group, the Ministry of Agriculture reacted strongly against some of the suggestions made in them and asserted a different point of view on quantitative regulation and on subsidies from that which British officials had upheld in Washington. The main impact of these differences was on trade policy and is discussed in another chapter. But the attitude of agricultural circles in the United Kingdom toward the regulation of production and trade in foods was more lenient than that of industrial and importing circles. Farming interests wished to limit the physical quantities of some imported foods. But other producing interests had little reason to support measures that would raise the prices of raw materials. Here was the making of a serious controversy within Whitehall.

Although all the experts—British, Canadian, and American—admitted that regulation of production and exports of certain raw materials might be necessary for a time to remove maladjustments between the supply of and demand for certain raw materials, there was little agreement between agriculturalists and others on the precise conditions in which it should be permitted. Some agricultural experts wished to apply it freely as part of organized efforts by governments to contract production of some commodities and expand that of others. Other experts pointed to the danger that high-cost producers would be bolstered up too long at the expense of low-cost producers, and recommended that quantitative regulation should be used sparingly and only in urgent cases.

The shadow of the Great Depression hung over the discussion of raw material questions as it did over international monetary questions. In the early 1930's the producers of raw materials had come off worse than the producers of manufactured goods. The position of countries dependent on exports of raw materials had deteriorated even further than that of countries with more diversified exports. It was indeed difficult for any experts to plan for the future without being influenced by the plight of raw material producers during the interwar period. The danger of preparing for a repetition of the last depression instead of preparing for new conditions in the postwar period was as great in this as in other fields. Some British officials, however, were more guarded than the American officials, no doubt largely because of the famous White Paper on employment of which preliminary drafts had been circulated in Whitehall and which showed confidence in the ability of governments to prevent the return of great depressions. In Washington there was little hope at that time of maintaining full employment after the wartime demand had fallen off.

However, a closely related controversy over the use of subsidies for the production of food and raw materials illustrates both the influence of the past and the expectation of changes in the future. Agricultural circles in Washington were strongly opposed to the use of direct subsidies on production. Their opposition was based on historical experience of the curtailment of European markets for North American exports of food and agricultural raw materials by the use of subsidies and other protective and preferential devices. They argued that such measures shut out goods produced at low cost in favor of goods produced at high cost.[6] They recommended that a limit should be set on the amount of subsidized production.

[6] Both in documents and oral discussions of the time the term "low-cost" production was generally abandoned for the term "more effective" or "most effective" production. It was considered unwise from a political point of view to use the term "low-cost."

This enthusiasm for supplying the market from low-cost or "most effective" production was not always pursued consistently. The Department of Agri-

Whitehall took a different view. Both for domestic and international reasons, British officials wished to leave the way open for subsidies on the production of a number of commodities. At home they had to contend with a demand for agricultural protection. Abroad they expected to be faced with a demand from underdeveloped countries for freedom to increase the protection of infant industries. They wished to meet both demands by insisting that any protection given should be given by direct subsidies and not by higher tariffs nor by quantitative restriction of imports.

But these differences did not overshadow the substantial agreement among the majority of British, Canadian, and American experts on the approach to raw material questions. All of them were prepared to recommend that the questions should be dealt with by an international organization and not left to the haphazard processes of the interwar period. The discussions on the nature of the international organizations were based chiefly on the detailed British plan which provided for a General Commodity Council made up of representatives of all the member countries, and a Commodity Commission of seven members appointed by the Council not as national representatives but as persons experienced in international economic matters. A Code of Principles was to be laid down followed by separate Commodity Councils which it was proposed to set up to deal with single commodities. A Corporation was to be established to buy and sell raw materials under direction of the Commodity Commission.

By the end of 1943 there was common ground between Washington and London on the desirability of an international commodity organization to work closely with the other organizations that might be set up to deal with food, trade policy, monetary questions, and investment. It was agreed both within and between Washington and Whitehall that all commodity agreements should come within the same organization instead of being split between the Food and Agricultural Organization and a separate body to deal with raw materials other than food. Individual commodity organizations, each dealing with a single raw material, might be set up or might be adaptations of previously existing bodies: on them countries "largely

---

culture held out for a higher export quota for the United States in the proposed international wheat agreements than was likely, apart from subsidies, to be supplied under free competition in normal times.

dependent" upon imports were to have equal representation with the exporting countries. Buffer stock schemes were to be given further study. Mr. Keynes and Professor Robbins fully agreed with Washington that buffer stocks would break down in a depression comparable with that of the early 1930's but they—and Whitehall generally—believed that such severe depressions could be prevented in the future.

When the British experts left Washington in the autumn of 1943, they looked forward to a continuation of informal discussions early in 1944. But 1944 passed without any further discussions between British and American teams on the principles of commodity agreements. This time it was Westminster, not Whitehall nor Washington, that was responsible for the delay. Bitter dissension arose between Westminster and Whitehall on questions of trade policy: raw material agreements were involved, if at all, only indirectly through policy on subsidies. The main differences were concerned with agriculture and with trade preferences, and are described in the chapter dealing with trade policy. But the discussions on raw materials had been parallel to the discussions on trade policy and both were held up as a consequence of dissension over one of them.

During the delay more study seems to have been given to the subject in Washington that in Whitehall. British officials, at odds with ministers, and unable to make progress on Article VII questions, turned for some time to different fields. But in Washington an interdepartmental committee pressed on with studies of commodity agreements, and by the close of the summer had completed a new report which brought Washington much nearer to a common policy. One sharp difference remained. The Department of State was now thoroughly in favor of the establishment of a single international organization which would cover international trade, commodity agreements and cartel practices. The Department of Agriculture, on the other hand, resolutely maintained that commodity agreements should not come within the same agency that dealt with trade policies, but should be dealt with by a separate international commodity organization. Clearly, the agriculturalists feared that a wider organization would be dominated by free traders hostile to commodity agreements. Washington officials outside the State Department were equally afraid that a separate organization to deal only with raw material agreements would be dominated by restrictionist planners.

A deadlock was reached for a time. But by the autumn of 1944 officials in Washington were in substantial agreement that the proposed international body, however it might be related to other international organizations, should investigate raw material questions and recommend to governments methods of dealing with international difficulties, and supervise international commodity agreements to hold them in line with a code of principles to be negotiated between the member countries. Limitation of production or exports was not to be imposed unless a preliminary investigation had demonstrated the existence of a "burdensome surplus" which "the price system" could not remove in a reasonable time, and unless an agreement had been reached on methods of readjustment. Countries largely dependent on imports of a raw material were to have an equal voice with producing countries in the controlling body.

So far these proposals were in harmony with those of the British plan. On buffer stocks, however, Washington still took a much more conservative view than London, and was prepared to recommend only that the proposed international organization should study their practicability.

No serious obstacle remained to the fruitful resumption of Anglo-American discussions on commodity agreements, and the further delay was merely a by-product of the controversy within London on trade policy.

In the autumn of 1944 the deadlock in London on Article VII questions was broken and Whitehall was in a position to resume discussions on trade and raw material policy. The circumstances in which the informal discussions were resumed in London in late 1944 and in the first-half of 1945 are discussed more fully in the chapters on trade policy. By this time there were few pronounced differences on commodity policy. In Washington the Department of Agriculture had less influence than formerly, and in London, while Lord Keynes was closely occupied with monetary questions, the buffer stock proposals languished. The next step was to prepare a draft statement of proposed principles to guide international commodity agreements. This was to be a chapter in a more comprehensive plan covering trade and cartel practices as well. The preliminary draft was tentatively agreed on in discussions between Harry Hawkins, Lloyd Steere, William Fowler and the present writer on the U.S. side, and Sir Percival Leisching, Sir Wilfred Eady, Professor Lionel Robbins, and G. Shackle on the U.K. side. William Clayton and some of his advisers joined in the discussion in July, and the final touches were added in Washington at the time of the early part of the negotiations on the British loan.

The resulting document may thus be taken as closing, a little belatedly, the stage of wartime planning on international commodity agreements. It embodied the substance of many of the proposals made in the British and American interdepartmental reports already described. Its text was published in November 1944 in the *Proposals for Expansion of World Trade and Employment*, Chapter V of which dealt with "Intergovernmental Commodity Arrangements." It is therefore unnecessary to describe it here in detail. It differed from the original British plan chiefly in its noncommittal attitude on buffer stocks, the establishment of which, under the influence of Keynes and the Colonial Office, had been at first the main aim of Whitehall. But it differed also just as sharply from the earlier views of Washington, shown in the original Draft Wheat Agreement and to a lesser extent in subsequent informal discussions. The main driving force behind these views, which had come from the Department of Agriculture, had spent itself; the cautious British attitude toward regulation of production and exports was accepted in Washington and the *Proposals* expressed a severely restrictionist policy towards restrictionist policies. No member country was to limit production or exports unless it had been determined by special investigation that a "burdensome surplus" had piled up and was causing "widespread distress to small producers accounting for a substantial proportion of the total output" and "widespread unemployment, unrelated to general business conditions," neither of which could be "corrected by the normal play of competitive forces rapidly enough to prevent widespread and undue hardship to workers. . ."[7] Under such tight conditions it would seem that the disease might go far while the doctors were studying the diagnosis!

For the rest, the *Proposals* embodied familiar material relating to the objectives, the operation, and the review of commodity agreements, the substance of which had been included in the earlier British and American informal proposals. More stress was laid, however, on the importance of making "special studies . . . of the position of particular commodities of which excess supplies exist or are threat-

[7] *Proposals for Expansion of World Trade and Employment*, Ch. V, par. 4.

ened, to the end that, if possible, consumption may be increased and the anticipated difficulties may thereby be averted."[8]

Finally it was now accepted in Washington as well as in London that international raw material questions would come within the scope of a single International Trade Organization. The Department of Agriculture's position had been rejected. But it was still left doubtful how far the Organization's powers of supervision would go. Member countries were "to undertake to adhere" to stated principles and conditions. They were "to undertake to transmit to the Organization, for review, intergovernmental commodity agreements in which they now participate or in which they proposed to participate in the future." But on the detailed relationship between the international trade organization and the organizations that operated the agreements on particular products nothing was said.

There seems to be little doubt that in those days it was expected that the difficulties which all these provisions were designed to meet would recur fairly soon after the war. From Hot Springs onwards, however, this expectation had been greater in Washington than in London. From the spring of 1944 to the end of the war I was frequently kept busy in London on the controversies that arose between the State Department and the Foreign Office regarding the food contracts which the United Kingdom was negotiating with other Commonwealth countries. These controversies were partly the result of differences between the opinions held in Washington and those held in London on the time when scarcities would give way to abundance and perhaps to overabundance. The experts of the Ministry of Food had contended that severe food scarcities would continue in the early postwar years and that the wartime policy of increasing agricultural production should be carried over into the early postwar years even in the food exporting countries. But Washington agricultural circles had been "surplus-minded" for more than a decade before the war and, though they changed their attitude for a short time in 1943, they lapsed again in 1944—of all times!—and near the end of the war expected an early return of postwar surpluses. More generally, American raw material experts tended to underestimate the strength and duration of postwar demand for most primary commodities. This is not surprising when we recall the esti-

[8] *ibid.*

mates of postwar unemployment that were widely accepted as the war was drawing to a close.

Thus in the later years of the war international commodity agreements were widely regarded as a question of the transition period and not merely of the long run. Their relevance to the early transition period was exaggerated.

CHAPTER V

Planning to Reduce Trade Barriers

THE controversy in 1941 and early 1942 over the text of Article VII of the Mutual Aid agreement had drawn wide attention in Washington and London to the question what sort of international trade policy should follow the war. It turned largely into a discussion of two supposedly alternative methods of trading among nations—"bilateralism" and "multilateralism." These widely used terms oversimplify the issues. Natural resources and technical skills are so unevenly distributed over the earth that equality of imports and exports between pairs of countries is impracticable and a wider network of exchange must be sought, even if it falls far short of a world multilateral system in which all currencies are interchangeable freely and the credits which each country obtains in its transactions with some countries can be used to offset the debts which it incurs in its transactions with other countries. Much of the argument turned on the question whether a leading importing country should be free in the postwar period to press the countries which supplied its imports to take directly in return as much of its exports as possible even if other countries could supply them more cheaply. The issue arose in an acute form out of the sudden large changes in the debtor-creditor positions of certain countries, notably the United Kingdom. It played a large—though not large enough—part in the move to establish new international organizations to deal with international monetary and financial questions. But even if the new and special obstacles to the restoration of a world trading system were removed by appropriate financial measures, arduous negotiations on the details of postwar trade regulations would be unavoidable.

From the beginning it was clear that after the Second Great War of the twentieth century international trade would restart under very different conditions from those which existed after the First Great War. In 1913 a world multilateral trading system was flourishing. Obstacles to trade were insignificant compared to those of later years. The new Democratic regime in the United States sharply reduced tariffs. The so-called quantitative restrictions that are familiar to the present generation were hardly known. If, therefore, the nations had simply resolved to resume peacetime trade after the war under the 1913 tariff there would have been little cause for complaint.

But from 1939 to 1945 no one concerned with postwar planning could calmly accept the idea of returning to the trading conditions of the 1930's. For world multilateral trade, though it had recovered in the 1920's, had been seriously impaired in the 1930's, first by the Great Depression and later by preparations for war. Restriction of imports, not only by high tariffs but also by limits on physical quantities, had grown rapidly. They were indeed more a consequence than a cause of the crumbling of the world multilateral system, but that did not make them any more supportable to traders or to nations particularly dependent on trade. No responsible officials in the departments concerned with trade could overlook the necessity of international cooperation on a greater scale than ever before if tolerable conditions of trade were to be established. The precedents from the interwar period were not encouraging: many efforts, embodying a variety of approaches, were made with little success to reduce barriers and to raise the volume of trade from the low levels to which it had fallen.

From the beginning, the discussion of postwar international trade was directed mainly to questions of trade barriers and government assistance to industries. There was strangely little analysis of the actual structure of trade in the past: what there was came from the outside and notably from the officials of the League of Nations, first at Geneva and later at Princeton. It seems to have passed almost unheeded in government circles and even among academic economists.

In 1942 Washington had a tentative postwar policy on international trade. But it was only the prewar policy of the United States with a few improvements in detail and an enlargement in scope. It was still based on the principle that trade treaties should be negotiated between pairs of countries in separate negotiations. This necessitated a long-drawn-out process of bargaining, product by product, with the aim of reaching a rough equivalence in concessions over the whole field. It had been cleverly adapted to the limited opportunities which the present constitution of the United States, inherited from the leisurely and parochial conditions of a bygone age, gives to the executive branch of government to undertake commitments abroad without the risk of prompt repudiation by the legislative branch at home.

In 1942 Whitehall did not move as far with plans for postwar international trade generally as with plans for postwar trade in raw materials. Keynes, who gave so much of the impetus to the international monetary and raw material plans, was less inclined to take the initiative in trade policy. In my conversations with him in 1942 I found that although at the beginning of the year he had dropped the idea that discriminatory bilateral bargains with other countries (accepting imports conditionally on the acceptance of exports) would be unavoidable, he looked for a solution to the Clearing Union plan, to the buffer stock plan, and to general policies to maintain domestic employment at a high level. He did not seem to think then that any considerable contribution could be made by Secretary Hull's policies on international trade, and when I pointed out to him the importance to Britain of better access to markets abroad if exports were to be increased to compensate for the loss of foreign investments, he placed more importance, in his reply, on the relation between the quantity of international trade and the quantity of domestic employment and economic activity than on the relation between the quantity of trade and the height of trade barriers.

But Whitehall had taken seriously the commitments on trade policy in Article VII of the Lend-Lease agreement. It did not agree then, and has not agreed since, that bilateral negotiations and agreements under the Reciprocal Trade Agreements Act could be considered as a complete or adequate fulfilment of the international trade obligations under Article VII, and it was casting around for plans to give fuller effect to these obligations. Before the close of 1942 the first move toward a definite constructive British policy on international trade was made and it was followed up steadily in the early part of 1943.

If any one event can be designated as marking the origin of the International Trade Charter and the International Trade Organization proposed at Havana in 1947, it took place in Whitehall in the latter part of 1942. If any one person can be described as the originator of the movement for an International Trade Organization it is

James Meade,[1] who at the time was a member of the Economic Section of the War Cabinet secretariat, then headed by Professor Lionel Robbins and responsible on civilian matters to Sir John Anderson, Lord President of the Council. In the latter part of 1942 Mr. Meade produced a plan for an international commercial union of countries that would reduce trade barriers to low levels. It was to adopt a convention specifying the necessary reductions, establishing an agreed code of international trading conduct, and providing machinery for interpretation of the convention and for dealing with complaints of infringements. It would also be equipped to carry out investigations, to supply information to member countries, and later to prepare amendments to existing agreements.

Mr. Meade's proposals gained the support of other members of the War Cabinet secretariat and engaged the interest of the Board of Trade. It was arranged that Mr. Meade should work with the Board of Trade to bring the plan to an acceptable form. The Board of Trade then sponsored the plan on the Interdepartmental Committee dealing with international economic questions. After much discussion and criticism a draft was adopted and recommended to the Ministerial Committee, to which the Interdepartmental Committee was responsible, as a suitable basis for discussion in international negotiations.

However, these discussions in Whitehall raised acute differences of opinion in some quarters concerning the practicability of removing discriminations and restoring unfettered multilateral trade, at least in the early postwar period. An able economist among the Treasury advisers opposed Mr. Meade on this issue and maintained that bilateral bargaining—discriminating between those countries which would and those countries which would not accept U.K. exports in the quantities desired—would have to be the U.K. policy after the war. This view was no longer supported by Mr. Keynes and failed to gain the support of the Board of Trade, the War Cabinet secretariat, and the majority of Treasury economists. But a vigorous discussion took place through memoranda, debates in committee, and individual discussions.

In December 1942 I summarized the position briefly in the course of a memorandum dealing with the state of preparations in Whitehall for Article VII discussions: "For a time the British proposed to

[1] Now professor of international trade in the London School of Economics.

wait for us to take the initiative in working out the details of a plan for the reduction of tariffs and the removal of discriminations. But owing to the initiative of certain government economists the Board of Trade, with the help of an economist drawn from the War Cabinet secretariat, is now working on a project for a sort of low tariff union of countries, which would agree to certain standards of conduct and take certain measures for the reduction of tariffs and removal of discriminations. . . . The plan has to pass through other departments and the interdepartmental committee and receive the green light from the Cabinet Committee which passes on documents submitted by the Interdepartmental Committee. I understand that good progress has been made and that there is a definite prospect that the British may be prepared to take the initiative in 1943 in submitting plans for freer trade."

Through the greater part of 1943 steady progress was made on the British plans for an international trade organization and a code by which trade policy should be guided in the postwar period. In Washington more difficulties were encountered. During visits to Washington in the spring, before and after the Food and Agricultural Conference at Hot Springs, I had opportunities to discuss trade policy with leading officials in the State Department during one of the biennial struggles of the Administration against recalcitrant congressmen for the renewal of the Reciprocal Trade Agreements Act which authorized the executive to negotiate bilateral trade agreements without ratification by Congress. In face of a growing Republican opposition, the administration would almost certainly have been defeated if its case had been in hands less skilled than those of Secretary Hull, Harry Hawkins, and their competent staff, aided by enlightened outside organizations. Some Congressmen and lobbyists for vested interests were deterred by no scruples and by no sense of the ridiculous from proclaiming outrageous falsifications. A representative from California asserted loudly that Nazi Germany had been forced into the war by the Reciprocal Trade Agreements Act. Angry replies and rejoinders were made until the press sought the opinion of Secretary Hull, who blandly replied that if it had not been a congressman who had made the statement he would have said it was piffle. The congressman from California was no match for such an experienced political hand and his attack fizzled out in spluttering incoherence. But the renewal of the act was never a foregone conclusion; opposition to it was a slight foretaste of what might be expected if far-reaching postwar reforms in the conduct of international trade were attempted.

It is not surprising, therefore, that, after the successful outcome of this gruelling struggle, I found State Department officials more anxious to make the fullest possible use of the existing powers of the executive in the next two years than to return soon to Congress and strive to obtain wider powers embodying a new and more drastic approach to the reduction of trade barriers. They were prepared to seek larger powers within the old framework when the act came up for renewal two years later—first the power to negotiate larger reductions of tariffs than the existing act permitted, and second an extension of the duration of the act from two to three years. But the fundamental basis of the act would be unchanged: it would still be confined to selective reduction of tariffs negotiated with one country at a time and would not permit the United States to join in a general reduction of tariffs that might be agreed on in an international conference of many nations.

From my knowledge of developments in Whitehall I was convinced that such an extension of the Reciprocal Trade Agreements Act, desirable and useful though it would be, would not go far enough to meet the views of the United Kingdom. In numerous personal conversations with leading officials since Article VII of the Mutual Aid agreement had been signed, it had been made unmistakably clear to me that the method of bilateral negotiations was not regarded by the British as an adequate means for reducing trade barriers immediately after the war, and that tariff reductions under bilateral trade agreements would not be accepted as a full discharge of the obligation arising out of Article VII to reduce trade barriers. It followed that the United Kingdom would not agree to the abolition, though they would agree to the reduction, of preferences in return merely for reciprocal reductions of tariffs under the Reciprocal Trade Agreements Act. Article VII provided for the reduction of tariffs and the abolition of preferences. But it did not give precise guidance on the question how large a reduction of tariffs would be required to call for the abolition of preferences. All the arguments and differences have centered on this undetermined point. British spokesmen did not deny the obligation to abolish discriminations under certain conditions. But they repeatedly declared, at first privately and later during negotiations, that they would abolish preferences only in return for a heavy all-round and not a "selective" reduction of tariffs and other trade barriers. Though they have not stated to this day, so far as I am aware, what in their opinion the extent of such a reduction would have to be, my impression from an early stage was that it would have to be much more than 50 per cent of the prewar height of all tariffs.

Another important postwar trade question would have been left untouched by the Reciprocal Trade Agreements Act. It was a central principle of the act that trade agreements should provide for approximately equal reductions on both sides. Fortunately, this principle had not been interpreted narrowly: no attempt had been made to work out "equivalence," product by product, but in a broad sense equality was sought over the whole range of concessions. But from 1941 onwards it became clear that in the postwar world the United Kingdom would have lost the creditor position which it had held before the war, while the United States would probably be more than ever a creditor country. If chronic instability in international accounts was to be avoided, adjustments would have to be made in the balance of trade in both countries, exports increasing proportionately to imports in the United Kingdom and imports increasing proportionately to exports in the United States. To assist in the difficult task of making these adjustments, trade barriers should be lowered on both sides but to a greater extent on the American than on the British side. The Reciprocal Trade Agreements Act contributed to the first but not to the second of these processes of adjustment. In recommending the bill to Congress, administration spokesmen stressed particularly the principle of equivalence in concessions. This may have helped to pass the bill but it also made it so much the more difficult for the administration to lay before Congress at a later stage any measures that could be used ultimately to increase imports more than exports.

Ambassador Winant held the view, and made it known in Washington, that the Reciprocal Trade Agreements Act, although it was useful as far as it went, would not in itself suffice to meet postwar needs, and that an attempt should be made, in spite of the risks of failure, to harmonize trade policy with the changed balance of payments position. But, as we shall see, those who were charged with the conduct of relations between the State Department and

Congress were never bold enough to attempt this difficult task. Perhaps it was an impossible task: we shall never know with certainty. But an essential first step would have been to explain to the American public the changed economic position of the United Kingdom with all its implications. It seems strange in restrospect, that a preliminary step so obviously necessary to a reasonable postwar policy in finance as well as trade should have been completely omitted, and that to this day the American public, not wholly through its own fault, has only the vaguest ideas of the sources of Britain's postwar troubles and has often been deceived by the propaganda of the press and other interests which misrepresented the work of the British Labor Government as unfailingly as they misrepresented President Roosevelt's great reforms in the 1930's.

However, the Ambassador was never disposed to throw away the half loaf because he could not obtain the whole. During the summer of 1943 he discussed with me the chances of negotiating a new reciprocal trade agreement with Great Britain. Some of the British Dominions, particularly Australia, desired a new agreement with the United States in which they hoped to obtain concessions on wool duties. But, since any comprehensive agreement between a member of the Commonwealth and the United States would affect preferences which had been agreed on within the Commonwealth, the most suitable procedure seemed to be to start negotiations simultaneously between the United States and the members of the Commonwealth. This was desired by Australia and Canada, and the question was discussed in London at a private meeting of economic representatives of the Commonwealth countries in the early summer.

The position of the United Kingdom did not coincide with that of the Dominions or of the United States. Since 1941 Whitehall had said that negotiations on postwar tariffs on particular commodities would be remote and unrealistic. In their view the proper approach to postwar commercial policy was to start with informal discussions between experts and in successive stages to lay the ground for a bold, far-reaching multilateral act to slash prewar barriers deeply by a given percentage and open the way for a large expansion of international trade. The details of their plan were explained to the Dominions officials. The plan called for a sharp reduction in tariff barriers by a percentage to be agreed on, a ceiling on tariffs for the future, and a severe curb on limitation of imports by physical quotas. The right was to be reserved, however, to maintain such limitations as were necessary to safeguard the balance of payments in the emergency period, the duration of which could be shortened if a suitable international monetary plan were adopted. It acknowledged that after the war state trading would be of sufficient importance to require the adoption of principles to govern its conduct and safeguard it from being used as a discriminatory weapon to serve political ends, and it discussed the problem of formulating such principles. It provided for the establishment of a permanent international trade body composed of members who accepted its principles and took the necessary initial steps to cut down trade barriers. Thus it covered most of the main points of what was to become, about five years later, subject to ratification, the International Trade Charter.

As to reciprocal trade pacts, the British stated unequivocally that, although they would welcome such pacts after the general international trade issues had been dealt with on comprehensive lines, they would not consider them as constituting in themselves a fulfilment of the commercial policy obligations arising under Article VII of the Mutual Aid agreement. In my conversations in Whitehall I had noted additional reasons why the U.K. was less attracted than some of the Dominions were by the idea of a new trade pact with the U.S. as a first step to reduce trade barriers. Australia stood to gain directly by U.S. concessions on wool, which were conditions of any trade agreement between the two countries. Canada also stood to gain considerably by U.S. concessions. But the U.K. did not look directly to the United States market as a leading field for expansion of its exports in the postwar period. It did not underestimate the importance of a reduction in the U.S. tariff as a prerequisite for unshackling international trade. But to Britain the value of such a reduction was considered at that time to be largely indirect, opening the way for more exports to the U.S. from countries which would constitute good markets for U.K. exports—the Latin American countries among others. Consequently a series of trade pacts between the Dominions and the U.S., each involving concessions by the U.K. on preferences, would not aid Britain nearly as much as it aided the U.S. and the Dominions. What Britain needed most was a general opening of world markets, particularly in the industrially younger countries.

Ambassador Winant was attracted by the British postwar international trade plan. He believed, however, that the British and American approaches were compatible, the one supplementing the other. To the end of his life he was a strong and active supporter of the trade policies of Secretary Hull and his aides, and on this occasion he hoped that their desire to use their powers within the time limits could be fulfilled. He therefore raised the matter with Mr. Eden, who was always anxious to advance U.S.-U.K. cooperation in postwar as well as war matters. Mr. Eden suggested that an arrangement should be made for me to take up the matter in technical detail with Mr. Law, the Minister of State, and Dr. Hugh Dalton, President of the Board of Trade. This was done and I put forward all available arguments for starting negotiations on new trade agreements promptly and without prejudice to the U.K.'s own trade proposals, including the point that if existing powers to reduce U.S. tariffs went unused until they lapsed it might be more difficult than it would otherwise be to persuade Congress to grant additional powers that might be needed to give effect to U.K. trade proposals.

But, for the reasons already outlined, Whitehall had made up its mind, and, as I was already aware, had reached agreement with the Dominions to raise its own comprehensive trade plans before entering into trade negotiations with individual countries. Fortunately, the standstill in Washington on postwar discussions had been broken by the time of the Hot Springs Conference, and agreement in principle was reached soon thereafter to begin informal talks on ways to give effect to Article VII.

In the late summer and early autumn of 1943 the long-postponed informal talks on Article VII matters took place in Washington after a delay of eighteen months since they had first been proposed by Ambassador Winant. As we have seen, discussions had already been held and papers exchanged on the international monetary plans. The conversations on that subject therefore started from an advanced position and were carried much further than those on other aspects of Article VII. The conversations on trade and raw material policy, on the other hand, were the first of their kind and broke new ground. No commitments were made, but the ideas of, and the documents produced by, each group were disclosed to the others and informally expounded and criticized. The principal authors of the proposed plans became acquainted with each other and excellent personal relations were established between them. The British plan for an international trade organization linking countries that would agree to reduce trade barriers, already explained to the Dominions, impressed Washington officials, who began energetically to study it in detail. Differences in approach and emphasis had appeared within each group and as yet there were no sharp cleavages on national lines.

In resumed personal discussions in Whitehall I kept in touch with the further development in British views on trade policy during the remainder of the year. When the British group returned to London and there was time for stocktaking I found that they had been well impressed with the Washington officials, notably with Mr. Hawkins, and that those of them who had not previously been in Washington and who had hitherto feared a repetition of the American withdrawal from European affairs after the First World War were reassured and convinced that Washington would not return to a policy of isolation.

In 1943, besides the Anglo-American discussions in the autumn, there were discussions on trade policy between the United Kingdom and the Dominions and between the United States and Canada. If an attempt were made to describe the course of all these conversations much repetition would be unavoidable. It will be more convenient, therefore, to analyze briefly the position reached by the end of 1943. This will be all the more appropriate as a breaking point in the discussion because of an unexpected delay in the resumption of the discussions in 1944.

By the end of 1943 there were encouraging signs that officials in both capitals were making great efforts to solve the most important problems of trade policy, particularly the form of attack on tariffs and other trade barriers, and the type of provision for continuous international attention to trade questions. Careful analysis was being made in London and Washington of all the administrative and political questions that would have to be solved if the sweeping approach to trade barriers which the British were proposing informally was to be adopted. A deep cut in tariffs "across the board" would raise many administrative difficulties. Some existing duties, commonly described as "ad valorem," were computed as percentages of the value of the product, and others, commonly described as "specific," as fixed sums per unit of product regardless of price. The first varied with variations in prices while the second remained constant. If a uniform cut were to be made in tariffs a criterion of equivalence between these types of duties would have to be agreed on. Presumably a general tariff cut would be expressed as a percentage reduction of the ad valorem duties and as a corresponding reduction in specific duties, to be worked out after calculating their ad valorem equivalents.

The chief "technical" difficulty in applying any general formula for the reduction of tariffs and any criterion for determining the ad valorem equivalents of specific tariffs is that more than one method is followed in valuing the articles on which duties are charged. In some cases duties are based on the value of the article in the country of origin, in others on the "landed value" in the receiving country. Within each category there are differences in detail and in the efficiency of administration. It should be the function of an international trade organization to obtain greater uniformity in valuation, but this takes time in countries with weak administrative machinery.

These difficulties were not new. They had beset the League of Nations in its efforts during the interwar period to reduce trade barriers by international agreement. But there were ways in which, with reasonable give and take, they might be surmounted: for example, a conversion rate might be agreed on to cover the difference between value abroad and value in the importing country.

Beyond the "technical" questions were differences in principle, raising important political questions that would have to be decided sooner or later by the heads of states. A number of formulas for tariff reductions had been drawn up experimentally by civil servants from 1942 onwards, and each of them was based, either explicitly or implicitly, on different assumptions regarding the contributions to be made by different countries whose trade barriers were at different heights. For example, a formula merely providing for a uniform proportionate reduction in tariffs is based on the principle that high-tariff and low-tariff countries should make the same proportionate reductions. Sinners and saints would be treated alike. On the other hand, a formula providing for a proportionate reduction to, but not beyond, a stated level is based on the principle that high-tariff countries should make a greater proportionate reduction than low-tariff countries. Virtue would bring some reward. By an extension of the same principle an upper limit could be fixed for all duties.

But two other types of approach were based on a markedly different principle. First, there was the approach in which a general agreement would be reached by a number of countries to negotiate with one another in pairs with a view to reciprocal tariff reductions, as under Secretary Hull's program. This is commonly described as "selective" tariff reduction. Some products are not affected at all and the negotiations aim at a balance between the total concessions on each side. This aim is not easy to achieve. At the outset each side argues that the other is giving too little and asking too much; in the end a compromise is reached. But by its very nature this approach tends to like treatment of both high- and low-tariff countries. An attempt was made to meet this difficulty by allowing an undertaking not to raise a low duty to be treated as equivalent to an undertaking to reduce a high duty. Second, there is the approach which attempts to apply "selective" tariff reduction following a single multilateral negotiation instead of a multitude of bilateral negotiations. Under this scheme it would be agreed to reduce by a stated percentage the ad valorem equivalent of the total tariff duties of each country, taking as a basis the import values in some past year.[2] This would leave each country the choice of the products on which duties would be lowered. In this form it would treat high-tariff countries and low-tariff countries alike, but a differentiation might be made by excluding duties below a given level.

It is easy to point to administrative difficulties and to inadequacies in the application of any of these methods of reducing trade barriers. So effective, indeed, has been the work of the armies of officials throughout the world engaged for several centuries in hindering or blocking the flow of goods, and so entrenched are the interests that have grown up around the restrictions, that the task of even mildly reducing them is an extraordinarily complicated one. The greatest difficulty is the apparent political necessity of demonstrating in every country that that country has not given away more than it has received in concessions. To devise a formula for a general reduction in tariffs that will satisfy every country on this point is extraordinarily difficult. The statesmanlike attitude would be not to seek

[2] During the war most plans of this sort suggested the last prewar year as the base year.

attainment of such a fine and detailed balance, but to recognize above all that the benefits of a general simultaneous reduction of barriers would be likely to outweigh by far for each country any small differences between the immediate effects of the application of the formula of reduction to the different countries concerned.

The end of 1943 came with the experts of the U.S., and U.K., and Canada still wrestling with the merits and defects of various formulas for the reduction of trade barriers. The British and Canadian officials were still insisting on the inadequacy of a mere agreement to negotiate bilateral pacts and on the necessity of making a sweeping multilateral reduction in a single act; the U.S. officials were willing to examine every possibility, intellectually attracted by the U.K. approach but uncertain and noncommittal about its political practicability in the U.S. No commitments had been entered into on any side, but the experts were "thinking together" on a common set of propositions and were striving not for sectional advantage but for the solution that gave the best prospect of a large reduction in trade barriers.

The limitation of imports by physical quantities, which had become one of the chief methods of restricting international trade in the immediate prewar years, seems to have aroused general condemnation among officials of all the countries up to this time. It had been fully recognized in London, Washington, and Ottawa that reductions in tariffs could easily be nullified if restrictions on physical quantities imported were imposed in their place. Such restrictions were more stifling to trade than duties on imports which could often be surmounted by enterprising exporters who made every effort to reduce their costs. From the beginning the postwar plans included a general prohibition of limitation by physical quantities or "quotas," except insofar as such limitation might be necessary to give effect to agreed allocations of scarce products in the early postwar period, or to give effect to commodity agreements involving export "quotas," as proposed in the Draft Wheat Agreement of 1942.

In 1942 and 1943 my work in London on inter-Allied committees had taught me that the types of economic regimes to be expected in Europe after the war might differ from those which existed before it. Public ownership and operation of a number of important industries previously under private control might be expected, and a movement which began in industry could not be excluded permanently from trade. A code of international trading conduct would therefore have to take state trading into account. The difficulty about state trading lay in the possibility that it might be used to discriminate between countries—the movement of goods following political rather than economic channels. The criterion of price could not be applied with the same assurance to a totalitarian country like the U.S.S.R. as to other countries, especially when exchange rates had to be used. In democratic types of socialist economy, prices and costs might be used in the manner envisaged by Professors Lange, Taylor, and Meade, as the main guide to operations, in much the same way as in capitalist economies. But would such blueprints be followed in the postwar world?

Some officials in London and more in Washington deplored all state trading in peacetime and were skeptical of the practicability of drawing up safeguards against discrimination and undue protectionism in state-trading countries. Others, including the present writer, conceived of the economic order as developing fitfully and with many setbacks toward greater cooperation, public control, and public enterprise, and held that it was vain to expect that the trading methods of the past would continue without change, and that it would be a grave error for the United States to give an appearance of interfering to prevent changes in the internal economic order of other countries. All alike agreed that we should have to learn how to live with a certain amount of state trading in the postwar world and must therefore work out principles to guide its conduct and invite countries to accept these principles as part of the code of future international trading.

Of the two dangers in state trading the first—that of opportunities for political discrimination—would be met by an undertaking to follow commercial considerations in making purchases abroad. Actually this danger is probably greater on paper than in practice. A scrutiny of the trading operations of the U.S.S.R. in the interwar period showed little or no evidence that commercial motives were subordinated to political motives. Economic self-interest will generally lead a state-trading country to use its limited foreign funds and gold to the best advantage. In such a country the alternative uses of exchange resources will be examined as a whole by those who determine what goods shall be bought and where they shall be bought. In countries where all trade is carried on by private buyers and sellers there is no such central examination of the uses to be made of foreign funds and it is only in retrospect that these uses are known. The second danger—that of excessive protection—is indeed difficult to remove except in the kinds of socialist states in which available criteria of prices and costs would be not very dissimilar to those in capitalist states.

No important change regarding trade discriminations occurred up to the end of the year. The question how much reduction of trade barriers should be considered as an offset to the abolition of discriminations remained open. Since there was widespread skepticism as to the willingness, not of the administration but of Congress, to agree to a very large cut in the United States tariff, the more significant question was how much reduction in preferences should accompany a given reduction in tariffs. The text of Article VII threw no clear light on this question. It has always seemed to me reasonable to interpret Article VII as carrying an obligation to make a greater proportionate reduction in discriminations than in tariffs, since the ultimate aim was abolition of discriminations and reduction of tariffs. But I am not certain whether the U.K. representatives were ready to accept this as a principle, even though they would have been ready to accept it in practice if a very large and comprehensive reduction in tariffs had been offered.

However, in 1943 it was impracticable to form any decisive views on the question how to deal with discriminations. There was no assurance and scarcely any likelihood that Congress would agree to reduce tariffs far enough to invoke the obligation to abolish discriminations. Nor as yet could any decision be made on the method of tariff reduction—whether by bilateral negotiation or by multilateral act, whether on selected commodities only or on all commodities. To my mind—though there were some in Washington who thought otherwise—there was never at any time even a remote chance that preferences would be abolished in return merely for a group of bilateral agreements to reduce tariffs on selected commodities. But the main point is that, although in a formal sense the obligations in respect to tariffs and preferences were reciprocal, in reality the fate of preferences depended on the fate of tariffs, not the fate of tariffs on the fate of preferences. There was little doubt that the U.K. would have abolished preferences in return for a very large all-round cut in tariffs, not merely by the U.S., but also by the other chief trading countries. Such a solution would have been highly beneficial to Britain. But if this solution was impracticable the next question was, by how much would the high-tariff countries reduce trade barriers? The key always lay with tariff concessions.

CHAPTER VI

Drafting Proposals on International Trade

THE Anglo-American discussions on postwar trade policy, which had been delayed by political difficulties in Washington in 1942, were delayed by political difficulties in London in 1944. Within the coalition cabinet there were sharp differences, not only over imperial preferences but also, and even more, over the suggestion, which appeared in the records of the informal talks in Washington in the autumn of 1943, that restriction of imports by physical quantities should be prohibited except as a temporary device to meet deficits in the balance of payments. The Minister of Agriculture, supported by a few other ministers, opposed this suggestion in principle and demanded that the way be left open to restrict imports of agricultural products by physical quantities. The struggle among ministers was long and strenuous. The leading civil servants vigorously pressed, but for nine months pressed in vain, for permission to resume the informal talks which had taken place in Washington in the autumn of 1943. Mr. Eden, Mr. Law, Dr. Hugh Dalton, and Sir John Anderson agreed with the civil servants but could not for some time overcome the opposition from agriculture, led by R. S. Hudson, and from supporters of imperial preferences, led by Leopold Amery. Constructive work on trade policy was halted for some months, and it was not until adoption of new provisions for dealing with agriculture, to be described later, that the deadlock was broken.

From early 1945, and in a much more concentrated way during the early summer of 1945, informal talks took place in Whitehall between a small number of leading British officials and United States officials from the U.S. Embassy. The British officials were led by Sir Percival Leisching, a distinguished civil servant who had been drawn from the Colonial Office to the Board of Trade by Dr. Hugh Dalton to head the preparations for postwar planning on trade policy. With him in the discussions were Sir Wilfred Eady, leading Treasury official, Professor Lionel Robbins of the War Cabinet secretariat, G. Shackle, an expert on trade negotiations, and a few others who attended intermittently to deal with special subjects on which they had expert knowledge. It would have been difficult to find a more capable group than the British officials who took part in these discussions. On the United States side Harry Hawkins was assisted by the present writer and later also by William Fowler, an expert of long experience on trade negotiations who joined the Embassy in 1945, and on agricultural matters by Lloyd Steere, agricultural attaché of the embassy, who was thoroughly experienced in international negotiations. Mr. Hawkins had been the right-hand man of Cordell Hull in the administration of the Reciprocal Trade Agreements Act, and the chairman of the interdepartmental committee on trade matters. He was therefore thoroughly acquainted with the views of Washington, and he had the confidence of those who would make the decisions on trade policy. He was singularly free from prejudice, and in negotiation was always unruffled. His modesty and freedom from vulgar ambition combined with his grasp of both principles and details to earn for him general respect both in his own country and abroad.

The object of the meetings was to find how far Washington and London were agreed on the main lines of postwar commercial policy; to work out tentatively a procedure for subsequent discussions with other countries; and to draft a statement of general principles to which the U.S. and the U.K. could subscribe and which might be used as the basis for discussion at an international conference.

It is not necessary to describe the discussions in detail in this study, since their outcome, after a further discussion in Washington at the time of the negotiations on the British loan in September 1945, which did little to alter the position reached in London, was embodied in the document published under the title *Proposals for an Expansion of World Trade and Employment.* However, a number of proposals in the discussions in London which were not included in the document drafted later should be recorded because of their intrinsic economic importance.

Of these the most important was the British proposal that tariffs should be reduced by a given percentage on all commodities subject to protective duties. As we have seen, this proposal was first made in the discussions in Washington in the autumn of 1943. It was renewed vigorously in the informal talks in 1945 and was regarded by British civil servants as the core of the entire postwar trade policy planning. It was and still is my conviction that this was a more effective method of reducing trade barriers than the method provided in the Reciprocal Trade Agreements Act. It could be put into effect at a single international meeting, while hundreds of meetings would be necessary to work out bilateral trade pacts among the United Nations. It would cut impartially into all tariffs and not merely into those judged to be of secondary importance by the country making the reduction.[1] Whitehall also laid great stress on its psychological value as a dramatic proof to the world of serious intention to cut down obstacles to trade. In 1945 the British negotiators pressed the advantages of such an approach even more vigorously than they had done in 1943. They considered that the success of the whole venture depended on its adoption and were more emphatic than ever on the inadequacy of the machinery of bilateral trade pacts to give effect to the obligations in Article VII of the Lend-Lease agreement.

The attitude on the side of the United States was still mixed. My impression is that most of the leading U.S. officials concerned with trade questions believed that a percentage reduction of all tariffs was a sounder and simpler method of reducing postwar tariffs than the method followed in the reciprocal trade agreements. There were indeed a number of difficulties of application, but they were not insuperable and it seems fair to say that if the decision could have been based on economic effects alone Washington and Whitehall would have been in substantial agreement on the subject.

The chief economic difficulty of reducing all tariffs by a fixed proportion was that countries with high tariffs would be treated more leniently than countries with low tariffs. However, as we saw in the preceding chapter, this difficulty could be partly overcome by exempting tariffs below a given rate or reducing them by a smaller proportion than that by which higher tariffs were reduced. Other refinements could be introduced. Of course perfect equity is unattainable and the closer the approach to it the more complicated the formula for reduction becomes: somewhere simplicity and admin-

[1] Of course reciprocal trade pacts cut into tariffs on some commodities of first importance but they leave the way open for sheltering others.

istrative practicability must be preferred to further refinement.

The outcome of the discussion on this question was determined, not by economic reasoning, nor on grounds of equity but by what the Assistant Secretaries in the State Department believed it possible to pass through Congress. Here again the administration spokesmen had committed themselves, in the hearings on the renewal of the powers to negotiate reciprocal tariff reduction, to the principle of reciprocity and to the principle that each country should be left free to select the goods on which it was willing to reduce tariffs. They did not believe that Congress could be induced to go beyond the limits set by the Reciprocal Trade Agreements Act. In retrospect the validity of their judgment on this matter is doubtful, and in any case it seemed to some of us at the time that the attempt ought to have been made even if it failed.

The final rejection in Washington of any attempt at a bold handling of tariff reduction by a single stroke was a great disappointment to Whitehall. A leading official told Mr. Hawkins and me that the abandonment of this approach would end all his hopes of achievement. What was needed, he added, was a simple, vigorous, and challenging approach to the whole attitude towards trade that had grown up in the preceding twenty or thirty years. Without this he believed that the British would go into any other approach with no heart and without expectation that much would come out of it.

However, British officials had been obliged since 1943 to modify their position on the uniform proportionate tariff reduction to meet strong pressure from the Ministry of Agriculture. Tariffs on food imports were to be exempted from this method of reduction and to be subject to an entirely different approach, which may be summarized briefly and crudely as follows. First, no protective measures of any kind should be used which would raise the price of food to domestic consumers by more than a certain percentage above the world prices. Second, if domestic production of any group of foods increased by more than a certain percentage of the average level in some past period,[2] the protection or direct payments to producers would have to be reduced. The significance of these proposals depended largely on the values to be given to the percentages. British officials held that these values should be negotiated at an international conference, and they proposed no figures to us. However, there

[2] This past period at the outset was to cover a few immediate prewar years.

is little reason to believe that they wished to set the domestic production of protected foods far above the prewar level. Even agriculturalists were well aware that after the period of scarcity had passed the domestic production of wheat, for example, would have to decline considerably. A leading official hinted to me that the proportion of prewar production to be permitted before protection was reduced might be appreciably less than unity. Another said in the discussions that both of the percentages in question should be attractive to primary producers overseas, including the Dominions. However, the question lost much of its importance when the proposal to reduce all non-food tariffs by a given proportion was rejected. Under the reciprocal trade agreements procedure each country chooses for itself the commodities on which it is willing to reduce tariffs.

Nevertheless, the discussions on agricultural protection were useful in bringing out the special claims of agriculture in both countries. In both Whitehall and Washington there were differences of opinion between the departments concerned with agricultural products and those concerned with other products. As we have seen, these differences in Whitehall and Westminster had been one of the main causes of delay in the resumption of the trade talks. But in Washington, also, the agriculturalists demanded special treatment both on imports and on exports. The policy of restricting the amount produced at home, or the amount of domestic production placed on the home market, to maintain agricultural prices at levels proportionate to non-agricultural prices had led to a demand for curtailment of imports into the United States, and to attempts to dump surpluses abroad with the aid of subsidies. We were conscious of inconsistency when we argued against the prohibition of export subsidies: if there is one thing on which writers, and particularly American writers, on trade policy have agreed it is that dumping goods abroad is a form of economic warfare which provokes import restrictions.

However, the subject of dumping or export subsidies had become far more complicated than it had been before the Great Depression. We found it impossible to separate it entirely from the question of subsidies on domestic production. Agricultural spokesmen in Washington asked why it should be considered a crime to subsidize exports if the importing countries demanded the right to exclude imports indirectly by subsidizing domestic production. But, as we have seen, the spokesmen for the whole British group, and not merely for agriculture, held that restriction of the right to subsidize domestic production would close the least harmful method of protecting infant industries in the underdeveloped countries and would increase the pressure from such countries to be exempted from tariff reductions and from the removal of arbitrary limits to the quantity of goods imported. In the first attempt to reach a compromise between these divergent views, it was proposed that after a transition period there should be no export subsidies except on commodities declared by the International Trade Organization to be "in world surplus." This was elaborated in the final *Proposals for Expansion of World Trade and Employment*: before resorting to export subsidies members were to try to find other solutions and if they failed were to adopt export subsidies only to regain the share of the world market which they had in a former period.

When finally the United Kingdom negotiators reluctantly gave up hope that the United States would accept the proposal to reduce all non-agricultural tariffs by a uniform percentage the tariff discussions turned on the possibilities of finding short cuts to the conclusion of bilateral trade agreements. The idea of over fifty nations attempting in a short time to negotiate such pacts in pairs was terrifying. Visiting Lord Keynes one day at the Treasury, I found him attempting to calculate the number of separate negotiations and meetings that would be needed to do this! I do not think that Whitehall ever again showed the zeal for tariff reduction which it had shown while hope remained for a comprehensive and fairly simple method of reducing tariffs at a single international gathering. It was only gradually that short cuts were devised, and there was no way of avoiding long-drawn-out higgling and bargaining over a multitude of different items. Mr. Hawkins wisely held that preliminary meetings of what he called a "nuclear group" of countries should be held at one spot and that negotiations between pairs of them should be carried on simultaneously. He wished to limit the group to a small number, but care had to be taken in the choice of the countries to be invited. It was decided that at least fourteen countries must be included.[8]

As we have seen, the so-called quantitative restrictions had become an even worse hindrance to world trade in some areas than tariffs

[8] Later this was increased to 16 and finally to 23.

had been in the 1930's. In 1945 all the members of the U.S.-U.K. group, except perhaps the British agriculturalists, deplored without qualification the stifling effect of such restrictions and readily agreed that they should be removed completely as soon as the difficulties of transition had passed. Here again the agriculturalists in Washington as well as in Whitehall were unwilling to accept provisions similar to those proposed for non-agricultural products. In the United States it would have been difficult to carry out measures for restricting the domestic production of farm products unless imports of the products were restricted simultaneously. In the United Kingdom marketing schemes to maintain the prices of some of the more perishable foods might be upset if imports from neighboring countries were freely admitted or were restricted only by moderate tariffs. An exception had to be drafted permitting "quantitative" limitation, when, but only as far as, it was necessary to the restriction of domestic supplies.

At these early discussions the difficulties of the transition period were recognized though they were underestimated. Since they affected particularly the willingness and even the ability of the European countries to abandon quantitative restrictions on imports and that of the overseas exporting countries to abandon the direction of exports, two important exceptions were made to the general principle that such restrictions should be abandoned. The first permitted the import and export restrictions needed to carry out international allocations of scarce goods during the period of postwar shortages of a number of important foods. The second permitted restrictions to meet adverse balances of payments in the immediate postwar period when increased exports of minerals and manufactured goods from the European countries depended on earlier increases in imports of food and raw materials from overseas. Thus the nature of some of the most important difficulties of the transition was recognized. But over-optimistic ideas on the magnitude and duration of the difficulties were held on both sides and particularly on that of the United States. More than that, the great difficulties of restoring a world multilateral trading network, even when early postwar scarcities had passed away, were largely overlooked. The only difficulty that was appreciated at this stage was that resulting from the loss of Britain's overseas investments, but even this was looked at too exclusively from Britain's point of view, and its widespread effects on other countries received less attention.

State trading was discussed in the informal talks, and the substance of the section ultimately adopted at Havana was drafted. Some opponents of the trade charter have accused its supporters of opposing state trading and of trying to establish private enterprise over all world trade. Such charges have no foundation. Having been present at most of the early discussions, I can state that no one who took part in them tried to exclude state trading or believed that it would be possible to do so. There were those who preferred private trading but they were not so politically immature as to believe that state trading would disappear. In fact everyone concerned in the talks sincerely desired to leave the way open for the Soviet Union to join the proposed international trade organization. The general principle adopted was that state-trading organizations should follow commercial criteria in their dealings. It was extremely difficult to determine exactly how this principle was to be applied but, as we noted in the preceding chapter, a state-trading country has the strongest motive to pursue the old commercial aim of buying in the cheapest market, allowing for quality and time of delivery, and so obtaining the best value for its outlay of foreign currencies or gold.

But if the dangers of discrimination under state trading have been greatly exaggerated the dangers of concealed protective measures under cover of state monopolies is real. How is it possible in such conditions for a country to play its part in general reductions of trade barriers? It was suggested that countries which adopted state trading should agree that the difference between the domestic price set by the monopoly and the price at which the product could be imported should not be greater than the tariff negotiated on the product through the international trade organization, or alternatively that as a counterpart to tariff reductions by other countries they should undertake to increase their purchases of goods by percentages to be agreed on. In the end, however, it was decided not to include such detailed points in the text of the proposals.

Whatever ingenuity may be shown in trying to devise safeguards against the abuse of state trading, the outcome depends on the good will and good faith of the countries concerned. If there were reasonable political harmony and confidence in the world a working solution could be found for the difficulties of establishing roughly comparable criteria of protection and discrimination among countries with widely different economic systems. On the other hand, when there is grave political mistrust among the nations and particularly when the lines of cleavage are associated with differences in the social order, it is difficult to devise indisputable criteria and still more difficult to secure the strict observance of any criteria that may be formally agreed upon.

It was doubtful whether the Soviet Union would enter into an international trade organization or subscribe to a code governing the conduct of international trade. During the summer of 1945 I had an opportunity to converse privately on trade with some Russian representatives temporarily in London. They showed no sympathy with the aims of Article VII of the Lend Lease agreement toward postwar trade questions, and they revealed suspicions of U.S. and U.K. motives, particularly in relation to the Central and Eastern European countries. The Russians were not alone in believing that the real object of the advanced industrial countries in advocating freer trade was to hold the markets for manufactured goods in the less developed countries and check their industrialization. Protection, argued my Russian friends, was necessary for the industrialization of Eastern European countries, and their industrialization was necessary to free them from economic domination by the capitalist countries. Their doctrines seemed to be a compound of those of Lenin and List.

During the informal talks in London I concluded that the differences between the U.S. and Britain would be far less serious than those between both of them and the protectionist countries of Latin America and Asia. There had already been and would continue to be some well advertised differences on preferences and discriminations. But the quantitative importance of this issue had been greatly exaggerated both by the extreme supporters and by the extreme opponents of preferences and discriminations; and although wrangling might break out again over them it would have little effect on world trade in the near future. A far more serious issue was likely to arise over the so-called infant-industry argument for protection in the less industrialized countries. In one of our informal talks we were joined by a British commercial attaché who had been attached over several years to a number of British missions in Latin America. He predicted serious trouble as soon as an attempt was made to draw Latin American countries into subscribing to a code that would prevent increased industrial protection. Some of the governments, he maintained, would kick at any limitation on their freedom to raise duties or impose import quotas. Much later I recalled these early forecasts when the accounts came in of the prolonged controversies at Havana.

The infant-industry or infant-country question was a real issue and not merely a symptom of political intransigeance. In the informal talks efforts were made to work out measures that would permit legitimate protection for genuine infant industries without starting a general increase or preventing a general decrease in trade barriers. The Australian Tariff Board had worked out some useful procedures, particularly in requiring any industry claiming protection on grounds of infancy to present a detailed case to prove that it was a genuine infant and was likely to grow up. British officials proposed at one stage that in the trade code temporary infant-industry protection should be permitted up to a stated level when an adequate case had been made for it, but that it should be diminished in stages and abolished after a certain period. This was an ingenious proposal and probably the best that could be devised if tariff protection were to be permitted for infant industries. We agreed, however, that it would be better if all aid to infant industries were given by subsidies alone: the taxpayer could be relied on to keep subsidies within proper limits more than he could be relied on to agitate against tariffs, the incidence of which was less clear to him. At the international conference which was to come later, concessions might have to be made on tariffs for infant industries, but it was decided to hold them in reserve and not to make them in advance in the text of the proposals to be issued as the basis for the discussions at the conference.[4] Postwar experience was to show that the British forecasts of future trouble with the underdeveloped countries were fully justified.

The cartel question caused more trouble than the question of commodity agreements. The vigorous officials who worked on it in Washington desired to press on London some drastic provisions by which each government would prohibit firms under its jurisdiction from joining combinations in restraint of trade, and would pass

[4] Although I agreed with this view at the time, in retrospect I believe that we were in error and would have been well advised to have admitted the principle of tapering tariffs for infant-industry protection into the *Proposals*.

legislation designating agreements between firms to restrict prices, to allocate markets and to limit production as illegal. In London, although we put forward these proposals in the discussions we were well aware that they would not be accepted either by the United Kingdom or by the Western European countries. The British, as we have seen, took a different view and aimed at building up a case law in the long run, based on experience in dealing with specific complaints: they were not convinced that price fixing and limitation were at all times anti-social practices and they wished to investigate each case on its merits. The outcome of the discussions was a draft proposing that the international trade body should accept complaints that might be made against private international combinations or agreements, that they should be empowered to make recommendations to the member states and to request information on the measures taken to carry them out. This would be a modest but useful start in the control of private enterprise in its international operations.

The draft of the *Proposals for the Expansion of Trade and Employment* was tentatively agreed on in substance and most of it in detail in the London conversations. It was worked over again in Washington at the time of the loan and Lend-Lease talks and the statement was not made public in final form until November 1945. It was delayed by the desire in Washington to announce it simultaneously with the conclusion of the loan agreement. The retracing of the ground in Washington was necessary not only for political reasons but also to satisfy the other agencies and departments that their points of view were adequately represented in the negotiations.[5]

On the other hand I remain convinced that it was not only unnecessary but also harmful to link these negotiations even loosely with, and to hold them at the same time as, the negotiations on the loan. Let anyone who doubts this read carefully the relevant Parliamentary

[5] During a visit to Washington in the preceding year I had tried to explain to an official who played an important role in the anti-cartel planning that the point of view not only of the British but also of the continental European Allies differed from that of Washington, that pressure for a sort of international anti-Sherman Act could only result in deadlock, and that it would be necessary therefore to work out a compromise. He listened skeptically and replied, "Well, you wait till we get those damned British over here. They will have to come through." Actually, when the time came the British negotiators stood their ground and the position reached in Washington was identical with that which had been reached in London.

Debates[6] and the files of the leading British newspapers at the time. There can be no doubt that wholehearted approval by members of Parliament and by the British public of the results of the international trade discussions was seriously impeded by the widespread though incorrect impression that Britain's negotiators had been pressed into acceptance of the agreement on trade by Britain's financial necessities. The linking of these discussions was wholly unnecessary. Doubtless the motive behind it was partly the fear that without some such form of indirect pressure the United Kingdom would hold back on trade discussions as she had done in 1944. I can testify, however, from close touch with Whitehall at the time that this fear was wholly imaginary in 1945. Cabinet ministers had agreed in the late summer of 1944 to the continuation of the discussions, and the British had taken a leading part in the formulation of the *Proposals.*

Thus, those in Washington who distrusted British motives and wished to reinforce persuasion by indirect pressure, achieved exactly the same agreement as would have been achieved by persuasion alone, but in addition alienated sections of public opinion in Britain which might have been won over if no suspicion of pressure had arisen. It is true, of course, that suspicion in some British quarters of the United States motives was unfounded or grossly exaggerated; but if the cards had been played more carefully no pretext would have been left for it.

[6] Hansard, *Parl. Deb.*, House of Commons, Vol. 417, pp. 422-558; House of Lords, Vol. 138, pp. 678-892.

CHAPTER VII

A Model Approach to Planning

THE preceding chapters have traced the origin and development of postwar planning on international monetary, lending, and trade matters. They have shown how the broader plans proposed at the outset would have created instruments for dealing with long-run questions that could also have been used to meet at least some of the needs of relief and reconstruction; but that these were gradually whittled down by criticism and political compromise until they had little relevance to the emergencies of the immediate postwar period and for the most part would become useful to the postwar world only after a period of transition in which the needs of relief and reconstruction had been met by other means.

It is necessary, therefore, to turn to an examination of the planning through other channels for relief and reconstruction. Before doing so, however, we may usefully examine an early approach toward world food questions that demonstrated the possibility of comprehensive and integrated planning for the short run, the transition, and the long run. It is concerned with food and agriculture, but the moral which it carries may be given wide application.

Early in 1943 the prospects for international discussions on post-liberation and postwar questions were improving. Confidence in ultimate victory was growing. But the war was still in a difficult stage, and in the highest circles in Washington it was believed that the time had not yet come to begin international discussions on the fundamentals of a world political settlement and on the question whether the League of Nations should be continued or what organization should succeed it. These subjects would have raised highly controversial issues, and it was not judged wise to call the United Nations together for the first time to deal with the most controversial as well as the most important of the numerous questions requiring international cooperation after the war.

President Roosevelt now judged that the time had come when the

United Nations could be invited, without danger of discord, to a conference on postwar questions if the subject chosen was of common interest throughout the world and might be expected to bring wide agreement at least in aims. If such a limited objective were achieved the prospects of successfully dealing with the more difficult political issues later would be improved.

Food was a subject which appeared to fulfil the conditions for a successful first conference. It was a matter of special concern to the masses of people in all countries during the Second World War as it had been during the First. "Food Will Win the War" was a slogan widely proclaimed in the First World War, and implicitly accepted in the Second. Like all useful slogans, it oversimplified the true position but directed attention to a matter of fundamental importance. Its application to the Second World War was less direct than to the First: there was little hope that the Nazi Empire could be brought down by starvation. However, the production of food within and its distribution among the Allied belligerent countries remained one of the leading economic problems of the war and one of the chief subjects of wartime planning.

But food took on a wider significance in the Second World War than in the First. The conviction spread that food would win the peace as well as the war. Early it became clear that food relief would be at once the most urgent and most difficult of the immediate postwar economic tasks of the Allies. Early, however, the idea spread also that food could win the peace in a much wider sense than is associated with the mere provision of immediate relief. The public interest in food and nutrition had been growing before the war in several countries. Striking advances had been made in biochemistry and in its application to animal and human nutrition. The work of the nineteenth century should not be disparaged but it had left the impression that good nutrition was chiefly a matter of proteins and of adequate energy intake measured in calories. Diets were judged chiefly according to the amounts of carbohydrates, fats, and total proteins which they contained. The diets of soldiers and sailors in the First World War were drawn up in these terms so far as they were scientifically planned at all. But in the interwar period research in nutrition, some of which had begun earlier, made rapid advances and opened wide fields whose existence was previously unknown or only vaguely suspected. These researches revealed the significance of mineral salts and of a number of "accessory factors" or vitamins whose chemical structures and precise functions were unknown when their existence was first demonstrated. Thus the needs of the human body were seen to be more varied and complex than had previously been believed, and the quality of a diet judged by the presence of a variety of nutrients was found to be as important as its energy value.

When the newer knowledge was used to judge the state of the people's nutrition the results were disturbing. In the Western World, where famine no longer existed except as the aftermath of war and revolutionary changes, and where the energy needs of most of the people were fully met, it nevertheless appeared that the diets of a considerable proportion of the people, even in the wealthiest communities, were deficient in a number of important nutrients, and that ill health and premature death were increased by these deficiencies. Stirred by the public statements of Sir John Boyd Orr and his associates in Great Britain, of Professor E. V. McCollum in the United States, and of Stanley Bruce and F. L. MacDougall, Australian representatives in Geneva, and by the interest of the workers' group in the International Labor Organization, the League of Nations and the ILO appointed a mixed committee whose work brought food and nutrition questions into the forefront of the social and economic questions requiring international cooperation. The technical reports of the committee marked the beginning of, and prepared the way for, the systematic accumulation of a body of knowledge on the actual state of food consumption and nutrition throughout the world.

The World War halted this work but did not destroy its fruits. Much that had been learned was applied to wartime food organization. The tentative schedule of human requirements of the different nutrients which the mixed committee had drawn up was used both in evaluating wartime diets and in planning for food relief after the liberation of the occupied areas. But the influence of the work of the mixed committee did not end there. It left a body of people, scattered over several countries, who had taken part in the work of the prewar period and who were determined that preparations for the postwar period should begin promptly when conditions permitted and should greatly exceed prewar efforts in scope and intensity.

Early in the Second World War a number of influential persons in London and Washington began to work for an early revival of international discussions on world food questions. Ambassador Winant was one of the strongest supporters of this movement. Stanley Bruce and F. L. MacDougall, who were stationed in London during the war, were untiring in their efforts to persuade the leading governments to give food a prominent place in postwar reconstruction. Several personal discussions took place among Ambassador Winant, Mr. Bruce, Mr. MacDougall, and Sir John Orr in London during 1942. The subject was raised in Washington by Mr. MacDougall and by the Ambassador. Mr. MacDougall engaged the active interest of Mrs. Franklin Roosevelt and Vice-President Wallace in it and perhaps through them it was brought to the attention of the President.

President Roosevelt's invitation took not only Washington but the world by surprise. Diplomats of many countries were puzzled over the precise character and scope of the conference and the type of delegation to appoint. Even in the embassy in London we had no detailed information on these questions. Ambassador Winant was in Washington for consultations on many questions. A telegram then arrived calling me and a colleague to Washington. Treasury officials in Whitehall asked me to meet them before leaving. Arriving at the Treasury, I entered a room to find not only Keynes but a group including Sir Wilfred Eady, Sir Hubert Henderson and Sir Arthur Waley, leading Treasury officials. Obviously Whitehall had been taken by surprise and questions came in abundance. Why had food been chosen as the subject of the first meeting? What would be the scope of the conference? Did "food" include agriculture? What type of delegation would be most suitable? But that evening remains in my memory largely because of Mr. Keynes. My first replies were that we had no more information in the embassy than the announcement gave, but that I had been for some time aware of quiet moves to give a prominent place to food and nutrition in postwar reconstruction questions, that President Roosevelt was a master in the art of "timing," that food was a subject that appealed to the masses of people, and was better understood by them, than were many of the intricate financial and other economic problems on which we were working, and that in an opening meeting food and nutrition questions would probably bring more agreement, at least on aims, than some of the other postwar questions.

Mr. Keynes looked more dejected than I had ever seen him and as I continued this ad hoc attempt at explanation his dejection deepened. For eighteen months he had worked unsparingly at his Clearing Union plan. He had piloted it through Whitehall, successfully meeting all the objections of the more conservative civil servants. He had brought over important ministers of more than one party to its side. But one thing had been lacking. A year had passed since Article VII had been signed but no discussions had yet taken place with the United States on the plan. Keynes at least expected that when postwar discussions did begin the monetary plan would have priority, striking as it did directly at the heart of Article VII. Food and nutrition as an alternative beginning was something he had never dreamed of!

When I had finished speaking, Keynes looked up and said in substance: "What you are saying is that your President with his great political insight has decided that the best strategy for postwar reconstruction is to start with vitamins and then by a circuitous route work round to the international balance of payments! It is a very ingenious strategy, but how long will it take to reach the balance of payments by this route and how many people will understand this roundabout way of doing things?"

In Washington my colleague and I found no readymade answers to the questions raised in London and presumably in other capitals. Clearly the initiative had come from the "top" and most civil servants in Washington knew little more than civil servants in Whitehall did! These details are worth recording because they show that in some circumstances an international conference may be successful even when no direct, prolonged preparations have been made. Dean Acheson took general charge of preparations, and a group of officials, drawn largely from the Department of Agriculture with a small number from the Department of State, with Dr. Howard P. Tolley as chairman, worked continuously for nearly three weeks on the preparation of a proposed agenda and on a series of detailed documents covering each part of it and including constructive suggestions on policy. This group did the work which would—or should—have been done by an international secretariat if the conference had been held within the framework of a permanent international organization.

It would not be within the scope of the present study to give a descriptive account of the conference at Hot Springs, but some important features of it were relevant to one of the central questions discussed here—that is, the difference between the short-term emergency postwar food problem of regaining lost ground and the long-term postwar problem of improving on prewar conditions. In early 1943 American agricultural opinion was still largely influenced by the fear of "surpluses" which had been one of the main preoccupations of the Department of Agriculture and the farmers in the prewar period. Our estimates in London of the probable extent of relief needs and those of the Tolley Committtee in Washington had had a sobering effect but in the short time since they had been made they had been studied more by the War Food Administration than by the peacetime divisions of the Department of Agriculture. Consequently, a considerable part of the U.S. delegation and staff concerned themselves more with the long-run questions than with the short-run. But the U.K. delegation and staff took a much more balanced view and vigorously stressed the urgency of the immediate postwar period. To a considerable extent their position was supported by the European Allies, and the U.S. group was impressed by the evidence which they presented. Two outstanding resolutions were adopted on the subject, the first dealing with "Changes in Production in the Short-Term Period," and the second with "Co-ordination in the Short-Term Period."

The first of these two resolutions embodied the supremely important principle that policies and practices which would be undesirable and even retrogressive from a long-run point of view should nevertheless be resolutely pursued during the period of scarcity immediately after the war. One of the chief conclusions reached by students of nutrition before the war had been that in most countries there should be an increase in the human consumption of foods of animal origin. The resolution, however, bluntly stated that countries in which expansion was possible should "increase the acreage under crops for direct human consumption, and even . . . hold back the rebuilding of depleted livestock herds—essential though this rebuilding will ultimately be. . . ." The next paragraph, dealing with countries whose agriculture had been impaired, stated that in the immediate postwar period they should ". . . bring about a rapid increase in food production, even if this involves a departure from the use of the resources which in the long run will be required, and even if it delays a return to production policies which are desirable for technical, economic, or nutritional reasons (for instance, in Europe there may need to be a concentration in the first years on vegetables, bread grains, and other products where production can mature quickly and which yield more calories per acre than livestock). . . ."[1]

This was straightforward and unequivocal: looking back over the time which has passed since it was adopted we can appreciate its soundness and foresight, and its combination of respect for principles and freedom from doctrinaire tendencies; and we can only regret that the admirable example set at Hot Springs in respect to food was not followed elsewhere on subjects other than food, particularly on trade.

Even in a more general sense the Hot Springs Conference supplied a model for the initiation of postwar reconstruction plans that might well have been studied and followed in other fields. It was called to deal with a subject of wide scope and it dealt at the same meeting with both the long-run and short-run aspects of the subject. Some members of the conference were well equipped to discuss both aspects. Consequently a well-balanced point of view was maintained, both in the discussions and in the recommendations. Actually there was no fundamental inconsistency between the short-term and the long-term recommendations. The InterAllied Nutrition Committee had faced a somewhat similar difficulty, though its concern was only with the short run.[2] In conditions of general scarcity, hunger must be removed or greatly reduced before detailed attention can be given to meeting the full needs of specific nutrients. Until this is done the population cannot work to full capacity or even to the capacity reached in the past, and since the long-run aim to improve nutrition can be attained only by an increase in output no progress can be made toward it until the short-run objective of removing hunger is achieved.

But, however straightforward such reasoning may be, it is greatly to the credit of a conference of the United Nations that it was accepted. In international as in national conferences on subjects which have a political bearing it seems to be the exception rather than the rule to face squarely and accept fully a diagnosis which for some

[1] Resolutions XII and XIII, Final Act of the United Nations Conference on Food and Agriculture, Hot Springs, Virginia, U.S.A., May 18-June 3, 1943.

[2] See Chapter VIII.

time to come dims the hopes and postpones the attainment of the goals that have inspired people in the past, and which sharply reminds the world of the difficulties and hardships of the near future and the labor and sacrifices that must be undertaken, not to reach new and as yet unrealized levels of comfort and well-being, but even to regain old levels long recognized as unsatisfactory for a large proportion of the population.

But the conference did not propose to return to an older status quo. The very conditions of scarcity had their beneficial side for mankind by spurring activity to improve the distribution of food. In the past economists with an inherited bias against government intervention have belittled plans for improved distribution on the strange ground that total production was too low to make it worth while to distribute what there was more evenly and equitably. This type of argument has no appeal to students of food and nutrition, except for a limited application to certain stages of famines. Fortunately at Hot Springs the conference was not confined to general reasoning on the question but had the benefit of the U.K. experience of domestic food rationing and allocation and of the experience of the Combined Food Board on international food allocation. A deep impression was made on the conference by the masterly work of the British Ministry of Food, Ministry of Health, and Advisory Committee on Nutrition, in the distribution of scarce supplies to the best nutritional advantage among the different groups of the population. In modern history there is no record of any country which has turned adversity to social advantage as Great Britain has done during and since the war. No other democracy and no communist country has yet come nearly as close as Great Britain has to a distribution of food according to need. This was an achievement of planning and not of "free enterprise." Under free enterprise the nutritional advances made in Great Britain in spite of a reduction in the national food supply might well have taken half a century or longer to achieve.

On the international side of distribution in the period of scarcity the Hot Springs Conference also took a firm and farsighted position. In a notable resolution the conference expressed the view that "despite all efforts to increase production, supplies of essential foodstuffs and certain other agricultural and marine products and of the necessary instruments of production, such as fertilizers and machinery, and the means of international transportation will all be inadequate to meet basic requirements in the transition period, which may extend for several years after the cessation of hostilities."[3]

Here was none of the false optimism which, under the influence of the fear of "surpluses," recurred in Washington in the next two years and weakened the application by the United States of the principles of the resolution. The practical conclusion drawn by the members of the conference was that governments should act in co-operation to increase production, to allocate supplies, and to prevent "violent fluctuations arising from unrestrained competition for inadequate supplies, in the prices of food, the instruments of production, and other necessities, including industrial goods."[4]

Thus the delegates at the Hot Springs Conference neither neglected the short-term period nor underestimated its importance but were clear and explicit in their recommendations for dealing with it and did not hesitate to restrain popular hopes of an early freedom from want of food after the end of the war. Their competence and courage were not in vain, for food questions have been met more intelligently than most postwar questions. But, as we shall see, some essential parts of their recommendations, though formally accepted, were not followed in practice by food-supplying countries—to the detriment of the whole field of reconstruction.

The conference made a useful distinction between the short-term period and the transition period. In the former the main problem was absolute scarcity, to be met by turning productive factors into different lines and in opposite directions to those that should be followed in the long-term period. In the transition period the principal problem would be how to move away from the short-term policy of producing an exceptionally high output of energy foods for direct human consumption to a long-term policy aimed at producing the best combination of foods from the point of view of contemporary knowledge of nutrition. Resolution XIV, dealing with "Adjustment of Production in the Transition from the Short-Term to the Long-Term Period," drew attention to the importance of making these changes "progressively" as the conditions of scarcity passed away. An example given pointed to the desirability in parts of Europe

[3] Resolution XIII, Paragraph 1 of preamble.

[4] See Resolution XIII, paragraph 3 of preamble and 1(c) of recommendations. It is difficult to see how the United States can be acquitted of an act of international bad faith in its reckless scrapping of price controls on and after V-J Day.

during the transition of "increasing the production of milk products as herds can be reestablished, accompanied by declining production of grains."

Long-run policy was then outlined in a comprehensive series of recommendations beginning with production policy and passing through agricultural credit, cooperative movements, land tenure and farm labor, education and research, conservation of land and water resources, land settlement for food production, to occupational adjustments in rural populations, to international commodity arrangements, to international distribution of food and to the organization of marketing. The recommendations on some of these subjects could be applied not only before the transition period had ended but even during the immediate period of scarcity. But the full application of others clearly would have to wait, perhaps for several years—notably those in the second and third sections of the comprehensive resolution on production policy[5] which called for "changes in the pattern of production, designed to give greater emphasis to foods rich in vitamins, minerals and proteins, and for measures to limit the production of energy foods in high cost areas."

It speaks well indeed for the American delegates at Hot Springs that they were ready to accept the postponement of the long-term production policies to meet the conditions of the scarcity period. It will be within the recollection of many of those working on postwar planning about this time that one of the strongest hopes in Washington commercial-policy circles, as well as in agricultural circles, was that the European countries might be persuaded to reduce the high barriers to imports of wheat which had been built in the 1930's, and to accept North American exports in replacement of high-cost domestic production, using a larger proportion of their land for the production of more quickly perishable foods. In its picture of future developments the Hot Springs Conference placed such a development in the long-term period, admitting that it had no place in the scarcity period.

Two long-period questions aroused considerable controversy, though not in plenary sessions, at Hot Springs. The first was international commodity arrangements and the second was "Special International Measures for Wider Food Distribution."[6] Since commodity agreements came within the scope of the direct discussions under

[5] Resolution XV.

[6] Resolutions XXV and XXVII.

Article VII of the Mutual Aid agreement, the discussion of them at Hot Springs has been considered in another chapter.

The second question was one of the most difficult of all questions at the conference but though it was not a matter of immediate importance, to some of us it seemed important that it should at least be squarely faced. It was the international counterpart of the national problem of unequal distribution of food within countries. The conference, notably impressed by the example of Great Britain, enthusiastically upheld the principle that governments should be responsible for improving the diets of the people wherever inadequacies are found, and particularly should undertake "positive measures" to improve the diets of "pregnant and nursing women, preschool and school children, adolescents, workers, and individuals receiving low incomes."[7] But if this was to be the attitude toward inequality of income and inequality of food consumption *within* a country what was to be said about the same inequalities when they were found on a great scale between nations! In the one case there were differences among the average conditions of different groups within the same nations: in the other there were differences among the average conditions of different national groups in "one world." If we agree that the first should be grappled with how long can we ignore the second? If the conscience of the national community is now roused over the consequences of great inequalities among its members, how long can the conscience of the international community remain unaffected by the immense inequalities among the nations?

It was not indeed the mere existence of inequality that aroused uneasiness so much as the combination of inequality with an absolute deficiency of ordinary necessities at the lower end of the scale. The human organism can thrive on various diets, some more varied and seemingly more palatable than others. There is no cause for worry if the diets of some peoples are simpler and more "austere" than those of others, so long as all of them can obtain enough to meet full energy needs and none show evidence of disease or ill health traceable to insufficiency of particular nutrients. Unfortunately, the evidence submitted to the Hot Springs meeting showed that then and in the prewar years considerable numbers of people in certain areas were far from being able to meet bare energy needs and that the

[7] Resolution IV.

physical development of some of these peoples appeared to be retarded by insufficient food. On the other hand, in the prewar period some of the large food-exporting countries were unable to dispose of their exportable supplies, and restrictive measures were taken in the effort to reduce these "surpluses."

But the question what should be done about these conditions was not as readily answered in the international as in the domestic sphere. This was not surprising: the inherent difficulties in the first are much greater than those in the second and—almost equally important—few people had yet felt a strong urge to overcome them. The question raised in ancient times, "Am I my brother's keeper?" was slowly coming to be answered affirmatively in the twentieth century within some national communities, but few were ready to accept, even in principle, the same obligations toward their fellow men —near or far—who acknowledged and lived under other sovereign jurisdictions.

In approaching the problem of food distribution within countries, the conference, as we have seen, had clearly affirmed the responsibilities of governments and public authorities to take all the steps within their power to ensure that adequate diets were in the reach of the low-income groups, even quoting approvingly "direct action to make protective foods available free, or at low prices, to groups with inadequate diets."[8] In approaching the problem of food distribution between countries the conference reaffirmed the substance of this principle and added that "this responsibility will be met primarily by national measures."[9] But it then admitted that certain countries might be unable to fulfil this responsibility from domestic resources and food imports until their agriculture and industry had passed through a long period of development. In a number of resolutions the conference recommended methods of increasing domestic food production and of international cooperation and assistance to spread improvements in production. But, like unassisted domestic efforts, all these take time and the question arises whether international measures can be devised to fill at least part of the gap in the intervening period.

At Hot Springs no agreement was reached on any particular measures, but the conference recommended that the permanent inter-

[8] Resolution XXVI, paragraph 1b of recommendations.
[9] Resolution XXVII, paragraph 1 of preamble.

national food and agricultural organization which it called on the governments to set up should "study the possibility of devising measures to meet the needs of countries with inadequate supplies, and the machinery needed for this purpose, distinguishing between methods which would be used in the case of famines following catastrophes, and in the case of countries where the available food supplies are generally inadequate."[10]

As there was little discussion of the subject in the general sessions, and as the subject is likely to arise again in the future as an important long-run question, it seems appropriate here to analyze briefly the main issues discussed informally outside the sessions.

There was general agreement on the desirability of international measures to help countries whose total food supplies were inadequate to increase their domestic production. Some of us, however, even during the preparation of secretariat papers on the agenda items had wished to go further and explore the practicability of international measures to supply certain foods temporarily to such countries on terms more favorable than those obtainable on a commercial basis.[11]

Members of the secretariat, including the present writer, made suggestions which, though they were not accepted in detail, served as a basis for some informal discussion. An extract from a memorandum of mine, written at the time, follows:

"International measures may consist (a) in helping a country to increase its domestic production of foods; (b) in supplying to the country certain foods on terms more favorable than those obtainable on a commercial basis.

"The first of these measures opens up wide possibilities of agricultural assistance. Skilled technicians might be lent to the country to deal with specific problems affecting crops, livestock, drainage, control of pests, methods of introducing new crops, and so on. This can be discussed in more detail elsewhere.

"The second of the measures may for convenience be divided into two parts: (i) arrangements for supply of grain or other bulk foods of high energy value to meet caloric deficits; (ii) arrangements for supply of certain types of foods needed to provide specific organic

[10] Resolution XXVII, paragraph 1 of recommendations.

[11] My records contain memoranda which I wrote at the time advocating a plan along these lines in considerable detail on the administrative as well as the economic side. There is however no space in the present study for such detailed examination.

and mineral constituents to meet qualitative deficiencies, especially among children and mothers.

"The bulk supply of (i) grains or other foods of high-energy value to meet caloric shortages could probably be carried out through an international buffer stock. There is likely to be considerable support for the setting up of an International Commodity Council with subcommittees dealing with particular products. The object would be to maintain buffer stocks of some of the basic primary products, with a view to reducing price fluctuations. Given an international buffer stock in wheat it should be possible to make special arrangements for drawing on the stock to a limited extent to supply grain on terms more favorable than commerical terms if an International Food Council agreed that the food position of a deficit area justified such a measure in the interests of the health of the population.

"An important issue of policy arises at this point. When it is said that there is a 'surplus' of a commodity what is meant in most cases is that at the market price supply exceeds demand. It does not follow that the *need* for the commodity is satisfied. When there is a wheat surplus in this sense it is possible that millions of people in Asiatic countries are subsisting on a diet below energy requirements. In these circumstances it has been argued, for example by Australians, that countries with a wheat surplus should be allowed to sell part of the surplus to China or India at prices far below the prices at which the rest of the wheat has been sold.

"If all wheat exports were sold at the very low price which is the highest that the deficit Asiatic areas could pay in the assumed conditions, only a fraction of the costs of wheat production would be covered and wheat producers, other than a section producing at very low costs, would face disaster. On the other hand, if only such wheat as cannot be sold at market prices were sold at the cut price to customers unable to pay more, the result would be a gain to the owners of the surplus. But the majority of the buyers of wheat would almost certainly object strongly to the discriminatory prices. Moreover, suspicions are likely to arise between the producers in different areas if producers in some areas where there is a surplus sell on their own initiative part of their wheat at knock-down prices. Under such conditions, moreover, the feeling may grow that the system of discriminating prices violates the spirit of liberal commercial policies.

"Therefore, there is a strong and I think a convincing case against permitting such discriminatory prices under ordinary commercial conditions.

"On the other hand, if an International Commodity Council and an International Food Council were set up it would be possible to work out methods of using a 'surplus' to meet unsatisfied needs in ways that would not encounter these objections.

"First, the disposal of surpluses at specially low prices should only be permitted under the following conditions:

"(1) A country which in a given year finds itself unable from domestic production and imports through commercial channels to meet the energy needs of its population should be entitled to place before the International Food Council a full statement of its position together with an estimate of the caloric deficit which would have to be met if the population were to obtain its bare energy needs.

"(2) The International Food Council would then examine the statement and if in its opinion the health and working capacity of a part of the population of the country making the application were dependent on imports of grain or other foods of high-energy intake beyond what could be obtained at market prices, then the Food Council would recommend to the International Commodity Council that from the buffer stocks there should be made available to the country in question a specified amount at a specially low price within the capacity of the country to pay. The price would be decided by the two Councils and the country in consultation."

In other papers I have expounded these ideas more fully and with some variations but it would be out of place here to discuss the subject exhaustively. However, it is important for the purposes of this study to examine the relations between such proposals and the other postwar plans which were gradually developing in London and Washington. The chief objection to the proposals was directed against the discriminating prices which they permitted. Some of the U.S. officials and delegation members held strongly that discriminating prices were inconsistent with the trade policies which the United States advocated. Some British officials and delegation members were concerned, first with the precedent which they feared would be created in favor of a wider application of discriminating prices, second with the effect of the precedent on the international trade policies which they had formulated and were waiting for an opportunity to discuss with U.S. officials, and third with the effects of discriminating prices, even if they were applied in a worthy cause, on the prices of Britain's large and indispensable wheat imports.

Those of us who believed that in the long run a constructive plan to remove semi-starvation from the earth would have to be adopted were ready to grant that discriminating prices under private enterprise were harmful and incompatible with sound trade policies, but maintained that it was quite another matter when special price concessions were made by international agreement for the purpose of preventing grave deterioration of health and working capacity. A large insufficiency of food inevitably lowers production both of food and of other goods, and decline in production is usually followed by decline in trade.

After studying the subject more closely since 1943 I have come to the conclusion that the British fears that such measures would tend to raise the prices of their wheat imports have more substance than the other objections to the "special international measures for wider food distribution." This has been confirmed by unofficial talks which I have had since the war with some of those concerned with British food policy. It has of course special force in the period in which the U.K. is struggling with balance-of-payments difficulties.

The Hot Springs Food and Agricultural Conference stands out as the most comprehensive and unified treatment of any of the chief postwar questions. Within its inescapable limits it shirked no issue and sidetracked no difficulties. Even where it failed to reach decided conclusions, as on special measures to meet peacetime inadequacies of whole nations, it recommended full examination by a permanent international body. With this excellent foundation for subsequent planning in detail we returned to our various stations in high hopes and with a range of vision that extended to the distant heights without overlooking the formidable obstacles that lay in the immediate path.

CHAPTER VIII

Food Relief Planning

IN 1942 a growing scarcity of food in most of the occupied countries aroused apprehension not only for the war but also for the immediate postwar years. International trade in fertilizer, in animal feedstuffs, and in agricultural equipment had been cut off by the blockade of Europe. Britain had kept the seas open, but the wartime demands for shipping and the destruction wrought by submarines had early forced her to restrict food imports to necessities. In the belligerent countries, agricultural workers had been drawn off the farms in large numbers into the armed forces and munition works. In Germany they had been replaced by prisoners of war but this depleted the labor and reduced the production of the occupied countries from which the prisoners had been drawn. Over most of Europe livestock were greatly reduced in order to turn cereal and root feedstuffs into direct human consumption. These changes were brought home to the public by the imposition and the enforcement with varying efficiency of drastic food rationing.

North America, in sharp contrast, was little affected by these conditions, and food consumption was rising above prewar levels. The increased incomes of workers who were now drawn into wartime economic activities were increasing the demand for the more expensive types of foods. But "surpluses" of a number of foods continued for some time after the war began, and the Lend-Lease Act was welcomed by the Department of Agriculture and the farmers as a means of reducing them. In 1941 and most of 1942 the purchasing missions of the Ministry of Food were pressed to buy freely and were given no hint of any shortages to come.

However, some of those who, like the present writer, were called on to deal with food questions in this period were impressed most of all with the widespread ignorance of the extent of these changes. Qualitative knowledge might set the direction of planning, but it could do little more: quantitative knowledge was indispensable to the preparation of working plans, both for the wartime and for the postwar period. At the end of 1942 no satisfactory quantitative data had been prepared in London or Washington on food consumption per head of population in the European countries or even in the United Kingdom and North America!

Such was the position when the first food plans were drawn up for the immediate postwar or rather post-liberation period. Late in 1942 both military and civilian quarters in London were concerned about the food conditions in the areas that would be liberated in the invasions that were being planned and the execution of which had already begun in the Mediterranean. The military authorities did not wish to be encumbered with any more civilian supplies than were essential to the prompt success of their operations. But it was believed that food supplies were low in many of the areas which it was hoped to liberate and it was realized that starvation or extreme distress among civilians behind the lines might impede the advance of the Allied troops.

In September 1941, the Inter-Allied Post War Requirements Bureau had been set up in London by the United Kingdom and the European Allied Governments in Exile.[1] In November 1942 the organization was requested to make a prompt report on the food needs of the liberated areas in an "emergency period" immediately after liberation. A committee was formed of which I was appointed chairman. It included a distinguished group of British and European agricultural and nutrition experts and F. L. MacDougall, an Australian who had played a leading role with Stanley Bruce in the outstanding work of the League of Nations on food and nutrition.

The experience of this committee brought out clearly the great difficulties that beset all efforts to formulate in advance plans for immediate relief or early reconstruction. Generally postwar planning for the short run seems to have been even more difficult than planning for the long run. Two months of incessant labors were necessary to reach agreement in a highly qualified committee all of whose members were imbued with a spirit of good will and a sense of urgency. We had no precedents and no examples to follow and were in the position of pioneers in an almost unknown territory. The countries for which we were requested to plan were, except for the activities of guerillas, entirely under the control of the enemy. None but clandestine movements and communications—at the risk of life—could be made between them and Britain. Information on

[1] See chapter ix, pp. 147-48.

the conditions of life in the occupied countries was scanty, often inconsistent, and sometimes contradictory. Even under prewar conditions and with full access to the countries, an appraisal of their food conditions would have been difficult and the results subject to much error. In 1942 the difficulties were so great that at the outset some members of the committee argued that the only method of work was to make a guess in round millions of the number of people who would have to be fed! To these members it was necessary to explain the procedures that would have to be followed to obtain food for relief. The chances were that when the first areas were liberated, and for some time afterwards, the war would still be going on and the demand for relief food would be one of a number of competing demands, military and civilian, some of which would be regarded until the war ended as even more urgent than civilian relief in the liberated areas. Hence there would be little chance of persuading the supply authorities to set aside food for civilian relief unless the demand were supported by the fullest information obtainable and by sound reasoning based on it.

Our plan of work may be summarized very briefly, since it was followed subsequently by the other bodies concerned with relief planning in Great Britain and the United States and in UNRRA. The needs of each country were estimated separately. They depended on the quantity of food that might be expected to be in the country at the time of liberation and the level of consumption to which it was decided to raise the civilian population. Each of these quantities was the subject of prolonged discussion and of many differences of opinion that could be resolved only after weeks of effort. Relief requirements were then calculated by subtracting the estimates of domestic food supply from the estimates of the supply that would be needed to bring the population to the appropriate level of consumption. To add to the difficulties, estimates of the civilian populations of the countries were far from reliable.

The estimates of domestic food production proved to be one of the most difficult tasks in drawing up food requirements, not only then but all through the war and for some time after it. In making them we faced not only technical but also political difficulties. Wartime work on international food questions called for as much diplomacy as technical skill. The representatives of the Allied Governments in Exile were in a difficult position. Haunted by doubts about the reception they would get in their own countries after the war, they wished to place it on record that they had striven for and where possible had obtained undertakings from the chief Allied powers to send adequate relief to their countrymen promptly after liberation. They hoped that when the time came to return to their countries they would be able to demonstrate that, although they had avoided the dangers and hardships of the occupation, they had nevertheless used their time in exile to the subsequent benefit of their countrymen who had remained at home.[2] All this made them predisposed to accept the lower rather than the higher estimates of the domestic food supplies in the occupied areas and the higher rather than the lower suggested levels of consumption to be established by relief shipments.[3] In all estimates of domestic production there was a considerable range of probable error. Generally the continental European members argued for figures in the lower part and the British and American members for figures in the higher part of this range of uncertainty. Reasonable compromises could be made so long as the Allied members did not press their estimates below the lower fringe of this sloping no man's land.[4] In spite of all the difficulties the committee in the end agreed on estimates of domestic supplies in each of the occupied countries of Europe.

When the committee turned from production to consumption it first reached the important conclusion, generally accepted subsequently in all work on food requirements, that in most areas the food-producing agricultural classes were able—in some areas too well able—to look after themselves, and would need no food relief. In many areas they seemed to have been holding back from the

[2] However during the periods when the bombing of London was particularly heavy we found that the Allied representatives were less worried over the attitude of those who had stayed home and who, on such occasions, were safer than people in London.

[3] The pressure to inflate estimates of requirements generally came from the Allied political representatives rather than the technical representatives, and I found it necessary on several occasions through the war to go to the higher political representatives who were not on the food committees and try to persuade them to change their instructions to their technical representatives and to allow technical bodies to function as technical bodies.

[4] Other difficulties arose over conversion factors to be used in calculating the calorie and protein values of carcasses and the available carbohydrate values of cereals. The average weight of carcasses had fallen in the occupied countries, but some of the Allied members suggested factors so low that, if correct, the animals must have been little more than walking skeletons! However, there were also differences due to imperfect knowledge and investigation in the past, apart from any political influences.

market enough food to supply their full caloric needs. There could be little doubt that they would continue to do this for some time after liberation; for the administrative controls, never wholly effective, would probably be weaker in the immediate postwar period than they had been during the war. Later experience confirmed the soundness of the assumption that the problem of food relief was chiefly an urban problem; except for certain areas such as the Dalmatian coast, the agricultural populations were excluded from estimates of requirements.

Turning to the level of consumption, the committee, after long discussion and much argument, adopted what came to be known as the 2,000-calorie level for the urban populations that needed food relief. This abbreviated phrase led to much popular misunderstanding. It meant that the caloric value of the relief food needed would be calculated by multiplying the relief population by 2,000 times the number of days in the relief period. The food would therefore be enough to give an *average* of 2,000 calories per person per day to the relief population. But the actual needs of individuals differed considerably according to age, sex, and occupation, and the total food supplies were to be distributed roughly according to comparative needs. For example, small children and old people would get less than 2,000 calories, manual workers more and heavy manual workers substantially more.

From this time "calories" became almost a political issue and the "2,000-calorie level" was frequently on the lips of Allied ministers, civil servants, and others, many of whom had only a vague conception of its significance. It was even mentioned in the dignified deliberations of the House of Lords. It attracted supporters and opponents—especially opponents—from various quarters where a new-found interest in the mysteries of nutrition suddenly appeared. It aroused indignation among humanitarians full of sympathy for the plight of the peoples in the occupied areas. And inevitably, through oversimplification, it led to gross misunderstandings and extraordinary misconceptions. Some thought it implied that brawny manual workers wielding pickaxes or sledgehammers would have to subsist on 2,000 calories. Others described it as a "starvation diet" that would turn the liberated peoples against their liberators. The idea that no one would get more than 2,000 calories, incredible though it appeared to those familiar with the subject, was widely accepted in popular discussions.

The question what caloric intake is needed to maintain health and working capacity is difficult to answer with precision. The necessary intake depends not only on sex and age but also on output of energy, which differs widely among individuals of the same age and sex. What we sought was a rough average figure, easily used in calculations, which would provide a diet sufficient to remove danger of starvation and to enable moderate working activity to be carried on. We estimated that the "2,000-calorie level" would probably supply rather more than two-thirds of full caloric needs, the exact proportion depending on the extent to which waste was taken into account. If no allowance were made for waste at any stage from production to consumption it would probably be close to two-thirds; if full allowance were made at every stage, it would probably be close to three-quarters.[5]

The case for the 2,000-calorie level was based at this time chiefly on the expectation of a continued scarcity of transport, especially of ships and landing craft. The necessity of landing large armies on the mainland of Europe dominated both naval and military strategy and the pattern of war production.[6] The greater the space given to civilian supplies the less there would be for military supplies,[7] and the longer the war would last.

Having completed estimates of domestic food supplies and determined the level to which the food consumption of the non-agricultural populations should be raised, we turned to the composition of the foods to be supplied, and decided to cast our recommendations in the form of requirements of specific quantities of a small number of staple foods, with cereals in much greater quantity than

[5] Waste occurs at the source, during manufacture, in wholesale and retail distribution, and in households and restaurants. In estimates during the war the practice was increasingly followed of calculating supplies and requirements "at the retail stage"—that is, allowing roughly for waste up to the point where the consumer receives the food for final consumption. Little is known of the extent of waste in households.

[6] Unfortunately for some time it did not dominate production as much as it should have done. See the illuminating study of General Sir Frederick Morgan, *Overture to Overload*, 1944, pp. 131, 143, 145, 170-171.

[7] It was more difficult than might have been expected to convince European allied representatives of this. At some stages I think the extravagantly large "PX" supplies to U.S. soldiers and civilians in Europe made a bad impression. The priority given to them seems to have arisen from a philosophy in the War Department that refused to treat the American soldier as an adult.

any other, in weight, volume, and energy value. The cereals were to be supplied as far as possible in the form of whole grain, and the receiving countries were to mill the grain at an extraction rate of approximately 85 per cent, the residue to be used as animal feedstuffs. Rationing was to be maintained, and special provisions were to be continued, or where they did not already exist were to be established, to safeguard the nutrition of infants, children, nursing and pregnant women, and sick persons.

It was already clear to us that there would be a serious world shortage of foodstuffs of animal origin and of fats and oils of both animal and vegetable origin, and that at least the shortage of animal foodstuffs would be likely to continue for several years after the war. Consequently the statement of requirements for these scarce foods was kept down to low levels which were determined partly by opinions about nutritional needs and partly by recognition of the importance of custom and habit. As to nutritional needs, there was some concern about the difficulty of obtaining enough vitamin A and, among some members, about the difficulty of obtaining enough protein of high quality. But the evidence on protein needs was obscure and conflicting, and those who argued for higher requirements of animal protein were apparently influenced more by the alleged need to make up for protein depletion under war food conditions than by current necessities in a short relief period. Over a large part of occupied Europe, however, the evidence of serious malnutrition among the Allied populations was scanty, and although there were a few ardent advocates of high requirements of animal foods and even of vitamin capsules the committee in the end came to a moderate and practicable plan that tried to cut the coat according to the cloth. But much concern was felt over the nutritional needs of infants, young children, and pregnant and nursing mothers. Here even short-run deficiencies might be serious, and careful plans were drawn for the supply of supplementary foods and nutrients and for their appropriate distribution among these groups. But shortage of milk was a grave handicap to these efforts, and although we recommended that all available milk should be reserved for the special groups our estimates left little hope that all the child population could be supplied. Hence we recommended the provision of chocolate fortified by vitamin A for the children who could not get milk.[8]

[8] Visiting Mr. Keynes one day about this time I found him reading our re-

The report of the committee was widely circulated in London and Washington departments. The magnitude of the requirements put forward impressed the supply authorities and helped to correct over-optimistic ideas still lingering from the days of surpluses. The estimates were of course subject to periodic change as harvest prospects changed. But a method of approach had been laid down which, with some improvements in detail, held the field throughout the war in the formulation of requirements.[9] This was unequivocal short-run planning with a clearly defined and limited objective. Its chief difficulties came from the scarcity of information and from the intrusion of political motives.

This report and that of the Tolley Committee in Washington had hardly been completed when President Roosevelt called for a United Nations food conference. As is shown in another chapter, the urgent food needs of the short run were strongly emphasized at Hot Springs. Unfortunately, the Interim Organization charged with the preparation of plans for a permanent food and agricultural organization moved very slowly, and when the organization was set up it fought shy for some time of short-run food problems.

But food planning for the short run became more and more urgent and went on through many channels, both military and civilian. First the new office set up within the State Department and headed by Governor Lehman, took up food along with other relief questions. Later in 1943 the plans for the creation of a United Nations Relief and Rehabilitation Organization were completed and the organization was set up in November. From the beginning it was clear that food would constitute the largest single item in international relief. The rehabilitation of agriculture as quickly as possible

port. He expressed approval of the report and recommendations and asked me to meet him in the Bank of England two days later. Arriving there I found both Mr. Keynes and L. J. Cadbury, another director of the Bank, in the room. Keynes asked me to expound the recommendation on vitaminized chocolate and then asked Mr. Cadbury whether enough capacity had been left in the chocolate industry to manufacture the quantities specified in our report. After some technical discussion conclusions were reached on the resources needed to produce the required quantity and Keynes wrote and circulated an interdepartmental paper embodying the conclusions and vigorously urging prompt action. When France was invaded in the next year the 21st Army Group took with them supplies of vitaminized chocolate as recommended. This incident illustrates both the catholicity of Keynes's interests and his deep humanitarian instincts.

[9] An able United States committee was working, unknown to us, about the same time in Washington with Dr. Howard Tolley as chairman.

after liberation of the occupied areas was therefore accepted as one of UNRRA's main objects in the field of rehabilitation, as food was in the field of relief.

But between the time of the reports by the Inter-Allied Committee and Tolley Committee in Washington and the time when UNRRA began its work there was a great and haphazard growth of food relief planning. A memorandum of mine sent to Washington in September 1943, which argued the case for the unification of food relief plans, showed that, taking London, Washington and Cairo together, there were eleven different bodies independently formulating relief requirements, all of them overlapping as to the areas covered and few of them knowing what the others were doing or even whether or not they were doing anything! Even within the War Department in Washington the International Division of the Quartermaster Corps was at odds with the Civil Affairs Division.

However, the confusion in food relief planning was due partly to a number of political decisions made in 1943. It was decided that in the early period of liberation food relief supplies should be the responsibility of the military authorities. But the so-called military period was never defined clearly enough for practical purposes, and UNRRA's early approaches to the allocating authorities were hampered by its inability to state precisely when the food which it was requesting would be needed. Such facile political decisions at the "top level," giving a deceptive impression of simplicity, often create insurmountable practical difficulties at the "working level," where general statements have to be interpreted to produce detailed operating plans. These difficulties were increased by the refusal of the War Department to cooperate with the civil agencies and with the international secretariat of UNRRA on the ground that military secrets concerning the place or places of invasion might be given away. Those of us who advocated the unification of food relief pointed out that there would be no danger of this if relief plans were made simultaneously to cover all European occupied areas.

In November 1943, the confusion was increased by the decision that UNRRA would procure and finance food supplies only for its Central, Eastern and Southern and not for its Western European members, who would procure and finance their supplies independently. Since this led to separate and independent formulations of requirements for the two areas, those of us who agitated for unified requirements raised the question what assurance there could be that, in applying for scarce food supplies and shipping space, common methods of formulating requirements would be followed. An attempt was made to meet this criticism by giving power to the Director General of UNRRA to comment on and, if he thought fit, to object to the requirements presented to the allocating authorities by the liberated countries that paid for their own supplies. But this appeared at the time to many of us to be an unsatisfactory compromise, and the fundamental objection remained which I expressed at the time as follows: "The existence of more than one plan becomes a definite hindrance when the supply authorities and financial authorities are called upon to allocate supplies and appropriate funds. Such authorities are naturally inclined to delay action until the plans are harmonized by their authors or submitted to another group of technicians for detailed appraisal or reworking. This takes time."

Behind the multiplicity of plans lay an assumption that requirements must be formulated by those charged with the administration or supervision of the area in which the relief was to be given. This assumption, always tenaciously followed by the military in Washington, has little but military tradition to support it. Much effort and time would have been saved and could have been turned to other purposes, if a single group of the best experts in London and Washington had been formed and given a monopoly of the task of preparing relief requirements,[10] always in consultation with the countries concerned.

In London we made strenuous efforts to accomplish this in limited aspects of food relief. We believed, for example, that once agreement was obtained on estimates of domestic food supplies in the areas to be liberated one of the main obstacles to agreement on food relief needs would be removed. Fortunately, for a time we found sympathetic officials in the War Food Administration (particularly Dr. John Cassels) and in the Department of Agriculture, and, through the support of Ambassador Winant and Philip Reed a Combined Food Working Party was formed, composed of U.S., U.K., and UNRRA experts, which met in London from time to time and

[10] I do not suggest that this should have been done at the very beginning. In blazing a new trail independent efforts may produce better results at the outset. But, this no longer applies when the basic methods are laid down and represent the consensus among competent experts. By the middle of 1943 the time for unification had come.

reached agreements on estimates of food in the occupied and later the liberated areas. Both UNRRA and SHAEF made substantial use of these data. The difficulties with the military were much reduced by a decision that the theater commander was to be the judge of requirements. SHAEF was much easier to work with than the Pentagon, and on an informal basis effective cooperation took place among embassy officials, UNRRA officials, and the SHAEF staff concerned with civilian needs in the areas to be liberated. The methods of formulating food requirements, the evidence concerning domestic supplies in occupied areas, and the level to which an attempt was made to raise the civilian populations were all markedly influenced by the experience gained in London.

New advances were made in the estimation of food consumption in the United Kingdom, Canada, and the United States, following a dispute within the Lend-Lease and War Food Administrations over the level of consumption in the United Kingdom. With the growing scarcity of food in the world as a whole, the allocating authorities in Washington began to look more closely into the basis of the claims that were brought before them. When British requirements were questioned the British Ministry of Food, with our support in the embassy, proposed an impartial inquiry by experts. There was extraordinary uncertainty about actual consumption in any country. The proposal was accepted and applied with great success. In meetings in London, Washington, and Ottawa of what came to be called the Food Consumption Level Inquiry, the most comprehensive investigation made up to then or since, covering the United Kingdom, the United States, and Canada, established complete agreement among British, American, and Canadian experts, opened new paths in its methods of approach, and aided planning in the postwar as well as the war period.

Thus, in spite of all the confusion and overlapping, notable advances in knowledge were made which later produced important practical results. With the growing habit and improving technique of making appraisals of the food situation on the European and American continents it became possible to foresee far better than ever before the probable postwar difficulties and dangers and, as far as political conditions permitted, to plan in advance to forestall or mitigate them.

In the spring of 1943 an ad hoc food committee of the Committee of the Council for Europe of UNRRA was appointed with instructions to lay down "the bases of requirements" for food relief. This did not mean estimation of the precise quantitative needs at any particular time but a statement of the principles which were to govern the formulation of food requirements. At the outset the majority of the committee insisted on planning only for the "post-emergency" period, on the assumption that SHAEF would look after the earlier period. This arose from the continued fears of most of the Allied representatives of the reception they would get in their own countries, and their unwillingness to have their names linked with any disagreeably but unavoidably low levels in the early days of liberation. Dr. Cassells and I, who represented the United States on the committee, proposed that three standards should be laid down as the objectives for three successive stages: first, the 2,000-calorie level for the emergency period; second, a 2,250-calorie level to increase working capacity; and third, a 2,500- or 2,600-calorie level to meet all or most energy needs. How far UNRRA should go would be determined by the resources given to it and the comparative urgency of needs for other goods. But opposition to this proposal for political reasons was intense and in the end a target of 2,650 calories was set up to be approached as nearly as circumstances would permit. Dr. Cassells and I considered that this target was unreal for working purposes but of secondary importance so long as it was understood to be merely a long-distance aim to be reached only if supplies permitted.[11]

The most difficult and important issue was that concerned with distribution among the Allies: on this question we were not willing to compromise. The difficulty arose out of the differences between the living conditions of the Western European countries and those of the countries to be supplied by UNRRA. The Western Allies wished to adopt criteria that would at least partly restore their prewar advantages over the rest of Europe. Although they would not be supplied by UNRRA they had an important interest in the UNRRA bases of requirements for food, for they were or would be-

[11] For a contrary view see J. Lindberg, *Food, Famine, and Relief*, Princeton, League of Nations, 1946, pp. 94-96. It should be noted that some of the Allied ministers who pressed for this high level changed their minds later when a choice had to be made between spending all their UNRRA funds for food and dividing them between food and other urgent requirements for restarting home production.

come claimants before the allocating authorities for the scarce foods that UNRRA sought for its members. If UNRRA were given funds to restore prewar levels fully it would be reasonable to agree to differential levels between the two groups of countries. But we did not believe that the funds or the supplies would permit this, and we believed that at low levels the principle of equality of treatment in calorie levels should be upheld. The composition of foods might differ: in fact the Southern and Eastern European countries did not seek to obtain the same amounts of animal foodstuffs per capita as the Western countries requested.

The idea that relief diets should resemble roughly the customary diets of each area was generally accepted, and the arguments of the Eastern and Southern European representatives for sharing alike were confined to calorie levels. It was generally recognized, too, that the principle of equality of treatment could be applied in practice only within the limits of the shipping and inland transport that would be available for transporting food at the time, and should therefore be interpreted or qualified to mean that the allocating authorities should refuse additional allocations to a country which had reached a specified level only when such allocations would hinder other countries below that level from reaching it. Thus, if Norway had reached the level and Poland was still below it, but land transport to, or port capacity in, Poland made it impossible to place more shipments in Poland for the time, it would be in order for Norway to receive additional shipments.

On the UNRRA committees my colleagues and I had advocated from the beginning that the committees on requirements should confine themselves to matters of policy and should leave to the secretariat the details of planning and the execution of policies. The conditions affecting relief and rehabilitation were continually changing and the secretariat should, we argued, be free to adapt requirements[12] and other details of planning to the changes without being obliged to obtain the sanction of slow-moving committees on every detail. This argument was reinforced by the difficulty of keeping political issues out of technical committees. What appeared to be innocuous details of planning and administration were sometimes transformed into,

[12] The requirements themselves changed with revisions in the estimates of indigenous supplies. The proper function of the committee was to agree on the principles of estimating requirements but not to be continually passing on the actual amounts to be sent to different countries.

or made the pretext for raising, far-reaching political controversies. However, the case for keeping executive and administrative work out of committees does not depend on this supplementary point: in my experience it applied with no less force to organizations in which the Russians took no part.

Food relief was the most urgent of all economic problems over the greater part of continental Europe in the first two years after the war and it was fortunate that early attention had been given to the methods of planning both on the side of supply and on the side of requirements. The methods devised and the estimates made, after further development, laid the foundation for new appraisals of the food position after the war over a large part of the world, and new efforts to improve the position of the countries in which food consumption had long been inadequate. Here some permanent gains were snatched out of the necessities of emergency planning to mitigate the wretchedness and want which the scourge of war had brought to millions of long-suffering peoples.

CHAPTER IX

Planning for International Relief

AFTER the summer of 1940 it became clear that most of the European countries would remain for some time under enemy occupation, cut off from trade with the rest of the world, restricted in their economic relations with one another, exploited to serve the war needs and maintain the living standards of the aggressor countries, deprived of the means to maintain or renew their capital equipment, and, in some areas, rent with civil strife and guerrilla warfare. Looking still further ahead it was to be expected that there would be much physical destruction and economic confusion during the period of liberation. And if liberation came through slow, hard-fought advances economic order would have to be restored in areas liberated before the war had ended everywhere.

Hence in the same period in which drafts of Article VII of the Mutual Aid agreement were being discussed across the Atlantic as a basis for the long-term international economic organization of the world, the first steps were being taken to prepare for the short-run international economic difficulties that would probably arise even before the end of the war and on a much greater scale after it.

London was the headquarters of the European Allied Governments in Exile and we were brought in close touch with them during the war.[1] The lot of the Allied ministers in exile was not an enviable one. They were ministers with little to administer. Depressed by the calamities which had overtaken their countries and unable to control the course of events at home, they at first lived a restless existence without satisfactory outlet for their energies. After the

[1] Ambassador Biddle was responsible for direct diplomatic relations with these governments, and excellent cooperation existed at all times between him and Ambassador Winant and between the staffs of the two embassies. We were called on to provide the majority of U.S. representatives on the Inter-Allied committees.

German invasion in Europe had reached its peak, at least in the West, their attention was gradually turned to questions of relief and reconstruction in their countries, and they asked the Foreign Office what views the United Kingdom government was forming on such questions, and the Treasury what plans it had to deal after liberation with the monetary chaos in Europe.

The first move was made by the Foreign Office, which invited the heads of the Allied Governments in Exile to a meeting at St. James's Palace, presided over by Mr. Eden, at which an "Inter-Allied Committee on Post War Requirements," with a bureau responsible to it and headed by Sir Frederick Leith-Ross, a distinguished British civil servant, was established. This was the first widely representative international organization set up to deal with postwar questions. The aim of the member countries was "to secure that supplies of food, raw materials and articles of prime necessity should be made available for the postwar needs of the countries liberated from Nazi oppression." The plans of the countries were to be coordinated through the committee and the bureau. Estimates of requirements were to be made, priorities among the different needs were to be established, and plans were to be prepared for "the most efficient employment" of Allied and other European shipping after liberation.[2]

Ambassador Winant had encouraged Mr. Eden to call this meeting, and the Foreign Office was in turn anxious that a United States representative should sit on the Inter-Allied Committee, since it would be necessary, unless the war ended much earlier than appeared likely, to turn to the North American continent for help in the immediate provision of relief supplies after liberation. Unfortunately the most the Ambassador could obtain was permission for an embassy representative to sit as an observer on the committee. The Ambassador designated Alan Steyne, an able and energetic foreign service officer, whose immense labors during the war led to a breakdown in health and premature death in 1946, for this position. Mr. Steyne, commendably, interpreted broadly the role of "observer," and made constructive contributions to the work of the committee and the bureau. Months later, after persistent representations to Washington, the Ambassador was able to raise the status of Mr.

[2] Resolution adopted at the Inter-Allied Meeting held in London at St. James's Palace, September 24, 1941. For full text see Report of Proceedings, Card 6315 of 1941, pp. 17-18.

Steyne and of U.S. representatives on various subcommittees of the organization from that of observers to that of full members.

The organization was handicapped by the difficulties of recruiting an adequate secretariat. The war was in full swing, victory was still distant, and the demands for trained staffs in the departments concerned with the war effort was so great that few persons could be spared to engage in preparations for postwar relief. Sir Frederick Leith-Ross was appointed as chairman of the committee and head of its secretariat. His knowledge was wide; he was popular with Allied ministers, and he became in practice as well as in theory an international representative who did not hesitate to oppose the views of his own countrymen when he believed that it was in the interests of the European Allies as a whole to do so. But it was difficult to recruit even a staff with general administrative qualifications and impossible to recruit a staff with specialized knowledge in many fields of consumer and producer goods. It was decided that the staff should be all British, since the Allied Governments in Exile were short of skilled and experienced officials to carry out their own work and would have been crippled by the loss of the few they had.

As if to compensate for the insufficiency of the secretariat, a massive structure of committees and working parties was erected. The advice of a large number of experts was obtained. Hundreds of meetings were held and many reports issued. Naturally, the quality of the work was uneven: both the committees and the secretariat were better equipped in some fields than in others. The small secretariat struggled heroically with the great numbers of papers, of calculations, of reports, and of meetings that arose out of so large a structure of committees, subcommittees, and working parties.

The question how to make estimates of future requirements for whole countries was to remain throughout the war, and for a time after it, one of the most important and most complex and difficult of all postwar questions of the short run. It was one of the main problems both of relief and of reconstruction. It was an intrinsically dull subject, but it aroused sharp differences of opinion; it engaged the labors of hundreds of officials, and at times it stirred up heated political controversies.[8] The difficulties were aggravated by the fre-

[8] There is no space in this study for a wide range of illustrations, but in Chapter VIII I have explained some of the central problems of requirements in a discussion of food relief plans.

quent failure of newcomers to study and profit by what had already been done before, and by the lack of an accepted set of principles generally followed. In 1943 I suggested that an experienced official should be released from all other duties for six months to prepare a textbook on "The Formulation of Requirements." This might have saved much time, prevented further repetition of the same initial errors by a constant stream of newcomers to the field, and economized the services of skilled workers urgently needed for many tasks.

The requirements formulated by the committees were so wide in scope that if they had been fulfilled they would have gone a considerable way toward meeting reconstruction as well as relief needs.[4] At that time no sharp distinction was drawn between relief and reconstruction. The Inter-Allied Committee, however, carefully avoided all discussion of the financing of the requirements and confined itself strictly to the mere statement of the goods which, in its opinion, were needed. In retrospect, much of the work appears valuable, and it would have been still more valuable if greater attention had been given to the probable supply position of some of the commodities and if the secretariat had understood the importance of producing recommendations that would impress the allocating authorities as being within a range of possible fulfillment in the immediate prewar conditions.[5]

Outside the Inter-Allied Committee and its bureau, important discussions took place in Washington and in London in 1942 and 1943.[6] In both capitals there were sharp and even acrimonious differences of opinion on the form which international relief and reconstruction should take after the war. In London one school of thought, represented by some of the British officials concerned in the work of the Inter-Allied Post War Requirements Bureau, took an ambitous view of the scope of the international organization which, it was generally agreed, would have to be set up to deal with relief. They saw in it much more than an organization to arrange for the procurement and distribution of relief goods among final consumers. They

[4] The committee claimed, however, that its estimates made no provision for the restoration of working stocks.

[5] The food committee with its "2,000-calorie level" (see chapter VIII) obtained a favorable reception for its report among army and civilian supply authorities. SHAEF later adopted that level as the aim of its own operations.

[6] They had, I believe, started in 1941 in Washington, but I am not acquainted with their earliest stages.

foresaw correctly that the European continent would need many other goods besides goods for direct consumer relief, and they would have given an active role to the proposed international organization in the fields of procurement, transport, and distribution of all such goods. Their opponents in Whitehall summed up their point of view as proposing that a United Nations organization should be set up which would "manage the whole import program of Europe." Officials in the supply departments in Whitehall were skeptical of these ideas and as time went on became actively antagonistic to them. At the other end of the scale, it was held that many of the postwar supplies could be arranged directly between the supplying and the receiving countries within a framework of allocations of scarce goods; another part might be carried out with the help of long-term international organizations; and only the residue should be entrusted to an international relief organization.

In Washington early differences were even sharper. At first there was only one point of unanimous agreement: it was that the American people generally respond readily to appeals from those in material distress. Provision of funds for straightforward relief would therefore be supported by Congress and the public. There the unanimity ended. How the relief should be given and where relief ends and reconstruction begins were questions on which wide divergences of view existed. At opposite ends of the scale were the views typically associated at the time with Milo Perkins, a leading official in the Department of Agriculture, and Herbert Hoover. Mr. Perkins was not interested in a narrowly restricted charitable organization. He desired an international organization that would not only bring relief to the destitute but would also reconstruct the whole economic life of the countries which had suffered under the Nazis. In contrast, Mr. Hoover was typical of an older school of thought which was not even interested in an international organization for relief, which was strongly opposed to one in which all countries had the same voting power, and which leaned toward the unilateral administration of relief by the supplying countries, mainly the United States, which might use the American Red Cross as its agent, limiting relief to final consumer goods and mainly to food and clothing. This outlook was common to most isolationists. Unlike the outlook of either side in the controversy in London, it was a challenge to the whole idea of establishing an international organization based on equality of status.

But Washington was more international in outlook than it had been in the First World War and in the period from 1928 to 1932. The State Department, with support from other agencies, and under the leadership of Dean Acheson, came out in support of an international organization with an international secretariat, in which the United States would be in a position of formal equality with other states.[7] This decision, like the later decision to accept the substance of the Acheson-Lilienthal report on atomic energy, was unmistakable evidence of the growth of a more generous spirit and a more mature international outlook in the United States.

This cleared the ground and put the internal differences in Washington on the same plane as those in London. The exact scope, functions, and structure of the international organization were the subject of prolonged discussions in both capitals and some of the differences of viewpoint in London, which have already been described, had their counterparts in Washington.

Ambassador Winant took a lively interest in the planning of the international organization and expressed his views in telegrams, in conversations in Washington, and in a comprehensive memorandum on postwar matters which he prepared for Secretary Hull early in 1943. In 1942 he requested me to study what form of organization was best adapted to international relief. In the same period Keynes, in personal conversations, impatiently referred several times to what he considered to be an unrealistic attitude in some British officials who wished to give wide scope and powers to the organization. After long consideration the Ambassador and I drew up suggestions for Washington. A brief and simplified summary will serve to bring out some of the main issues on which decisions had to be made.

The demand for relief would begin early when some territories were cleared of the enemy but the war continued elsewhere. It would increase enormously when the Axis as a whole, or at least the European part of the Axis, collapsed. Hence unified and comprehensive estimates of needs should be made and accepted by all parties as soon as possible, subject to frequent revision. The proposed scale of relief should be decided early, though in practice shipping might

[7] This approach was strongly advocated by Ambassador Winant who frequently communicated with Washington at length on it.

be the chief determining factor until hostilities ceased in Europe. Food and medical supplies would usually come first but sometimes manufactured goods might be needed early to draw food out of the local farmers. Supplies would have to come chiefly from the U.S., the U.K., the British Commonwealth, and Argentina. They would at first be drawn largely from stocks, but the size of stocks could be affected by deliberate policies that took future relief needs into account.

Existing machinery was inadequate to deal with relief supplies. The administrative structure for obtaining relief supplies must begin with government departments in the supply countries, in each of which a coordinating body was necessary. A committee for this purpose had been set up in Whitehall but met only at long intervals and was too unwieldy to transact business. In some quarters in London it was thought that the Inter-Allied Post War Requirements Bureau should serve as a coordinating body. This was absurd: neither the Bureau nor a United Nations relief body could perform the functions of a national coordinating body, for policies on relief supplies would raise controversial domestic issues, such as the question how far the civil population of the supply country should be rationed to build up relief stocks. A small interdepartmental national body was needed in each supply country, but this was only the beginning. International coordination of supplies was equally necessary. Here again it was widely, but in our view wrongly, held that the proposed international relief organization should be the coordinating body. Most of the goods needed for relief would be goods needed also, while the war lasted, for the armed services, the civil populations in the supply countries, and armed services and civil poulations in Allied countries engaged in warfare. International relief constituted one competitive demand out of many, and allocation among competitive claimants could not be acceptably made by one of the claimants! The Combined Boards seemed to be the most appropriate international coordinating body for the purpose. During their deliberations on relief they might include representatives from supply countries not then represented.

The functions of the international relief organization would be to prepare requirements for the countries to be liberated, to act as claimants before the Combined Boards for those countries, to arrange procurement of allocations from the supplying countries, to transport supplies to the areas where relief was needed, and to ensure that distribution of supplies within those areas would be as fair and efficient as possible.

This approach was wholly on the side of those who sought a genuinely international handling of the relief problem, but it proposed a much more modest role for the international organization than was desired in some circles in London and Washington. Many of those who, then and since, advocated the creation of new international organizations, failed to see the necessity of first analyzing clearly the functions which an international body can properly perform and their relation to the functions which can only be performed by national bodies. They had erred, too, in underestimating the difficulties of starting a new international organization. These difficulties were at their height in 1942 and 1943, when the demand of governments for trained officials and experts was intense and when it was extraordinarily difficult for an international body to recruit a competent new staff.

However, if the international relief body were to be given more limited functions than its idealistic advocates desired, it would not be prevented from interpreting relief in a wide sense to include much reconstruction of local productive capacity. There were in reality two largely separate issues behind the controversies in London and Washington: first, the question precisely what functions the international body should discharge in assisting the liberated areas, and second, what should be the scope of the assistance given. It was possible to argue for strictly limited functions in the international organization, which clearly would be only one of a number of organizations assisting the liberated areas, and also to argue that the assistance to be given should be wide in scope and should cover a large part of reconstruction as well as relief. A third position was held strongly in some quarters, particularly in the supply departments in London and Washington; it was that there should be an international organization with strictly limited functions confined mainly to relief in the form of food and clothing, and a separate reconstruction program covering repairs, replacement, and even improvement of the productive equipment of the liberated areas, and organized by the supplying countries, perhaps through some temporary coordinating international machinery such as the Combined Boards.

These cross currents, each of them flowing strongly in different directions, kept the final outcome uncertain, not only up to the time when the representatives of the United Nations met on November 9, 1943, to sign the instrument which established the United Nations Relief and Rehabilitation Administration but even until the first meeting of the Council of the Organization which was not closed until December 1. In contrast to the practice followed in setting up the long-term organizations, the agreement setting up UNRRA was a short document, expressed in general terms except where it outlined the internal structure of the organization. The agreement had been reached in negotiations through diplomatic channels and was not debated at a conference. The chief purpose of UNRRA was to be "the relief of victims of war in any area under the control of any of the United Nations through the provision of food, fuel, clothing, shelter, and other essential services, and to facilitate in such areas, so far as necessary to the adequate provision of relief, the production and transportation of these articles and the furnishing of these services."[8]

The detailed policies to guide UNRRA's operations were not drawn up at the start and embodied in a charter; they were to be laid down by resolutions of the council, which was to meet twice a year. In this way a number of fundamental decisions of policy were made at the first council meeting, which settled for the time the controversies that had preceded the formation of the organization. The functions of UNRRA were to be closely similar to those we had suggested in London: the Director General was to be the claimant before the Combined Boards for the countries receiving relief, and was to secure "a fair distribution of goods which are in short supply and of shipping services to and among the various areas liberated or to be liberated."[9] But the discharge of this responsibility was to be a much more complicated task than we had foreseen: it was affected by another decision of the greatest importance.

In earlier discussions it had generally been supposed that the international relief organization would aid all the liberated countries impartially. It was true that the assets held abroad by some of those countries would be restored to them after the war and could be used to pay for relief. But the aftermath of the First World War had inclined most of us to oppose their dissipation to meet emergency needs

[8] Agreement for United Nations Relief and Rehabilitation, Article 1a.
[9] Resolution No. 17.

of consumer goods. There was a healthy impulse among Washington officials, which we shared in the embassy in London, to avoid the accumulation of debts and the dissipation of international assets in order to meet the emergency economic needs either of war or of the immediate aftermath of war. Lend-Lease was the outcome of this impulse during the war, and many of us hoped that there would be an equally bold approach to the early postwar period. Unfortunately, the supplying countries were not yet ready for such a move.

The question how to finance UNRRA supplies had perplexed the U.S. and U.K. Treasuries for a time. Eventually the solution was found in a suggestion which, Keynes told me, had been made by Dr. Harry White in a luncheon conversation with him, that each contributing member country should give an amount equal to 1 per cent of its estimated national income. This suggestion was taken up enthusiastically by Keynes and was accepted at Atlantic City.[10] For the first time it was possible to form an idea of the size of the funds that would be available for the new international organization. On the other side, by selecting the estimates of the more sober among the Allied committees in London, a rough idea could be formed of the extent of probable demands on the fund.

The results of these comparisons were disturbing. The fund resulting from a 1 per cent levy on the national incomes of the countries which had not been occupied might amount to roughly $2,500 million. This was an immensely larger sum than had ever before been voted for international relief or entrusted to an international organization. But it looked a small sum in comparison with the needs of the countries to be liberated.

The results of these estimates were far-reaching. First they—far more than any abstract doctrines—set sharp limits to the extent of UNRRA's efforts in the field of rehabilitation or reconstruction. Political considerations had indeed led to the rejection of the word "reconstruction" in UNRRA's title and terms of reference. Several congressmen in Washington had bitterly assailed the point of view illustrated by Milo Perkins' demand for an international body that would reconstruct as well as relieve. They identified this position with that of the New Deal in domestic affairs. Civil servants

[10] Estimates of the national incomes of some of the member countries were no more than window dressing. But this signified little in comparison with the political advantages of the formula.

in supply departments in Whitehall looked with suspicion on the idea, which they attributed to Sir Frederick Leith-Ross, of an UNRRA which would "manage the whole import program of Europe."[11] In the end, however, it was the size of the fund which determined the scope of UNRRA's activities. Article 1 (a), quoted above, left much formal scope for reconstruction. It appeared that if UNRRA were able ". . . to facilitate the production and transportation of . . . food, fuel, clothing, shelter and other basic necessities," and "the furnishing of . . . medical and other services," even only "so far as necessary to the adequate provision of relief," it would cover a wide area of reconstruction. Actually, however, the demands for food relief were so large, so urgent, and so costly that only a small proportion of the funds would be left for "rehabilitation."[12]

The second decision, taken at this meeting, that greatly affected the scope of UNRRA was the decision that the Western European Allies would not apply to UNRRA to meet their relief needs. Thus arose the distinction between the "paying" and "non-paying" members of UNRRA. It made UNRRA an agency for assisting Eastern, Southern and part of Central Europe. The consequences of this step were far-reaching. As we shall see later, it increased the drain of external assets from the Western European countries in the immediate postwar years which brought some of them, particularly France, close to economic collapse.

The question therefore arises, how was it that the French representatives took a prominent part in the movement to exclude from UNRRA financial aid those countries which possessed, or at the end of the war would possess, assets abroad? There is no doubt that they were impressed with the insufficiency of the funds to meet the needs of the liberated territories as a whole. Probably this was the

[11] This phrase was used by a prominent British official who took part in the controversy in Whitehall, in a conversation I had with him shortly before leaving London for Atlantic City. The United Kingdom delegation was sharply divided within, and the controversy which had begun in Whitehall was continued at Atlantic City for some time behind the scenes in delegation meetings, the "big UNRRA" forces being led by Leith-Ross and the "little UNRRA" forces by John Maud of the Ministry of Food. A British delegation seriously split on fundamental policy was an unusual occurrence such as I had not seen before and have not seen since.

[12] This word, taken from the jargon of American social workers, was politically preferable to "reconstruction." There are of course degrees of reconstruction, and "rehabilitation" may appropriately be used to designate the earliest stages of reconstruction, including particularly the repair of damaged or deficient equipment.

main but not the complete explanation. When the council meeting opened at Atlantic City the shape of things to come was only partially discernible. Those who held that UNRRA's role in the immediate postwar period should extend widely over Europe's external economic relations were still making their voices heard. The Western European Allies were anxious to maintain autonomy in external economic affairs and feared that an UNRRA of large scope would have too much say in their affairs. Some of them possessed considerable foreign exchange funds or gold or both, which would be released to them in Washington and London at the end of the war, and their governments in exile still hoped that these assets would be sufficient to meet their relief and reconstruction needs. If the estimates of requirements for which their representatives had pressed on the Inter-Allied committees were roughly correct these hopes were indeed ill founded. But the Allied invasion of northwest Europe had not yet begun and much might happen before the Western Allies would be called on to finance their relief needs. It was understood that supplies would be brought in by the armies during the military period.[18] In more than one country, including the United States itself, there were many who hoped that Lend-Lease in a modified form might be continued for a time to meet some of the immediate postwar needs. There was indeed no warrant for this belief or hope in the act itself or in the debates and hearings on it. Nevertheless, the hope of a change in the attitude of the United States on the matter seems never to have faded until the day when President Truman, without previous notification to the recipient countries, announced that Lend-Lease had ended.

Whatever weight may be given to these and other factors that may have influenced the Western European countries, there is no doubt about the significance of the decision that was reached. It released more funds for the Eastern and Southern European countries than would otherwise have been available. But in the end it was to throw a greater burden on the Western European countries than they could bear, and the optimism which prompted it hindered the realization that comprehensive measures to deal with the postwar difficulties of Western Europe would be indispensable.

When these fundamental issues were settled there were still many

[18] I do not think it was yet realized that these supplies would be accompanied by bills!

difficult questions of organization to decide. The regional division of functions was more difficult for UNRRA than for most international organizations. The sources of supply and the field of operations were widely separated. On technical grounds there was a strong case for placing the seat of authority near the field of operations. On political grounds there was an equally strong if not a stronger case for placing it close to the largest sources of supply. The political view prevailed so far as the headquarters was concerned, but concessions were made to the regional principle in the establishment of a European regional organization in London, and another for the Far East, which, however, could not move away from Washington. As we shall see later, this form of organization raised many difficulties in practice. Moreover, as countries came to be liberated the regional organization was no longer the nearest point to the field of operations, and the country missions, placed in the areas in which relief was distributed, were to play an increasingly important role.

The arrangements for the procurement of supplies placed on the UNRRA administration the responsibility for securing "a fair distribution of goods which are in short supply and of shipping services to and among the various areas liberated or to be liberated." The Western Allies who were procuring and paying for their own supplies had therefore to keep the UNRRA administration informed of their proposed purchases, so that the Director General could raise objections if the paying countries attempted to get so large a share of scarce products that the non-paying countries would go short. It was recognized, however, that the war effort must not be hindered by relief demands, and the UNRRA administration was to appear before the Combined Boards as the accredited applicant for relief whose claims would be weighed alongside other claims, especially those for meeting war needs. There was much discussion and some controversy over these arrangements. Governor Lehman, who became director of UNRRA, was concerned over the danger that the relief claims of the countries whose supplies would be financed by UNRRA might not be given adequate weight, especially since the Western European countries were going their own way outside UNRRA.

Following the council meeting at Atlantic City, the European regional machinery of UNRRA was set up in London and Ambassador Winant was appointed as United States representative on the chief organ, the Committee of the Council for Europe. Fighting was going on in Italy but the main part of Europe was not yet liberated. Nevertheless, in London we became deeply involved in the work of relief planning in 1944. Space will permit only brief analysis of some of the chief issues of principle that arose from this time to the end of the war.

The first issue was concerned with the estimation of requirements, which became increasingly important as it was more and more realized that demands would not only exceed supplies of some commodities but would also exceed the funds of UNRRA. Strong efforts were made to induce the Committee of the Council for Europe to accept en bloc the requirements prepared by the Inter-Allied Post War Requirements Bureau, which was now closed. It was only the diplomatic skill of Ambassador Winant that induced the committee to reject this by a narrow margin. We believed that many of these requirements had been prepared without sufficient attention to the supply position: they would also have exceeded UNRRA's resources and placed the Director General in a difficult position.[14] An alternative was accepted which charged a group of subcommittees to agree rapidly on the "bases of requirements." They were not to make quantitative estimates but were to lay down principles to be followed by the secretariat in the preparation of requirements. This proved to be a difficult task, but it was accomplished after exhausting labors.[15] The result was that the work of estimation was transferred from committees to a secretariat—a consummation for which all of us who had gone through the rigors of committee politics were thankful.

In postwar planning activities during the war we were frequently faced with the choice of either opposing proposals which everyone of good will believed to be desirable if practicable, or of supporting them even though we were convinced that they could not be carried

[14] The United Kingdom representatives agreed that the estimates were too large but thought it unwise to risk antagonizing the Allies by refusing to endorse a program which they had helped to produce. For a time the British proposed that revision should be delayed until the impracticability of the program had been demonstrated by events. To avoid dissension on the committee we reached a solution of these difficulties at a meeting in the Foreign Office at which the Ambassador and I were able to persuade the British not to oppose the preparation of revised estimates.

[15] Some reference is made in Chapter VIII to the "bases" worked out by the Food Committee. But in clothing and industrial rehabilitation it was much more difficult both to obtain information on existing deficiencies and also to lay down standards or levels of assistance.

out, at least without detriment to other equally or more important aims. There were two schools of thought on this matter both in Washington and London. The one believed that it did not matter what the committees did: necessity, and not previous committee decisions, would determine what was to be done when the time for action came. Why, therefore, trouble to argue with the Allies and arouse irritation by holding out against impracticable proposals? The other school believed that it would be dangerous as well as insincere to agree to plans that would arouse expectations which could not be fulfilled, and that the adoption of useless plans would leave gaps which would have to be filled by hasty improvisation at the last moment. In the embassy we took the second view.

But the estimation of relief requirements had scarcely been "taken out of politics" when another still hotter political issue came in by a different route. The Soviet Union had sent a delegation to the first council meeting of UNRRA and subsequently appointed representatives to the London committees. Most of these representatives were able and reasonably well informed. They did not appear to be bound by rigid instructions on technical matters. They supported our position on the "bases of requirements," and from their interest in this question I inferred early that they would seek UNRRA aid for their own territories later. On certain political issues, however, their position was defined early and pressed tenaciously.[16]

The first of these political issues arose on a Soviet proposal to give the highest priority and the largest relief supplies to countries which had been most active in resisting the enemy. In an effort to prevent open political controversy at the council meetings I carried on prolonged conversations privately with the Soviet representatives for several months on this issue. But their instructions were insistent and the philosophy behind them was narrow and simple. When I said

[16] Before UNRRA was set up, I had seen Russian representatives at work, first in 1942 in London on the committee which drafted the Allied declaration refusing to recognize transfers of property in enemy-dominated territory and second at the Hot Springs Food Conference. On each occasion they had taken little direct part in the meetings but had shown a cooperative attitude and had neither hindered the proceedings nor made attacks on any of their wartime allies. At the London meeting the Russian representative had first stated that he could not sign the draft declaration because the U.S.S.R. was not at war with Japan. Our first draft used the term "Axis." When this was altered to "enemy" the Russian representative obtained a change of instructions and joined the rest of us in approving the declaration.

that their proposal would base relief on deserts and not on needs they were ready to accept and defend rather than to repudiate the characterization. When I pointed out that it was impossible to measure degrees of resistance to the enemy they replied in simple though evasive illustrations that everyone knew that Yugoslavia actively resisted the enemy while France and Czechoslovakia did not. Privately they often expressed contempt for Czechoslovakia and sometimes for France.

Ambassador Winant was firmly opposed to any departure from the principle of relief according to need which had been the foundation of all our work on relief requirements. If political discrimination were admitted in any form there was no knowing where it would end. The word "priority" must be excluded at all costs. However, he agreed with my suggestion that a general statement might be acceptable to the effect that particular attention should be given to the needs of those countries which had suffered great damage and loss in resisting the enemy. Unfortunately, Washington would not agree to such a compromise at that time. Finding the voting prospects doubtful, I moved in committee that the matter be referred to the full council meeting at Montreal in October. This motion was passed by a narrow margin.

At that meeting the Soviet delegates again stubbornly pressed their motion in its original form and again we discussed the issue privately with them to avoid open dissension. The State Department was now ready to agree to an innocuous form of words such as we had suggested in London. But several days and nights of argument and the consumption of much vodka were necessary before Russian agreement could be obtained. Fortunately, the Russian representatives were as anxious as we were to avoid open controversy, particularly on the eve of the final convergence of the Allied armies on Germany.

It was important that this issue should be handled with tact as well as firmness at Montreal, for one of the main objects of the United States delegation was to obtain the consent of the council to a limited form of relief for Italy. Relief in any form for ex-enemy countries could be given by UNRRA only after special resolution of the council in each individual case. In the autumn of 1944 memories of the unprovoked Italian aggression against Greece, and Mussolini's "stab in the back" of France and Great Britain were still strong and vivid.

At another conference in another Canadian city a destructive and revengeful plan for Germany was being pressed on Mr. Churchill by a high-ranking United States representative. Mr. Acheson, the United States representative on the UNRRA council, was therefore in a difficult position at Montreal, and his difficulties were increased by well-meaning supporters among the Latin American representatives who enlarged eloquently on the glories of the Latin traditions which they and Italy shared. The chagrin of the Greek and Yugoslav representatives, whose countries bore painful evidences of the seamy side of the modern representatives of Latin civilization, was not concealed. And in the background lay the Italian vote in the United States which had reinforced humanitarian sentiment in determining Washington's policy. But Mr. Acheson's sincerity, skill, and prestige carried through the proposal and shipment to Italy of food for children and other special classes of the population soon followed. This was the first breach in the doctrine that UNRRA aid was for wartime friends and not for wartime enemies. The Soviet Union's attitude had been uncertain at first, and it would not have been surprising if, in the face of claims on behalf of ex-enemy countries, the Soviet representatives had made claims on behalf of their own country which could not have been contested on grounds of equity but would have raised grave financial difficulties. But they accepted Mr. Acheson's explanations, given privately to them as well as stated in the sessions, and, without taking a prominent part in the debates, voted affirmatively. In the end even the Greeks, after referring justifiably to their sufferings from Italian aggression, accepted the proposal.

Although the motives behind this move were a mixture of humanitarianism and domestic political expediency in the United States, there can be little doubt that the principle of extending relief to ex-enemy countries was sound and that it would have been even better still if the needs of ex-enemy countries as a whole had been recognized at the start and brought within the scope of an UNRRA provided with additional funds for the purpose.

The question whether the Soviet Union would itself apply for UNRRA aid was not raised in the last winter of the war, and in Washington and London the impression grew that the Russians would align themselves with the rest of the Big Three in contributing to rather than drawing on UNRRA's resources, or at least would refrain from asking for UNRRA aid. It was widely realized that no country had been devastated as much as the U.S.S.R., and that without external aid her recovery would be slow and painful. But because Russian needs were so great it appeared to many that they could be met only by large-scale loans exceeding the total funds of UNRRA.

In the closing months of the European war there was much discussion on the problems of displaced persons, and the role of the military authorities and of UNRRA in restoring them to their homes. The occupation of most of the European continent by the enemy and its exploitation to serve the plans of the conquerors for further agression had led to a migration of several millions of workers into Greater Germany. Many were drawn there by force and some by the hope of gain. They labored in the fields and factories of Germany, releasing German workers to meet the insatiable needs of an army fighting simultaneously on three fronts. The return of these workers to their homes would be a large undertaking. The reestablishment of those who had no homes to return to or who for political reasons feared to return to their homes would be an even larger undertaking. Many in both categories would have to be at least partially maintained for a time. Should all this be a task of the military authorities or of the relief organization or first of the one and later of the other? The respective roles of the two had not been determined when the first concentration camps were overrun by the Allied armies, and cesspools of German iniquity were revealed which exceeded the worst horrors of the Dark Ages.

The operations of SHAEF were carried on chiefly in Western Europe and in Germany and, apart from displaced persons, had little direct effect on the receiving countries of UNRRA. Consequently the "military period" was of less importance to UNRRA's task than it had first appeared likely to be. Except for Greece and Italy the UNRRA receiving countries had been liberated largely by the armies of the Soviet Union. Yugoslavia owed its liberation mostly to its own exertions and to material and technical aid received from Britain and the United States. But the whole of Eastern and most of Central Europe were difficult to reach with large supplies immediately after the fighting ceased. Difficulties of transport delayed UNRRA aid. Nevertheless, the fall of Germany rather than the fall of Japan was the turning point in UNRRA's transition from the mainly planning stage to the stage of operations in the liberated areas.

This discussion would be incomplete without reference to the internal difficulties of UNRRA.

In the earlier stages UNRRA was severely handicapped by the decision, which, so far as it affected food relief, was discussed in the preceding chapter, that the military should be responsible for the procurement and shipping of early relief supplies and that UNRRA should start operations only at the end of an unspecified "military" period. The President apparently believed that by this arrangement it would be easier to obtain the necessary appropriations from Congress for wartime relief, and possible to obtain a larger total amount for wartime and postwar relief than could be obtained if UNRRA were the sole claimant both during and after the war. Winant considered this to be a sound political judgment but recognized the difficulties in which it placed the UNRRA administration. It postponed the day when UNRRA would be in effective operation, and as time went on gave an opening for critics to ask derisively what UNRRA was doing and why it had been set up if it was not intended to operate when the need for relief was so clear in the territories that were gradually being liberated in Southern and, later, Western Europe.[17] It prolonged unduly the stage of paper planning which was difficult and laborious in any circumstances and which became thoroughly boring when there was no opportunity to test and amend the plans from experience gained in attempting to apply them. As in the case of food, so in the case of other aspects of relief, the function of planning should have been separated from that of administration and a single comprehensive plan should have been drawn up to be applied, with appropriate adjustments to changing conditions, both by the military and by UNRRA and the civil authorities. This would have narrowed the distinction between the military and civilian periods to one of administrative responsibility and, if political conditions in Washington made it necessary, to procurement.

[17] Lord Keynes, notwithstanding his early interest in UNRRA and his strong approval of my memorandum in 1942 outlining proposals for the structure and functions of UNRRA, later joined these critics. We had a number of vigorous arguments on the question. I thought that Keynes did not appreciate its political aspects sufficiently. His political insight fell far short of his economic insight.

A second difficulty which hampered UNRRA from the beginning was the difficulty already mentioned of recruiting a qualified secretariat. It is hard enough in ordinary times to recruit a good staff for a new international organization. In 1944 the difficulties were extraordinary. Britain and the European Allies were using almost all available persons in urgent work of immediate national importance. There was hardly any labor market outside government service in which suitable persons could be found. In the United States there were still some reserves to draw on, but few persons with international experience were available.

Those who from prewar experience had learned of the difficulties of staffing an international organization were seriously concerned over UNRRA's prospects. On several occasions in 1944 and 1945 I raised the subject with the Ambassador and always found that he was fully aware of the needs of UNRRA and was doing what he could to bring them to the attention of the highest government authorities both in Washington and in London. His first concern was to assist Governor Lehman in finding a first-rate British Deputy Director General. He tried repeatedly to persuade the Foreign Office and the appropriate ministers to release for this post Mr. (now Sir) Oliver Franks, later the U.K. Ambassador in Washington, who was at that time in a leading post in the Ministry of Supply and who had been a university don before the war. The Foreign Office was sympathetic but the Ministry of Supply would not agree to release Franks. The Ambassador also urged certain cabinet ministers to take the initiative in facilitating release of a certain number of competent government workers for UNRRA. At the same time, in conversations with British officials, I argued that the U.K. government had given no assistance to UNRRA in its efforts to build up a competent staff.[18]

Unfortunately, our hopes that Washington would do its part were not realized. Although the shortage of administrative staff was less in Washington than in London, neither the State Department nor any other department, then or later, stirred itself seriously to shake loose first-rate administrators from their existing posts and encourage them to go to UNRRA. On several occasions in 1944 and 1945

[18] I gathered that Mr. Churchill was somewhat lukewarm toward UNRRA while the fighting lasted, but Mrs. Churchill showed considerable interest in it.

Ambassador Winant strongly but with little success urged the State Department to use its influence to obtain specified individuals, some of whom were willing to come to UNRRA if satisfactory arrangements could be made with the organizations in which they were working.

Gradually UNRRA improved its recruitment and in time built up a reasonably good staff in what might be called the middle positions, and later in its "country missions" which worked in the areas to which relief was sent. But in recruiting for the higher administrative ranks it was, with some exceptions, less successful. Moreover, it suffered during part of its life from an excessive number of "reorganizations" involving substantial changes in staff and radical readjustment of functions within the organization.[19] Reorganizations are sometimes necessary, but they may do more harm than good if they uproot not only the parts of the old organization that are working badly but also those that are working well. The "new broom that sweeps clean" is a bad model to copy in dealing with human organizations. Inefficiency in government departments and in international organizations usually springs from weakness in particular posts rather than from weakness diffused over the whole. If reorganizers would search diligently for the weak spots and remove them directly instead of upsetting everything and reshaping it according to a preconceived blueprint they would have greater chance of success.

Much of the growing criticism of UNRRA in London and Washington in 1944 and early 1945 was directed against Governor Lehman. In the embassy we refused to join in these criticisms and did our best to defend UNRRA from outside attacks. At the same time we studied the internal structure and operations of the European Regional Organization of UNRRA and did not hesitate to make direct informal criticisms to UNRRA officials of what appeared to us to be defects in the work of the organization. We also instituted a regular series of reports to Washington on UNRRA matters, analyzing the difficulties of the European Regional Organization and the steps taken from within to improve its structure and working.

Finally, UNRRA had to face the unwillingness of some of the British and American officials in the supply departments in London

[19] This point applies largely to the European Regional Organization of UNRRA, but the workings of that organization cannot be separated wholly from that of headquarters in Washington.

and Washington to cooperate wholeheartedly with it. The earlier disputes over the role of UNRRA in Allied relief, which had even been carried into the British delegation at Atlantic City in December 1943, were not ended with the beginning of operations by UNRRA. They remained as a source of friction between officials in UNRRA and officials in supply departments. "Ministerial levels" were not involved, but unfortunately chose to ignore instead of suppressing them. In reality, the disputes were jurisdictional disputes analogous to those going on between different agencies in Washington.

The choice between the national and international approaches to relief affected the respective roles played by national civil servants and international civil servants in Inter-Allied relief operations. The division of functions actually adopted, as well as the structure of the national organizations to deal with relief, gave no undue share of activities to the international organization, but it gave enough to arouse jealousy and rivalry in some of the national officials in supply departments. This could have been checked by ministers or heads of departments if they had been so disposed. But in practice they did not follow the working either of national or of international relief activities closely enough to enable them to intervene with confidence and to secure the practical everyday cooperation among the national and international officials that was essential if the virtuous professions of support for UNRRA from the lips of highly placed government spokesmen in the United States and Britain were to be in harmony with the practices followed in actual operations.

CHAPTER X

The Problems of Transition and Reconstruction

STILL another sphere of postwar planning remained. The creation of a temporary international body to dispense immediate relief, and the creation of permanent international bodies to guide normal peacetime economic relations between the nations were all to the good so far as they went. But even on the most optimistic assumptions wide gaps remained. They lay mainly within an area that may be broadly designated by the term "reconstruction."

But postwar reconstruction should be interpreted to cover the immaterial as well as the material, the organization of services as well as the organization of physical production, finance as well as industry and agriculture, the economic activities of central and local government as well as of private business firms and their associations. Reconstruction, so regarded, lay in an area between that covered by the plans for UNRRA and for emergency aid supplied by the armies on the one hand, and that covered by the plans for permanent international monetary and trade organizations on the other. It was as indispensable to the initiation of the work of the permanent organizations, like the Bank, the Fund and the International Trade Organization, as it was to the completion of the work started by the temporary relief organizations.

There is no rigorous dividing line between these categories and, as we have seen, in the earlier stages of postwar planning the functions proposed for the permanent organizations were extended far back, while the functions proposed for the relief organization were extended well forward, into the period of transition and reconstruction. In the preceding chapters I have shown how the rearguard of the one and the vanguard of the other were pared down in 1943 and 1944 until an immense gap lay between the two areas of postwar planning on which the greatest progress had been made. The present chapter discusses the heterogeneous collection of limited plans designed to cover this middle area of postwar preparations.

In the earlier stages of postwar planning, as we have seen, no sharp distinction was drawn between plans for organizing the supply of consumer goods and plans for organizing the supply of producer goods for the areas that would be liberated. The distinction between relief and reconstruction was hastened, if not initiated, by differences over the scope of the proposed relief organization. In Washington the strange and to outsiders the unintelligible connection made between the idea of reconstruction in liberated territories and the idea of President Roosevelt's New Deal confused counsels and hindered serious consideration of international issues on their own merits. Both during and after the war some congressmen, following Mr. Hoover, argued that only consumer goods should be sent to the liberated areas. Fortunately, this extreme position was never accepted. Its absurdity and wastefulness were obvious: what sense would there be in pouring in large quantities of consumer goods from outside, and leaving domestic production crippled for want of moderate or small quantities of producer goods? Whatever satisfaction it might bring to the combination of philanthropic, laissez-faire, and isolationist impulses of its advocates, it was certain to be costly for the supplying countries and only a temporary panacea for the receiving countries. But though the new isolationists did not get their way, neither did the thoroughgoing supporters of large-scale reconstruction get much of what they wanted. The "rehabilitation" functions of UNRRA were not to be dismissed lightly as of no account, but it was soon realized that a very large part of UNRRA's funds would have to be spent on food supplies.

Clearly, the gaps in reconstruction measures would have to be filled from other sources and by different methods. But as with relief, so with reconstruction; the political atmosphere in Washington set limits on what could be done, with little regard to the ideas of planners on what ought to be done. And the limits were sharpest in those aspects of reconstruction for which large funds were indispensable. The United States contribution to UNRRA was larger than any contribution made up to that time by any country for international purposes. It would not have been easy for the administration to have gone to

Congress again soon afterwards to seek large additional funds for reconstruction, even if the postwar planning groups in Washington and London had given much more attention than they did to the study of reconstruction needs and had made greater efforts than they did to convince the higher political personages of the necessity of far-reaching measures to assist liberated countries to rebuild their productive capacity, restore normal working stocks, reestablish their fiscal and financial systems, and ultimately bring their external trading and financial transactions into equilibrium. Actually, except perhaps for monetary reconstruction, very little time seems to have been given by civil servants and almost none by the higher ranks to the systematic investigation of these questions during the war. In the field of reconstruction there was no counterpart to the well-organized, forward-looking groups that worked on the long-run aspects of international monetary and trade questions.

But if there was little or no attempt to consider reconstruction as a whole, and nothing analogous to the comprehensive efforts to give effect to Article VII of the Mutual Aid agreement, there was nevertheless much useful if scattered work on particular aspects of reconstruction. For the most part this work was started and guided by civil servants, both temporary and permanent, and the progress made in certain directions was mainly due to the initiative and energy of individuals with enough imagination to look beyond the routine work of the day. These qualities are distributed unevenly in government departments as they are in other walks of life. The largest scope for them lay in those aspects of postwar reconstruction in which much could be done without seeking large financial appropriations from supplying countries. This was a larger field than is sometimes realized.

Of these aspects of reconstruction one of the first to be discussed in London by an international group was European monetary reconstruction. In the early months of 1942 I found that Foreign Office, Treasury, and Board of Trade officials were considering what preparations could be made to deal with the monetary confusion which would be found in the occupied territories immediately after liberation. Keynes remarked to me on the number of luncheons and dinners to which representatives of the Allied Governments in Exile were inviting him. Though he appreciated the personal compliment, he suspected that an important motive behind these invitations was the hope of learning something about the government's attitude on post-liberation monetary questions. Soon Nigel Ronald, tireless Foreign Office missionary in all postwar economic causes, told me that the Foreign Office was convinced that Anglo-American cooperation in such matters was essential, and was reluctant to begin discussions with the Allies without United States participation. In their view the proper procedure was to form a group of U.S., U.K., and Allied financial experts to "think together" and discuss the issues informally as early as possible, rather than study and formulate in isolation plans which might be difficult to reconcile later. Ambassador Winant shared these views, which were almost identical with those which he had expounded to me in 1941 in discussing Article VII of the Lend-Lease agreement.

But it is never safe to assume that things which appear reasonable on one side of the Atlantic will appear reasonable on the other side, or that economic common sense will be regarded as political common sense. Besides the generally cautious attitude of the Secretary of State in 1942 regarding discussions of postwar matters with other countries, it was doubted in some Washington circles whether the representatives of the governments in exile would carry much weight with, or even be acceptable to, their countrymen after liberation. What then, it was argued, would be the use of reaching agreements with ministers in exile who might be repudiated in their own countries when the time came to give effect to the agreements? But quite as important as this general question was the uncertainty regarding the future government of France, and President Roosevelt and Secretary Hull were particularly sensitive on this point, not only in 1942 but for some time later.[1] There was much suspicion of the United Kingdom attitude toward the Free French. The Foreign Office view, expressed to me in informal discussions on the proposal to set up an Inter-Allied financial committee, was that it was too early to predict which of the governments in exile would become the governments of their countries after liberation, but that it was important to uphold the legal position that no break had occurred in the continuity of the free governments of the temporarily occupied countries. The United King-

[1] For a brief discussion which goes to the root of the matter see J. G. Winant, *Letter from Grosvenor Square* (Boston, Houghton Mifflin), pp. 250-52. The passages should be taken as a whole. Some reviewers have created a misleading impression by citing the first part in isolation.

dom believed that the best way to do this was by carrying on business with the governments in exile without regard to the question whether the ministers in those governments would maintain their positions after the war. The Germans tried to belittle these governments and to deny their legal status, but their desperate efforts to capture King Haakon were evidence of their anxiety to prevent legally constituted free governments from being set up abroad.

This subject cannot be pursued here, but it should be noted that the differences described above delayed full United States participation in economic discussions with the Allied Governments in Exile. For some time the U.S. Treasury attaché and the present writer could attend the meetings only as "observers"—a status unpleasantly reminiscent of the days of isolationism.

The discussions on financial reconstruction of the liberated areas were carried on in a committee composed of the finance ministers of the European Allied governments and of British Treasury and Bank of England representatives. The meetings were designed not to prepare plans but to exchange information and analyze the issues. Nevertheless, some of the results appear significant in retrospect, notably in revealing early the intention of some governments to adopt drastic measures to deal with the menace of postwar inflation resulting from the scarcity of goods and the expansion in bank notes, bank balances and, in some areas, Treasury bills, and the dangers of further deterioration in economic controls.[2] Some of them were already having new currency notes printed to take into their countries at the time of liberation. Others were considering as a temporary device the "overstamping" of a certain proportion of existing notes. In 1942 it was too early to decide on the ratio of exchange between old and new notes or the proportion of notes to be overstamped.

The second question on the supply of money was whether or not to block all bank deposits immediately after liberation. Some Allied

[2] The increase of money had already been large in all the occupied countries, but the increase of prices varied in different countries. Greece had fallen into economic chaos, but in some countries the Germans were concerned to prevent a monetary collapse that would have injured their interests. In the sectors of the economy producing war materials or defense works for the Germans the supply of money was abundant and its turnover considerable, but even here a large part of monetary receipts merely increased cash reserves, scarcity of raw materials preventing an increase in production and stocks apart from German demands. Economic controls prevented the cash reserves from flowing into increased wages and dividends.

finance ministers proposed first to block all deposits, then to release a certain proportion for essential working uses, and subsequently, after scrutiny[3] of large accounts, to release an additional proportion to be determined in the light of the price level which it was hoped to establish. The remainder would be cancelled or exchanged for government bonds.

From the attitude of the Belgian experts I inferred that the Belgian government, more confident than some of the others of its reception after liberation, had already decided to perform this type of surgical operation on the currency. Other Allies were seriously considering it. But it did not pass unquestioned:[4] some feared that it would hamper reconstruction and reconversion; others pointed to the difficulties in establishing equitable and administratively workable criteria for determining the extent and incidence of blocking. Forced loans or capital levies were suggested as alternatives. It was agreed that much short-term debt would have to be funded and that the cashing of bills at maturity might have to be restricted.

Some of the differences in detail on domestic economic reconstruction arose out of the differences between the internal conditions of the areas concerned rather than from divergences of principle. Differences between the behavior and attitudes of the peoples in monetary matters as well as differences in the structure of banking and in monetary habits had to be taken into account.

In the background of the discussions lay great differences in the extent of communication and coordination between the governments in London and the active and passive resisters at home who were making surreptitious postwar preparations. The greater confidence of the Belgian government in London arose out of the effective communication which they maintained with noncollaborationist government personnel at home, and which enabled common postwar plans to be prepared.[5]

No more difficult exercise of judgment faced the postwar planners

[3] At this point a political motive was added to the economic motives: it was desired to examine the accounts of suspected collaborators and others who had become rich under the German occupation.

[4] The Netherlands representatives doubted its expediency.

[5] See the illuminating study by L. H. Dupriez, *Monetary Reconstruction in Belgium* (New York, King's Crown Press), 1947. Professor Dupriez, with whom the present writer was able to check his impressions in London after the liberation of Belgium but before the war ended, took an active part in the surreptitious planning in Belgium during the occupation.

of monetary reconstruction than that involved in fixing a postwar exchange rate. These early discussions revealed the difficulties without leading to solutions. It was indeed on this point that the importance of United States and British cooperation in planning was most clearly demonstrated. Much could be done on domestic financial policy in any liberated territory without knowing what all the rest of the world would do, but the fixing of exchange rates could never be a one-sided process. The fixing of an exchange rate in a liberated area raised questions of future costs and prices abroad as well as at home, and the Allies quickly pointed out that costs and prices in dollars and sterling would be of immediate concern to the liberated countries because the dollar and sterling areas would provide a large part of relief and reconstruction materials. The committee agreed that in the immediate postwar period the question was not what permanent rates should be fixed but what provisional rates should be used in reviving international trade. Any lasting exchange rates must bear some relation to costs and prices in the trading areas. But which costs and prices could be taken into account in setting up provisional rates at the time of liberation? In most of the occupied areas a large volume of transactions took place at black market prices much higher than official prices. It was agreed that existing controls must be maintained or new controls substituted for them and that black markets would not disappear overnight.[6] Nor could the effects of currency reforms on the price level be estimated precisely in advance. At this point Mr. Keynes appeared with a brilliantly phrased contribution maintaining that the best criterion to use in practice was the change in comparative wage levels since the prewar period. This simplified the question: there were not as many different wages for the same kinds of work as there were prices for the same kinds of goods. But although it was important to take account of changes in wage rates or earnings the prospects of maintaining stable wages after liberation were doubtful and varied greatly within the occupied area as a whole. The discussions on exchange rates stopped at this exploratory stage: it was too early to attempt to lay down provisional rates.[7]

[6] In reading this highly compressed discussion the reader should remember that there is not space here to take account of the wide variations in different parts of the occupied area.

[7] A general proposition that seemed to draw assent from most of the committee was that as nearly as possible there should be neither inflation nor

Although these exchanges of views among Finance Ministers were tentative and exploratory they show that active planning was already in progress long before the war ended. They show, too, that financial experts from the start were well aware of the decisive importance of "real" as distinguished from monetary factors. The effects of the supply of goods and of the efficiency of "real" controls and the attitude of the people toward them were rarely lost sight of. But war aims and peace aims are not always complementary. While the Finance Ministers were emphasizing the need to maintain strict economic controls in the early postwar period their counterparts in other ministries, broadcasting to the occupied territories, were exhorting their peoples to sabotage the German economic controls. "C'était la guerre," but some habits formed in war are not immediately thrust aside when peace comes.

Thus it was recognized early that monetary reconstruction was an essential basis for agricultural, mining and industrial reconstruction but that the monetary mechanism alone was not enough to control economic transition from war to peace. The outstanding characteristic of the transition period would be scarcity both of essential producer and consumer goods. Monetary controls could not in themselves cope with scarcities and it was doubtful whether they could be maintained at all without aid from "real" controls. In the aftermath of the First World War this had not been understood, and the inflation was much worse in almost all countries during the early reconstruction period than it had been during the war.

During periods of unavoidable scarcity, distribution is of supreme importance—the distribution of scarce producer goods as well as of consumer goods.[8] The all-round recovery of production depends largely on the control of distribution. The more thorough control of distribution during the war years after 1939 made this clearer than it had been to the men of 1914-1918. An extensive machinery of allocation had been set up by the United Kingdom, the United States, and Canada for war purposes, and the question soon arose whether it

deflation after liberation. This proposition did not appear to me to be useful in the circumstances of the times and I have omitted discussion of it in this account.

[8] It is strange that many have held the opposite view, contending that if there is not enough to go around it does not matter much how the inadequate amounts are distributed; the important thing is to produce more.

should be scrapped abruptly at the end of the war or continued through the transition period.

The first discussions appear to have centered on transport. The Inter-Allied Post War Requirements Committee set up a committee on European inland transport which included distinguished British and continental European experts. Its members quickly perceived that they had to do with a subject which, though it affected the distribution of relief goods, was chiefly a question of reconstruction. When the Inter-Allied Committee was disbanded and its work taken over by UNRRA, the transport committee continued independently for a time pending the adoption of its own recommendation—that a European inland transport organization should be set up. The committee showed that with adequate planning and organization the losses of and damage to transport equipment during the war could be largely offset by more intensive use of what remained. Before the war wagons and coaches on international trains were often obliged to return empty or incompletely used by the same routes over which they came, instead of returning by other routes on which they would attract more freight and passengers.[9] International negotiations would be necessary to achieve this reform. In addition, there were numerous questions of repair and reconstruction both on railways and on inland waterways, and on these also international cooperation would be necessary. Great difficulties were to be expected over the restitution of transport equipment which had been widely dispersed over the continent by the Germans. All governments in the liberated territories would strive to get back their prewar equipment, and in the disturbed conditions of the transition period there was a danger that, as in 1919, they would order the unloading of goods at the frontiers for fear that their wagons would not be returned. Finally, there was the question how new equipment could be obtained for liberated areas in competition with domestic and with other international demands in the supplying countries abroad, and how to allocate it among the European claimants. The supply would certainly fall short of the demand in the earlier stages of reconstruction, and the United States and United Kingdom would have to meet a heavy demand for replacement of their own rolling stock and equipment,

[9] This had been true of the earlier stages of United States railroad history, but in the earlier part of the twentieth century it had been remedied by agreements among the railroads.

which had been greatly overworked during the war. The Allied countries would gain by the maintenance of orderly allocation and procurement in the postwar period of transition.

In 1942 Ambassador Winant began a long struggle to persuade Washington to send one or more experts on transport to London to discuss these questions with the British and the European Allied experts. For a long time he was unsuccessful, but when I visited Washington on two occasions in 1943 I was encouraged to find that a small group of officials in the Departments of State and Commerce were closely following the work in London and had started work of their own in the same field.[10] However, they were not permitted for many months to enter into discussions with other countries. In London both ministers and officials were prepared to negotiate as soon as the United States and the Soviet Union were ready. Thus planning in Inter-Allied circles, in Whitehall, and in Washington in 1942 and 1943 laid the foundations of the European organization which it was hoped to establish later.

But preliminary negotiations through diplomatic channels were long-drawn-out. After early delays in Washington no serious differences arose among the United Kingdom, the European Allied governments, and the United States. But all sought the cooperation of the Soviet Union without which the organization could not discharge its functions adequately for the whole of the European continent. The Russian railways were constructed on the broad gauge, and when Russian armies advanced into Europe later they would doubtless extend broad-gauge lines into the Eastern European countries through which they advanced. Germany stood in a central position of great importance for through traffic in Europe. Agreement with the Soviet Union would be necessary for the reestablishment of unified German railway services. The representatives of Central and Eastern as well as those of Western and Southern Europe were already well informed and needed no further persuasion to convince them of the uses of a European transport organization after liberation. The main problem was to impress on the U.S.S.R. the

10 Throughout the war the State Department was well served by a small but competent group of officials working on shipping, inland and air transport questions. They maintained a sense of continuity and consistency lacking in some of the other sections of the Department where a high rate of turnover led to discontinuity in policy and preparations.

importance of the subject and to persuade them to send representatives to a European international meeting.

In London and Washington the officials who were concerned with shipping showed no less foresight than those who were concerned with inland transport. Outstanding administrators in the Ministry of War Transport and the War Shipping Administration saw as early as 1943 that preparations must be made to continue, with appropriate modifications, the wartime machinery for the allocation and routing of Allied shipping and perhaps for a time even the specification of particular ships for particular cargoes. Here, however, was a question for skilled international negotiation. The Combined Shipping Adjustment Board was an exclusively Anglo-American body. It was the most informal of wartime international bodies. Of its constitution and proceedings there is little formal record but it provided the necessary link between the Ministry of War Transport and the War Shipping Administration. Under the stress of wartime conditions the Allied Governments in Exile of the continental European shipping countries agreed that their merchant fleets which had escaped from the enemy should be placed under the control of the Combined Shipping Adjustment Board, even though they were not themselves represented on the board. But it could not be expected that the European Allied shipping countries would allow this arrangement to continue after the European war had ended. If their ships were to remain during the transition period as part of an Allied pool they would at least demand representation on the international body which operated the pool. As they had agreed during the war to the use of their ships first to assist in the defeat of the enemy, so, at the coming of peace, they would demand that their ships should be used first to assist in supplying the needs of the liberated countries.

Yet it was essential that shipping controls should not be abandoned suddenly when the war ended in Europe, as, on the insistence of the United States, they had been when the First World War ended. First, a large quantity of shipping might be needed in the Pacific. Second, there would be a great demand for shipping to return the overseas armies of the Allies to their homelands. Third, the liberated areas would be urgently in need of shipping to bring overseas supplies to them. Fourth, traders would seek shipping to resume peacetime trading operations all over the world and especially in seas freed from enemy submarines and mines. Priorities would have to be agreed upon and enforced to deal with these demands in an orderly manner. A new agreement and perhaps the formation of a new organization would have to be negotiated among all the Allied countries which possessed merchant fleets. The intense demand for shipping in the immediate postwar period would create confusion unless the use of ships were regulated carefully in accordance with a new order of importance of different uses; otherwise the interests of shipowners under free competition would differ greatly from the interests of the United Nations.

By early 1944 memoranda had been exchanged between London and Washington on early postwar shipping questions, and preparations were being made to take up the matter with the shipping countries among the Allies.

However, the authorities in control of Allied shipping did not themselves determine the order of importance of the movements of different cargoes and passengers: their function was to give effect to the decisions of other authorities when the supply of shipping was sufficient to do so, and to call attention to the necessity of modifying those decisions when it was not. Some of the decisions on the order of importance of the different uses of transport for the aim of defeating the enemy might be made by the heads of state, and most of the details were decided by other "appropriate authorities" within the war government organizations of the U.S. and the U.K. Again, within a few broad categories of goods there were other U.S.-U.K. bodies designed to assist in deciding on allocations, particularly the Combined Food Board (in which Canada joined), the Combined Raw Materials Board, and the Combined Production and Resources Board. Some of the decisions of these bodies might affect directly or indirectly the kinds and the amounts of goods to be transported between different Allied and neutral countries.

The future of the Combined Boards was therefore a matter of importance for the early postwar period. Were they to be continued and, if so, in what form? As with the Combined Shipping Adjustment Board, it could hardly be expected that the Allied countries not represented on the boards would agree, after the war ended, to allocations which determined what they would receive, or, in some countries, where their supplies would go, unless they could take part in deciding the allocations. This applied particularly to the Combined

Food Board. But it was easier to agree on the necessity of changing the form of the boards at the end of the war than it was to agree on the precise changes to be made, and there was much argument in both Whitehall and Washington concerning the structure and uses of the boards immediately after the European war. An exploratory letter went from Washington to London seeking British views on the subject.

Returning to London at the end of 1943 from the UNRRA Council meeting I found Ambassador Winant worried over the slowness of postwar planning. The Second World War had already lasted as long as the First, and the Allies were still unready for the peace. The invasion of Northwest Europe which was to end the war would soon begin. The complexities and uncertainties of the coming land, sea, and air operation were a constant source of anxiety. The Ambassador had fought in Europe as a volunteer from early in the First World War and well knew where the brunt of war fell. He was conscious, in those anxious months of waiting for the final grand assault, of the thousands of young men who were soon to be cut off in the morning of their lives. Their sacrifice, he believed, was the price of failures in high places in the prewar years, of the illusions of appeasement and isolationism, and of the loss of opportunities to reconstruct the world in a new image after 1919. He spoke of the immense responsibilities that lay on those few individuals in high places to leave nothing undone to win the war without unnecessary loss of life and to create after it a world in which such conflicts would not recur. He expressed confidence in the Allied war leaders and their direction of the war but feared that they were giving no comparable attention to the conditions of the peace. He was aware of, and did what he could to assist, the earnest efforts of the groups of officials in Washington and London to hasten preparations for the postwar period. But he deplored the difficulties of getting broad and unified consideration of these plans in the highest quarters. His mind was constantly ranging ahead, conscious of the risk that in absorption in the pressing affairs of the day the dangers of the morrow would pass undetected and that unforeseen emergencies might arise for which no preparations had been made. He liked his advisers to concentrate not only on immediate issues but also on issues which they thought might become important six months or a year or two later. In economic matters he frequently reminded me of this, and in the early months of 1944 I attempted to make a new appraisal of the future of postwar preparations. By this time I was convinced that planning for reconstruction was at once supremely important and seriously deficient.

The chief result of my study was to bring out the danger that the establishment of UNRRA would create the illusion that the financial needs of the transition period had been provided for and that the new permanent international organizations which were planned to deal with short-run balance-of-payments difficulties, with long-term international investment, and with international trade and raw material questions under normal peacetime conditions, would be able to take on where UNRRA left off. It seemed to me that there was an enormous gap between UNRRA and the new organizations designed to fulfil the commitments made in Article VII of the Mutual Aid agreement. As we have seen, the original British plan on international monetary organization was much more far-reaching than the plan that was taking shape early in 1944 in the whittled-down form in which alone, in the opinion of its U.S. sponsors, it stood any chance of acceptance by the United States Congress. Studying the tentative drafts of the plan and estimating the probable outcome of the points still in dispute among the negotiations, I concluded that no contribution to reconstruction or to the solution of the difficulties of the transition period could be expected from the international monetary organization, and that if an attempt were made at this stage to change the plan drastically its sponsors would probably be defeated in Washington. Hence it seemed best to put through the plan in its strictly limited but politically acceptable form and seek a solution of the reconstruction problem through other means.

The reconstruction problem was a problem of finance and of international organization to deal with the difficulties of the transition period. If the Western European Allies were to pay for their immediate needs of consumption goods out of their foreign exchange funds, and mainly out of their dollar funds, it could not be expected that they would be able to meet their reconstruction needs unaided. In addition there was the special U.K. balance-of-payments difficulty which had worried Mr. Keynes and his colleagues in the Treasury from 1941 and which, though it gave the first impetus to the formation of the international monetary plan, later was left outside the scope of the plan and had not yet been dealt with in any other plan. Yet it had lost none of its importance since 1941: in fact the liquidation of U.K. foreign balances had been increased considerably by the necessity of paying for deliveries for which contracts had been made before Lend-Lease started and which continued to flow in until January 1944.[11]

Thus the two fundamental questions of international finance appeared to be, first, how to finance the requirements of the continental European Allies for external aid in reconstruction, and second, in view of the loss of a large part of U.K. foreign investments, how the U.K. could obtain a sufficient volume of imports to meet the needs of its people for essential goods for home consumption and for raw materials for its export industries? No effective attempt had been made in the first four and a half years of the war to deal with either of these questions! As to the second question, I still believed that the simplest and most effective immediate remedy was to make Lend-Lease retroactive and reimburse the United Kingdom for the assets which it had liquidated in the common cause. But it seemed useless to suggest this in 1944: the political education of congressmen, of large sections of the public and even of official Washington in these matters had been wholly neglected. There had been a well organized movement to inform the British people about the United States but little or nothing had been done to inform the people of the United States about Great Britain. In the interwar period isolationists and pacifists had created the myth that the United States had been drawn into the First World War by clever but wicked "British propaganda." As if to give no excuse for the extension of this myth to the Second World War, the British for some time refrained from circulating in the United States adequate information about or explanation of their position. In their anxiety to obtain the fullest United States participation in the war and in world affairs after the war, they often ignored misrepresentations from anti-British critics in the United States and carefully refrained from drawing comparisons between the part played by Britain and that played by the United States between September 1939 and December 1941. This may have been wise restraint, but it drew a veil over the fundamental basis of the balance-of-payments

[11] R. G. D. Allen, "Mutual Aid between the United States and the British Empire, 1941-1945," in *Journal of the Royal Statistical Society*, 1946, pt. III, p. 283.

difficulties which would bring an economic crisis in the U.K. immediately after the war. I have always thought that the administration and the wiser men in Congress would have been well advised to have given a full public explanation of the coming economic difficulties of the U.K., showing particularly the extent to which these difficulties arose out of Britain's early stand against the common enemy. But the opportunity to do this was lost.

The sources of the help both for Great Britain and for the continental European Allies would have to come largely from countries far from the battlefields. To the countries over which the battle raged or which were within range of aerial bombardment, the Second World War had been much more widely damaging than the First. The area occupied by the enemy, and therefore completely cut off from economic relations with the rest of the world, was much wider. The American continent, because of its distance from the war area and—except for Canada—because of its late entry into the war, was certain to end the war with great economic advantages over Europe. Its consumption of essential products had not been curtailed, and in some directions had even increased. Much of its equipment was improved: innovations were introduced in 1940 and 1941 which Europe could not afford to adopt during the war.

But these world changes were never clearly explained to the American public, and many congressmen were more concerned to find useful weapons in party political controversy than to form a clear, unprejudiced view of world prospects after the war. Consequently, at that time it seemed useless to suggest any large generous act, such as later took the form of the Marshall Plan, to follow rapidly on the UNRRA contributions.

The alternative form of help lay in large loans to meet the reconstruction needs of the continental European Allies and to close the gap in the U.K. balance of payments until British exports could be increased to the necessary extent. Looking at the measures that seemed likely to be adopted, I was impressed with their inadequacy to meet either of these needs. The lending operations of the proposed international investment organization were mainly intended to meet long-term needs in normal peacetime conditions and not reconstruction needs immediately after the war. Of course, a large volume of outstanding international loans had come to be looked on with disfavor after the interwar experience of loans contracted during and just after the First World War. But in the Second World War the genius of President Roosevelt, by substituting Lend-Lease for commercial loans, had prevented the accumulation of unmanageable debt, and reconstruction loans would not have to be superimposed on a large wartime debt. Moreover, the interest rates and terms of repayment on reconstruction loans could be adjusted to world conditions. If political conditions permitted, some reconstruction loans could be made on such easy terms that they would not differ widely from grants-in-aid. But in the temper of the times it seemed politically necessary to preserve the forms and conceptions of the marketplace.

However, there were a number of different ways in which the British balance-of-payments difficulties and the reconstruction needs of the European Allies could be met, and in early 1944 it seemed to me that the most urgent task was not to press dogmatically any one solution but first to call attention forcibly to the existence of large gaps in the most immediately important parts of reconstruction planning and to the necessity of filling those gaps without delay if existing postwar plans were not to be set back. Nor was it merely a question how the gaps should be filled—by loans, by grants, or by other methods. There was the further question what international channels should be used for applying whatever method was approved. An examination of existing plans which were on their way to adoption showed that for the most part the permanent international economic organizations were to play little or no role in reconstruction and in the troubles of the period of transition immediately after the war. The piecemeal approach to postwar economic questions, which for political reasons could not be avoided in the years before general agreement was reached on the principle of a United Nations Organization, was being carried too far. Prewar experience in Geneva had impressed on the Ambassador and on me the inherent difficulties of establishing international organizations and the great skill and strong sense of moral purpose that were needed to make them work effectively. It seemed unwise to create a large number of separate new organizations or to set up organizations not intended to exercise significant functions immediately after the war.

CHAPTER XI

An Attempt at Stocktaking

IN APRIL 1944 a State Department mission on postwar planning visited the embassy. Among its members were the late Dr. Isaiah Bowman, H. Freeman Matthews,[1] and John Lee Pratt, who were interested in the economic as well as political aspects of postwar problems. At their suggestion I summarized my views in the following memorandum.

ORGANIZATION OF INTERNATIONAL ECONOMIC RECONSTRUCTION

I

(i) The United Nations Relief & Rehabilitation Administration has been set up and is in the early stages of organization.
(ii) An International Conference has been held on Food and Agriculture and an International Food and Agriculture Organization is to be established.
(iii) A conference of the International Labor Organization is being held on the postwar international program for labor.

Discussions have taken place on:
(iv) An international monetary organization.
(v) An international commercial policy organization.
(vi) An international commodity (raw material) organization.
(vii) An international long-term investment organization.
(viii) Policies with respect to international cartels.
(ix) International commercial aviation.

The discussions have gone far in respect to (iv), considerable progress has been made with (v) and (vi), while the discussions on (vii) and (viii) are in the earliest stage.

Discussions are about to begin on:
(x) Oil.

Memoranda have been exchanged on:
(xi) Shipping.
(xii) European inland transport.

[1] Now Under Secretary of State.

At the Moscow Conference and in a communication from Washington to London the question has been raised of:

(xiii) An overall steering committee in respect of measures for international economic reconstruction.

A communication has passed from Washington to London on

(xiv) The future of the Combined Boards.

II

Many of these subjects are closely interconnected and there is much more unity than appears on the surface in the work that has been done. The following regrouping of subjects will help to make this clear:

I. Relief and Emergency Rehabilitation
II. Food and Agriculture
III. Labor
IV. International Monetary Organization
    International Investment for Development Purposes
    International Trade, including
        Commercial Policy
        Commodity Policy
        Oil Policy
        Cartel Policy
V. International Transport, including
        Shipping
        Inland Transport
        Commercial Aviation

I suggest there are good reasons for adopting some such classifications as the above in actually setting up international organizations. Thus in Group IV there would be three organizations only, and in Group V one organization only. This would make the task of overall coordination much simpler than it would be if there were ten or eleven separate organizations in groups IV and V.

III

How far does the preceding classification cover the fields of essential postwar economic measures?

The answer depends mainly on the scope which is given to the subjects outlined in the classification. It is possible to give the subjects a sufficiently extensive scope to cover the major part of the essential fields.

In practice, however, the discussions have left important gaps which must be filled if grave difficulties are to be avoided in the postwar period, particularly during the transition from war to peace conditions. Many of these gaps could be filled by extending the scope of the discussions of some of the subjects on which discussions have already taken place or are likely to take place in the near future.

The main gaps are:

(a) Little provision has been made so far for the transition period between relief and the early stages of "rehabilitation" on the one hand and the application of long-term economic measures on the other.

(b) The subjects discussed under Article VII have been treated largely from a long-term point of view. In some cases there seems to have been a tendency first to take up long-term measures and policies many of which it is agreed can only take effect after a transition period.

This tendency is not in itself necessarily open to adverse criticism. One of the main objects of the discussions is to agree on the establishment of international economic bodies in certain fields, and in some of these fields—for example, monetary policy and commercial policy—it is impracticable to reach such agreement without a careful analysis of long-term as well as transition problems. Moreover, it would be dangerous to adopt transition measures on a day-to-day basis without regard to their long-run effects.

But the time has now come when measures for the transition period must be considered on a comprehensive scale without delay. The question arises whether problems of the transition period shall be dealt with through separate discussions and the use of separate machinery from those of the Article VII discussions or whether the scope of the latter discussions and of the international organizations which it is proposed to establish as an outcome could be enlarged to cover at least a substantial part of the measures that will be necessary during the transition period.

I suggest that the second of these alternatives should be adopted where practicable, for the following reasons:

(1) The working experience gained in dealing with transition problems would increase the efficiency of the organization when it came to deal with long-term reconstruction.

(2) There would be greater continuity between transition and long-term policies and the personnel administering them, and less danger that hastily improvised measures would be adopted in the transition period which would prejudice long-term policies.

If the principle is accepted of combining where practicable discussions and organizations dealing with transition problems with those dealing with long-term problems, what would be the scope of its application?

The clearest cases are in the broad field of trade policy, especially in commodity—particularly raw material—questions. My suggestion is that when the Article VII talks are resumed the discussions of commodity and cartel questions and of quantitative restrictions on trade as well as tariffs should at an early stage deal systematically with the probable conditions that will arise immediately at the end of the war. This would cover some of the most acute of the immediate postwar economic problems.

If this course is not adopted what are the alternatives?

1. It may be argued that commodity questions in the transition period can be dealt with by the Combined Boards. When the structure and func-

tion of the Combined Boards are examined, however, this does not appear to be a satisfactory solution, for the following reasons:

(i) The Combined Boards were set up as Anglo-American advisory administrative bodies concerned chiefly with allocation of scarce materials and shipping in the interests of the war effort. It is essential that they should continue to concentrate exclusively or primarily on this function not only until the war in Europe is ended but also until Japan is crushed. It seems inadvisable in these periods to add any substantial functions to those at present carried out by the Boards.

(ii) Raw material problems in the transition immediately after the war will by no means be simply problems of dealing with scarcities and recommending measures to increase production: in some cases—especially in minerals—they will be concerned with the disposal of stocks excessive for peacetime needs and with methods of curtailing excessively high-cost production. The types of skill and personnel required to deal with these questions differ widely from those required to carry out the present functions of the Combined Boards.

This does not mean that the role of the Combined Boards will end as soon as peace comes. On the contrary, the Boards possess administrative machinery which is indispensable in the transition period as an instrument for international control and allocation of scarce commodities and services. The retention of such controls for some time after the war is essential if conditions of international economic anarchy are to be avoided. In carrying out these functions the Combined Boards will have to work in close cooperation with the International Commodity Organization in respect to plans for allocating scarce materials and increasing their production. But they will not be suitable bodies for dealing with other aspects of commodity questions.

2. Another alternative is to deal with the transition period by separate ad hoc governmental negotiations on the numerous questions that will arise.

At present there seems to be a drift in this direction. But improvised and ad hoc arrangements to deal piecemeal with transitional questions may create dangerous precedents and give rise to inconsistencies and confusion which will prejudice the chances of the successful operation at a later stage of the permanent economic bodies.

I suggest, therefore, that at the resumption of the talks on the international commercial policy organization the subject might be discussed with reference to transition measures as well as long-term measures and the objective be adopted of establishing the international commercial policy organization at as early a date as practicable with a view to using it as an instrument for international consultation on transition as well as long-run measures.

The same considerations might be applied to the resumed talks on the international commodity organization, which should preferably be a subgroup of the international commercial policy organization.

Cartel policy should be taken up as an aspect of commercial and commodity policy. It is essential to achieve as much consistency as possible between cartel and commodity policy, and cartel policy should be considered from the starting point of the immediate postwar period.

International Monetary Policy

The lines on which progress has already been made limit the scope of application of the main thesis of this paper to the field of monetary arrangements. Section X of the agreed statement on the International Monetary Fund shows recognition of transitional difficulties in the monetary field, but it does so by exempting member countries from some of the provisions of the plan until transitional difficulties have passed. It specifically states that "the Fund is not intended to provide facilities for relief or reconstruction or to deal with international indebtedness arising out of the war."

In view of the progress already made in obtaining technical agreement on the monetary plan, it would be unwise at this stage to add functions to the International Monetary Fund. But the dangers of ad hoc arrangements in the transition period are serious and there is a gap to be filled in this field, especially since many new governments in liberated countries will be faced with the necessity of making difficult adjustments. In such conditions organized international machinery is most desirable.

International Investment

Present proposals are for a separate organization dealing with long-term investment (this is stated before I have had time to look at the latest British views) for development purposes. Such an international organization is of the greatest importance, but it will be readily recognized that both it and the International Monetary Fund cover only a limited portion of the field in which international lending may be necessary after the war. Probably there are advantages in some specialized organization dealing with lending for long-term development, and it is well to go ahead with the discussion of this field. Later, however, it may be that the international organization dealing with it could conveniently become a subdivision of a wider organization including other forms of lending.

Moreover, one of the neglected fields is that of lending for immediate reconstruction purposes after the war. In the continued talks on the international investment body, attention should be given to this, at least in so far as long-term loans for development can be applied to long-term projects dovetailed with essential capital reconstruction projects.

Transport

The trend in this field on the whole has been in a different direction from that of the talks on monetary and commercial policy. Transition problems have been taken up at the start and more attention has been given to interim and transition than to long-run arrangements. The

British view on an inland transport organization for Europe is that it should be set up promptly with a view to unified treatment of transitional questions and that out of the experience thus gained it may be possible to retain the organization in some form for long-run purposes. They fear resistance from European Allies if long-run plans are put in the forefront at the outset.

On the other hand, it seems essential that the long-run as well as the transition problems of shipping should be discussed at an early date. They will no doubt come up in the Article VII talks on commercial policy. It seems desirable that there should be a systematic discussion in which both those familiar with overall economic policy and also technical shipping experts should be present. Could not this be arranged in connection with Article VII talks? Close links are needed, and it is to be hoped have already been established, between those concerned with commercial policy and those concerned with transport.

IV

The suggestions made above would fill important gaps but would still leave a wide gap in the field of rehabilitation and readjustment.

UNRRA's terms of reference permit it to undertake limited rehabilitation. But its scope is narrow and its funds still more restricted. In practice it is not likely to be able to cover more than a small part of rehabilitation and that part will be confined to equipment needed for producing urgent consumer goods for relief purposes.

How will reestablished governments in Europe be able to obtain essential imports, especially of raw materials needed for industries which produce for exports as well as for domestic consumption? Some of them in the early stages will have little or no foreign funds, and their export occupations will be disorganized. Britain, likewise, will be unable to finance readily many of its necessary imports in the first two years.

In some circles it has been argued that Lend-Lease should be renewed and extended for the early postwar period. Even apart from the great political difficulties in the United States in the way of such a course, it does not appear that such a measure could fill the gap adequately in view of the limitations on the use of lend-lease materials for export purposes. Until the export industries of European countries are reestablished the transition period will be prolonged.

The alternative would seem to consist in international loans for specific purposes of reestablishment of economic life in the widest sense, including a high level of employment.

The question arises whether this should be done by bilateral arrangements through direct intergovernmental negotiations or whether international machinery should be established to serve as a standing instrument for negotiations.

Here again ad hoc arrangements seem inadequate, and the most needy countries would have the greater difficulties in negotiating loans under such conditions.

If the impression were spread abroad that the United States would supply large loans to Britain or other countries there might be a tendency for existing creditors to press for high terms of repayment in the belief that the funds would be available from other sources. Hence great care is obviously needed in planning and in respect to publicity on planning for international credits. Organized international machinery would have some advantage in this respect since it might facilitate compositions between creditors and debtors in some cases.

These views are embryonic and alternative measures for filling this gap in rehabilitation and early reconstruction should be carefully examined. It is clearly most urgent to reach decisions at an early date since these problems will come right in the forefront of public attention quickly after liberation.

London, April 29, 1944

A critic might object that this memorandum gives almost equal attention to questions of organization and to questions of substance, and that the precise form of organization matters little so long as the questions of substance are dealt with somewhere. Unfortunately, however, in the conditions of the time there was no assurance, nor even much likelihood, that the diverse questions of substance relating to the postwar period would inevitably find their places in appropriate organizations. The importance of some of them was not yet widely recognized. That of others, as we shall see, was even denied in some quarters in 1944. Thus the extent to which the important issues were covered was affected greatly by forms of organization that were adopted. Even if an international body is charged only in general terms to study or otherwise deal with a particular subject, the chances that something will be done about the subject are far greater than they would be if no organization were instructed to take it up. If the trade organization had been set up promptly, with broad terms of reference covering both the immediate postwar years and the long run, and without waiting to prepare an elaborate charter in advance, the chances are that concerted action to revive trade during the transition period would have come earlier than it did.

But the trend was in the opposite direction. On a visit to Washington in October 1944 I found surprisingly little concern over the difficulties of immediate postwar reconstruction. Many officers in the Department of Agriculture were "surplus-minded" and feared overabundance more than scarcity. In other departments disturbing symptoms appeared of a desire for haste in returning to prewar conditions, particularly in trading and financial arrangements, as the war entered its last stage. Some officials were suspicious of Great Britain and thought they saw hidden intentions in every proposal that came out of London. Suspicion was heightened by a fundamental difference of outlook between London and Washington. Few officials in Washington were fearful of postwar scarcities. At the UNRRA Council meeting at Montreal, the Combined Food Board had presented an optimistic report on grain supplies. Business concerns were agitating against wartime international as well as national economic restrictions. The short-sighted attitude of some government officials and of the Secretary of Agriculture was due not only to lack of insight but also to bitter and sustained attacks from congressmen and businessmen, the former pushed on by the latter and both moved by selfish individual aims which even in wartime some of them could not transcend. Officials in London were in a different position. By 1944 they were thoroughly experienced in the art of making the most of scarce resources and were well informed on the prospects and dangers of continued and perhaps increased scarcities in the postwar period. In a civil service in which advancement was less dependent than it was in Washington on attracting favorable notice from those who stood above it, they were more outspoken and more ready to bring unpalatable facts before ministers than Washington officials were at that time and on that subject. Again, the form of government in Great Britain gave little or no scope for ill-informed and self-seeking representatives in the legislature to harass officials in the exercise of their duties.

To sum up: business interests pressed congressmen to obtain early relaxation of economic controls, abandonment of the sterling pool, reduction of taxation; and congressmen made their views known forcibly to Secretaries, Under Secretaries and Assistant Secretaries, who, in turn, became reluctant to broach new proposals which would necessitate continued restrictions at home and new unrequited expenditures abroad. Civil servants had few opportunities to gain a thorough hearing for unpopular proposals, and some of them, sensing the reception that would probably be given to such proposals, refrained from making them. Others, notably in respect to food, went so far as to give assurances that no serious shortages existed!

The difficulties in Washington were greatest in respect to postwar measures for which large financial appropriations would be required from the United States, and Washington officials were able and willing to cooperate with London in preparing a number of special measures for the transition period which required only small financial contributions from the countries taking part in them. The negotiations on shipping and inland transport were continued and new negotiations began on proposals, which originated in London, for the establishment of a European Coal Organization and a European Economic Committee.

In August the negotiations on shipping came to a head at an Inter-Allied meeting in London which led to an "Agreement on Principles having reference to the continuance of Coordinated Control of Merchant Shipping."[2] This was a model of postwar planning for the short run. It was in effect an acceptance of continued shipping controls in the period between the end of the war in Europe and the end of the war in the Far East and as long as might be necessary after the end of the war everywhere to bring supplies to the liberated areas. No ships under the authority of the contracting governments were to be released from control or to be employed for cargo that was not essential "unless the total overall tonnage is in excess of the total overall requirements, and then only in accordance with a mutually acceptable formula which shall not discriminate against the commercial shipping interests of any nation. . . ." Controls were to be exercised by methods similar to those of the U.S. and U.K. ship warrant schemes. A ship warrant served as a pass which enabled its possessor to obtain the use of necessary shipping facilities. It was issued only in return for undertakings regarding trading areas, voyages, cargoes, freight rates, and other matters, and made possible the allocation of particular vessels to particular purposes.

But, as we have seen, it could not be expected that, when the war with Germany ended, all the Allied countries which owned ships would continue to be ready to place them under an organization on which only Britain and the United States were represented. A new

[2] Signed by representatives of Belgium, Canada, Greece, the Netherlands, Norway, Poland, the United Kingdom, and the United States.

body was to be set up with a council on which all member countries were to be represented and an executive board whose members were to be the U.S., U.K., the Netherlands, and Norway. Like the War Shipping Administration, the board was to have two branches, one in Washington and one in London. In short, the new body was to be the Combined Shipping Adjustment Board with broader membership and a more detailed constitution.

The agreement was a great achievement which ensured that the muddle of 1919 would not be repeated. The continental European Allied governments which possessed ships might have demanded—and in the absence of an agreement would have directed—that immediately after the collapse of Germany their ships should all be used for bringing supplies to their liberated countries. It was clearly perceived that in the early postwar period the demands for shipping would remain very high and confusion would follow the sudden removal of controls. But there were numerous vested interests and political motives pulling in the wrong direction, and the agreement was a triumph of reason and the cooperative spirit.[8]

The extraordinary importance of coal in the period of reconstruction was recognized early in Whitehall, mainly through memories of the confusion and international friction that followed the First World War, when supplies of coal were scarce and high-priced in the period of reconstruction. But two members of our embassy in London were as active as Whitehall in arguing that urgent measures would be essential to prevent an even worse position from arising at the end of the Second World War. Mr. Notman, a mining expert attached to the supply mission, and Samuel Berger, who later became labor attaché at the embassy, should be credited with arousing Washington to the imminence and dangers of a grave shortage of coal in Europe. They had studied the decline in the output of coal in the U.K. and its significance for the countries which, before the war, had relied on Britain for coal supplies. They could see no substitute sources of supplies immediately after the war, and had come to the startling conclusion that the United States must export coal to Europe, perhaps even to Great Britain, for a time. In visits to Washington they made an impression on those concerned

[8] Much credit should go to Huntington Morse of the War Shipping Administration, who was an outstanding delegate at the meeting and combined the qualities of a first-rate administrator with a thorough grasp of principles.

with coal questions in the wartime agencies. Colonel Koenig, the head of the solid fuels section of SHAEF, added his influence to those who urged Washington to join in the efforts to avert a disastrous shortage of coal in Europe. In Whitehall leading officials of the Ministry of Fuel, with the backing of Nigel Ronald of the Foreign Office, obtained government support for British initiative in opening negotiations for the establishment of a European Coal Organization.

The principal aims of these missionaries were, first, to establish an orderly system of allocations of the scarce supplies after the war, and, second, to organize an emergency export of coal from the United States to Europe in the early transition period. Allocations required agreement among the supplying as well as the receiving countries, and an international body would have to be formed which would include representatives of all the important countries in both catogories. If American coal were to be exported to Europe the United States must be represented on the international body and her exports must be brought within the system of allocation.

At first it was believed in the Foreign Office and in our embassy that the proposed coal organization should be a subdivision of a more comprehensive European Economic Committee. The high officials of the Ministry of Fuel and Power, however, seemed to prefer an independent organization. Much depended on the course which the negotiations might take. Most of us believed that it was important to set up the organizations as promptly as possible and that if a hitch occurred in the negotiations on one of them the establishment of the other should not be delayed.

The proposal to establish a European Economic Committee encountered greater difficulties among Washington officials than the proposal to establish a coal organization. From the beginning, Nigel Ronald and I had discussed it in detail[4] and I was therefore taken

[4] I exchanged ideas also with Lord Keynes, asking him particularly about his experiences on the Supreme Economic Council in 1919. He stressed the need for provision to bring deadlocks to higher authorities, usually Foreign Ministers, promptly if anything was to be accomplished rapidly, as it must be if it were to be useful in postwar emergencies. He added that a difficulty on the Supreme Economic Council was the immediate occasion for his resignation in 1919. He had asked Mr. Lloyd George for permission to make a certain proposal on the Council. The Premier had agreed that Keynes could raise it but if it was not accepted by the other members he was not to expect Lloyd George's backing.

aback when, in a meeting which I attended in Washington in October 1944 to draw up a draft reply to the British note which proposed the setting up of such a committee, some officials expressed the view that the proposal was a British attempt at "domination" of the European countries! The real difficulty at this time was the immense gulf between London and Washington on the question of postwar scarcities. Some Washington officials, under pressure from congressmen, were more concerned to "return trade to private channels" than to provide against postwar scarcities; only with difficulty were they dissuaded from introducing this subject into the reply to the British note! Notwithstanding the rain of flying bombs falling on London during this period, I experienced a sense of relief on landing in London again later in October.[5]

It now appeared high time for the embassy to take the initiative if the European organizations were to be set up in time for the peace, and I took up the matter early with the Ambassador and my colleagues. Mr. Winant was not only anxious to press forward but immediately sensed that the chief obstacles were diplomatic and lay with the Soviet Union.

Washington's attitude was disconcerting on some points, but would not hinder the establishment of the organizations, though it might affect the subsequent operations of the European economic committee. Coal, transport, and other urgent economic questions could not be dealt with comprehensively unless Eastern and Central as well as Western and Southern Europe were brought into consultation, and the willingness and perhaps even the ability of Eastern and Central Europe to cooperate with the West on postwar measures would depend largely on the attitude of the Soviet Union. Ambassador Winant held that every effort should be made to bring the Soviet Union into the negotiations and into the organizations when they were formed. He hoped that the Russians would cooperate with the West in the postwar world and believed that the stability of the peace depended on their willingness to do so. But he was never willing, at any time or on any subject, to "appease" the Russians when he believed them to be wrong in principle. No American negotiator during or after the war could be depended on more than he could to give no ground on fundamental principles in negotiating

[5] The attitude of Washington on these subjects has changed so radically since early 1947 that the position in 1944 seems remote today.

with the Russians. On this occasion he agreed that if the Russians delayed their response to Allied invitations unreasonably we should aim at setting up the organizations without them, always leaving the way open for them to join later. At so late a stage in the war we could not afford to procrastinate indefinitely on measures so urgently needed when the fighting ceased in Europe.

We then drew up the following proposals and placed them before the State Department and the Foreign Office. First, we proposed a preliminary meeting in London among the U.S., U.K., U.S.S.R., and France to discuss the formation of a European coal organization. It seemed preferable to negotiate with the Russians in a small rather than in a large group. Second, if agreement were reached in principle at this meeting a second meeting should be called to which all the European Allies would be invited, and at which terms of reference would be agreed on and the organizations would be established. Third, if within a reasonable time no reply came from the Soviet Union to the invitation to the preliminary meeting, the invitations should be sent out and the meeting should, if necessary, proceed without the Soviet Union. Fourth, if the Russians came to the preliminary meeting but refused to agree to the establishment of the organizations on acceptable conditions, we should reach agreement with the U.K. and France, close the meeting, and immediately join in sending invitations to a meeting of all the European Allies, the purpose of which would be to establish the organizations and set them in motion straightway.

This plan was generally in harmony with Foreign Office ideas, though both the Foreign Office and the State Department expressed a strong desire that every effort should be made to obtain the agreement of the U.S.S.R. Representations were made in Moscow and invitations to a preliminary meeting were sent out. In the end the Russians agreed to appoint representatives, and the meeting was held in London.

The Russian attitude was not clear at the outset. The Soviet delegation appeared at first to side with us on a difference that arose between us and the United Kingdom delegation. We contended that the coal organization should be a subgroup of the economic committee, while the British, under the influence of the Ministry of Fuel and Power and against the advice of the Foreign Office, wished it to be an independent organization. However, in the opening meetings the Russian delegation had no instructions from Moscow. When the instructions came the meeting entered on a time of trouble. Moscow took not an isolationist but a doctrinaire point of view. First, it declared that the proposed European economic committee would overlap with the Economic and Social Council provided for in the Dumbarton Oaks plan for the United Nations Organization. Second, it approved of the idea of an international coal organization but insisted on the introduction of a clause in its terms of reference directing that first priority over German coal shipments should be given to reparation deliveries.

Strenuous days and nights of negotiation followed. The Russian proposals were not acceptable to any of the other delegations. The Economic and Social Council did not yet exist and probably would not be ready to start until 1946. It was to exercise long-term functions relating to the whole world. It had been decided that reparation policy was to be drawn up in Moscow by the Reparations Commission. The Soviet amendment with respect to the coal organization would prejudge the question whether reparation should be made from current production or from capital equipment and might leave no Ruhr coal available for any purpose but reparation.

Every effort was made to persuade the Russians not to press their amendment, but the delegation had inflexible instructions which permitted no compromise of substance. Next we moved to amend the title of the proposed economic committee to the "Emergency Economic Committee for Europe," thus stressing its temporary nature and opening the way for abolishing it if and when a regional group of the Economic and Social Council were set up for Europe. It was all to no purpose. The Russians appeared to believe themselves indispensable to any organizations that might be set up. During this intensely controversial part of the negotiations I happened to be acting head of our delegation, and when the Soviet delegates received their instructions I was invited with two colleagues, Samuel Berger and Winthrop Brown, to dinner with them. When the head of the Russian delegation made it clear that he would oppose the idea of a European economic committee I restated the case for setting it up before the war ended, and after expressing the hope that the Soviet Union would appreciate our viewpoint, added that in any case it seemed to us necessary to complete preparations before the war ended. He looked at me with an air of surprise and laughed heartily. "Do you really think," he said incredulously, "that the other countries will agree to set up such an organization without the Soviet Union?"

Notwithstanding every effort to induce the Russians to change their minds, the conference ended without agreement and we immediately proceeded with the plan which Ambassador Winant had proposed and which had gained acceptance in Washington. The first step was to approach privately some of the smaller Western European Allies to find whether they could be relied on to support our position. Nigel Ronald quickly obtained the agreement of the Netherlands and Belgium. The second step was to issue invitations to all the European Allies, including the U.S.S.R., to attend conferences for the purpose of establishing a European Coal Organization and a European Economic Committee. The Soviet Union did not send representatives and the organizations were successively established without it, on the understanding that the way was open for it to join at any time.

CHAPTER XII

The Interregnum

THE end of the war in Europe brought indescribable relief to London, which had been in the firing area for five years. If external signs had been a reliable guide, there would have been some excuse for not hastening the preparation of postwar plans in the final year of the war. Up to a short time before the collapse of Germany the work on postwar planning had been carried on in lively and dangerous surroundings. In discussions on postwar planning in the embassy, in Whitehall, and over restaurant tables in Picadilly, Mayfair, and Soho, voices had sometimes to be raised above the sound of flying bombs passing overhead to explode deeper in London. Casualties were heavy: many who had survived years of intermittent bombardment died in sight of victory. It needed an effort of imagination to realize that, notwithstanding the intensified visible signs of war and the precariousness of life in Britain's capital, preparations for the peace were far in arrears and the end would come before we were ready to deal with the conditions of the changed world which it would bring.

But the range and scope of the Second World War were far wider than those of the First. It is even doubtful whether the First World War has been appropriately designated. Overwhelmingly it was a war of Europe and the Near East. In the Second World War the Far East was deeply involved. Large areas were overrun by the enemy; regimes were overturned, and the seeds of social upheaval were scattered widely. The peacetime flow of trade and migration was changed in direction and diminished in volume.

However, the two theaters of war were widely separated. When General Rommel was thrown back from the gateway to Egypt and the Japanese army from the gateway to India the attempts of the Axis to unite were finally crushed. When President Roosevelt and General Marshall wisely decided to give priority in men and equipment to the European over the Far Eastern theater of war, the stage was set for the earlier defeat of Germany than of Japan, although, unfortunately, the end was delayed through diversion of some kinds of equipment, especially landing craft, to the Pacific theater.

The period between the defeat of Germany and the defeat of Japan may be considered as an interregnum between full wartime economy and peacetime economy. Wartime conditions had to be maintained so far as they were necessary to the deployment of additional forces to end the war in eastern Asia. But not all the forces that had been brought to bear on Germany were needed for or could be turned into the war against Japan. Thus additional men and equipment could be used for relief, reconstruction, and reconversion. Moreover, there was an opportunity to expedite postwar plans and fill the gaps left in the plans that had already been made during the long period of total war on all fronts when the energies of statesmen and civil servants had been absorbed mainly in day-to-day emergencies. But, contrary to widespread expectation, the time was short and the use made of it was disappointing.

With the approach of the German collapse, the position of Lend-Lease had to be reconsidered. At this stage it might reasonably have been expected that the problems of postwar reconstruction and particularly the problem of Britain's external financial reconstruction, would have been thoroughly analyzed and discussed. But the close of the European war at first raised scarcely a ripple on the surface of Anglo-American relations. British negotiators pointed out in Washington that the conditions of Lend-Lease during "Phase 1" (the European war) needed some modification during Phase 2 (the completion of the Far Eastern War). When Britain had redeployed all the forces that were needed and could be turned from the war in Europe to the war in the Far East some of the remaining productive factors could be turned back to the reconstruction of industries part of whose output was exported. Under the terms of the Eden-Winant agreement of July 1941, the United Kingdom was precluded from exporting goods made of Lend-Lease or *similar* materials.[1] Washington was now ready to modify these conditions as long as the Japanese war lasted. Military Lend-Lease aid was to continue on a scale reduced to the needs of the war against Japan, and civilian aid on much the same scale as before.

Unfortunately, the attitude of many in Washington on the dollar reserves of the sterling area was as narrow at the end of the German

[1] See p. 190. In my memorandum written a year earlier I had argued that for this reason the extension of Lend-Lease would not be an adequate solution to British reconstruction problems.

collapse as it had been earlier. In the last year of the war sharp attacks were made on the British for building up their gold and dollar reserves at the time when they were receiving Lend-Lease aid. These attacks, which seem to have originated largely among congressmen and businessmen, were unfortunate from every point of view, and the attempt to put pressure on the British to keep their reserves below $1,000 million revealed serious misconceptions of the international financial order. Such a reserve would have been only about a third of the prewar reserves of the United Kingdom; yet it would have had to serve for the whole of the sterling area and during a period when prices were much higher than they had been before the war and the network of world trade had been torn apart. Washington was rapidly being forced unwillingly into a position of international leadership, but the dominant views of many of its politicians and businessmen on international finance were still primitive.

But the arrangements made to deal with "Phase 2" of the war seem to have lulled both London and Washington, and particularly London, into a false sense of immediate economic security instead of rousing them to the peril that planning would be overtaken by events and that they would be caught unready at the close of the Far Eastern War.

"The war we are engaged in is one war," said Acting Secretary Grew on May 14, 1945, "and the end of organized resistance in Europe is not the end of the war." This was said to justify the continuation of Lend-Lease. But it was also a caution against a letdown following the collapse of the chief enemy country. It was doubtless from the same motive that other warnings were issued against the danger of underestimating the task that remained. Unfortunately, however, the warnings were carried too far and an estimate became widespread that eighteen more months would be needed to defeat Japan. However stirring such warnings might be to the armed forces, they had the effect of lulling the economic planners into a false sense of security from which they were soon to be rudely awakened.

The most important gaps in the planning, mentioned in my memorandum written a year earlier,[2] still remained open, nor had any serious attempt yet been made to close them. Among high-ranking statesmen in the United States, President Roosevelt, Mr. Stimson,

[2] See pp. 187-91.

and Mr. Morgenthau had shown some appreciation of the coming British balance of payments difficulties. But Mr. Morgenthau had set back the chances of a genuine remedy by propounding a spurious one[3] and President Roosevelt had carelessly allowed himself to be drawn momentarily by Mr. Morgenthau into a blind alley and on coming out of it became absorbed in war tasks and in a presidential election. Mr. Stimson held the most intelligent views of them all on postwar aid to Britain, but the subject was not the primary concern of a Secretary of War. Cordell Hull, at the time of the Morgenthau controversy, had failed to take the statesmanlike view on the U.K. postwar difficulties that might have been expected of him, and had allowed a minor long-run question concerning imperial preferences to divert him from a major short-run emergency. But after his retirement there was even less leadership on and understanding of the subject among the highest ranks of the State Department.

Nor was there any more progress on the matter in Whitehall than in Washington. There was indeed greater awareness of the dangers ahead, but action was halted by sharp disagreement over an acceptable means of escaping from those dangers. All understood the nature of the difficulty and the necessity of temporary external aid to overcome it. But one group held that, since the difficulty had arisen through Britain's earlier and greater contribution to the common cause of her allies, the only acceptable aid would be an outright grant. The other group agreed with the ethics of this position, but considered that in the world as it was, it would be difficult and perhaps impracticable to gain acceptance for it in the United States: hence it might be necessary to seek a loan on the most favorable terms obtainable. These were legitimate differences of opinion or judgment. Unfortunately, the argument persisted too long: it would have been better to have decided arbitrarily in favor of one of these views and then to have taken diplomatic action on it, than to have prolonged the debate when time was so short.

The second great gap in postwar planning lay, as we have seen, in the failure to make provision for organizing and financing reconstruction. In the interregnum between the fall of Germany and that of Japan no move was made to fill this gap. Some of the Western European countries had external funds which would tide them

[3] See Chapter XIV.

over the first few months of the postwar period; and for the Central, Southern and Eastern European countries UNRRA was ready to pour in large quantities of relief goods and small but valuable quantities of transport equipment and "rehabilitation" goods. These measures saved Europe from starvation but touched only the fringes of the general reconstruction of its economic life.

After the successful conference at Bretton Woods in July 1944, only formal ratification by national legislatures was needed to establish the International Monetary Fund and the International Bank for Reconstruction and Development. The movement to establish an international organization or organizations to deal with international trade policy and international raw material policy had met with greater obstacles, but advances were made in London in the last few months of the war: the groundwork was being prepared for a joint U.S.-U.K. statement of the aims to be pursued and the fundamental principles of a code to govern international trading were being steadily worked out.[4] But these, like the central functions of the International Monetary Fund, were not adapted to the immediate conditions with which the world would be confronted when peace returned.

One of the greatest economic errors of the peace after the First World War had been already largely guarded against when Germany collapsed in April 1945. Provision had been made, or was shortly to be made, partly through the retention of war machinery in modified form and partly through the establishment of new machinery, to ensure the best use of scarce materials and services in the early postwar period. Both the older and the newer bodies performing this function were made widely representative and covered coal, shipping, food, and other indispensable needs of reconstruction. These bodies were remodelled or newly set up only after patient and arduous negotiations in which the views of countries in widely different positions had to be reconciled, and it was one of the little advertised triumphs of international cooperation that fancied sectional interests and opportunities of gain were subordinated to a common policy of sharing by international agreement in those materials and services of which all stood in need but of which there was not enough to meet all needs.

Finally, when the German collapse came, the Allies were not more

[4] See Chapter VI.

ready to deal with a shattered Germany after surrender than they had been to deal with an aggressive Germany when the war began. This subject will be discussed in detail in the chapters which follow.

President Roosevelt died on the eve of the triumph of the Allied arms, to whose success he had contributed so much. But he died also on the eve of important new decisions which the coming of peace would necessitate, and the decisions had to be made by others of lesser stature, less experience, and less appeal to the masses of people at home and abroad. In this study, which deals with a limited field in some parts of which President Roosevelt was not at home, it has been necessary to record certain failures on his part. But nothing is further from the aim of this book than an intention to disparage the great President who led and inspired the American people in the New Deal and in the Second World War, and whose influence, both in war and peace, extended far beyond American shores.

If Roosevelt made serious errors, as I have argued in the following chapters that he did in regard to Germany and the Far East, his stature and prestige were such that, given longer life and better health he would have done more to repair those errors than his successors did, or could have done. As it was, preoccupied with the conduct of the war, he never seems to have given his mind to the problems of Germany's future. When Ambassador Winant tried to impress on the President in February 1945 the urgent need to prepare a reasonable policy for postwar Germany, the difficulty he found was not so much that of overcoming an antagonistic attitude as that of inducing the President to bring his mind wholly to bear on the question. This may have been largely the result of exhaustion and failing health. But it was also characteristic of the President's earlier attitude: it seems as if there were certain future contingencies which he was reluctant to consider deeply much in advance, preferring to rely upon his unrivalled powers of improvisation when the time came. And there is little doubt that if he had lived and retained his health those powers would have been exerted to their limit in the critical summer and autumn of 1945 and he would have salvaged much that was lost, and would have started new constructive measures that were never tried, in the early days after the collapse of Germany, by those who took over after his death.

The economic preparations for the peace would certainly have been hastened in some directions if London and Washington had not expected the war to continue considerably longer. Next to the President's death the greatest surprise for most of the world in 1945 was the speedy collapse of Japan following the collapse of Germany. It ought not to have been so. There was justification for surprise at the President's death but it is difficult to understand the widespread belief that Japan would greatly prolong its resistance.[5] First, the prewar tendency to underestimate greatly Japan's economic strength had given way to an opposite view that greatly overestimated it. Second, the terrain of Japan was widely different from that of Germany: manufacturing industry was, and had to be, concentrated in four plains, the Kwanto, the Nobi Plain, the Kwansai, and a part of Kyushu. Third, Japanese shipping was particularly vulnerable to submarine and naval attack and the islands could not carry on without trade. Fourth, the actions of selected Japanese military units who fought to the end on certain islands was no guide whatever to the actions of men, women and children in the crowded, specialized, vulnerable communities of Japan proper.[6]

In the early summer of 1945 I had several conversations with Ambassador Winant on these matters. He was worried by the lack of preparation for the conditions which the end of Lend-Lease would bring, and I believe that if President Roosevelt had been alive Winant would have made one of the direct and vigorous appeals to him which in the preceding four years he had reserved for matters of the greatest urgency.

The more we reflect on the errors in the military estimates of what would be required to defeat Japan, the more impressed we are likely to be with the limitations of military experts. Experience seemed to show that Germany could not be reduced by air bombardment and blockade alone; therefore it was apparently assumed that the same conclusion applied to Japan. The analogy was inept. In deciding on the strategy to be used against Japan, a naval and air analogy with the German attacks on Britain would have given better results than an analogy based on the Allied attack on Germany. Japan was in the position in which Britain would have been if it had lost

[5] Medical indications gave no ground for forecasting the early death of the President. See Ross T. Macintire, *White House Physician* (New York, G. P. Putnam's Sons), 1946, pp. 14-29, 239-40.

[6] As a former resident in Japan, I could not believe that the Japanese people "would fight to the last man" when thrown back on their homeland.

both the Battle of the Atlantic and the Battle of Britain. And of the two the loss of control of the seas was the worst setback: the crippling of Japan's merchant marine doomed her in any case.

Even a priori economic and geographical reasoning should have disposed of the argument[7] that Japan could only be defeated either by a large scale invasion costing hundreds of thousands of lives or by a wholesale slaughter of civilians by atomic bombs; but if empirical support is needed in retrospect it is given by the careful investigation of the Strategic Bombing Survey, which concludes:

"The responsible leaders in power read correctly the true situation and embraced surrender well before invasion was expected."[8]

"Based on a detailed investigation of all the facts and supported by the testimony of the surviving Japanese leaders involved, it is the Survey's opinion that certainly prior to 31 December 1945, in all probability prior to 1 November 1945, Japan would have surrendered even if the atomic bombs had not been dropped, even if Russia had not entered the war, and even if no invasion had been planned or contemplated."[9]

The economic consequences of these military errors were far-reaching. Instead of having time to complete preparations for total peace, the U.S. and U.K., relying on exaggerated estimates of the strength of Japan and the time needed to defeat her, were caught unready and forced to improvise hurriedly. Unfortunately, the genius at political improvisation, who had successfully led his country through its greatest peaceful revolution at home and its greatest military and naval struggle abroad, was no longer in the White House. And in London, the economic fortunes of war had gravely handicapped Britain in circumstances in which, less than any country, and less than at any other time, she deserved to be handicapped.

The solution of the British balance-of-payments difficulties was the most urgent single question in the summer of 1945. The moment Lend-Lease stopped Britain would be in extreme economic danger. It was unfortunate, therefore, that just at this time some circles in

[7] It should be added that this view was not held unanimously in the armed services. Naval and air commanders in the field were less inclined to accept it than were the U.S. Chiefs of Staff in Washington.

[8] U.S. Strategic Bombing Survey, *Japan's Struggle to End the War*, 1946, p. 12.

[9] *ibid.*, p. 13.

Washington were inclined to link any aid that might be given to Britain to concessions by Britain in entirely different fields. This was an old subject of contention: from early in the war there were officials in Washington as well as politicians who were ready to use the pressure of British needs to obtain political and economic concessions on long-standing controversial questions. In the embassy in London we had opposed this from the beginning, believing not only that it was a form of diplomatic sharp practice justifiable only in exceptional circumstances—as for example, in dealing with neutrals in wartime or with countries suspected of politically agressive intentions—but also that, where British people were concerned, it increased opposition within Whitehall and Westminister to the very policy which it was designed to advance. For British officials and ministers whose ideas on policy were not far from Washington's when a subject was considered on its intrinsic merits, and who would support them against those of their colleagues in the government departments and the cabinet, would immediately join the opposite camp if an attempt were made to force acceptance by a threat of opposition to other measures which were important to Britain. This is well understood by those who know Britain well at first hand, and attempts to use Britain's necessities in one direction to get concessions in another were usually rejected through wiser counsels in Washington. Unfortunately, the turnover of Washington officials and heads of departments is always high, and the newcomers sometimes fall into errors which their predecessors have learned to avoid. In the summer of 1945 the question of aid to Britain to tide over her balance-of-payments difficulties was in danger of becoming entangled with problems of trade policy which were the subject of quite separate discussions. Ambassador Winant had a clear understanding of the dangers of linking these subjects, but Washington opinion was divided. Some officials, including the present writer, urged that no connection at all be made between the subjects. In the end a vague and, as I think, spurious connection was made between them by Washington.[10] It was held that, while financial aid should not be used as a weapon to force concessions on commercial policy, nevertheless the two sets of negotiations should be carried

[10] I do not wish to disparage those who formulated this point of view: they certainly staved off some deplorable alternative points of view that might have had serious political repercussions.

on simultaneously, on the ground that financial aid could effect lasting improvement only in a trading world shaped according to the principles of the proposed trade charter. There might have been something in this point of view if adequate provision had been made at the same time for the reconstruction of the Allied and the ex-enemy countries. But this was not attempted until two years or more later, and the economic world for which the trade charter was prepared was remote from the economic world in which the British loan was negotiated.

During the summer Ambassador Winant several times expressed his eagerness to get some leading spokesmen over from Washington informally in the hope that they would become more impressed with the need to hasten postwar preparations in several fields. Fortunately, it was decided that the Council of UNRRA was to meet in London in August. This would bring William Clayton to London and since he would take the leading part for the State Department, both in plans for aiding Britain and in the final stages of negotiation of an international trade charter, there were opportunities for an informal discussion of these subjects in London.

Except for the UNRRA Conference, the discussions in London in August 1945 were only informal and exploratory, but they marked an important stage in the development of postwar measures in three widely separated fields.

The first of them had to do with relief. UNRRA was in the midst of its operations in Europe. A steady stream of goods was pouring across the oceans and taxing the capacity of the damaged ports and inland transport equipment of Europe. The work of rescuing Central, Southern and Eastern Europe from an economic disaster that would have brought immense human suffering was under way. But the first UNRRA appropriation, fixed at 1 per cent of the national incomes of the contributing countries, was almost all engaged, while recovery was far from complete and provision for the continuation of aid was urgently needed.

At the same time two important new demands on UNRRA funds were made at the meeting. The first and the largest was for the extension of full UNRRA aid to Italy, thus placing an ex-enemy country in the same position as the Allied countries which received UNRRA aid.

The United States was the chief sponsor of this demand. The arguments for it—based on humanity, on convenience, and on the close relation between the economic fortunes of Southern and Western Europe—were reinforced by its popularity among the large body of voters of Italian origin in the United States. Since the United States was the largest contributor to UNRRA, its readiness to make a second contribution, and the vigor of its support of full aid for Italy, seemed to many of the delegations to be tacitly related. However, while this increased Italy's chances it by no means insured her against opposition. The countries which had been victims of what President Roosevelt had aptly described in 1940 as a "stab in the back" had not forgotten the destruction and disorganization caused by Italian aggression. At the previous UNRRA Council meeting at Montreal in October 1944 they had agreed on partial aid for Italy, but had keenly resented the glowing oratory in support of this policy from the Latin American representatives, who had watched the war at a safe distance. It would have been unfortunate to have been forced to rely at the London meeting on the Latin American vote to put through Italian aid.

The demand of the Soviet Union for UNRRA aid raised even more difficult questions and indirectly affected the prospects for full aid to Italy. At an earlier stage, when the Western world was filled with admiration for the struggle of the Russian people against the German invaders who stripped, pillaged, plundered, and murdered both as they advanced and still more as they retreated, it seems to have been widely assumed, both in government circles and among the public, that relief would be given to Russia as well as to the European Allies. But for some time after UNRRA was set up, Moscow made no specific request for UNRRA aid. As we have seen the total funds were insufficient to meet the total relief needs of Europe without Russia, and it was decided that the Western European Allies should not receive appreciable aid from UNRRA. Even with this limitation of demand, UNRRA was unable to meet fully the requirements of Central, Southern and Eastern Europe.

Two questions had to be dealt with immediately by the Council: first, the question whether new claimants should be accepted for UNRRA aid; and second, the question how to distribute the total resources among the claimants if new demands were to be added without new resources to meet them. For political reasons, the United States was bent on the acceptance of Italy, but the first position taken among leading members of the U.S. delegation who came from Washington was that the U.S.S.R. ought not to be a claimant. The reasons for this position seem to have been, first, that Great Powers should be above the acceptance of relief, and when in need should seek loans and not grants; second, that if the U.S.S.R. were granted relief the funds left for the other claimants would be so reduced that the UNRRA program would be wrecked.

Some days before the delegation from Washington arrived, I had received advance notice from a Russian source in London that the U.S.S.R. delegation would request a specified amount of UNRRA aid at the Council meeting. This was not surprising to those of us who had taken part in the prolonged discussions in London on the principles to be followed in the formulation of requirements and had noticed the interest of the Russian representatives in the question how the principles proposed would affect estimates of Russian needs. When I inquired of this source whether the Soviet Union was interested in securing reconstruction loans I was informed, to my surprise, that this question had already been raised by the Russians in the United States, and that the reception given to it had been unfavorable and was interpreted in Moscow as a rejection of loans for the Soviet Union.

Here was a reconstruction question the political significance of which was as great as if not greater than its economic significance. It came, too, at a time when doubts whether the Soviet Union would be willing to cooperate with the West in the postwar world were increasing in government circles, but when hopes of Russian cooperation had not died, even among those who had direct knowledge of the immediate difficulties. Hopes remained strong among the public in Britain, Canada, and—perhaps to a slightly lesser extent—the United States.

When the delegation from Washington arrived in London I mentioned to the Ambassador and to William Clayton the difficulties of supporting the Italian claim to full UNRRA aid while denying the Russian right to any UNRRA aid at all. Unquestionably, the Soviet Union had suffered immensely greater loss of life and destruction of property than any other Allied country. Whatever troubles the Western Powers had experienced in dealing with the Russians—and we had had our share of them in London—they could not afford to lay themselves open to the charge that they were already discriminating unfairly against the Soviet Union on one of the most important postwar issues.

However, at the beginning Mr. Clayton and his immediate advisers were strongly against UNRRA aid to the Soviet Union, for reasons described above. They were surprised when I reported my conviction, based on private conversations with reliable Russian representatives, that Moscow believed that it had already been turned down on a request for a loan, and they promptly drafted a telegram to send to the American Embassy at Moscow that evening on the subject.[11] Later I heard that it uncovered an error of omission.

In view of the indiscriminate hostility shown in some Washington political circles later toward all assistance, past or present, to the Soviet Union, the following extract from a memorandum of mine written at the time for Mr. Clayton and Ambassador Winant will show the strength of the case for reaching agreement with the Russians without giving them all that they asked for, which amounted to $700 million or half of the proceeds of a single UNRRA contribution by the member countries.

"... I suggest, therefore, that we should take a position as follows: (a) We cannot afford to have a split in the Council and a rejection by majority vote of a Soviet request for aid, because this would place us in an unfavorable position with world opinion and would prejudice our policy respecting aid for Italy and Austria, while in addition it might deprive UNRRA of wholehearted Soviet cooperation with its operations in Central and Eastern Europe.

"(b) In view of the publicity given to the Soviet request and the immense damage Russia has sustained, it is politically desirable that there should be at least some token UNRRA aid to the Soviet.

"(c) If possible, the financial committee should report favorably on a limited amount of UNRRA aid to certain parts of the U.S.S.R. which have sustained particularly severe damage during invasion. The grounds might be that Soviet gold and ability to obtain credits should be used to obtain the greater part of the assistance they need,

[11] The question of aid to Russia for reconstruction purposes had been raised by Ambassador Winant in August 1944 in a telegram to the President in which he recommended that an effort should be made during the war to reach a comprehensive settlement with the Soviet Union on postwar matters. Aid in reconstruction would be included if a satisfactory political settlement could be reached. See pp. 241-42.

but that the extent of their need is such that limited and localized UNRRA aid is justifiable.

"(d) There should be a clear understanding, (a) that there can be no guarantee of aid to the extent of $700 million,[12] that it is most unlikely that aid on that scale would be possible, that requirements as submitted are subject to cutting down in the light of the supply position and of other claims on UNRRA supplies; (b) that the Soviet will cooperate to supply full information on conditions in the areas concerned and will admit the necessary UNRRA staff in the same way as other countries have done."

Long and strenuous negotiations on this issue took place during the conference. In the end a compromise was reached: UNRRA aid to the value of $250 million was allocated for use in the Ukraine and Byelorussia. The Soviet delegation were disappointed that the amount was not greater, but were in no sense obstructive during the conference and did not oppose full aid to Italy.

The compromise over the Russian claim was, I believe, a statesmanlike act for which much credit should go to Mr. Clayton, Lester Pearson of Canada, and the Soviet delegation. There were some in Washington and in the American Embassy in Moscow who did not approve of it. Already the Soviet Union were failing to fulfill some of the obligations they had undertaken at Yalta, notably those concerned with Poland. But the real break between East and West had hardly yet come, and the public in Great Britain, Canada, and the United States would certainly not have approved of a blank refusal of aid to the Soviet Union. The outcome was wholly favorable. The conditions for the UNRRA aid were fully complied with in the Russian areas, including facilities for an UNRRA mission to observe distribution on the spot. The administration of the relief by the Russian authorities was honest and effective.[13]

[12] The amount requested by the Russians.

[13] As an example of the seamier side of political life in Washington, it should be recorded that an imaginative but incorrect and unsubstantiated story to the contrary was circulated later, when relations between the U.S.A. and the U.S.S.R. had become more strained and the more rabid controversialists in both countries were looking for more fuel to add to the fire. An American in the UNRRA mission in the Ukraine and Byelorussia who knew the facts communicated with Washington to correct these allegations. Later still the present writer, taking part in some informal discussions on suitable candidates to direct a new and temporary specialized international agency, suggested this individual, who was an experienced administrator. He soon learned, however, that such an appointment would be blocked by congressmen because of the

The second important achievement of the conference was the agreement of the member countries to make a second contribution, amounting to an estimated 1 per cent of national income, to UNRRA funds. This act was a recognition that the amount of postwar aid needed in Europe was much greater than optimists had predicted. The new contribution raised no real economic difficulties for the United States, but it was a serious burden on Great Britain. I recollect an important informal meeting at the Treasury in Whitehall at which certain members of the U.S. and Canadian delegations met leading British civil servants to discuss Britain's position with respect to a second UNRRA contribution. In reply to our expressions of hope that the U.K. would join in the second contribution, the chief British civil servants frankly outlined the difficulties of Britain's position. Only a few days before, President Truman had announced publicly in Washington, without previously informing the countries concerned or the American missions to those countries, that Lend-Lease had ended. Ambassador Winant and William Clayton were dismayed by both the content and manner of this announcement, and transatlantic telephone conversations followed, but the step hastily and impulsively taken by the new President, apparently to a large extent on the advice of Leo Crowley, could not be revoked. In the Treasury room it came to my mind that we were asking the British people to give away goods to the value of $320 million just at the time when they were faced with an enormous deficit in their balance of payments, which threatened a complete breakdown of their economy and which could not possibly be closed by their own resources. Yet, having outlined their difficulties, they went on to say that they could not refrain from making their full contribution to UNRRA for the second time. And when later the matter came up in Parliament not one voice was raised against that decision. Throughout the whole country the people considered it as a duty to play their part in relieving the peoples of the countries that had been occupied by the enemy. I believe that a similar view was held by the great majority of the American people, but this did not prevent bitter attacks by a noisy

earlier action by the proposed candidate to correct the false report concerning the use of UNRRA relief in the Russian areas! Is it any wonder that competent and courageous candidates for public offices, with a good chance of successful nomination, are so often difficult to find?

minority in Congress and sharp heckling of administration spokesmen who presented the case for the new contribution.

Following the UNRRA Council meeting Mr. Clayton engaged in informal discussions with Whitehall on financial aid for Britain and on trade, raw material, and cartel policy. These preliminary explorations were designed to pave the way for a meeting in September in Washington at which formal negotiations would take place concerning financial aid, the urgency of which had been brought home to Washington as well as London by the sudden collapse of Lend-Lease. There were at the same time a number of urgent questions regarding the final settlement of Lend-Lease which would have to be dealt with at the time when financial aid was taken up in Washington. Terms would have to be agreed upon to cover those goods which were already on the way or arranged for when Lend-Lease ended, and those durable goods in the hands of Great Britain which had been supplied under Lend-Lease and might either be returned or bought.

The British spokesmen indicated that in Washington they would state the case for a grant rather than a loan to meet their balance-of-payments difficulties. The case for a grant has been explained previously and need not be repeated here. Mr. Clayton, however, was able to discuss only credits. It may be said at once that there was no hope that the British point of view on this question would be accepted in Washington—mainly, I think, because the American people had not been prepared for such a step and did not understand the past history of Britain's financial sacrifices in a common cause. Nor at the time did the President and the Secretary of State possess the vision, the economic insight, and the determination needed to win over Congress to the bold and generous measure that would have been justified in the circumstances.

CHAPTER XIII

Germany: Reconstruction or Revenge?

THE chief enemy countries in the Second World War played leading economic roles in the two most densely populated areas of the world. Germany in Europe and Japan in Eastern Asia not only were well developed in agriculture but also supplied other countries both near and far with large quantities of manufactured goods. Their economic systems were interlocked with those of less developed areas near them. If Japan was less advanced industrially than Germany, she was also situated among other countries less advanced than those which surrounded Germany. In some respects she had greater economic strength than Italy, the third and weakest member of the Axis. If comprehensive plans were to be prepared for early postwar reconstruction, the enemy countries had therefore to be taken into account. If they were omitted the work of reconstructing the economic life of the liberated areas would be immensely complicated and long delayed.

But the political and psychological obstacles in the way of planning the economic reconstruction of the enemy countries of the present or the ex-enemy countries of the future were immense. The unprovoked aggressions, the brutality, and the oppressive rule of which every Axis country was guilty had aroused the just indignation of the civilized world. Unfortunately, in some quarters it had aroused also a desire for revenge which, however natural or understandable it might be, was wholly destructive in its effects, and undermined the moral leadership of the Allies.

But this deterioration came gradually, and in the early part of the war created in itself few obstacles to postwar planning. If the planners had pressed forward earlier in this field, particularly after the Atlantic Pact was drawn up, the course of events might have taken a much better turn and the open and cynical disregard of the Pact in the later period of the war might not have gone as far as it did.

Nevertheless, from the beginning such planning as there was for reconstruction in the ex-enemy countries was done in almost complete isolation from the planning for reconstruction in Allied countries. Hence it has been necessary to discuss it as a special subdivision of the whole field of reconstruction and to devote separate chapters to it.

The economic aspects of the question what to do with Germany after the war engaged the attention of Whitehall early. Sir William Malkin, a leading senior civil servant—later killed in an airplane disaster on the way to Yalta—presided over an interdepartmental committee of civil servants which, I believe, was the first official body in any of the Allied countries to make a systematic examination of the question. In 1942 and early 1943, when this group carried on its work, it was faced with many unknown factors. The shape of things to come in Germany could be seen only in dim, blurred outlines. The main work of destruction from the air was yet to come. The form of the collapse, the positions of the invading Allies when it came, the extent to which enemy civilian administration would survive, the size of food and raw material stocks, the amount of remaining industrial capacity—none of these things could be guessed with hope of even reasonable accuracy at this time.

But the memory of the economic confusion in Germany after the First World War and of its effects on neighboring countries was still vivid in Whitehall, and, as in other fields of postwar economic policy, officials were anxious not to repeat the mistakes of the past. There were a number of questions of policy which would have to be settled whatever the circumstances in which the war ended. It was all to the good that an early start was made and a tragedy that it was not followed up by ministers in Great Britain and their nearest counterparts in the United States.

Two aspects of the postwar economic position of Germany were considered at length in Whitehall from an early stage—reparations and what came to be called "economic security." This last phrase meant the security of the rest of the world from future German aggression, if and insofar as it could be secured by making and keeping Germany incapable of the economic preparations necessary to wage a modern war. Of course it could hardly be claimed that postwar economic checks on Germany would in themselves ensure the security of the rest of the world. Until Mr. Morgenthau came into the field on his own initiative those who studied the question of future economic security against Germany wished merely to explore the possibility of devising economic measures to increase the effectiveness of the measures of political security that it was taken for granted would be established. Measures for economic security were conceived of not as a substitute for, but—if on investigation they were found to have a place at all—as an aid or supplement to, measures for political security.

But the idea of reparation and the idea of economic security as defined here did not necessarily lead either to identical or to complementary economic proposals. Reparation strictly means to repair damage and make up losses. This can be done on a large scale only if the country making reparation has a strong and well-organized economic order, including in its productive capacity many of the things needed to wage war. Thus it seemed possible that economic security and reparation might up to a point be competitive and irreconcilable. This, however, depended on whether economic security was attainable and, if it was, in what form and to what extent.

To complicate matters still further, these economic issues could not be separated from political issues. If large-scale reparation involved a large-scale deterioration in the conditions of life of the masses of people in the country making reparation, and if measures designed for economic security prevented the ex-enemy country from making essential goods for domestic consumption and export, there was a danger that widespread resentment and discontent would arise to form a soil in which demagoguery and autocracy would grow and flourish.

A group of British officials, including high-ranking senior civil servants and temporary wartime civil servants drawn from several walks of life, gave much thought to these questions during the war. From an early stage I kept in close touch with some members of this group. The senior permanent officials were particularly concerned at the outset to avoid the worst errors of the 1920's. They favored reparation in kind over reparation fixed in monetary terms, though they were not so naïve as to imagine that reparation in kind completely sidestepped the monetary mechanism. Nor did they discard the idea of monetary payments from Germany to the Allies, to be used by the Allies to make, at least within limits, whatever purchases they thought fit. But the place which they proposed to give to unilateral payments was a special one, outside the ordinary conception of reparation. Assuming that fairly stable economic conditions might be restored within ten years after the war, Germany would have an economic advantage in being unable, by treaty obligation, to maintain armaments. On the other hand, the leading Allies would be under an obligation to maintain, if necessary by force, international security, and for this purpose would still be diverting part of their capital and labor into the production of goods that would yield no services to consumers. In an attempt to offset these future differences between the economic positions of former Allies and former enemies, some of the U.K. officials suggested that Germany should be required to make payments to the Allies, beginning only after reparation proper had been completed—perhaps about ten years after the end of the war. These payments would resemble in form the old-fashioned reparation in money payments, but would be very moderate in amount and would be characterized not as reparation but as payment toward collective security.

As to reparation proper, my impression is that Whitehall, with the aftermath of the last war in mind, deliberately limited its proposals to what it believed the public would be willing to support under the changed conditions of peacetime. The payment of reparation over a long period would be likely to break down over the reluctance of the British public in the future to enforce penalties on a generation which had not reached maturity when German aggression started the Second World War. Nothing could be worse than a drastic program of penalties that would be recognized as harsh after the heat of victory had passed and would fizzle out by default as the will to enforce it declined with the declining memory of the war and the restoration of a spirit of charity among men.

This concern with the attitude of the public greatly affected the form as well as the duration of reparation proposed. It made for reparation in kind rather than through the transmission of free purchasing power. In a short period in which monetary stability would probably not be firmly reestablished, certain types of reparation in kind might be easier to administer, especially if care were taken as to the types of goods removed. British officials at that time thought that there might be certain stocks of raw materials at the time of defeat which would be drawn on for reparation. However, this form of reparation, they held, must be strictly limited in scope and in time. Moreover, Whitehall still remembered the confusion caused after the First World War by the export of coal as reparation from Germany.

From the beginning, the conception of economic security raised great difficulties. The range of products essential to the conduct of total war is very wide, and if economic security were given a broad application German civilian industry would be crippled and the conditions of life of the people would be permanently lowered to a dangerous point. This was the last thing desired by the government and the people of the U.K. Notwithstanding all they had suffered from unprovoked German aggression, the spirit of revenge and retaliation had little place in their attitude to the future peace. They had to live in the future with the Germans as near neighbors, and however hopelessly sunk in evil Hitler's Germany might be, a stable peace in the future depended on an ultimate reconciliation being reached with a new and more civilized generation of German people. This could not be attained by heavily visiting the sins of Hitler's generation on future generations.

Economic security, if it means anything, is essentially a conception of the long run. The difficulties of reparation might be partially removed by turning reparation into a short-run affair, but no similar escape from the difficulties of economic security lay open. In the short run, indeed, economic security is of little importance. A defeated Germany could not in any circumstances revive its capacity to wage war again for some years to come. Moreover, the Allied peoples would be alert to take action if any signs of renewed aggression appeared in the early postwar period. If Germany again became an aggressor country, it could be only after a fairly long period of recuperation and by taking advantage of an unsuspecting generation that had not lived through the previous war. It is in this fact—or probability—that the chief obstacle to the application of measures of economic security lies. Of what use is it to devise measures today which would restrict the economic freedom and limit the economic sovereignty of a former aggressor country, but which would be superfluous in the near future and, if they were to serve their purpose, would have to be rigorously enforced in the more distant future when conditions would have changed and wholly different governments would be in power.

To my mind no satisfactory answer has been given to this question either in Whitehall or elsewhere during or since the war. However, the British civil servants rendered an important service by examining concretely the possibilities of economic security. These studies were started in connection with the work of the Malkin Committee and continued later by the Economic and Industrial Planning Committee, an interdepartmental committee under the leadership of the Foreign Office. A large volume of work was carried out by men of great ability, some of whom in peacetime had had direct experience of German industries and German economic conditions.

It seems appropriate at this point to analyze briefly some of the possibilities of specific regulatory measures over the German economy. They may be divided into two classes. First, there are the measures applied directly to the internal economic order in Germany and, second, those which concentrate on the nature and amounts of imports into Germany. As to the first, the practicability of prohibiting or limiting the size of specific industries or the manufacture of specific products that serve war purposes has to be considered early. This approach is more attractive at first glance than it is after prolonged scrutiny of particular cases. In modern total war the industries or plants which can be used only for peaceful purposes are very limited: a large number which produce essential civilian goods can either produce for direct war uses in their existing state, or can be adapted without great difficulty or long delay to those uses. The chemical and the iron and steel industries are only two of the more spectacular examples: there are many others. Thus widespread prohibition or limitation of industries would cause great deterioration in the conditions of life in peacetime, and could hardly be maintained over a long period without continued military occupation in great strength.

A more limited approach is to single out a very few industries for complete prohibition, for example the manufacture of airplanes and of synthetic oil. It is hardly conceivable that a country without the capacity to manufacture airplanes could wage modern warfare. Nor could Germany wage large-scale war under present conditions without producing synthetic oil.

However, in any attempt to obtain economic security by limiting or prohibiting the production of certain products or the use of certain processes, two difficulties have to be faced. The techniques of warfare change frequently: prohibitions and limitations therefore tend to become obsolete when the products which are prohibited or limited lose much of their importance through the growth of substitutes or the invention of new and superior products for use in war. If a general prohibition of substitutes and of new products is laid down, the civilian economy will be crippled. Second, inspection and enforcement are extremely difficult when the prohibited processes can be carried on in very small plants.

If productive equipment and processes can be found which are essential in wartime but not in peacetime, and which are difficult to conceal, their prohibition or limitation may serve a useful purpose in supplementing measures for political security. The British officials early considered the practicability of banning the production of synthetic oil in Germany. Clearly this measure is no general safeguard against aggression, since some countries possess enough natural oil for all purposes. But in Germany's special position it might be useful in the present state of technique. Moreover, the plants necessary to produce synthetic oil must be large and visible even to inspection from the air.

But not many products can be put in this category, and, in the main, economic security through internal controls would seem to require limitation of production or productive capacity of a number of staple products essential in both war and peace, among which many of the products of the steel industry, the chemical industries, and the machine tool industries are outstanding. But limitation of output or of capacity necessitates close supervision and doubts seem justified as to the probable willingness of future Allied governments to enforce, and future ex-enemy governments to accept, close supervision for many years ahead. Next, there is the difficulty of estimating an appropriate amount of output and of capacity. The volume of future economic activity, the direction of future technical developments, and the changes in the demand for raw materials resulting from them, cannot be predicted closely. If mistakes of underestimation were made, the civilian economy and hence the economic conditions of life would be depressed and political discontent would be aroused.

The difficulties of long-term internal economic control by supervising powers led to a careful exploration of the possibilities of controlling ex-enemy economic activities largely from the outside. These possibilities depend on the needs of the country concerned and the extent of its domestic resources. The control of Japan in this way is a simple matter. Japan was able to take aggressive action, not because of any inherent economic advantages of its position, but because of the gross negligence and inertia of the Western powers which deliberately threw away opportunities to control her with small risk of bloodshed. The case of Germany, with its greater natural resources, is different, but even Germany could not become self-sufficient.

The most obvious method of external control is through control of imports. However, a minute control of all imports would be difficult and burdensome and might not be tolerated for many years. As an alternative there is the possibility of confining regulation to a few "strategic" or "key" imports. The exclusion of oil and scrap iron from Japan in the early 1930's would have crippled the war plans of the militarists. As regards Germany, if it be assumed that large quantities of steel will continue indefinitely to be indispensable for war purposes, and if direct control of steel output over many years is difficult from a political and inconvenient from an administrative point of view, a substitute form of control might be found in the regulation of the import of scarce minerals that go into the manufacture of high-speed steel—tungsten, molybdenum, chromium, and others—in which Germany is deficient. The physical quantities of these scarce minerals that go into steel production are small. It is therefore easier in some ways to supervise them than to supervise a commodity of which large volumes are produced or imported. On the other hand, the smaller the physical quantities of an import and the higher the monetary value of each physical unit, the greater is the likelihood of successful smuggling.[1] After much study the British experts concluded that if this form of control were to be made effective it would have to be established by the United Nations as a world-wide control of the minerals concerned. This is not to say that the imports of other countries would be regulated: the control would be mainly statistical. But it would be essential to have a reliable balance sheet showing world production and an accounting of the disposition of the entire supply.

[1] It would be extraordinarily difficult, for example, to enforce limitation of the import of diamonds for cutting purposes.

Whitehall's exploration in these fields led to some preliminary recommendations by officials in the report of the Malkin Committee. Unfortunately, this valuable start, which had put the U.K. in the lead in preparation for what was almost certain from the beginning to be the most difficult of all the economic problems of the peace, seems to have been thrown away by the failure—or perhaps we should say the refusal—of ministers to study, and take at least a tentative position on, postwar economic questions relating to Germany. Repeated efforts by leading civil servants to draw the attention of cabinet ministers to the subject and to get approval of their paper as a basis for informal non-committal discussions with Allies failed throughout 1942 and I think through most, if not all, of 1943.

In Washington, postwar planning on Germany was more concerned with political and administrative than with economic questions. However, economic plans must always rest on political foundations and fit into a political structure: consequently, some examination of the chief political issues is essential to an intelligible account of the economic issues.[2]

The first and most important of these issues was the question whether Germany was to remain as a single state or to be divided into several independent states. From the beginning, civil servants who realized the desperate urgency of economic planning for postwar Germany and who with the help of junior ministers in London and a few assistant secretaries in Washington attempted to move forward without waiting for directions from above, were acutely conscious of the ambiguities and limitations arising from the absence of a political framework within which a detailed economic structure could be built. Consider, for example, reparation. How could any reparation plan be drawn up unless a decision were made on the question what territory would remain to Germany after the war and whether there would be a single Germany or separate German states. The Malkin Committee in 1942 tried to meet the difficulty by assuming that Germany would be "substantially a unitary state." This did not neces-

[2] By far the best account of the political planning is to be found in two articles by Professor Philip E. Mosely, "Dismemberment of Germany," *Foreign Affairs*, April 1950, pp. 487-98, and "The Occupation of Germany: New Light on How the Zones were Drawn," *op.cit.*, July 1950, pp. 580-604. These articles are indispensable and completely dispose of some misconceptions on the part of other writers, including Sherwood and Clay.

sarily mean that no territory would be taken from Germany. The committee recognized that certain areas on the outskirts of Germany—for example the Saar, East Prussia and Upper Silesia—might be transferred to other powers. But it did mean that Germany would not be split up into separate states and disappear as a single country.

Yet this was the very question on which, more than on any other, the heads of state in the United Kingdom, the United States, and the Soviet Union fumbled, vacillated, and went astray. The assumption made by the Malkin Committee was neither confirmed nor denied by any political decision until the Potsdam Conference in 1945! President Roosevelt, in the earliest discussion on the subject, seems to have expressed himself in favor of the dismemberment of Germany. Sumner Welles apparently encouraged him in this view and introduced the subject into the discussions of the Advisory Committee on Postwar Problems in 1942 and into the work of the research staff of the State Department. Professor Mosely states that "Projects for the partition of postwar Germany into three, five, and seven separate states were drawn up. . . ."[3] But the studies and discussions gave rise to strong opposition to dismemberment, not only among the staff but among the leading advisers, particularly Dr. Pasvolsky and the late Dr. Isaiah Bowman, who had been one of the leading American writers on territorial questions for a decade after the First World War. But this did not change the views of President Roosevelt. The notes of Harry Hopkins referring to a dinner with the President and Mr. Eden on March 14, 1943, state that the President "thought that we should encourage the differences and ambitions that will spring up within Germany and, in effect, approve of a division which represents German opinion." When Hopkins asked what would be done if no desire arose in Germany for separation, "both the President and Eden agreed, that, under any circumstances, Germany must be divided into several states. . . ."[4]

In conversations with Foreign Office officials on German economic matters, I had found no evidence of sympathy with, and much evi-

[3] "Dismemberment of Germany," *Foreign Affairs,* April 1950, p. 488. I also had the advantage of detailed discussions with the late Dr. Bowman on this subject at Johns Hopkins University.

[4] Robert E. Sherwood, *Roosevelt and Hopkins* (New York, Harpers), 1948, p. 711.

dence of disapproval of, proposals for the dismemberment of Germany. Hence, it was as surprising to me to learn that Mr. Eden had concurred with President Roosevelt in a categorical statement in favor of dismemberment, as it was to learn of the political naïveté of both Eden and Roosevelt in supposing that a spontaneous desire would arise within Germany to break up the Reich. Possibly Mr. Eden, if he was correctly reported, was merely expressing a personal opinion on the spur of the moment, for in Quebec on August 21, 1943, he informed Secretary Hull that, "while some members of the British government felt that Germany should be dismembered, he himself—and he felt, in general, the cabinet also—were not in favor of imposing dismemberment, largely because of the impracticability of carrying it out. He said it would be well to bring about a separation of the different states of Germany if it could be done voluntarily."[5]

The first sentence in this statement confirms what officials confidentially informed me at the time, but I should add that I never found among them the slightest indication of a belief that the German people would voluntarily strive to split up their country. It seems that in London ministers were divided, with a majority against dismemberment, but a minority active enough to prevent a collective decision from being reached, or at any rate to influence the Prime Minister not to seek such a decision because of the dissension that might be stirred up.

In the spring of 1943 a promising start was made on postwar planning for Germany. President Roosevelt discussed the postwar treatment of Germany with Secretary Hull on March 30, 1943, and three days later sent the Secretary a note requesting him to discuss with Secretary Stimson and the British "the question of what our plan is to be in Germany and Italy during the first few months after Germany's collapse."[6] The discussions which followed led to the document which Secretary Hull presented to Mr. Eden and M. Molotov at the Moscow Conference in October 1943. Its text is available and need not be repeated here. It covered much indispensable detail concerning the rights of the occupying powers, demobilization, political prisoners, maintenance of economic controls, delivery of war materials, elimination of the manufacture of arms, and provision for an inspection sys-

[5] *The Memoirs of Cordell Hull* (New York, Macmillan), 1948, II, 1233.
[6] *ibid.*, II, 1284.

tem. On the broader issues of policy it accepted the idea of unconditional surrender. It recommended "decentralization of the German political structure" but made no definite recommendation on dismemberment. It held that the future government of Germany should be democratic but included among the conditions of successful democracy "a tolerable standard of living" and "restrictions of measures of control to the requirements of general security."[7]

The question whether or not Germany should be dismembered was discussed inconclusively at the Moscow Conference of Foreign Ministers. Both Mr. Hull and Mr. Eden admitted that there were differences of opinion within their governments on the question, and Mr. Hull recommended caution and further study.[8] Only a month later at the Teheran Conference the heads of state were all for dismemberment, each of them, however, having a radically different idea of the form it should take. The left hand scarcely seems to have known what the right hand was doing either in London or in Washington. The President and the Prime Minister held views opposed to those of their Secretaries of State and still more to those of the capable advisers and civil servants who, in both capitals, had thoroughly studied the subject. Mr. Sherwood's account of the Teheran discussion is an illuminating account of confusion, disunity, and indecision in high places:

"There was extensive discussion of the dismemberment of Germany. Roosevelt submitted a plan for five autonomous states: (1) Prussia (reduced), (2) Hanover and Northwest, (3) Saxony and Leipzig area, (4) Hesse-Darmstadt, Hesse-Kassel and the area south of the Rhine, (5) Bavaria, Baden and Würtemberg—whereas the Kiel Canal and Hamburg, and the Ruhr and the Saar, to be under United Nations control. When Roosevelt offered this suggestion, Churchill exclaimed, 'To use an American expression, the President has said a mouthful!' Churchill agreed that Prussia should be separated from the rest; he believed that the southern states should be detached to become part of a Danubian Confederation.

"Stalin was not enthusiastic about either proposal, but said that of the two he preferred Roosevelt's. He felt that dismemberment meant dismemberment—that the Prussian officers and staffs should be eliminated but that otherwise he saw little difference between the

[7] *ibid.*, II, p. 1286. [8] *ibid.*, II, p. 1287.

people of one part of Germany and another. As to putting any parts of Germany in any Confederation, he said that, whatever form it might take, if there were Germans in it they would soon dominate it and the threat of a greater Germany would be revived. He said that there would always be a strong urge on the part of the Germans to unite and that the whole purpose of any international organization must be to neutralize this tendency by applying economic and other measures including, if necessary, force. This discussion ended up nowhere; it was decided that the subject should be considered further by the European Advisory Commission in London."[9]

Such was the position at the end of 1943. Little effective economic planning could be carried out when it was not even known whether Germany was to be one country or two countries or five countries after the war, or, if Germany was to be carved up, what the sizes and shapes of the slices would be!

But earlier in 1943 another important political decision had affected economic planning. In January the President told the newspaper correspondents at Casablanca that "he and Churchill were determined to accept nothing less than unconditional surrender of Germany, Japan and Italy."[10] In Washington on March 17 the President told Secretary Hull and Mr. Eden that ". . . we should insist on total surrender with no commitments to the enemy as to what we would do or would not do. . . ."[11]

From time to time during the remainder of the war, weighty reasons were brought against this decision both from within U.S. and U.K. government circles and from outside. Its wisdom was questioned by General Eisenhower and I believe by most military authorities in the field. The tenacious adherence to it by the Allies throughout the war must be attributed first to the influence of President Roosevelt and second to that of Mr. Churchill. Premier Stalin's attitude, however, was significantly qualified:

"As a wartime measure Marshal Stalin questioned the advisability of the unconditional surrender principle with no definition of the exact terms which would be imposed upon Germany. He felt that to leave the principle of unconditional surrender unclarified merely served to unite the German people, whereas to draw up specific terms, no matter

[9] Sherwood, *op.cit.*, pp. 797-98. [10] *ibid.*, pp. 693-94.
[11] *ibid.*, p. 715.

how harsh, and tell the German people that this was what they would have to accept, would, in his opinion, hasten the day of German capitulation."[12]

M. Stalin is a ruthless man, but these reasoned judgments of his show more political understanding than is shown by the more dogmatic statements Roosevelt and Churchill reiterated during the war without heed to the weighty objections of men closer to the scene of action. The lives of many human beings hung on this decision: it surely ought at least to have been made, if at all, only after the fullest discussion with the many well qualified advisers to be found both in the capitals and on the field of battle.

In the present study it is not necessary and indeed would be irrelevant to follow all the ramifications of the demand for unconditional surrender. The importance of this demand from the point of view of the economic planning for the peace, however, was very great, for it removed much of the incentive, which would otherwise have been present, to hasten the preparation of plans for the postwar German order. If M. Stalin's desire to clarify the demand and "to draw up specific terms" had been fulfilled, Mr. Roosevelt and Mr. Churchill would have been obliged to give directions to civil servants at the end of 1943 to hasten the completion of plans for postwar Germany. In fact, however, the efforts of civil servants were frustrated by the refusal of the highest statesmen either to take the initiative themselves or to endorse the initiative which civil servants attempted to take. And so the months passed between the meeting at Teheran and the launching of the great offensive in Normandy. Then, at that late hour, in the words of Mr. Stimson and Mr. Bundy, ". . . as General Eisenhower's forces advanced towards the German border it became clear that the armies had outrun the policy makers."[13] The war was being won; the peace was in imminent danger of being lost.

At the beginning of 1944 the European Advisory Commission, provided for in the Moscow Protocol, was set up in London with Ambassador Winant as the United States representative. It was designed to take up a number of questions left undecided at the Moscow Conference. Its terms of reference did not confine it to questions con-

[12] *ibid.*, pp. 792-93.

[13] Henry L. Stimson and McGeorge Bundy, *On Active Service in Peace and War* (New York, Harper), 1947, p. 566.

cerning ex-enemy countries, but unanimous consent was required before it could take up "European questions concerning the termination of hostilities" and in practice its chief business was to prepare surrender terms and the machinery needed to fulfill them.[14]

There has been little public understanding of the work, the difficulties, and the accomplishments of the European Advisory Commission. Soon after the death of Ambassador Winant a number of wild rumors and myths grew up around the almost unknown history of the commission. Professor Philip E. Mosely has disposed of these in two authoritative articles which will be indispensable to future historians: his is the most important contribution yet made to the study of the formation of occupation policies.[15]

The misunderstandings have not been confined to the public: they can be found among writers who did not watch events wholly from the outside. It has been said by a number of writers, including a former highly placed diplomat, that the representatives on the EAC were not at a sufficiently high level. For example, Howard Zink, although appreciative of the accomplishments of the EAC, states that, "It had the disadvantage of being too low in political level to decide important issues itself and found that referring matters to four capitals for decision led to serious difficulties."[16] Mr. Zink's experience appears to have been mainly in the War Department. But the former diplomat might have been reasonably expected to be familiar with the workings of the governments of the Great Powers. This makes it all the more surprising that it could seriously be supposed that any single individual, no matter how highly placed in rank, could be given the authority to make decisions on his own responsibility, and without discussions with his government, on vital and far-reaching issues concerning the postwar disposition of Germany. Modern democratic governments do not function in that way. In Great Britain and France every vital issue of policy must be brought before the cabinet; in the

[14] The origin of these terms of reference is explained in Professor Mosely's illuminating article, "The Occupation of Germany: New Light on how the Zones were drawn," *Foreign Affairs*, July 1950, pp. 581-2. London wished to settle during the war many questions which Washington desired, for internal political reasons, to postpone until after the war. This was a fundamental issue which is discussed elsewhere in this study.

[15] *Foreign Affairs*, April and July 1950.

[16] Harold Zink, *Allied Military Government in Germany* (New York, Macmillan), 1947, p. 68.

United States, depending on the scope and nature of the issue, it may be decided by the President, but even when the approval of the legislature is not required immediately the President is hardly in a position in practice to ignore all his advisers, especially when his Secretary of State has a mind of his own. Thus it is inconceivable that any representatives, even the heads of states, could have been appointed to the EAC with a free hand in practice to make prompt personal decisions on the spot on the far-reaching issues of policy as they came up. Moreover, the records of the heads of state give rise to apprehension rather than confidence regarding the soundness of their judgment on policy towards Germany. As we have seen, President Roosevelt, encouraged by Sumner Welles, favored the drastic dismemberment of Germany. Mr. Churchill seems to have followed him in principle though not in method for some time. M. Stalin also independently followed the same course until the later stages of the war. In other respects, as will be seen later, mistakes were made by President Roosevelt, Mr. Churchill, and M. Stalin on German questions. If the heads of states had been free to follow their personal inclinations there is reason to believe that greater disasters would have occurred on German matters than those which actually did occur. Heads of states are fallible human beings, daily harassed by multitudinous cares, without time to study deeply questions that lie beyond the scope of their previous experience.

Some of these points apply to other high-ranking statesmen in the capitals of the great powers. If the Foreign Ministers or Secretaries of State had been the representatives on the EAC it is inconceivable that they could have taken decisions on the spur of the moment on a great number of important new issues without communication with their capitals. If this applies to the statesmen who are supposed to specialize in external affairs, how much more does it apply to other high-ranking statesmen, most of whom are ministers or secretaries of departments dealing chiefly with internal affairs.

In short, it is an illusion to suppose that a speedier or a sounder settlement of postwar German affairs could have been achieved by the appointment of any of the higher-ranking statesmen from the capitals of the great powers as representatives on the EAC or any other body to work out the details of a German settlement. There can be no short-cut which will by-pass internal machinery for consultation and for the formation of policy, by giving a free hand to any statesman, however eminent, to decide a mass of detailed controversial questions solely according to his personal opinions.[17] Not only is it unlikely that the effectiveness of the European Advisory Commission would have been greater if the representatives on it had been drawn from the "top level" at the Allied capitals, but in the last resort the main obstacle to greater accomplishments by the commission came from the indecisiveness of the heads of state and leading ministers on some of the issues relating to Germany and their stubbornness on others.

Secretary Hull's promising start at Moscow raised hopes that during 1944 rapid progress would be made toward the completion of plans for Germany. At Teheran a step backwards had been taken, but it was an indecisive step which might be reconsidered in the European Advisory Commission. However, it was obvious from the beginning that no progress could be made unless positive decisions were reached in the capitals of the three great powers on policy toward postwar German questions.

Within the State Department efforts were made to work out such a policy. After the Moscow conference the Interdivisional Committee on Germany began to consider the chief questions that seemed likely to come up on the EAC.[18] But the State Department was not the only department with a say in the formation of policy for the EAC, and a joint State, War, and Navy indepartmental committee was formed at the end of 1943 for this purpose. Thus the necessary machinery of government existed, with the important exception that there was no cabinet secretariat in Washington to see whether the machinery was working, and no War Cabinet to make it work if through negligence or ill will any of its members was obstructing the fulfillment of its functions. Lacking these safeguards, the working of the machinery depended on the foresight and good will of each of the departments whose cooperation was necessary. Unfortunately, the War Department, which was represented by its Civil Affairs Division, showed neither foresight nor good will in this enterprise.[19] Month after month went by, and the Civil Affairs Division refused to cooperate

[17] There have been similar misunderstandings regarding the Council of the Organization for European Economic Cooperation.

[18] Mosely, *op.cit.*, in *Foreign Affairs*, July 1950, p. 386.

[19] Mosely, *op.cit.*, *Foreign Affairs*. July 1950, pp. 583-96. This article is indispensable to students of recent international affairs.

with the State Department, blocked the transmission of instructions to Ambassador Winant, and brought the work of the EAC to a standstill for some time.

During this period I kept in touch with British officials who were working on the economic aspects of postwar German questions, and on several occasions I discussed with the Ambassador the need of informal economic discussions on Germany with the British and if possible the Russians, particularly on reparations. On one occasion I explained at length to the Ambassador the work that had been done in Whitehall on reparations and pointed out that as yet nothing comparable had been done on the United States side. The Ambassador had a clear recollection of the reparations muddle after the First World War; his inclination was to avoid reparations altogether after the Second. But he accepted my argument that there would inevitably be a strong demand for reparations from countries pillaged by the Germans, and that it was advisable to prepare and present reasonable reparations plans to forestall the unreasonable and impracticable schemes which the spokesmen for the devastated countries, particularly Russia, might advocate.

Unfortunately, the obstruction that came from the War Department blocked the political decisions on which the economic decisions had to be based. The future historian will look back in wonder on those times during which an outstanding American representative was appointed to an important post abroad on a commission which the United States had taken a leading part in establishing, and was left stranded without instructions on the policy that he should follow, without freedom to propose a policy of his own, and without a mandate to comment on the policies proposed by other member countries. The War Department officials were able to veto all the proposals formulated in the State Department.

In the first half of 1944 the division of Germany into zones of occupation was one of the chief tasks of the EAC. Economic planning could not go far until this task had been completed. But behind it lay fundamental decisions of principle.

In most of the literature on the subject, the principle of occupation by zones has been taken for granted, and no attention has been given to alternative forms of occupation. Actually, however, there were other possibilities, and the Foreign Office suggested a single Inter-

Allied occupation of the whole of Germany. Professor Mosely points out that, "The State Department planning group gave it serious consideration but felt that it could not support it in opposition to the unanimous military opinion."[20] The proposal also ran counter to Russian ideas. But its rejection left many questions open. If there were to be separate zones, and if there were to be as many administrative systems as there were zones, Allied policies would have to be unified through an Allied control body or each zone would be left to go its own way.

Again, if language, administrative systems, and the philosophy of law and of government in the Soviet Union were so unlike those in the Western countries that a unified occupation of the whole of Germany was impracticable, it did not follow that unification of the Western Zones was out of the question. The unification of the armies of the United States and the British Empire had been successfully achieved in Italy and was to be maintained in the invasion of Northwest Europe. There was a strong case for continuing into the postwar occupation of Germany the magnificent Anglo-American cooperation which was soon to carry the Allied armies to the borders of Germany. In January 1944 General Eisenhower saw President Roosevelt and expressed "objection to dividing Germany into national sectors." He admitted "the difficulties of true joint occupation but argued that the U.S. . . . should insist on that plan as the only practicable one."[21] Mr. Hull, who was Secretary of State at the time, and Captain Butcher have shown that General Eisenhower was "deeply convinced" and urged strongly in April 1944 that "the British and American zones should be combined in one Anglo-American zone of occupation." He pointed out that "to set up each zone with its own transportation and supply programs in separate American and British zones would be very confusing administratively."[22]

Here again the War Department view dominated the foreign policy of the United States. It was influenced by a number of factors. There seems to have been an underlying bureaucratic assumption that responsibility must be undivided and that if the army were to be re-

[20] Mosely, *op.cit.*, *Foreign Affairs*, July 1950, p. 589.

[21] Dwight D. Eisenhower, *Crusade in Europe* (New York, Doubleday), 1948, p. 218.

[22] *The Memoirs of Cordell Hull*, *op.cit.*, II, p. 1613. See also H. Butcher, *My Three Years with Eisenhower*, p. 545.

sponsible wholly or partially for the occupation of Germany it must be in complete control, in an administrative as well as in a military sense, of the area which it occupied. It must be remembered also that the desire for the closest working cooperation or integration with Allies was probably not widespread in the armed forces but rather resulted from the clear insight and the incisive leadership of General Marshall, General Eisenhower, and a small number of other far-sighted leaders. The traditional sentiment may well have remained close to the older and now obsolete view of General Pershing. But apart from these influences some circles in the Pentagon had theories of their own on foreign policy. It seems likely that Hajo Holborn gives a fairly accurate representation of the predominant views in the War Department at that time. Mr. Holborn, though "not representing the views of any government agency" in his book, "was favored by holding a front seat" in the War Department during the formation of the U.S. military government organization. He says:

". . . inevitable as combined Anglo-American operations were in the combat phase, the continuation of this arrangement would have severely limited the freedom of American policy in Germany and Europe. From the American point of view cooperation with Soviet Russia was as important as association with Britain. In certain respects the United States had to pay even greater attention to Russia. Allied military government of Germany was to become the first practical test of the ability of the United States and the Soviet Union to work together intimately in the practical solution of an intimate task of the first magnitude. To the Russians the future of Germany appeared as the foremost problem of their national security. Russia's attitude to American policies in the Far East and to American-Soviet cooperation in the development of a world-wide security organization was bound to be profoundly affected by the relations which Russian and American administrations would be able to establish in discharging a common mission. It was also to be expected that British and Russian policies would not be easily harmonized and that American policy would be unable to mediate between the two powers if American military government was not separated from that of the British . . . the creation of national zones in Germany was inevitable."[23]

[23] Hajo Holborn, *American Military Government* (Washington, Infantry Journal Press), 1947, pp. 23-24.

This is determinism with a vengeance! But such use of the term "inevitable" will hardly carry conviction. Neither combined Anglo-American operations during the war nor separate Anglo-American operations after it were inevitable in the sense that, no matter who controlled policy or who directed operations, the same decisions would have been made. In the First World War there were no combined Anglo-American operations and not even combined Anglo-French operations until late in the war, although the need for them was just as urgent then as at any time. In the Second World War there were many obstacles to combined operations not only among the Allies but also among the different United States armed services, and this disunity sometimes hindered operations in the Pacific and in Southeast Asia. Combined operations were nowhere inevitable and were achieved in the offensive Allied war operations in Europe only because far-sighted American and British military and civilian leaders set their wills against the forces of disunity. General Marshall and General Eisenhower had long studied the subject, even before the war, and had made up their minds that General Pershing's cardinal policy of separate command must be discarded. Their strength of character and understanding and the support of the great wartime President decided the issue on the American side. If others had occupied their places the outcome might have been very different. Nor was the dissolution of combined operations inevitable after the surrender. It was partly the result of the ideas and surmises of a group of men in the Pentagon. It was partly the result of the special political structure and traditions of the United States government, under which in wartime the military power and influence become much stronger in the counsels of government than they do in Great Britain or indeed in any country of the British Commonwealth.

The theories of external policy partly stated and partly implied in the passage from Mr. Holborn's study, and which were tenaciously held in War Department circles, notably in the Civil Affairs Division, rested on the foundation that agreement with the Soviet Union was more important than agreement with the United Kingdom and the British Commonwealth, and that where there were differences between the Russians and the British Washington should play the role of intermediary between London and Moscow and would be able to negotiate a middle position that would be acceptable to American as well as to British and Russian views. This theory was sometimes put forward outside the War Department. Occasionally it was advocated in political, though never in government circles in London, that Britain should play the role of intermediary between Moscow and Washington! I have a clear recollection of Senator Pepper of Florida, visiting London on a return journey from Moscow, and expressing scorn at the prediction, which he said he had heard from an Englishman, that Britain would be a go-between in disputes between the U.S. and the U.S.S.R. Not content with justifiably criticizing that prediction, he followed it with the opposite prediction that the United States would be the go-between among the three countries!

The attitude regarding the Soviet Union described by Mr. Holborn appears to have been held for a time not only in certain army circles in Washington but later by James Byrnes, who, when he became Secretary of State in 1945, seems to have started with a confident determination to reach agreement with the Soviet Union, and might have been prepared, as some War Department circles were prepared, to place British interests below Russian interests, if by so doing a "deal" could be made with the Soviet Union. It was, however, a singularly naïve attitude that showed inexperience in the ways of the Soviet Union. Russian favors were not to be won by sacrificing British interests unless the United States was ready to sacrifice its own interests as well—to say nothing of the shabbiness of ranking the Ally who made war voluntarily against aggression and held the fort alone in the decisive hour below the Ally who was forced into the war after having made terms with the enemy to share the spoils of aggression. International harmony cannot be achieved by bribing an obstreperous nation with concessions made at the expense of an orderly nation. The philosophy and practice of the governing minority in the Soviet Union were indeed remote from those either of the United Kingdom or the United States—so remote that the differences between the English-speaking peoples, real though they were, appeared small by comparison. What reason was there for believing that the Soviet Union would cooperate with the one while refusing to cooperate with the other? Our experience in London seemed to me to support the view that if the Soviet Union intended to cooperate with the West it would cooperate with both the United States and the United Kingdom, and if it intended to pursue a hostile and obstructionist line it would do so against both the United States and the United Kingdom. This and not any preference for one foreign country over another was the decisive issue.

It follows, also, that the contention in some Washington circles that the willingness of the Soviet Union to cooperate generally in international affairs would be "profoundly affected" by Russian-American relations in the military government of Germany, probably reverses the true sequence of events. An illustration cited by General Eisenhower could be supported by other experience with the Soviet Union. After describing a period when social visits were exchanged successfully between Americans and Russians in Berlin, General Eisenhower continues:

"We learned another lesson when at the Council of Foreign Ministers in London sharp official differences repeatedly developed between Secretary Byrnes and Mr. Molotov. Instantly a strained and stiff attitude became apparent among the Russians in Berlin. Red Army officers who had already accepted dinner invitations from Americans either sent their regrets or failed to keep the engagement. Formerly pleasant faces clouded up; it seemed that no Russian was any longer allowed to smile at or talk pleasantly with, an American."[24]

Later this attitude suddenly changed again. The conclusion, which is supported by experience in London, is that Soviet representatives in the field follow and do not lead the policy of the Kremlin. If they had been left to themselves or given sufficient leeway there is little doubt that most of them would have cooperated with the representatives of the U.S. and U.K. Everything depended on what was in the minds of the members of the Politbureau.

The basic decision in determining Germany's future was not the later decision to dissolve SHAEF but the initial decision to support the division of Germany into separate national zones, not only for stationing the Allied occupying troops, but also for economic and political administrative purposes. Once this decision had been taken, General Eisenhower had an uphill task in arguing against the dissolution of SHAEF after hostilities ceased. Not only in the War Department but in other parts of the government there were many who held that since agreement had been reached on occupation according to zones, the occupation would start badly if its first step were to be the

[24] Eisenhower, *op.cit.*, pp. 445-46.

creation of a common U.S.-U.K. zone which would appear to the Russians to be a "gang-up" against them.

It has been necessary to analyze these issues at this point in order to make clear that the pattern of occupation was set irrevocably by the beginning of 1944 in a way which presented formidable obstacles to economic planning and to economic reconstruction. In international affairs the early decisions in a long chain of operations are often the most difficult to analyze in retrospect, and there is still some detailed research waiting to be done by future historians on the origins of the zonal system.[25] Behind this lay an even earlier decision, whether taken consciously or adopted with little argument, that there should be an occupation for a considerable period. It would have been possible to make a case against it that would have deserved careful examination.

In the spring of 1944 some headway was made in the political work of the European Advisory Commission through direct communication with President Roosevelt by the Ambassador and his political adviser, Professor Mosely. But it was difficult to make headway on economic matters. Meanwhile, I arranged with the Ambassador to prepare a series of messages to Washington on the machinery which had been set up and the ideas which were developing in Whitehall on reparation and economic security. He hoped that these periodical statements of what was being done in London would serve to remind the State Department of what would have to be done in Washington. I had suggested, and he had heartily agreed, that informal discussions between British and American experts, similar to the Article VII discussions, should be held on reparation and economic security. Foreign Office officials agreed with this view and from then until the spring of 1945 I maintained regular discussions with them on the prospects. In Washington at the end of 1943 I had raised the question with State Department officials who shared an interest in German economic questions, but at that time insufficient progress seemed to have been made in Washington to justify the dispatch of a team to exchange views with British officials.[26]

In the first half of 1944 marked advances were made in the State Department in planning for postwar Germany. A committee composed of representatives from all the appropriate divisions within the depart-

[25] It is of little use to characterize a decision as a major error without suggesting an alternative approach, and in another chapter I have outlined an approach which seems to me to have been feasible. See pp. 196-99.

[26] On the political side much more had already been done.

ment examined the principles of postwar policy toward Germany and produced a document on the treatment of Germany which, in a carefully reasoned argument, opposed the forcible dismemberment of Germany, recommended decentralization of the future structure of German government where practicable, demilitarization, punishment of war criminals, control of education, and moderate reparations to the United Kingdom, the Soviet Union and some of the other allies. It stressed the importance of negotiating uniform policies with the other occupying countries to govern all the zones of occupation alike.

Unfortunately this represented only the policy of the State Department and not that of the United States government.

In addition to this memorandum on general policy toward postwar Germany, a document on reparation policy was prepared in the State Department and subsequently discussed by the Executive Committee on Economic Foreign Policy on which other departments were represented. It was a moderate and reasonable statement which was influenced by the ideas of Whitehall but which rejected Whitehall's suggestion that "contributions to peace keeping" should be paid by Germany after reparation had ended, to offset the economic advantage she would enjoy in being relieved of the cost of armaments. It provided for moderate reparation in kind, limited to a short period. In view of the attitude of the Foreign Economic Administration at a later stage it should be noticed that at this stage their representatives not only held moderate views, uninfluenced by the sentiment of revenge, but took the lead in opposing some of the quite moderate suggestions of Whitehall as being too severe.

Thus the State Department under Secretary Hull made a genuine attempt to prepare the outlines of a reasonable policy for postwar Germany. Whatever shortcomings it may have had, it stands in retrospect as the only department or agency in Washington of which this can be said. If the position which it had reached by the middle of 1944 had been approved by the White House and accepted as the foundation for a more detailed structure of postwar planning for Germany to follow, the history of the early occupation of Germany would have taken a very different course from that into which it was precipitated by other hands after July 1944.

Meanwhile, Ambassador Winant, lacking the sort of mandate which the State Department documents, if they had been United States government statements of policy, would have given him in his work on the European Advisory Commission, made marked progress in the work of delineating the zones and the Berlin sectors, and by August he set himself to assess the position and prospects of postwar planning on Germany. This gave me an opportunity to bring before him again in detail the urgency of the need for early informal discussions with Britain and the Soviet Union, or at least Britain, on the vital questions of reparation and economic security which would be likely to dominate the economic aspects of postwar policy toward Germany.[27] Professor Mosely has recently summarized the message sent by the Ambassador embodying his comprehensive estimate of the situation:

"In mid-August, in a telegram of some seven thousand words, Mr. Winant set before the President the position which had been reached in attempts to settle policy toward Germany. He pointed out that the EAC had reached agreement on the terms of German unconditional surrender, that it could complete the agreement on zones as soon as the assignment of the two Western zones was decided, and that there was good prospect that it could shortly complete an agreement concerning the future machinery of Allied control. These three agreements, he emphasized, would provide the machinery for dealing with Germany but would not supply the content of future policy towards Germany. He urged that every effort be made on the American side to go forward to negotiate the widest possible measure of agreed policies to be enforced jointly by the future occupying Powers. It was not enough to set up the machinery of joint Allied administration; every effort should be made to work out agreed Allied policies which this machinery should carry into effect.

"Mr. Winant went on to point out that the Russian need for material aid in repairing the vast destruction in the Soviet Union was bound to make the Soviet government particularly eager to receive reparations deliveries from Germany on a large scale. Since the major part of German industry was located in the western zones, the Allies must try to work out, in advance, a reparations policy which would satisfy a part of the Soviet demands without involving an undue burden for the United States. He urged that Washington hasten the formula-

[27] Ambassador Winant's chief adviser on EAC matters was Dr. Philip E. Mosely (now professor of international relations at Columbia University). My role was a limited one since obstacles in Washington prevented the EAC from taking up the central economic questions of reparation and economic security which I followed in the embassy and on which I kept in touch with the development of Whitehall's views.

tion of a reparations policy and then bend every effort toward reaching the earliest possible agreement with its Allies while the war was still in progress. He warned that it would be almost impossible to achieve such an agreement after the close of hostilities and that if no agreement had been reached on reparation the proposed system for the joint control in Germany would break down. Rivalry for control over Germany, he said, would rapidly follow. He urged that the United States consider ways of helping the recovery of the Soviet economy, such assistance to be linked to the achievement of a satisfactory settlement of the problem of German reparations and of the most important political issues between the two governments."

Thus the State Department papers approved in July by Secretary Hull and Winant's statesmanlike review and recommendations in the middle of August had laid down in the face of many obstacles an enlightened approach to postwar Germany which, if adopted, would have raised the credit of the United States in the world and helped to start all Europe on the road to early economic recovery.

Meantime, in Great Britain the "German country unit" of SHAEF, unable to obtain guidance from Washington and Downing Street in the preparations which it was charged to make for the duties of Allied Government in Germany after the end of hostilities, showed unusual initiative in going ahead with its plans as best it could, following constructive principles similar to those independently drawn up in the statement of the State Department on the treatment of Germany,[28] but in addition providing a plan for the administration of Germany and an operational handbook. The American and British officers, most of them drawn from civilian life and many of them with experience in German matters, worked with vigor and enthusiasm and would have formed a most valuable nucleus for military government in civilian matters.[29] Thus, in the military as in the civilian field, a promising start on sound lines was made.

However, it was just at this time, when enlightened counsels had been given and the correct course to follow had been clearly charted, that a catastrophe occurred which upset all previous calculations, undid the preparatory work, aroused bitter and prolonged controversy, and set back the prospects of future European reconstruction.

[28] See pp. 239-40.

[29] See especially Dale Clark, "Conflicts over Planning at Staff Headquarters," in Carl J. Friedrich and Associates, *American Experiences in Military Government in World War II*, pp. 211-37.

CHAPTER XIV

Disaster to Economic Planning on Germany

IN AUGUST 1944 Mr. Morgenthau arrived in London accompanied by Dr. Harry White. His first business had to do with finances and currency in areas liberated and areas about to be liberated. He had made journeys with this object before—it was on one of them that Dr. White and Mr. Keynes, on Ambassador Winant's initiative, had held their first meeting on the international monetary plans.

Earlier in the war and even before the United States entered it, Mr. Morgenthau had visited Britain more than once. His business had ranged from airplane engines to currency preparations for the invasion in North Africa. The Secretary of State at the time, Cordell Hull, had complained of Mr. Morgenthau's incursions into State Department fields. It is true that Mr. Morgenthau ranged far beyond the legitimate domains of the Treasury. But some of his efforts in fields that, in a departmental sense, were none of his business, had been inspired by disinterested zeal in a good cause, had shown foresight and accurate judgment, and had borne good fruit. This applies to his work on airplane output and airplane engines. On other matters in which his department had a legitimate but not exclusive concern he had shown more vigor, more imaginative insight, and more enlightened generosity toward gallant Allies than some of his colleagues in the administration.

Thus the condemnation of some of Mr. Morgenthau's subsequent activities which is expressed in the following pages arises not from personal prejudice or lack of appreciation of the many valuable services which he rendered in the Allied cause. On the contrary, I can regard it only as a tragedy that one who did so much on so many issues on the side of the children of light should have injured his record by siding with the children of darkness on another great issue directly affecting the lives and well-being of millions of people. The recording angel will have difficulties with Mr. Morgenthau's record.

When his earlier business was completed, Mr. Morgenthau invited Ambassador Winant to the country house in Wiltshire where he was staying during his visit to Great Britain. He suggested that the Ambassador should bring with him his advisers on German questions. The Ambassador requested me to accompany him, along with Dr. Philip Mosely, his trusted political adviser on European Advisory Commission matters, and Walter Radius of the State Department, an expert on questions of transport and communication. On a bright Sunday in August during the period of flying bombs over London we drove through the countryside beyond Andover to a country house with large grounds. Mr. Morgenthau was awaiting us with Dr. Harry White and a number of Treasury staff members, including one who had been attached to the Army planning group in London.

Soon after our arrival we sat down to luncheon, and a few minutes later Mr. Morgenthau called on me to begin the discussion with an account of British views on the treatment of Germany after the war. I had no inkling of his views then or throughout the luncheon—nor, as far as I am aware, had any of my colleagues. Knowing the catholicity of his interests and his inclination to extend his operations as far as possible over the field of his interests, I took it for granted that, having contributed greatly to the advanced stage reached in preparations for the establishment of the International Monetary Fund and the International Bank, he was looking for additional fields of postwar economic reconstruction to conquer. In view of the anxiety which I had felt and had expressed to the Ambassador concerning the slowness of ministers in London and Washington to give concerted attention to the economic policy to be followed toward Germany after the war, this at first gave me more hope than alarm. Some of us disagreed with Mr. Morgenthau and Dr. White on particular points regarding the Fund and the Bank, but all of us were bound to acknowledge that their great energy, taken in conjunction with that of Mr. Keynes, was the most important single reason for the progress already made. It would be all to the good if similar, though at times more tactful energy were put into the formation of a sound postwar economic policy towards Germany.

My account of the development of Whitehall's views on the economic aspects of postwar Germany followed the lines already described,[1] though in much more detail. A question put by Mr. Morgenthau at the end had significance that was not apparent to me at the time. He asked whether in my opinion the British were likely, in spite of the horrors of the war, to forget and forgive speedily after it was over. I expressed the opinion that the British were not a vengeful people. After further questions and a purely descriptive summing up by Dr. Harry White, the party broke up with the understanding that it would reunite at three o'clock.

During the adjournment, Dr. Mosely and I held a discussion in the grounds with Dr. Harry White on the documents prepared in Washington regarding the treatment of Germany and reparation and economic security.[2] Mr. Morgenthau apparently knew nothing of them. When Dr. Mosely asked Dr. White whether he had read them, the latter replied that he had not but that he believed that copies had been placed among his papers just before he left Washington. He went back to the house and after a search returned with the documents. Mosely expounded the papers in detail. White made no adverse comment at any point and maintained a most agreeable attitude throughout our talk. There was nothing to indicate that up to this time he had studied the subject or formulated even the bare outlines of any "plan" on it.

In the afternoon the group reassembled, and we listened to the first exposition of the Morgenthau "plan." The discussion took place in bright August sunshine, on the wide lawn which surrounded the house. As we lounged on the grass Mr. Morgenthau in brief, simple terms expounded his views on what to do with Germany. In substance they were as follows: He feared that both the British and many Americans favored a "soft peace." This attitude had in the past led to the Second World War and would lead to a third if it were accepted again. The only way to prevent a third war was to make it impossible for Germany ever to wage war again. This could be done only by destroying her economic as well as her military capacity to wage a modern war. He did not believe that after 10 or 20 years the peoples in the Allied countries would remain willing to use force to prevent Germany from building another war machine. The only hope was to cripple Germany economically and deprive her for as long as possible of the power to take aggressive action again.

[1] See above, pp. 218-24.

[2] See above, pp. 239-40.

The way to accomplish this was to destroy German industries and convert Germany into a pastoral country. As long as she was without an industrial machine Germany could not wage war. Though there was little likelihood that the American people would be willing to keep troops long in Germany or to enforce sanctions against Germany for many years, the destruction of German industry would cripple for a long time Germany's power to rearm.

Chaos in Germany was inevitable and the Germans must be made to understand that they alone were responsible for it and that they could not expect any help whatever from outside in reconstruction. The occupying forces were there to teach the Germans that they were a defeated and conquered people. There must be no nonsense like the WPA program for Germany which the SHAEF planners in military government had been preparing.

There must be no fraternization of American troops with the Germans in any form. American and British troops were generally inclined to fraternize in any area which they were occupying, and strict directives would have to be enforced to prevent fraternization from occurring after this war.

The British would be in a very difficult position after the war. The loss of their foreign investments would force them to increase their exports greatly if their standard of living was not to go down disastrously. The destruction of German industries would enable them to take over Germany's former export markets.

Such was the substance of Mr. Morgenthau's "plan" as it was expounded by Mr. Morgenthau and Dr. White. Mr. Morgenthau expressed his ideas less systematically than they are summarized here, but Dr. White followed him later and brought sequence and interconnection into them. My impression at the time was that Dr. White had given little serious thought to the question before Mr. Morgenthau expressed his views at the afternoon meeting. This would not have been surprising in view of his immense labors and responsibilities on a variety of questions during the war.

Whatever might be thought of the opinions of Mr. Morgenthau, it was impossible to deny the resourcefulness of Dr. White in mastering the main points of the interdepartmental committee's report just before the meeting, and in transforming the Secretary's sketchy and spasmodic exposition of his views into a clear, amplified, and well-organized restatement composed in fifteen minutes after Mr. Morgenthau had finished speaking, and coming as nearly as possible to clothing a bad thesis with an appearance of intellectual respectability. Dr. White's arguments, however, were effectively challenged by Dr. Mosely at certain points.

In the course of the discussion the likelihood of postwar inflation in Germany was discussed. Mr. Morgenthau and two of his advisers held that since the Germans were responsible for bringing on inflation in the occupied areas, they should be given a taste of their own medicine and the occupying powers should have no responsibility for financial reconstruction.

Mr. Morgenthau then revealed the main purpose of the meeting. After expressing alarm at what he misleadingly described as the policy for a WPA in Germany (which he alleged that a SHAEF group were preparing), he asked what policy was being formed by the European Advisory Commission.

Ambassador Winant had quickly perceived that an inter-agency row was in the making. He was greatly concerned about the effects which it might have on the prospects of confirmation by the White House of the agreements already reached on the European Advisory Commission. Knowing that Mr. Morgenthau was frequently with the President, he was anxious to avoid premature involvement in a controversial issue just about to be joined and which, if it were not carefully handled in London at this stage, might spill over into the fields of discussion on which substantial progress had already been made in the EAC.

The Ambassador, therefore, at the outset confined himself to clearing up a misapprehension which Mr. Morgenthau was not alone in entertaining. The EAC, he pointed out, was a body of representatives of the U.S.A., the U.K., and the U.S.S.R. which had been set up to negotiate tripartite agreement on a common policy among its members toward surrender terms and the initial objectives and organization of the occupation. The representatives on EAC, however, did not individually formulate the policies on which they attempted to obtain agreement. The policies were formed by the governments of each of the countries which took part in the work of the organization, and the representatives negotiated on the basis of these policies. Obviously such far-reaching questions as those concerning surrender and occupation arrangements would not be left to three individuals but must be passed on by the whole machinery of government to the highest levels. Washington was clearly the place in which to raise questions regarding the national policy to be adopted by the United States.

Clearly the Ambassador was on firm ground in taking this position, not only for these reasons but also for another reason of which he was acutely conscious but which it would hardly have been appropriate to state. He was responsible to and received his instructions from the President and the Secretary of State in matters relating to negotiations on policy toward Germany, and he would not have been acting in accordance with his responsibilities if he had entered into an argument in London with the Secretary of the Treasury on these matters which were the subject of contemporary negotiations with the other countries concerned and of discussions within the administration in Washington.

Nevertheless, he took care not to associate himself in any way with Mr. Morgenthau's views, and at one point he turned to Mr. Morgenthau and Dr. White to ask them not to express to Mr. Eden certain views which they had expressed at the meeting.

Though we left no doubt of our dissent from the Morgenthau approach, the surprise and displeasure of the advisers to Ambassador Winant could not be fully expressed during the discussion because of the difficult position in which the Ambassador, through his position on the European Advisory Council, was placed. Moreover, the nature of Morgenthau's arguments discouraged attempts at serious analysis. When, after we returned to the house, Mr. Morgenthau asserted that Germany should be converted into a purely agricultural country I remarked that aside from other aspects of the questions such a change was impossible because of the ratio of population to cultivable land. His rejoinder was that the surplus population should be dumped into North Africa! Such a discussion was not worth pursuing.

The day after the meeting the Ambassador expressed concern to me over Morgenthau's intervention in postwar German questions. On most matters, he said, it was possible to reason calmly with Morgenthau and White. But they were so deeply aroused over the unprovoked aggression and the horrifying crimes of the Germans in occupied countries that they were not open to reason when it came to postwar German questions. In his opinion a major conflict was in the making in Washington and would have international effects. As we have seen, he was anxious first of all to consolidate the gains already made in negotiations on the European Advisory Council, and hoped that the row would not break out in full force until the White House had confirmed the results of past negotiations. He did not believe that he could exert any useful influence by becoming involved at that stage in the personal conflicts that were about to begin. This did not mean that he would not take a strong position on specific issues of principle. The record will show his stand against later instructions that reflected some of the influences of Morgenthau's intervention in Washington. But he saw at once that the outcome lay with President Roosevelt. Intensely admiring the President and serving him with unsparing energy and devotion, he yet recognized that on postwar Germany Roosevelt's attitude had so far been doubtful. It was this which stood in the way of a prompt overruling of Morgenthau in his self-appointed role of arbiter on United States policy toward postwar Germany. Unfortunately, the Ambassador's role in the war effort kept him—except during occasional visits—thousands of miles from Roosevelt during the war, while Mr. Morgenthau was a constant visitor to the White House. Indeed it was not until the President was returning from Yalta at the beginning of the next year that Winant was able again to speak directly to him on Germany.[8]

In the few days following this meeting Mr. Morgenthau and Dr. White carried their ideas into British circles, notably in a conversation with the Foreign Secretary. From what I have been able to gather they modified none of the points they had stated to us, even though Mr. Morgenthau had not contested some of our criticisms of these points. Mr. Hull in his memoirs has referred to the surprise that Mr. Morgenthau expressed later when Mr. Eden, arriving in Quebec to be confronted with a copy of the memorandum on the Morgenthau plan dictated by Mr. Churchill and initialled by him and by the President, made a heated protest. Mr. Morgenthau said that the Foreign Secretary had not spoken against his plan when he had expounded it to him in London.

The reason why Mr. Eden made little comment when Mr. Morgenthau visited him in London to explain his plan seems simple enough. Mr. Eden was naturally embarrassed when the United States Secretary of the Treasury approached him, unknown to the

[8] See p. 205.

United States Secretary of State, to urge on him a violently controversial plan on a matter which lay within the province of the Secretary of State but on which Mr. Morgenthau had not consulted any cabinet officer or member of the administration in Washington, nor even informed any of them that he intended to approach the Foreign Secretary on it. Mr. Eden was aware that any definite statement he made might be repeated, correctly or incorrectly, in Washington. On such major questions he could not afford to enter into negotiations impromptu and through unauthorized channels. If he had assented to Morgenthau's ideas his remarks would have been triumphantly quoted to President Roosevelt or Secretary Hull. If he had attacked Morgenthau's views he might have been held up to denunciation in Washington and his statements might have been misrepresented to the President as those of the SHAEF group had been. The Secretary of the Treasury's questions to me had revealed suspicion that the United Kingdom would take a "soft" attitude toward Germany once the heat of combat had passed. Mr. Eden, like Ambassador Winant, was experienced enough to keep out of premature and futile controversy with unauthorized and self-appointed spokesmen coming out of Washington.

On returning to Washington, Mr. Morgenthau began his attempt to give a harsh turn to American policy toward Germany. His opportunities of meeting the President informally gave him an advantage over the principal cabinet officers in whose department German affairs belonged far more than they did in the Treasury. From the memoirs of former Secretaries Hull, Stimson, and Morgenthau the reader can now follow for himself in considerable detail the developments that took place in Washington before and after and during the Quebec Conference.[4] It is a sorry story. As the accounts came through to the embassy from both British and American sources we were at first incredulous, then dismayed, and finally filled with apprehension for the future.

The first definite step at the top level in Washington came with the appointment by the President of a "Cabinet Committee on Germany," consisting of Hull, Stimson, Morgenthau, and Hopkins. This appears to have originated in a suggestion to the President on August 25 by Secretary Stimson, who was seriously concerned

[4] See especially *The Memoirs of Cordell Hull*; Stimson and Bundy, *On Active Service in Peace and War*; Sherwood, *Roosevelt and Hopkins*.

over the lack of preparation for dealing with German questions just at the time when the troops were entering Germany.[5]

A preliminary meeting of the deputies of the three secretaries and Mr. Hopkins took place on September 2. Dr. Harry White presented a "Morgenthau plan" which included most of the points outlined earlier by Mr. Morgenthau to us in London, but added some drastic territorial provisions designed not only to strip Germany of certain areas on the west and east but also to dismember the rest of Germany into "two autonomous independent states" and an "International Zone" to include the Ruhr and adjacent industrial areas, and to be governed by the United Nations, which was not then in existence. No trade was to be permitted between the "International Zone" and the two independent German states! All of the areas would be stripped of manufacturing industry, and Germany would supply compulsory labor in the devastated countries.[6] The policing and administration of Germany would be carried out mainly by the continental European Allies, and U.S. troops would soon be withdrawn.

To these provisions the following was added, referring to the Ruhr and surrounding industrial areas:

"This area should not only be stripped of all presently existing industries but so weakened and controlled that it cannot in the foreseeable future become an industrial area—all industrial plants and equipment not destroyed by military action shall either be completely dismantled or removed from the area or completely destroyed, all equipment should be removed from the mines and the mines shall be thoroughly wrecked."[7]

If this recommendation of large scale looting and destruction seems incredible to some readers I should add that typewritten copies of the statement still exist in the State Department and elsewhere. Although Mr. Hull and Mr. Stimson have published such illuminating discussions of the meetings of the Cabinet Committee that it is unnecessary to add much here, there is one point which may not have been as clear to them as it was to those of us who had

[5] Stimson and Bundy, *op.cit.*, p. 569.

[6] See especially *The Memoirs of Cordell Hull*, II, p. 1605.

[7] Quoted in *ibid.*, II, p. 1605. The random variation of tenses is evidence of the hasty way in which this "plan" was prepared. According to an oral account I have heard, the whole document was prepared in 48 hours.

listened to Mr. Morgenthau in London. Both the proposal to loot the Ruhr and the proposal that the Soviet Union and the continental European Allies should police and administer Germany were based partly on Mr. Morgenthau's estimate of the future attitude of the American people. In talking to us in London, the Secretary of the Treasury clearly asserted his disbelief in the willingness of the American people either to keep troops in Germany beyond a very brief period or to cooperate with other countries to prevent future aggression. It does not therefore appear to me wholly accurate to ascribe Mr. Morgenthau's advocacy of looting and destruction to the simple desire for revenge alone. One important aim behind the recommendation to loot and destroy is missed unless it is realized that in this way Mr. Morgenthau hoped to delay for some years the resurgence of and renewed aggression by Germany—an aggression which he despaired of preventing by civilized means.

The meeting of deputies on September 2 broke up in complete disagreement except on one proposal, that a State Department official should perform the impossible task of drawing up "a further memorandum attempting to reconcile the views of the three departments, which the Secretaries of State, Treasury, and War might be willing to sign and submit to the President as their recommendation."[8]

On September 5, the Cabinet Committee met but the principals were no more able to agree than the deputies had been. Accounts of this meeting have been published by both Mr. Hull and Mr. Stimson.[9] They do not coincide precisely, but the outlines are clear enough. The Morgenthau plan has already been described. Secretary Hull presented a memorandum of which some account is given in both Hull's and Stimson's memoirs.[10] It followed some of the provisions of the State Department document on the treatment of Germany which had been agreed on in July,[11] but added others not found in that document. It opposed forcible partition of Germany and recommended decentralization in the future structure of German government, demilitarization of Germany, punishment of war criminals, control of education, and reparations to the U.K., the U.S.S.R., and

[8] *ibid.*, II, p. 1607.

[9] *ibid.*, II, pp. 1608-09: Stimson and Bundy, *op.cit.*, pp. 569-73.

[10] *The Memoirs of Cordell Hull, op.cit.*, II, pp. 1608-09: Stimson and Bundy, *op.cit.*, pp. 570-71.

[11] See pp. 239-40.

some of the other Allies. Its attitude on German industry, however, seems to have been ambiguous. It disclaimed the idea of making Germany a purely agricultural country, and urged that the German economy should be made dependent on foreign trade. But it recommended that German living standards should be "held down to subsistence levels" and that "Germany's economic position of power in Europe must be eliminated."[12]

It is not brought out in any of the writings of the principals concerned in these discussions that not only the position taken by Mr. Morgenthau but also that taken by Mr. Hull differed from the attitude and recommendations in the documents produced by civil servants in Washington—chiefly in the State Department—to which I have already referred.[13] It would seem that Mr. Hull dictated the main points to a member of his staff and that the provision to hold down the German standard of living to a "subsistence level" and possibly also the provision to eliminate "Germany's economic position of power in Europe" were his personal ideas and not those of his advisers in the State Department.

It is difficult to reconstruct from the available evidence Mr. Hull's precise attitude on the future of German industry. When Mr. Stimson, in a memorandum to the President, stated that, "The position frankly taken by some of my colleagues was that the great industrial regions of Germany known as the Saar and the Ruhr with their very important deposits of coal and ore should be totally transformed into a nonindustrialized area of agricultural land,"[14] he seems to have had in mind Mr. Hull as well as Mr. Morgenthau. To keep Germany at "subsistence level" and to eliminate her "economic position of power in Europe" certainly would seem to necessitate a considerable measure of "deindustrialization."

To make confusion worse confounded, Mr. Hopkins, according to Mr. Stimson's account,[15] advocated the prohibition of steel production in the Ruhr and the Saar. If the prohibition of any single product could destroy the whole structure of industry in the Ruhr it would be that of steel.

The next day the Cabinet Committee met the President. Mr. Hull seems to have moved close to Mr. Stimson's position, but Mr. Mor-

[12] Stimson and Bundy, *op.cit.*, p. 571.
[13] See pp. 239-40.
[14] Stimson and Bundy, *op.cit.*, p. 571.
[15] *ibid.*, p. 570.

genthau had not budged and the meeting ended without agreement and without decisions.

Thus, at a time when an important conference was to begin at Quebec in a few days, when the Allied armies were entering Germany, and when enemy resistance in Europe might collapse at any time, the President had not made up his mind on what should be done with Germany after the war, and the four highly placed advisers whom he had designated to help him were hopelessly divided. One of them wished to wreck Germany's industries and flood her mines, a second wished to prohibit her from manufacturing her most essential industrial material, a third wished to eliminate her economic power and keep her people at a subsistence level, and a fourth was left to struggle for a humane and statesmanlike attitude. With such hopelessly divided counsels, producing a medley of conflicting opinions and advice, the great wartime President, ill and harassed with many cares, left for Quebec with the sounds of domestic discord in his ear and without the semblance of a firm position on which he might stand in his talks with the British Prime Minister.

The astonishing developments at the Quebec conference have been made known to the public in brief outline, though there are no doubt many details to be filled in later. The document on Germany which came out of the conference was brief—and disastrous. After referring to the convertibility of the metallurgical, chemical, and electrical industries and the devastation in Allied countries, it declared that these industries "in the Ruhr and the Saar would . . . be necessarily put out of action and closed down." The damaged Allied countries would take the machinery to repair their own losses. The Ruhr and the Saar would be put under an international body which would prevent any revival of the industries. The document concluded by stating that the program "is looking forward to converting Germany into a country primarily agricultural and pastoral in its character" and that, "The Prime Minister and the President were in agreement" on it.[16]

In retrospect, the actions of the President and the Prime Minister seem almost incredible, as indeed they appeared to us in London at the time. It seems likely that the atrocious misdeeds of the Germans under Hitler had aroused in the President a sense of horror and a sharp resentment that led him to favor strong measures to

[16] *ibid.*, pp. 576-77, *The Memoirs of Cordell Hull, op.cit.*, II, p. 1610.

prevent a revival of German aggression; that in his preoccupation with matters requiring immediate decisions he had not reflected deeply on the most practicable methods of reaching this aim; and that in his preoccupation with the vital war decisions made at Quebec he carelessly initialled an outrageous document without grasping its implications and its political repercussions. His subsequent remark to Mr. Stimson that "Henry Morgenthau pulled a boner"[17] undoubtedly represents his mature judgment. Whatever his feelings toward Germany may have been, his political judgment would never have allowed him to accept after careful reflection a proposal at once indefensible from a moral and disastrous from a technical standpoint.

The strong opposition aroused in London and Washington by the news of what had happened in Quebec quickly led to the repudiation of the memorandum by President Roosevelt. The responsible officials in the Foreign Office were aroused and the Foreign Secretary promptly flew to Quebec, indignantly denounced the Morgenthau plan and hotly attacked Mr. Churchill for having fallen in with it, pointing out that the Cabinet had given no mandate for such an action. "Anthony stands up to the P.M.," the Ambassador—who held both of them in high regard—remarked to me. A quiet mannered man generally, the Foreign Secretary would not be browbeaten, as some of the other ministers were at times, by Mr. Churchill.

But President Roosevelt was not the only lost sheep at Quebec. Mr. Churchill cut a poor figure there in the light of what he had said before and what he has said since the war as well as on the merits of the question. At the time it seemed almost unbelievable to us in the embassy in London and also to the British Foreign Office, that he could have not only initialled but even dictated the memorandum drawn up at Quebec, which, indeed, but for the eminence of its original sponsors and the gravity of the issues would have deserved to rank as a bad joke.

If it seems difficult to explain Mr. Churchill's actions we must turn to another purpose of his visit to Quebec. Whitehall had impressed on the cabinet the necessity of American assistance to deal with the precarious position of the U.K. balance of payments which would arise when Lend-Lease ended at the close of the war. The

[17] Stimson and Bundy, *op.cit.*, p. 581.

cabinet had agreed that the Prime Minister should take this up with the President at Quebec in the hope of obtaining an extension of American aid in a suitable form for a period after the war long enough to enable Britain to increase its exports, and perhaps reduce its imports, to the extent needed to reach a new equilibrium in its international transactions.

In much of the gossip that followed the Quebec Conference it was suggested, and is still widely believed in the United States, that Mr. Churchill, who began by sharply opposing Mr. Morgenthau's views on Germany, changed his attitude in the hope that by doing so he would increase the chances that Mr. Morgenthau would use his influence with the President in favor of extensive aid in the solution of the U.K. balance of payments problem.[18]

Although it may be readily agreed that the Prime Minister's actions were consistent with this hypothesis, I remain skeptical of its accuracy. In fairness to Mr. Morgenthau it must be said that, so far as I am aware, there is no evidence that in his dealings with the United Kingdom he was in the habit of threatening to use his influence to make aid in emergencies dependent on the willingness of the British to accept his views on other political issues. Some time after the controversy over Germany had begun, an able British treasury official, who took part in many negotiations with the U.S. Treasury, told me that Whitehall remembered and appreciated that Mr. Morgenthau had always upheld the fullest aid to Britain even when he had sharp differences with the British government on other issues. At no time, the official added, had Mr. Morgenthau attempted to use British necessities as a means of compelling Britain to accept his ideas of policy on matters unrelated to U.S. aid. Certainly in our meeting with him in early August 1944, Mr. Morgenthau said nothing suggestive of a wish to blackmail the British into accepting his plan on Germany.

A different and, as I think, a more reasonable explanation of Mr. Churchill's change of position at Quebec was given to me in London at the time by a British official. It is that after Mr. Churchill's initial rejection of his plan Mr. Morgenthau persuaded Lord Cher-

[18] This view has been widely accepted in uncritical fashion. As an example see Samuel Flagg Bemis, *A Diplomatic History of the United States*, 3rd edn. (New York, Henry Holt), 1950, p. 889; also *The United States as a World Power* (New York, Henry Holt), 1950, p. 418.

well, who had accompanied Mr. Churchill to Quebec, that by removing future competition from Germany in export markets, the "plan" offered the only way in which Britain could increase its exports sufficiently to restore its balance of payments. Lord Cherwell is said to have embraced this argument with enthusiasm and in turn to have converted Mr. Churchill to it.[19]

Lord Cherwell was a physical scientist of uncommon ability who had gained the confidence of the British Prime Minister by his achievements in the application of science to warfare and his skill in expounding relevant scientific developments.[20] He was an adviser at the right hand of Mr. Churchill and doubtless gave sound advice on many matters. But at times he strayed far from the fields of his studies and experience and gave advice to the Prime Minister which went counter to the views of more qualified advisers in Whitehall. In London, Lord Cherwell's own secretariat contained an outstanding Oxford economist, who unfortunately was not present at the Quebec Conference.

Thus at Quebec the heads of state, instead of seeking the advice of well-qualified Britons and Americans, some with a knowledge of Germany and others with a knowledge of international economics and perhaps a few with both, followed the advice of a physical scientist and a politically appointed head of a department who, though men of ability in some fields, had neither the equipment nor the temper, when left alone, to give sound advice on one of the most difficult of all postwar economic and political questions. It was indeed to the lasting credit of Mr. Morgenthau that he recognized, far more than any of his colleagues in the administration, except the President and Mr. Stimson, the magnitude and urgency of Britain's postwar needs. But in propounding a harsh policy toward Germany as a remedy for the difficulties of Britain he succeeded only in diverting attention away from the needs of Britain to the

[19] See Stimson, *op.cit.*, p. 526: "It appeared . . . that Mr. Churchill had been converted by the argument that the elimination of the Ruhr would create new markets for Britain. . . ." A more detailed account is given in Secretary Hull's memoirs, describing Mr. Morgenthau's own statement to the Cabinet Committee after the Quebec Conference: "He said that Mr. Churchill had at first been violently opposed to the Morgenthau policy towards Germany. . . . Morgenthau said he then took up the subject with Lord Cherwell . . . and apparently convinced him. Cherwell discussed it with Churchill and won him over." (*Memoirs of Cordell Hull*, p. 1615)

[20] See Winston Churchill, *The Gathering Storm*, Boston, Houghton Mifflin Co. pp. 150-151, 234, 468.

problem of postwar Germany, and, with others at home and abroad, in well-nigh drawing Germany and with it continental Europe into a common ruin.

The lamentable mistakes of President Roosevelt, Mr. Churchill, Mr. Morgenthau, and Lord Cherwell at Quebec have again and again brought to my mind the remarks of a leading British civil servant who, earlier in 1944, had privately expressed to me his fears and those of his colleagues that British ministers might go off by themselves and make foolish decisions on policy regarding German economic questions. With a few exceptions, neither British ministers nor American secretaries of departments had made the study and gained the experience necessary to form a competent judgment and draw up a statesmanlike policy on the economic future of Germany. In quiet times of peace, ministers might have prepared themselves to deal with this great and intricate question—but during the fiercest conflict the world has ever known, harassed by a thousand cares, worked to the verge of exhaustion, they never brought themselves to a calm, thoroughgoing analysis of all that was involved in the question. It was all the more important, therefore, that they should heed the advice and study the conclusions of the groups of temporary and permanent civil servants who had carefully examined the issues and after months of deliberation had drawn up reports containing recommendations on them.

Yet at Quebec no use was made of the work of advisers by the heads of State. The labors of highly qualified officials, given to this subject—notwithstanding the demands of other urgent subjects—out of a well-founded belief in its intrinsic importance in determining the results of the war, were either ignored or cast away overnight and replaced by technically amateurish and morally indefensible substitutes.

CHAPTER XV

JCS 1067 and All That

THE blocking of all attempts to obtain agreement in Washington and between Washington and the Allies on the reparation and economic security was the next disaster that overtook attempts to plan for postwar Germany. The efforts of Whitehall to prepare a policy had begun early, and the State Department had followed later. The informal conversations which I had carried on with leading Foreign Office and Treasury officials had often turned to the question what reparation demands were likely to be made by the Soviet Union and how we should meet them. Although in my earliest conversations with the Ambassador, he had shown distaste for reparations, fearing that it would tend to disorganize rather than to reconstruct the postwar world, his keen sense of politics had led him to accept the argument that the immense damage done on Soviet and other Allied territories would make it impossible to obtain Allied agreement to wipe the slate clean. And in 1944, we had in London a growing knowledge of Russian attitudes, through the UNRRA committees, the European Advisory Commission, and ad hoc negotiations on other matters. We thus learned Russian attitudes not only toward the enemy but also toward the Allied countries in which resistance to the enemy had appeared to the Russians to be weak, and it became clear that large demands would be made by the Soviet Union upon the ex-enemy countries. If Russian ideas on how relief should be distributed[1] were any criterion of the quality of their ideas on how reparation should be made, we might expect the greatest difficulty in reaching agreement. If the time consumed in reaching agreement on the simpler relief question was any indication of the time that would be required to reach agreement on the much more complicated reparation question, little opportunity remained even early in 1944 to reach agreement by the end of the war.

The wanton and unprovoked German attacks on peaceful countries, and the destruction and oppression which followed, were ample

[1] See pp. 160-61.

justification, on grounds of equity, for the demands of the Soviet Union and other European Allies for reparation, but past experience had shown that if such demands were excessive in amount and ill-considered in method they would hinder instead of advancing the economic reconstruction of the world. Unfortunately, the representatives of injured and suffering peoples, in the heat of their resentment against the source of their injuries and suffering, were all too likely to carry their demands too far and into the wrong channels. Consequently, the only prudent strategy for the United States and the United Kingdom was to take the initiative and put forward as the first item in a discussion of reparation a plan of their own which would attempt to meet the reasonable claims of devastated Allied territories as far as was compatible with general economic recovery in both Allied and ex-enemy countries. For in an interdependent world economic order you cannot distinguish between one country and another, retarding recovery here, hastening it there, in accordance with a scheme of rewards and punishments. To attempt it is to invite a common retardation in which suffering will be widely distributed with little regard to deserts. And in 1944 the Allied air arm was spreading devastation in German cities on a hitherto unknown scale: it was unlikely, therefore, that the abstract case in equity for making those who destroy responsible for repairs could be applied to a defeated enemy on whom even greater destruction had been heaped than he had been able to inflict on his earlier victims. Never was there greater need for initiative by Britain and the United States to persuade the Allies to accept a well-considered and moderate plan.

Ambassador Winant, impressed with the dangers of delay, gave an important place to reparation questions in his comprehensive message to the President in August 1944. He placed the issue in a broad setting and linked it with the question of economic aid for Russian reconstruction and the outstanding postwar political issues between the Soviet Union and the West.[2] He held that the best procedure for discussing the form and content of reparation was to arrange first a meeting of British, Russian, and American experts which might take place in Moscow if it seemed that better cooperation could be secured there from the Soviet Union. These experts

[2] See pp. 241-42.

might constitute a subcommittee of the European Advisory Commission, which had been understood from the time of the Moscow Conference to be the appropriate body to discuss reparation questions.

Secretary Hull and the State Department, in accordance with the understanding reached at the Moscow Conference, had accepted the European Advisory Commission as the proper body on which to carry out negotiations on German matters. But the conclusion is inescapable that this part of the Moscow agreement was never really accepted or even understood in the War Department or in the White House. Even when the Soviet Union was ready to expedite negotiations on EAC, the War Department and the White House on several occasions held the EAC at a standstill. At a time when the question whether or not the Soviet Union would cooperate with the West after the war hung in the balance, the example set by the United States, through no fault of the State Department or Ambassador Winant, was discouraging.

So far as I have been able to ascertain, Mr. Churchill was hardly more helpful than President Roosevelt on EAC matters. But Mr. Eden and the Foreign Office, like Secretary Hull and the State Department, did their best to make the EAC work. The form of government in Great Britain gives less play for the indulgence of whims either by the Prime Minister at one end of the scale or by irresponsible members of Parliament at the other, than the form of government of the United States gives to the President at one end and to irresponsible congressmen at the other.

Following the Morgenthau affair, I continued my messages concerning the work and opinions of Whitehall officials on Germany, reporting their opposition to destructive measures such as Mr. Morgenthau had proposed. Ambassador Massigli, the French Ambassador to Britain, in a conversation with Mr. Eden, tentatively raised the question whether parts of Western Germany should be placed under a *régime spéciale.* Foreign Office officials feared that the French suggestions might be a camouflage for the partition of Germany, but they adopted an attitude of inquiry and pointed out to me that, whatever ultimate motives the French might have, at least they did not seek to destroy the economic structure of Germany but rather to preserve the productive power of the Ruhr for the benefit of all Europe. For this reason the French proposals, while ultimately unacceptable in the form in which they were put forward, might serve for a time as a useful counterweight to the Morgenthau plan.

These evidences of mounting French interest in the economic as well as the political future of Germany made it all the more important to start informal conversations as soon as possible on the fundamental postwar economic issues concerning ex-enemy countries. During the autumn negotiations went on which brought the French into the EAC by the middle of November. Thus the stage was set for informal discussion of German economic issues.

But the players never appeared on the stage.

Secretary Hull admirably stated the case for proceeding without delay to complete plans through established international channels in cooperation with the United Kingdom and the Soviet Union:

"We have thus far . . . acted on the basis that every action followed with respect to Germany, particularly in the post-hostilities period, would be on an agreed tripartite basis. It has also been our understanding that the Soviet government has also acted on this general assumption, and of course the European Advisory Commission, established by the Moscow Conference, was set up for the purpose of working out the problems of the treatment of Germany. We must realize that the adoption of any other basis of procedure would enormously increase the difficulties and responsibilities of our soldiers in the immediate military occupation period but also of our officials in the control period following. . . .

". . . Our information up to the present has been to the effect that the British government no doubt has ideas of its own with respect to the application of economic controls to Germany, and we have not yet had any indication that the British government would be in favor of complete eradication of German industrial productive capacity in the Ruhr and Saar. We have no ideas as yet what the Soviet government has in mind. Would it not be well at this time for the State Department to sound out the British and Russian views on the treatment of German industry either through the European Advisory Commission or otherwise?"[8]

Unfortunately, President Roosevelt, after realizing his mistake at Quebec, instead of examining the contending and irreconcilable views which had been urged on him, and deciding which of them or what

[8] *The Memoirs of Cordell Hull*, *op.cit.*, II, pp. 1616-17.

combination of them, or what alternative views, should be adopted as United States policy, turned away entirely from all planning for the future of Germany. The sands were running out. The German military organization was falling apart. The structure of Nazi domination was crumbling at its foundation. Yet the President replied to Mr. Hull's statesmanlike request that he did not think "that in the present stage any good purpose would be served by having the State Department or any other Department sound out the British and Russian views on the treatment of German industry. Most certainly it should not be taken up with the European Advisory Commission which, in a case like this, is on a tertiary and not even a secondary level. . . ."[4]

The President's extraordinary ignorance of the terms of reference of the EAC is difficult to explain. The EAC was of course created by the Foreign Ministers of the Big Three at Moscow. Can it be that Roosevelt's—and at times, I believe, Churchill's—indifference and confusion on the subject were due to a preference for carrying on foreign policy in personal meetings of the heads of state and a subconscious reluctance to sanction vigorous initiative from "lower levels"?

However, the central error lay in the President's refusal to countenance any conversations with our chief Allies. In the embassy we believed—as the State Department and the Foreign Office believed—that the EAC was obviously, by the terms of the Moscow agreement, the proper channel for the discussions. But if agreement could have been more quickly obtained to carry them on through other channels we should have welcomed such an opportunity. Above all, speed and initiative were essential. We dreaded leaving the initiative to the Allies which had been most damaged by the Germans and which were, in consequence, least likely to put forward at the start a moderate and workable plan as the basis for discussion.

A clue to President Roosevelt's action may be found in the evidence we have on the origins of a memorandum signed by the President a few days after his note to Secretary Hull. Professor Mosely refers to it as follows:

". . . an F.D.R. memorandum, *elicited by the Civil Affairs Division*, put a complete stop to postwar planning for Germany and even

[4] *ibid.*, pp. 1619-20.

placed in question the U.S. draft directives which had already been cleared in Washington and circulated to the EAC. Although Mr. Winant was in America in late October, he apparently was told nothing of this decision, which cut the ground completely from under the EAC and from under the policy which he had advocated so forcefully on every possible occasion and particularly in his long telegram of mid-August to the President. The momentum which the EAC had been building up was halted. Progress was not resumed until the beginning of April, 1945, when time was already running out."[5]

Thus the order to "stop planning" and to avoid even informal discussions with the British was instigated by the Civil Affairs Division of the War Department and was not the result of spontaneous initiative by the President. For the second time Roosevelt carelessly signed papers placed before him during great pressure of business.

It was not long before our fears concerning reparation were, unfortunately, justified. When the Yalta Conference opened on February 3, 1945, neither the United States nor the United Kingdom had any concrete policy on reparation and economic security, nor had they exchanged ideas among themselves, nor had either of them exchanged ideas with the Soviet Union. To my mind the unreadiness of Britain was even less excusable than that of the United States. Britain's experts on German economic matters were more experienced and qualified than American experts, and, under the eye of the Foreign Office and the War Cabinet Secretariat, their work had been much better organized than the work in Washington. Nor had they been victims of a "cease planning" order as their American counterparts had been. Yet Mr. Eden had to admit to M. Molotov at Yalta that while "the British had studied the German matter at the technical level . . . the War Cabinet had not discussed it."[6] For more than two years previously studies and suggestions by competent civil servants had been waiting cabinet consideration!

Postwar planners had always to face the danger that a complicated postwar question would be thrown suddenly into a top-level meeting

[5] Philip E. Mosely, "The Occupation of Germany, *Foreign Affairs*, Vol. 28, No. 4, July 1950, p. 597. The italics are mine.

[6] E. R. Stettinius, *Roosevelt and the Russians: The Yalta Conference* (New York, Doubleday), 1949, p. 119.

without preliminary investigation and exchanges of ideas among officials who had studied it in detail. Even when qualified officials had studied and reported on a controversial question, there was no assurance that the top level would not plunge into a discussion of the question at an international meeting without knowledge of the studies and without seeking the advice of those who had made them.

So it was at Yalta.

When M. Stalin claimed large-scale reparations in kind, both the President and the Prime Minister, according to Mr. Sherwood, ". . . said that public opinion in their countries was opposed to the whole concept of reparations in view of the unfortunate results of the Treaty of Versailles."[7] Presumably this is based on the late Mr. Hopkins's notes. The more detailed though still incomplete account in the late Mr. Stettinius's work shows that the Soviet Union always had the initiative and that Roosevelt and Churchill were continuously on the defensive. Mr. Eden launched a counterattack. Apparently British advisers, though they had been unable to get a hearing from ministers on this subject for over two years nevertheless succeeded in warning them at the conference against the crude and staggering Russian demands. The most detailed Russian statement came from Mr. Maisky, who advocated removals of "factories, heavy machinery, machine tools, rolling stock, and investments abroad" from German ownership. German industry should be reduced by 80 per cent! Here the Russians rivalled Mr. Morgenthau. Reparations in kind were to be paid over ten years. Reparation to the Soviet Union alone should amount to $10,000 millions.[8]

This was followed later by a Russian document in which it was proposed to fix total reparation at $20,000 millions, the Soviet Union to receive half this amount.[9]

These figures were opposed by the British delegation and at first by President Roosevelt. It was then suggested that they were to be taken only as a basis for discussion by a proposed Reparation Commission which was to meet in Moscow. The outcome of the controversy illustrates sharply the marked difference between the British and American forms of government. Notwithstanding the absence of both the Prime Minister and the Foreign Secretary in Yalta, a stream of

[7] Sherwood, *op.cit.*, p. 861.
[8] Stettinius, *op.cit.*, pp. 130-32.
[9] *ibid.*, p. 105.

detailed messages passed between the British delegation and London, and the cabinet discussed the issues that had been raised. It decided that the British delegation should not agree to the naming of any reparations figures even as a basis for discussion. Mr. Churchill and Mr. Eden adhered to that decision throughout the conference, and at one stage M. Stalin actually accepted a draft without any figures. But he receded from this position, apparently under pressure from his advisers, and raised the question again. The President had no cabinet to guide or control him. He was inclined to agree with the British view but late in the Conference he weakened and accepted the advice given in a note passed to him by Mr. Hopkins, reproduced by Mr. Sherwood:

"The Russians have given in so much at this Conference that I don't think we should let them down. Let the British disagree if they want to—and continue their disagreement at Moscow. Simply say it is all referred to the Reparations Commission with the minutes to show the British disagree about any mention of the ten billion."[10]

The President agreed, but Mr. Churchill and Mr. Eden, bound by a cabinet decision made during their absence, firmly adhered to their reservation against any reference to the amount of reparation. This and other examples could be cited to show the fundamental misconception of the British form of government that underlay Mr. Hopkins's jocular remarks at a dinner during the Teheran Conference ". . . telling the Russians that he had made a long and thorough study of the British Constitution, which is unwritten, and the War cabinet, whose authority and composition are not specifically defined. He said that as a result of this study he had learned that 'the provisions of the British Constitution and the powers of the War Cabinet are just whatever Winston Churchill wants them to be at any moment.' "[11] It is one of the great strengths of the British form of government that this interpretation was wholly wrong.

The figures inserted in the Protocol returned to plague Washington later. Top-level negotiations were so infrequent that those who took part in them were apt to overlook pitfalls with which humbler representatives sitting on working committees with the Russians were all too familiar. Before reassuring themselves that the mention of this amount did not commit them to anything, the President and Mr. Hop-

[10] *ibid.*, p. 860.

[11] *ibid.*, p. 793.

kins might have asked themselves why the Russians were so desperately anxious that the figures should be inserted in the Protocol.[12] In any case, it is no light matter to bind a commission in advance to start from a particular basis of discussion: inevitably the initiative goes to the negotiators who proposed that basis. Washington's interests were certainly closer to London's than to Moscow's in regard to reparations. The danger of a late upsurge of sympathy for a country many of whose proposals have been successively rejected at a conference was very real at international gatherings up to the time when Russian intransigence was carried to such extremes that all but the satellite countries became thoroughly alienated.[13] It was not confined to American delegations: for a time the French were markedly susceptible to it. The sentiment behind it was often worthy of respect, but after witnessing many international discussions I believe that in international affairs the wise rule, with rare exceptions, is to vote according to the intrinsic merits of each issue.

The formal repudiation of the Morgenthau plan by President Roosevelt was far from ending the controversy or repairing the damage that had been done. The State Department might be prohibited from entering into the proposed informal Inter-Allied discussions on the economic future of Germany which, in the judgment of Secretary Hull and the State Department, of Ambassador Winant and his advisers on the one hand, and of the Foreign Office on the other, were necessary if the Allies were to be ready for the peace. But work had to go forward on the preparation of a directive to the Commander-in-Chief who was to bear the responsibility for governing the United States zone and who would have to represent the United

12 This is not to imply that anxiety on the part of a Soviet representative to obtain acceptance of what might appear to be an innocuous form of words was always evidence of sinister intentions. In some cases it was due merely to a desire to show something to his superiors when he had been given rigid instructions to press for acceptance of a Soviet demand. In these cases it was sometimes good policy to accept such innocuous additions. But this situation could not arise at a top-level meeting.

13 The present writer and his colleagues encountered it in extreme form throughout 1946 during the negotiations to establish the International Refugee Organization, when it was necessary to organize as far as possible the defeat of 75 hostile amendments proposed by the Soviet Union and Yugoslavia. Late at nights there was a particular danger that some representatives would relax and say in effect, "We have knocked them down so many times today: cannot we let them have this one?"

States on the Allied Control Council after hostilities ceased. As long as the War Department and the State Department were the principal departments concerned in the preparation of the directive, a reasonable agreement was in sight. But after the Cabinet Committee had been set up, and especially after the Quebec Conference, Mr. Morgenthau succeeded in placing the Treasury in a prominent position in the discussions on the directive, and the discord which had split the Cabinet Committee was carried into the group of deputies who were charged to prepare the directive. The Treasury representatives made aggressive and pertinacious efforts to put the Morgenthau plan into effect through the directive. In this way they hoped partly to offset their defeat on the Ruhr issue by imposing their destructive policy on the U.S. zone. After the President had repudiated the Morgenthau plan the meetings on the directive reached a complete deadlock. Clearly, no genuine compromise was possible between such inherently incompatible and even contradictory views as those held by the Treasury on the one hand and the State and War Departments on the other. No intelligible and consistent policy could be adopted unless one side or the other was overruled and a choice made between a destructive and a constructive policy.

The President seems never to have faced and weighed these alternatives. According to an oral account which I heard at the time, the renewed deadlock was brought to his notice after his repudiation of the document which he and Mr. Churchill had initialled at Quebec. But instead of dealing with the issues behind the deadlock, the President is said to have impatiently brushed aside the matter, exclaiming that he would not tolerate such disunity among his advisers and that members of the Cabinet Committee must "get together."

The outcome of this refusal to arbitrate was the notorious "basic directive," JCS 1067, which was supposed to guide the United States occupying forces in the initial period of occupation. It was a pseudo-compromise containing elements of irreconcilable viewpoints inharmoniously blended to produce the greatest confusion among the greatest number. It may well rank among the most discreditable state documents ever written. The real authorship of some sentences is clearly traceable to Mr. Morgenthau and his aides, that of others to the representatives of the State and War Departments. The sentence "Germany will not be occupied for the purpose of liberation but as a defeated enemy nation" might have been taken from Mr. Morgenthau's remarks in London. It is followed immediately, however, by the sentence, "Your aim is not oppression. . . ." But by no means all the destructive sentences were offset to some extent by contradicting them or providing a loophole of at least temporary escape. Even where a loophole was left it was often a vague and ambiguous one which timid administrators might fear to adopt though their more courageous colleagues would make the most of it. Thus administration would be uneven and fluctuating.

The chief loopholes of escape from the worse provisions of the directive lay in the vagueness of the "Basic Objectives of Military Government." The drafting of these supposed "objectives" was disorganized, loose, and rambling.[14] It was stated that the principal objective was "to prevent Germany from ever again becoming a threat to the peace of the world." This of course was capable of innumerable interpretations. Some details were specified—"the elimination of Nazism and militarism" and other such obvious measures. But the phrase "industrial disarmament" was dangerously ambiguous. The loose drafting of this section had far-reaching effects because of the many later clauses in the directive which permitted or exhorted the Commander-in-Chief to carry out certain measures to the extent necessary to achieve the "basic objectives." Fortunately, the ambiguity was to prove useful to the more enlightened administrators.

The most deplorable and subsequently the most anachronistic provision was that which directed the Commander-in-Chief to "take no steps (a) looking towards the economic rehabilitation of Germany, or (b) designed to maintain or strengthen the German economy." This might indeed be modified if "necessary" to carry out the "basic objectives." But an administrator would be at his wit's ends to see how to relate such vague general objectives to the question of economic rehabilitation and the effect was disastrously negative, as we shall see in a later chapter.

The financial clauses were in the same strain. At the outset they directed the Commander-in-Chief to "take no steps designed to maintain, strengthen or operate the German financial structure except in so far as may be necessary for the purposes specified in this di-

[14] Part I Section 4. It is not clear whether sections a and b are supposed to be "basic objectives" or whether they are merely exhortations to administrators.

rective."[15] Naturally the Treasury exerted a particularly strong influence on this section of the directive, and as the financial administration would be headed by officers who were really Treasury officials transferred temporarily to the army and in frequent communication with Mr. Morgenthau, financial policy was predestined to be, in its earlier stages at least, an instrument of revenge and not of reconstruction. American and British taxpayers are still paying for the consequences of this early and major error of the peace.

The efforts of the State Department officials who, though they were placed at a great disadvantage after the retirement of Secretary Hull, did what they could to combat the influence of the Treasury, were not all lost. The confused and inconsistent nature of the directive left openings through which intelligent administrators could, and later did, avoid the full application of the worst clauses. Forced into a defensive position, a few able officials, notably H. Freeman Matthews, to some extent mitigated, though they could not escape completely, the consequences of the failure of the President to rule decisively on the differences which could not be resolved by his advisers.

When Mr. Hull retired, early in October 1944, the State Department ceased to be an important influence on the determination of policy towards postwar Germany. Mr. Sherwood has related the circumstances which determined the selection of Mr. Hull's successor. "Roosevelt was going to be his own Secretary of State, particularly in direct dealings with Churchill and Stalin. . . ." With this object in view, Hopkins advised against another suggested nominee on the ground that the latter ". . . was not one to conform placidly to the role of a mere mouthpiece."[16] Thus the criterion on which the appointment was made destroyed all chance that President Roosevelt's lack of understanding and foresight on postwar Germany might be at least partly remedied by the initiative of a Secretary of State who would see the breakers ahead and insist that the ship's course should be changed. Consequently, the State Department played a negligible role on policy toward Germany at a critical stage during and immediately after the war.

The War Department embodied the most baffling contradictions. Of all the members of the Roosevelt cabinet, Secretary Stimson held the most enlightened, the most statesmanlike, and the most

[15] Part III, par. 44.

[16] Sherwood, *op.cit.*, p. 835.

humane views on German matters. But the record of the Secretary of War and the record of the War Department on policy toward Germany were not one and indivisible. Any historian who assumed that as Mr. Stimson preached, so all the administrative officials of the War Department practiced, would miss an essential part of the history of American policy toward Germany. Both Sumner Welles, with his policy of dismemberment, and Mr. Morgenthau, with his policy of revenge, had their counterparts within the vast organization whose intricacies are symbolized by the interior of the Pentagon Building. Early in the history of the European Advisory Council, a high-ranking officer privately argued with me that as long as Germany remained a unitary state periodical world conflicts were inevitable. He may not have influenced the formation of policy on the question, but he did represent a viewpoint held in some circles in the War Department. More important was the presence of persons in the War Department who sympathized with Mr. Morgenthau's views and played an active role in shaping the detailed application of policy. They, and others who were unduly concerned with jurisdictional matters, influenced the Civil Affairs Division in directions that hindered the efforts of others to plan comprehensively, and turned important segments of the planning into wrong channels. More things go on inside the Pentagon than are ever dreamed of by Secretaries of War or Defense.

The effects of the bitter controversies in Washington were quickly felt in London, both in the embassy and in U.S. military circles. There was no longer any hope of a response to the Ambassador's comprehensive telegram sent in mid-August.[17] The refusal or inability of the leading statesmen to give early attention to the postwar treatment of Germany destroyed the chances, which otherwise would have been favorable, of an early Anglo-American agreement in detail on the postwar economic measures to be applied to Germany during the period of occupation. For economic plans could not be made in complete abstraction from political plans. As to international monetary organization, it was possible to proceed on the assumption that the nations would share a common desire for stable world economic conditions. As to trade, it was possible to proceed on the assumption that there would be agreement on the need for expansion of

[17] See pp. 241-42.

both the production and the exchange of goods. But as to the postwar German economic order there could be no common assumptions until it had been decided whether to suppress or to reconstruct, whether to exact penalties or to draw a veil over the past, or what intermediate course to follow. London and particularly Washington were rent apart from within on fundamental questions, and the heads of state, who had gone far toward the adoption of disastrous expedients from which they were rescued only with difficulty, instead of using the authority and supplying the initiative to break the deadlocks, fluctuated uncertainly in their own views and ignored their most qualified advisers.

Mr. Churchill's record appears little better than the President's. Both on dismemberment and on the economic treatment of Germany he appears at several meetings to have taken positions neither then nor later sanctioned by the cabinet. It is a curious commentary that the views, apparently improvised hastily, which he adopted on those occasions, were concerned with the very same subjects on which the British civil servants were unavailingly attempting to get the ear of the cabinet, and on which they were in constant dread that the Ministers of the Crown would commit serious errors through making "snap" decisions without taking advice.

Though Mr. Churchill's actions contributed to the muddle over Germany, it must be admitted that London had a better record than Washington on postwar German matters. But the credit for this should go mainly to civil servants rather than to ministers, to Whitehall and not to 10 Downing Street. Among ministers, however, Mr. Eden and Mr. Richard Law maintained a firm and intelligent position, once Mr. Eden had dropped support for dismemberment, which I do not believe to have ever been favored by Foreign Office officials. Unfortunately, while the organization set up under the War Cabinet ensured both initiative and coordination on German matters among civil servants in the appropriate departments, the disagreement and lack of foresight and interest in the cabinet itself spoiled the chances of British leadership among the Allies. Great as a war premier, Mr. Churchill lacked both an interest in and a clear insight into postwar economic and social matters.

Though the hope of preliminary Inter-Allied conversations on German economic matters was deferred for many months after the

Quebec meeting, steps were taken in Washington to undertake certain studies on Germany for internal use. Before the end of September 1944 a letter from the White House charged the administrator of the Foreign Economic Administration to organize studies "from the economic standpoint of what should be done after the surrender of Germany to control its power and capacity to make war in the future." This work was to assist in the task of "seeing to it that Germany does not become a menace again to succeeding generations."[18]

Such terms of reference, which were obviously influenced by the Morgenthau plan, pushed the FEA studies into purely negative channels. During the interdepartmental discussions on reparation in the Executive Committee on Economic Foreign Policy, the FEA had taken an even more moderate position than the State Department: its representatives had insisted on limiting reparations to a very short period and had opposed acceptance of the U.K. suggestion that after ten years annual payments should be made by Germany to offset partly her economic advantage in having no armaments to maintain. But the influence of the FEA was subsequently thrown on the opposite side, and some of the committees which it set up rivalled the Treasury in destructive recommendations.

The bitter internal controversies which Secretary Morgenthau had started in Washington soon spread to American Army circles abroad and disrupted the constructive work of the past. Dale Clark says:

". . . a group of officials in the Treasury and others near the Secretary of the Treasury had actively participated in the military government planning to the point where officials in the State Department and officers in the Civil Affairs Division, War Department, were complaining of the necessity for clearing papers with the Treasury. A former Treasury official who occupied a key position as Director of the Finance Division of SHAEF was commonly referred to in London as a Treasury representative in uniform. Contact with his former chief, the Secretary of the Treasury, and thence to the White House, gave him a pronounced advantage in negotiations in England. . . .

". . . to put into effect the military and foreign policy sponsored by the Secretary of the Treasury it was necessary to secure the rejection of the draft directives prepared by the European Advisory Coun-

[18] From paragraph 7 of letter of September 28, 1944, from President Roosevelt to Leo Crowley.

cil. The planning done by SHAEF's German Country Unit and of its successor, the U.S. Group Control Council, was largely discarded. . . ."[19]

[19] Dale Clark, "Conflicts over Planning at Staff Headquarters," in Carl J. Friedrich and Associates, *American Experiences in Military Government in World War II* (New York, Rhinehart), 1948, pp. 224-25.

CHAPTER XVI

Reparation or "Deindustrialization"?

When the war ended in Europe, the Allies of 1945 were no more prepared to deal with the thorny and difficult problem of reparations than the Allies of 1918 had been at the end of the First World War. No plans or policies on reparation had been agreed on among the Allies or even by the governments of the United States and the United Kingdom. The Reparations Commission provided for in the Yalta Agreement had not even begun its work. Washington was still unprepared with a clear, well-thought-out policy, embodying a consensus among the appropriate government departments and studied and approved at top levels. Apart from the earnest but unsuccessful efforts of small groups of civil servants in London and Washington, and the strong recommendations in Ambassador Winant's telegrams to Washington, more than five years of wartime opportunities to plan for this vital issue of the peace had been thrown away. As we have seen, Washington's inaction had prevented discussion of reparation on the European Advisory Commission and had frustrated our desire in London to arrange preliminary informal talks in 1943 and 1944 between British and American and, if possible also French and Russian, experts to clear the ground for final negotiations at political levels.

In the winter of 1944-1945, despairing of any initiative in Washington, I tried to impress on Lord Keynes the desperate need of initiative among British ministers in the preparation of reasonable plans on reparation and other German economic questions. This appeared to me to be a far more important subject at the time than Bretton Woods and its aftermath, to which Keynes had given so great a proportion of his energies, and I hoped that Keynes would use his influence in the right direction. But this time he was not only unresponsive; he was perverse. His attitude was defeatist, and, while admitting that there was a muddle, he spoke as if it were a hopeless muddle, and as if nothing could be done about it. The Morgenthau plan was wrong, of course, he said, but even the Morgenthau policy, if pursued consistently, might have been less harmful than the existing hodgepodge which was neither one thing nor the other but a confused blend of inconsistent ideas.[1] Now the position was hopeless. I dissented strongly, and, though our cordial personal relations were unbroken, we remained in flat disagreement on this question.[2]

When the Russians took the initiative and at Yalta broke the prolonged inaction with their abrupt demands for immense reparations, the Western Allies were placed at a lasting disadvantage in negotiations on the question.

Although it had been agreed at Yalta that a Reparations Commission, composed of British, American and Russian representatives should be set up in Moscow, the Commission had not met and its work had not begun when the war ended in Europe. It was not until the war was drawing to a close in March 1945 that the United States component of the commission was set up. At first the way was open for cooperation between it and the State Department and the United States representative and staff on the European Advisory Commission.

But the work on reparation and the policy adopted by the United States component of the Allied Reparation Commission developed independently of the work of the United States component of the European Advisory Council. The reparation group was appointed by the White House, and Edwin Pauley, who was placed at its head after President Roosevelt's death, paid little attention either to the State Department or to the United States group on the European Advisory Council. Contrary to the intention at the Moscow meeting of Foreign Ministers in 1943, reparation was now wholly severed from the EAC. The lack of leadership in the State Department in these critical earlier months of 1945 was a disaster. Repara-

[1] History may have appeared to him to be repeating itself. Austin Robinson, in his illuminating essay, "John Maynard Keynes" (*Economic Journal*, March 1947, p. 24) states that, "He had certainly said more than once in my hearing that the fault of Versailles was that it had failed either to be sufficiently Carthaginian or sufficiently liberal."

[2] On one occasion, in giving me an account of a dinner meeting with Bernard Baruch, who was visiting London, he commented on Mr. Baruch's cordiality and added with a twinkle, "He seemed to have almost forgiven me for writing a book." This was a reference, of course, to the famous *Economic Consequences of the Peace*. Mr. Baruch in 1919 had deplored, not only Keynes' book but also his resignation, apparently on the ground that it would not have been too late to save the situation. For a fair discussion of this question see Austin Robinson, *op.cit.*, p. 19-25.

tion, if it was to be made, was bound to affect the whole economic order in Germany and it was unwise to place the formation of U.S. policy on it in the hands of a new and separate group which pursued its own way with little attention to other groups which had worked on German questions for some time and were still working on aspects of German economic matters other than reparation.

A striking illustration of the disorganization in Washington on German matters arose over the question when the U.S. and U.K. delegations should go to Moscow to begin the discussions provided for in the Yalta agreement. A sharp difference had arisen with the Soviet Union over the question whether France should be admitted to the discussions. Since France had suffered severely from German aggression and was represented on the European Advisory Commission, the State Department and the Foreign Office strongly held that she should be represented on the Reparation Commission at Moscow. Ambassador Winant asked me at this time to take up with the Foreign Office a request he had received from the State Department to endeavor to obtain British agreement not to send the U.K. delegation to Moscow until this issue had been settled. The State Department officials feared that if the U.S. and U.K. delegations went to Moscow without previous understanding on the issue there would be no hope of getting the U.S.S.R. to agree to the admission of France. At the Foreign Office I reached an understanding with Mr. (now Sir) Reginald Hall Patch that the British delegation would not leave London until I informed the Foreign Office that the State Department considered the time had come to do so. A few weeks later, when no change had occurred in the U.S.S.R. position on France, the Ambassador asked me to deal with another telegram which he had received from Washington stating that the U.S. reparations group was leaving for Moscow in a few days, and asking blandly what the British group was doing and when it intended to go to Moscow! The first message had come from the State Department and the second from Edwin C. Pauley. From the beginning, Mr. Pauley considered himself to be responsible directly to President Truman. At least in the early months he seems to have habitually bypassed the State Department. After a time this became public knowledge: it added to the existing confusion and lowered further the prestige of the State Department.

The complicated question of restitution of property looted by the enemy or which had changed hands through enemy action was another economic issue thrown into confusion by the dualism in the practice of foreign policy on reparations which followed Mr. Pauley's appointment.[3] In London we had the earliest acquaintance with this subject when an Inter-Allied committee, on which I sat as U.S. representative, was set up in June 1942 and produced the Allied declaration of non-recognition of forced transfers of property.[4] It was understood later that the subject would be dealt with by the European Advisory Commission.[5] The State Department considered, even after the reparation group had been set up, that restitution should remain within the EAC. Working members of the reparation staff under Mr. Pauley expressed themselves in London as satisfied with this arrangement. But Mr. Pauley himself, after he had gone on to continental Europe, seems to have made a direct and successful appeal to President Truman that restitution should be transferred from the European Advisory Commission staff to the reparation group. Actually, of course, there was no close connection between restitution and reparation. When a looted object had been destroyed completely, restitution might, on one interpretation, consist in the transfer of a similar object in compensation if one were available. But a large part of restitution consisted in highly technical legal questions concerning ownership and transfer, involving the European Allies and neutrals. It was above all desirable that machinery should be set up to deal with this promptly, since the longer the delay the more difficult it was to trace the looted objects—many of which had crossed national boundaries—and the more complicated became the legal questions involved. The Foreign Office held that a separate administrative organization should be established to deal with restitution. They pointed out that the decision after the First World War to place the administration of restitution in the hands of the Reparations Commission had delayed action on restitution

[3] In a formal sense, of course, all external matters are the responsibility of the President, and the Secretary of State is merely an adviser to the President. But in practice it would be impossible for a President, even if he wished to do so, to pass on the countless issues in external policy that arise from day to day and on most of which he has no experience or knowledge.

[4] See p. 160.

[5] Since it involved all the European Allies it could not be disposed of by the members of EAC alone. But provision had been made in the terms of reference of the EAC to set up appropriate machinery to consult and reach agreements with the other European Allies.

until it became extraordinarily difficult to trace, to prove the origin, and to provide for the return of stolen property. Ambassador Winant and his advisers on the European Advisory Council agreed with this viewpoint, and an informal paper on restitution had already been placed before the EAC for early discussion when all previous arrangements were overturned by Mr. Pauley's action. The only result was to delay progress.

In the preparations for the peace no subject was more bungled than that of reparation. In seeking an explanation we must consider not only the nature of the machinery for the formation of policy but also the ideas in the minds of those who framed the policy. To those at the top level in the governments concerned, reparation was one question out of very many competing questions, and it was far from being a leading question, except perhaps to M. Stalin. They had no time to examine it fully and were always prone to make snap judgments. But the impulses of President Roosevelt and Mr. Churchill were undoubtedly humanitarian, and they both believed that the attempt to exact reparation after the First World War had been a disaster which they had no desire to repeat after the Second. At Yalta the President seems to have been reluctant at the start to consider reparations at all.[6] Neither the President nor the Prime Minister seemed well acquainted with the views of his advisers. There is no reason to suppose that the President ever desired reparation to be used as an instrument for revenge or for ulterior purposes. He seems to have been concerned most of all to stave off extravagant Russian claims.

The reparation measures drawn up after the Second World War were shaped largely by motives that had little to do with reparation. The Soviet Union was genuinely interested in reparation. France, though she was kept out of the reparation discussions, was anxious to obtain coal but was more concerned that priorities for exports over domestic consumption should be enforced on Germany than that the coal should be delivered free. The doctrinal basis of the measure finally drawn up may be found in the belief, first, that reparations "in money"—that is, in periodic payments by Germany that might be used to purchase goods in Germany at the discretion of the receiving country or to purchase other currencies to buy goods

[6] Sherwood, *Roosevelt and Hopkins, op.cit.*, p. 861-62.

elsewhere—were chiefly responsible for the failure of reparations after the First World War and must be avoided after the Second; next, that if reparations were made only in specified quantities of goods, currency and exchange difficulties would be avoided;[7] and, finally that the goods assigned to reparations should be mainly producer goods dismantled from German factories.

The idea that reparations in kind avoided all financial and exchange difficulties seems to have been carelessly adopted without careful consultation with experts who had thoroughly studied the experience of the 1920's. An idea which had a strictly limited application was elevated into a dogma. In the present machinery of government, this has frequently happened, especially in the stress of wartime, when the leading statesmen are called on to make rapid decisions on a variety of matters in a short time. An adviser or a group of advisers state a proposition or an idea and carefully qualify it in detail. The statesman, who has other matters urgently awaiting attention, remembers and later acts on the opening proposition but forgets, if he ever grasped, the qualifications and limitations. Thus are great affairs of State sometimes disposed of.[8]

To explain the origin of the third aspect of reparation policy it is necessary to go beyond reparation. There were two aims behind the idea of stripping Germany of capital equipment. One was to make reparation for the capital equipment destroyed by Germany: this played a large and, one suspects, the main part in Russian policy. The other was to destroy German manufacturing industry in the belief that by doing so a future war could be prevented or postponed. This aim appears to have influenced United States adoption of the policy of concentrating reparation wholly on the removal of capital equipment from Germany. During the meeting in Wiltshire in August 1944, at which Mr. Morgenthau expounded his ideas of policy toward postwar Germany, he reacted against the British views on reparation which I described at the outset, and seemed to oppose reparation on the ground that it would maintain or increase Germany's capacity to produce, which he desired to curtail drastically. But he later perceived that reparation could be

[7] This position was held by the U.S.S.R. as well as the U.S. and U.K. and was explicitly stated by Marshal Stalin at the Yalta Conference.

[8] Jacob Viner has clearly pointed out the error of assuming that all the difficulties of transfer of reparations are removed by the adoption of reparation in kind. See *Foreign Affairs*, "German Reservations Once More," July 1943, pp. 659-73.

reconciled with "deindustrialization" by dismantling industrial plants and removing them to other countries instead of destroying them with explosives where they stood. When the special reparation group was formed in March 1945 and began to look around for ideas on reparation policy, Dr. Harry White tried to convince them that reparation should take the form of large-scale removal of German industrial equipment. Reparation in the form of periodical deliveries of raw materials or manufactured goods would only preserve or increase the productive capacity which Germany could turn to war purposes later. This explains an important difference in principle between the U.S. and the U.S.S.R. reparation policies at the outset: both aimed at the removal of capital equipment, but the former desired also, while the latter opposed, periodical transfers of raw materials and manufactures. The Russians wanted coal but Mr. Morgenthau wished to wreck the German coal mines.

The Russian proposals were expressed in their most extreme form at the Yalta Conference in February 1945, the month before the U.S. reparation group was formed in Washington. Mr. Byrnes reports Mr. Maisky as stating:

"Our plan foresees that reparations in kind should be demanded from Germany in two ways. First, withdrawals from the national wealth of Germany. That means factories, land, machinery, machine tools, rolling stock of railways, investments in foreign enterprises, and so on. Second, yearly payments in kind. . . .

"The removal of capital wealth was to be completed in two years and the yearly payments in ten years. Eighty per cent of German industry should be removed."[9]

But a policy which originates in one reason is often continued for another. Morgenthau's indirect influence was strong when the reparation group was formed but waned after the death of President Roosevelt. It would undoubtedly have declined in any case in 1945: if President Roosevelt had lived he would have had to turn his full attention to postwar German matters for the first time and his constructive mind would have set aside the remnants of the Morgenthau plan. But the reparation issue came to be dominated more and more by the attitude and the practices of the Sovet Union, and the opposition of the United States to reparation deliveries of raw materials and manufactured goods continued, although the grounds on

[9] James F. Byrnes, *Speaking Frankly, op.cit.*, p. 26.

which it was originally based had been first modified and then rejected. The necessity of checking Russia's exorbitant demands on Germany and her efforts to get a foothold in the Ruhr, and the realization that while the U.S. and the U.K. were pouring relief into Germany the payment of reparation by Germany would be made at the expense of the British and American taxpayer, later supplied valid grounds for a policy originally advocated on grounds now unacceptable.

The attitude of the Soviet Union dominated the course of the critical reparation discussions of 1945. In May Mr. Pauley and his group arrived in London on their way to Moscow and held a brief informal discussion with the U.K. reparation group. Before he left I heard Mr. Pauley express his intention of trying to clear up the business of the Reparation Commission in Moscow in about three weeks! His ability in the oil business had brought him wealth and prominence but he was new to inter-governmental negotiations, which require very different qualities and experience. Above all, he did not yet understand the peculiar difficulties of negotiating with the Russians. In this he was no worse off than Mr. Byrnes was in his early days as Secretary of State. Apparently Mr. Pauley and Mr. Byrnes both conceived of negotiations with the Russians as a process of bargaining in which real compromises were made by both sides. Mr. Pauley understood the art of bargaining in such conditions: he played his hand astutely, not allowing his opponent to read his mind or foresee how far he would go. Yet his ventures into reparations were as great a failure as his ventures into oil had been a success.

There were, I suggest, two reasons for this. First, he did not have the patience required in negotiating with the Russians. Presumably, in negotiations on oil both sides desire to reach decisions within a reasonable period of time, and Mr. Pauley was taken aback when he found that Russian negotiators are in a hurry only when they hope to obtain unilateral concessions from the other side, and are capable otherwise of sticking woodenly to their position day after day, week after week, and month after month; of evading, procrastinating, and (if they give ground at all) of seeking to regain it by outflanking manoeuvers. Second, it may be presumed that a negotiator on oil always knows what he wants and sets a precise aim before him. But in the reparation negotiations Mr. Pauley showed no evidence of any strong convictions of what ought to be done; he seems to have taken over an essentially negative, sketchy, hastily conceived, and imprecise plan to combine reparation with partial deindustrialization of Germany. In the end he abruptly dropped the subject and went home, leaving to others the herculean task of attempting to build a workable scheme out of vague and ambiguous "principles."

The discussions of the Reparation Commission in Moscow were long-drawn-out but ended in complete failure, and the Potsdam Conference started on July 17, 1945, with reparation as an open question on which decisions were urgently needed but not even the most rudimentary agreement had been reached, although Germany had been occupied about three months. In these circumstances it is not surprising that the agreement on reparations at Potsdam was hastily drafted, vague and unsound, and destined to touch off international controversies which have not yet been resolved harmoniously. It was a last-moment improvisation made in a desperate effort to break a prolonged stalemate. It is a page of history which does no credit to any of the countries involved in it.

The future historian who surveys both World Wars will find hardly more wisdom in the reparation provisions of the Potsdam Agreement in 1945 than in those of the Versailles Treaty in 1919. Both conferences affirmed an unlimited responsibility of Germany to make reparation. Both recognized—the Versailles Treaty explicitly and the Potsdam Agreement implicitly—that this responsibility could not be discharged fully. The Versailles Treaty specified an amount to be paid over the first 2⅓ years[10] but for the rest it set up a Reparations Commission to estimate the amount of "damage done to the civilian population of the Allied and Associated Powers" by German aggression[11] and to "draw up a schedule of payments prescribing the time and manner of securing and discharging the entire obligation" by 1951.[12] The Potsdam Agreement was extraordinarily vague as to the total amount. Section IV, headed "Reparations from Germany" specified no total amount but indirectly limited the "amount and character of the industrial capital equipment" that might be taken as reparations to that which was "unnecessary for the German peace

[10] The Reparations Commission was to determine the manner of payment which might be in goods or "money."

[11] See Articles 232 and 233 and Annex I to Section VIII of the Treaty.

[12] Article 233.

economy."[13] The reader seeking light on this has to turn away from the section on reparations to the section on "Economic Principles," where he finds among the aims of Allied controls to be imposed on the German economy the following:

"To assure the production and maintenance of goods and services required to meet the needs of the occupying forces and displaced persons in Germany and essential to maintain in Germany average standards of living not exceeding the average of the standards of living of European countries. . . ."[14]

From these scattered statements it seemed to follow that reparations in the form of "industrial equipment" were to amount to the difference between the existing equipment and that which was considered necessary to maintain a "standard of living" equal to the average of that of Europe.

If it were not for its grave effects on economic reconstruction, this astonishing formula would be an excellent subject for wit and humor at the expense of its authors. It would be difficult to find in the recorded history of international relations a more intellectually disreputable and administratively unworkable formula for determining the economic fate of a nation. It abounded in ambiguity and was fertile in opportunities for dissension. The satirists who parody the vagueness of language of international diplomacy would be hard put to find, when it comes to measurable quantities, a vaguer term than "standards of living." But the human imagination stands baffled at the conception of an "average standard of living" among the heterogeneous peoples and countries of Europe. And human ingenuity and resourcefulness would be exhausted long before a way could be found to impose such an imaginary "standard" on a population of seventy million people. Not the most socialistic of socialists could conceive of successful economic planning on such a scale as this. Regimented production and consumption would have to be enforced on a scale that would reduce the seventy million victims to automatons.

It has been said by apologists for the Potsdam Agreement that some sort of agreement on reparations was essential because the Russians were already removing capital equipment from the zone which they

[13] Section IV, par. 6.

[14] This formula should be compared with that in JCS 1067 (pt. II, par. 21) which specified the lowest instead of the average standard of living among Germany's neighbors.

occupied. This hardly appears convincing. The effect of the agreement was, first, merely to legalize Soviet looting of their zone without giving the Western Allies any control over its extent; and, second, to present the U.S.S.R. with a claim on the production of the Western Zones—a claim which was to become a source of future trouble for the Western Allies. In international affairs generally it is dangerous to assume that any agreement is better than no agreement: in this particular case it is difficult to discover that the conclusion of the agreement had any advantages over an adjournment without agreement, leaving negotiations to be continued elsewhere. Acceptance of a hasty agreement for the sake of agreement is the worst possible way of dealing with the Soviet Union.[15]

The vague formula for reparations in the Potsdam Agreement had to be interpreted in one way or another. A peremptory clause (IV,5) stated that, "The amount of equipment to be removed from the Western Zones on account of reparations must be determined within six months from now at the latest." Doubtless those who drafted this clause felt assured the labors needed to put it into effect would be performed by others. Just after the Potsdam Agreement was signed, Mr. Pauley made the extraordinary statement that the reparation policies were "clearly defined and complete, though of a very general character."[16] In a letter to General Lucius Clay he stated, "There is left with you and the Control Council . . . the whole problem of administering the reparations plan and deciding both when and what production facilities shall be removed from Germany as reparations."[17] With that Mr. Pauley and his staff gave up and went home, and Mr. Pauley, before moving on to fresh fields, told the American public[18] that "the reparations plan is thoroughly workable and . . . embraces all the basic policies required for active administration. For this administration the responsibility rests solely with the occupying authorities. . . ." He repeated the fallacious historical interpretation

[15] In view of the high quality of the work of British civil servants, both temporary and permanent, on German reparation and economic security it is puzzling to me that the U.K. assented to the agreement and apparently took little initiative at any stage during the conference to produce a better one and fight for it.

[16] B. U. Ratchford and W. D. Ross, *Berlin Reparations Assignment* (Chapel Hill, University of North Carolina Press), 1947, p. 45.

[17] *ibid.*, p. 46.

[18] See Department of State Bulletin, September 2, 1945, pp. 308-09 for the full statement.

which had become fashionable: "We believe we have avoided the errors that rendered the settlement after World War I a failure. We are not going to rebuild a strong Germany in order to pay reparations. We are giving out no blank checks without knowing what is in the bank. We are dealing in things which we have at hand or which we know we shall have. Where we have steel mills, we are dealing in existing steel capacity, not in hypothetical or unearned dollar values."

The strange conception that difficulties arising out of the use of monetary measurements and the operations of monetary institutions were avoided by the arrangements made at Potsdam is not easy to account for today. It is sometimes forgotten, however, that, so far as American acceptance of the plan to seize and remove capital equipment as reparation was influenced by those who wished to destroy German industry, the monetary question was irrelevant. Mr. Morgenthau as well as the FEA group, the War Department group and certain members of the reparation group who sympathized with him would not have been moved by arguments on the economic merits and demerits of different methods of obtaining reparations. They were interested, not in reparations but in the deindustrialization of Germany. Even if it could have been shown that this was a costly method of obtaining reparations, they would have been in favor of paying the price.

As it was, however, no study seems to have been made in any quarter of the economics of stripping factory equipment, moving it from one country to another, and attempting to bring it into production in a new environment. Yet this was the fundamental question on which the decisions of policy should have been made. And "hypothetical or unearned dollar values"—or other currency values—were essential to the inquiry. The cost, including the labor, of pulling down factories and heavy machinery, transporting them to distant places, reconstructing them, and bringing them into operation there should have been set off against the hypothetical earnings. But even this could not be worked out by taking each item in isolation. The industrial wounds of Europe could not be healed by wrenching apart the great industrial area of the Ruhr, with its intricate network of relationships between industry and industry, between plant and plant, between production and finance, and by scattering the equipment over various parts of Europe and the Soviet Union. An industrial area is an organism rather than a conglomeration of small, self-contained units, and the sum of the fragments that would be set up would not be equal to the whole that had been torn down.

The officers in the U.S. military government on whom the task of shaping a reparation plan was thrust were far from sharing Mr. Pauley's "keen satisfaction"[19] with the Potsdam Agreement. They faced the formidable task not only of building up a detailed plan from a few vague and ambiguous general statements but also of coming to an agreement on every detail with the British, French, and Russians on the Control Council. Moreover, the text of the treaty itself provided that the work "must" be completed in six months. Fortunately, the history of their efforts has been fully written by two of those who took part in the work.[20] These writers point out that, "Not a single representative from the U.S. reparations group remained in Berlin to explain how the group had functioned and to provide continuity in the work. Only a handful of documents and materials was left . . . there was a complete break in U.S. reparations work, and the task was transferred to an organization which was neither prepared nor equipped to carry it on."[21]

Notwithstanding the large U.S. staff in military government, it was extremely difficult to assemble even a skeleton staff to do the necessary spadework. An improvised staff, described as the German Standard of Living Board, attempted to estimate for Germany a standard of living "not exceeding the average of the standards of living of European countries."[22] This was the first of the innumerable phony estimates made in answer to a phony question. It was made in good faith by conscientious and competent workers who, however, were called upon, not only to make bricks without straw, but to make them according to a formula that would ensure the speedy collapse

[19] *ibid.*

[20] B. U. Ratchford and W. D. Ross, *Berlin Reparations Assignment* (Chapel Hill, University of North Carolina Press), 1947. This work, which is written from a refreshingly independent point of view, will be indispensable to future historians. It throws much needed light on the actual processes by which decisions were made, notably at "high levels," as well as the extraordinary shifts to which less exalted working officials were obliged to resort at times in order to carry out their instructions. It is a valuable corrective to many academic studies on international relations. However, the reparations muddle should not be taken as characteristic of government operations!

[21] *ibid.*, p. 70.

[22] Potsdam Agreement III, B, 14 (b).

of any structure that might be built with them. As Ratchford and Ross state, "With only a month in which to produce the first report, the . . . board could not allow itself to be held up by problems which, because of their complexity, lack of data, etc., could not be solved quickly."[23] The assumptions and methods are described by these authors, and space cannot be given to them here.[24] It should be said, however, that even they give little idea of the jumps and the imaginative feats involved in the determination of the "average standard of living of Europe." These extraordinary computations led to the conclusion that, "the German standard would have to be reduced to about 74 per cent of its 1930-1938 average. . . ." This was found "by coincidence" to be approximately equal to the actual standard in 1932.

"It was decided, therefore, that the pattern of German production and consumption for 1932, with certain important exceptions because of distortions caused by depression conditions, might be taken as a guide to the production and consumption which should prevail in the postwar economy . . . this basic formula . . . became the basis of all future negotiations, and no other comparable formula was ever offered by any other group."[25]

This was surely an unfortunate coincidence and if the political insight of the American group had been equal to their statistical ingenuity, they would have carefully concealed it and stated their basis as a hypothetical one. It is no wonder that Mr. Stolper pointed out that, ". . . the economic conditions of 1932 were just the environment that brought Hitler to power. It was the year of 6 to 8 million unemployed, about half of Germany's industrial working force . . . the wisdom of the Level of Industry Plan boiled down to perpetuating a revolutionary situation which had once thrown the world into its worst catastrophe."[26]

The next step, which was to obtain agreement on the Control Council on a detailed plan of action, was even more strewn with pitfalls. The details are described by Ratchford and Ross. To my mind, one of the most important lessons for posterity is that it is not only

[23] Ratchford and Ross, *op.cit.*, p. 74. They were working in a ruined city without access to substantial source materials even on Germany!

[24] *ibid.*, Ch. VII.

[25] *ibid.*, p. 79.

[26] Gustav Stolper, *German Realities* (New York, Reynal and Hitchcock), 1947, p. 145.

futile but internationally disastrous to make the construction of a "technical" scheme the subject of political bargaining. Even if the basis of the reparation scheme had been sensible and intelligible, no workable plan could have been drawn up if each figure had been made the subject of what Ratchford and Ross have aptly described as a poker game.[27] The "permitted levels" of the different industries were of course supposed to be interdependent, but the bargaining showed little trace of it. The level of steel production was perhaps the most disputed of all.

Recent American critics, particularly members of Congress and of the ECA, and American journalists abroad, who have sharply attacked the British and French for not being ready at once to cancel all reparation deliveries, would do well to study the history of American policy. It was the British and not the American plan which proposed much the highest levels of German industry, notwithstanding the greater losses the British had suffered and the greater extent to which they were open to German competition. Notably the U.S., under direct insistence by General Clay, lined up with the Soviet Union in insisting that the annual production of steel be limited to 5.8 million tons, as against strong British pressure for at least 9.0 million tons.[28] The scheme as it came out of the Control Council made little sense. Stolper no doubt exaggerated but one can feel much sympathy with him when he said, "The Level of Industry Plan will long be remembered as a unique specimen of human folly clothed in the pretentious garb of scholarly terminology. If anything was needed to discredit the authority of economists and statisticians, this document did it."[29]

I am not quite sure whether Ratchford and Ross are indulging in elaborate irony or expressing pent up feelings of satisfaction and relief at the end of a task to which they had given such unsparing and thankless service, when they conclude their account with ap-

[27] ". . . if some total stranger had been brought into the conference room on that afternoon, completely unaware of where he was or what was going on, he might well have thought that a poker game was in progress." Ratchford and Ross, *op.cit.*, p. 172.

[28] I followed the course of this controversy from London, being in touch with the British expert who reached the figure of 9 million tons. He is well known for his thorough knowledge of the techniques of the iron and steel industry and of its organization and history in continental Europe and the U.S. as well as the U.K. The U.S. figure of 5.8 million tons was decided on by General Clay against the recommendations of his advisors.

[29] Stolper, *op.cit.*, p. 145.

parent solemnity by saying, "The Plan for Reparations and the Level of Postwar German Economy in accordance with the Berlin Protocol was announced to the world at 18:00 hours on March 28, 1946.

"An historic document was written."

However, the stripping of capital equipment was by no means the only form of reparation which Germany was called on to make after the Second World War. The Potsdam Agreement provided that the German merchant marine was to be divided first among the U.S., U.K., and U.S.S.R., each of them being obliged to give appropriate quantities to other Allies which had lost shipping during the war.[80]

Next, the whole of Germany's external assets were to be seized by the countries in whose jurisdiction they lay. This seems to have been taken for granted in postwar plans on Germany, and no discrimination was made between ordinary business assets and assets acquired through German looting. In the Inter-Allied Reparations Agency, which had been set up to decide on the proportionate shares of the Western Allies in reparation removals from the Western Zones, it was agreed that the enemy assets seized in the countries concerned should be "charged against" the reparation shares. An additional provision—that the U.S., U.K., and France should "dispose of" or liquidate enemy assets in neutral countries and hand them over to the Reparation Agency for distribution as reparation —later gave rise to much friction and argument.

Both German external assets and German shipping were to be seized, ostensibly as reparation.[81] Although the desire for reparation in these forms in some countries was genuine, it was not the sole motive. First, the wording of the Inter-Allied agreement shows an anxious insistence that the assets should be "removed from German ownership or control" and their "return to German ownership and control" should be "precluded." This arose partly from a desire to weaken Germany which was akin to the desire for deindustrialization and partly from a desire to prevent Germans from enjoying the

[80] Section IV of Potsdam Agreement. This was obviously a form of reparation, yet it is not mentioned, nor is any cross reference given to it, in the section on reparation. The Potsdam Agreement was as faulty in form and draftsmanship as it was unsound in much of its content.

[81] In view of the huge shipping losses of the Allies, there was poetic justice in the seizure of German ships.

fruits of past looting. Second, though German ships were a suitable form of reparation—much more suitable than disembodied industrial plants—their seizure must also be considered as part of a plan to strip Germany of shipping for motives other than reparation. The Potsdam Agreement included the production of "sea-going ships" among the industries to be "prohibited and prevented" in order "to eliminate Germany's war potential."[82]

Thus we may conclude that reparation after the Second World War was largely a by-product of an attempt to deindustrialize Germany, in the belief that by doing so the Allies could prevent her from waging a future war. It was both a mistaken and a costly attempt, and British and American taxpayers paid a heavy price for it. Actually, the idea that Germany could wage another aggressive war in the near future was ridiculous, and, as to the more distant future, not even the advocates of the Morgenthau policy believed that restraints could be continued indefinitely. The U.S. government view, which was an unholy compound of the Morgenthau policy and a milder view (the former predominating), made the worst of both worlds. It claimed that a large measure of deindustrialization was necessary for the security of the Allies for a few years, but it held out the hope that these restraints would be lifted after reparation had been made, after the Allies had recovered, and after Germany had formed a democratic government. Reparations were to end in five years: "standards of living" in Allied countries were destined to return fairly close to prewar levels in that time, and a provisional democratic government was established in the Western Zones even earlier. Thus, as a measure of security for the Allies the deindustrialization policy was unnecessary and even futile—a source of resentment rather than a protection against aggression. It provided security when no security was needed, and made no provision for it in the days when aggression would be physically possible.[83]

[82] Potsdam Agreement, II B, 11.

[83] The account given in this study of the origin and development of the Morgenthau Plan and the reparation plan should dispose of the insinuations, made during the hearings of certain congressional committees, that Dr. Harry White was a disguised communist following instructions from Moscow in the part which he played and the influence which he exerted on the Morgenthau Plan and the reparation plan. The reader will observe that neither of these plans was consistent with communist policy and that the first of them was propounded before the Soviet Union had formed any policy on the economic future of Germany. In all their plans the Russians advocated and Mr. Morgenthau and Dr. White uncompromisingly and even bitterly opposed, reparation from current production. The Russians demanded

that reparation should be a first charge on German coal output, while Mr. Morgenthau and Dr. White demanded that the German coal mines should be "thoroughly wrecked."

Equally unfounded allegations have been made that Professor Owen Lattimore of Johns Hopkins University invented, under Russian direction or influence, and persuaded Mr. Pauley to accept, the method of reparation by uprooting and transferring capital equipment. As I have shown, Mr. Pauley adopted this form of reparation for Germany long before he went to Japan, and, it should be added, long before he met Professor Lattimore.

CHAPTER XVII

The Struggle to Change a Policy

THE economic errors of the peace with respect to Germany had been so far-reaching that it was not long before a movement to repair them began, which showed itself particularly in the fields of reparation, of zonal unification and of currency reform. But when the wrong steps have been taken in international matters it is impossible to go back on them overnight. Improvement was slow at first. The mistakes of Potsdam, the level-of-industry agreement, the narrow nationlism of the zonal organization, and the taboo on assistance in the reconstruction of Germany, returned time after time to plague Washington and London long after the United States administration became more enlightened.

However, the surprising repetition of the same errors, and the slowness in repairing them, arise out of many other factors besides the difficulty in changing agreements. One less recognized factor lies in the sketchy knowledge and understanding of detailed issues on the part of some of the political leaders. A study of Mr. Byrnes's account of the development of policy on Germany leads one to suspect that, like President Truman, he had no idea how far the Potsdam policy resembled the Morgenthau policy. He makes the important disclosure that the U.S. proposals on the Economic Committee at Potsdam, which, he says, "formed the basis of the program of economic and political principles for Germany and was approved by the heads of government,"[1] had been drawn up in an interdepartmental paper which was "prepared by the State Department after consultation with the Secretary of the Treasury and the Secretary of War, was signed by the representatives of the three departments" on March 25, 1945, "and then was approved by President Roosevelt."[2] The Secretary of the Treasury who signed it was Mr. Morgenthau! Yet Mr. Byrnes apparently believes sincerely that he was not influenced by the Morgenthau plan, for he adds that the paper

[1] James F. Byrnes, *op.cit.*, p. 187. [2] *ibid.*, pp. 186-87.

"... said nothing about making Germany an agricultural and pastoral state. Nor did Mr. Churchill, who had initialled the Quebec program, mention it to President Truman or to me. The fact is, it was not mentioned to us by anyone at Potsdam."[3]

It is no wonder that Mr. Morgenthau has argued that the Potsdam Agreement put most of his proposals into effect. So far his claim is largely justifiable: it is only when he goes further and maintains that President Roosevelt and other high-ranking statesmen gave them considered approval that he is distorting historical facts. As I have shown earlier, it was President Roosevelt's failure to adjudicate decisively between incompatible views among his cabinet officers that led to a "compromise" drawn up at "lower levels" which permitted large parts of the Morgenthau plan to creep in.[4] This pseudo-compromise was embodied in the paper used at Potsdam. In the end, it was combined with other elements thrown in by the reparations group whose members had been influenced in their turn at the higher levels by Dr. Harry White.

Thus the evidence leaves little doubt that President Truman and Mr. Byrnes did not see clearly where they were being led at Potsdam, particularly in economic matters. Their intentions may have been good, but they did not grasp the issues at stake, nor did they understand the nature of the inheritance that had been passed on to them.

None the less, as Mr. Byrnes gained experience in his new office, his views on Germany showed an intelligent development, and before he left office he helped to turn American policy on Germany into more constructive channels, in which the United Kingdom, which had followed an enlightened policy in its own zone, readily joined. The constructive elements in military government were anxious for changes in policy, while many of those with destructive aims had returned to civilian life.

But it was probably the indirect influence of the Soviet Union which did most to prod Washington to change its ways. M. Molotov delivered a speech on July 10, 1946, which was well calculated to gain support from the German people for the Soviet Union. The purpose of the U.S.S.R., he said, was "to transform Germany into a democratic and peaceloving state which, besides its agriculture, will have its own industry and foreign trade." He called for an in-

[3] *ibid.*, p. 187.

[4] See pp. 244ff.

crease in the levels of industry permitted to Germany. Mr. Byrnes comments that M. Molotov omitted to say that it was the U.S.S.R. representative who pressed for the lowest figures for German production on the Control Council. This was true, but Mr. Byrnes himself does not mention, and may not even have been aware, that the U.S. representative joined the U.S.S.R. in insisting on the lowest figure for steel production—5.8 million tons, over the emphatic protests of the U.K. representative and to the consternation of the Foreign Office (as I heard at first hand in London at the time). And the low figure for steel was the worst of many bad features of the level-of-industry agreement.

The unstatesmanlike and backward-looking policies of the Soviet Union have made her a convenient object of blame for all that has gone wrong in the postwar world. Certainly the Russians have much to answer for, and, apart from their great struggle against Germany, are unlikely to receive much praise at the bar of history for their conduct in our time. But the blame for the postwar failures in Germany has been cast too exclusively on them in many quarters. I do not believe that any fair critic who avoids national bias and examines the evidence can deny that the United States and France bear a considerable share of responsibility for the errors of the peace in Germany. Russian propaganda, insincere though it was, on this occasion struck a weak spot in the American armor.

The changes in U.S. policy between the Potsdam meeting and the Stuttgart speech a year later were by no means drastic. Halfway between these landmarks in U.S. policy toward Germany, a "Policy Statement on Reparations" was issued by the State Department, on December 12, 1945. It was written in the cumbersome, indirect, and verbose style that too often characterizes official statements in Washington, but it serves a useful purpose in showing that much of the Morgenthau spirit survived for many months after Mr. Morgenthau had left the administration, and also in marking the beginnings of a change. It reaffirmed the American intention "to abide strictly by the Berlin Declaration, which imposes a severe reparation obligation on Germany. . . ." It asserted that ". . . in removing equipment from plants declared available for reparation, no consideration should be given to withholding portions of the equipment desired by a reparation recipient in order to retain remaining installations and structures in more effective condition for peacetime uses."[5] It revealed once more that the motive which guided U.S. policy from the beginning was not so much a desire to exact reparation for its own sake as a desire largely to deindustrialize Germany.[6] Thus it described the first aim of the Potsdam reparation clauses as being "to weaken effectively the economic base from which war industry could be derived until a peaceful democratic government is firmly established in Germany." It called for the destruction—"in the security interest of the United States"—of "structures and installations" in shipbuilding as well as aircraft and munitions.[7] It repeated the naïve doctrine that, "Since capacity in the metal, machinery and chemical industries in excess of German peacetime needs is to be transferred to countries entitled to receive reparations from Germany, it is expected that the industrial capacity lost in Germany will after an interval be recovered in large part elsewhere in the world, and for the most part in Europe."[8]

On the other hand, it attempted to soften by a new interpretation the more drastic provisions of the Potsdam Agreement. This interpretation is contained—a literary critic might say half concealed—in the following sentences:

"In the view of the Department of State the Berlin Declaration is not intended to force a reduction in German living standards except as such reduction is required to enable Germany to meet her reparation payments. In effect the Berlin Declaration merely provides that Germany's obligation to make reparation for the war damage which her aggression caused to other countries should not be reduced in order to enable Germany to maintain a standard of living above the European average."[9]

According to this interpretation the hypothetical "standard of living" equal to the "European average" was to be imposed on Germany not as an end in itself but only as far as it was necessary to enable reparation to be made. This view was sharply attacked by the U.S.S.R. and it is therefore important to reexamine the documents with care.

As we have seen, the section on reparations of the Potsdam Agreement did not fix the total reparation to be made, but stated that, "the determination of the amount and character of the industrial capital

[5] Par. 3. I have assumed that the ambiguity in this clumsy sentence is due to bad drafting.

[6] Pars. 1-3.

[7] Par. 3.

[8] Par. 8 (c).

[9] Par. 5.

equipment unnecessary for the German peace economy shall be made by the Control Council under policies fixed by the Allied Commission on Reparations, with the participation of France, subject to the final approval of the zone commander in the zone from which the equipment is to be moved."[10]

In the section on "Economic Principles," it was stated that "Allied controls shall be imposed upon the German economy but only to the extent necessary . . ." to fulfill certain purposes, which were then listed. The list contained the following: "To assure the production and maintenance of goods and services required to meet the needs of the occupying forces and displaced persons in Germany and essential to maintain in Germany average living standards not exceeding the average of the standards of living of European countries. . . ."[11]

On these clauses hang all the law and the prophets concerning reparation. As to the first, however, the provision that the Allied Commission on Reparation should fix the policies for determining the amount of capital equipment for reparation was a dead letter from the beginning. That commission never fixed anything, unless it can be given credit for the agreement reached in Paris on December 21, 1945, which fixed the proportionate shares of the different Allies in the total reparation that might be taken from Germany. But this was an agreement not of the commission—for the U.S.S.R. was not present—but of nineteen countries, which formed a new Inter-Allied Reparation Agency, of which only two were members of the commission.[12] Of all the war and postwar international agencies, none was as sterile as the Allied Commission on Reparation. No policies on reparation were fixed by it: the clause in the Potsdam Agreement referring to it was ignored, and no reference to it appears in the "Plan of Allied Control Council for Reparations and the Level of Post War German Economy."[13] Therefore the only "policies" to guide the Allied Control Commission were those contained in the sketchy,

[10] Potsdam Agreement IV, 6.

[11] III, G. The U.K. and U.S.S.R. were to be left out of the average.

[12] The old U.S. reparation group had fallen apart, and the U.S. delegation was headed by Professor James W. Angell of of Columbia University. The Paris meeting set up the Inter-Allied Reparation Agency, which was concerned with the distribution of reparation among the Allies other than the U.S.S.R. and Poland.

[13] It should be noted also that this important point was ignored in the *Special Report of the U.S. Military Governor for Germany* made in November 1948. This report is reproduced in Department of State, *Germany, 1947-49. The Story in Documents* (Washington), 1950, pp. 420-24.

ambiguous provisions of the Potsdam Agreement just quoted! The Control Commission only put the finishing touches on a plan the main part of which, as we have seen, was worked out by the Level of Industry Committee and completed by the Economics Directorate and the Coordinating Committee. Here, as in so many of the negotiations on Germany, the lower the level of negotiation, the greater the accomplishments.[14] The work of interpretation was therefore done mainly by the Level of Industry Committee, but some thorny issues remained for the higher committees.

The State Department memorandum of December 12, 1945, took up two related conflicts of interpretation which remained, and one of which remains to this day. The first had to do with the level of the "peaceful" industries and the second with periodical deliveries of reparation goods from contemporary production. The Russians took the position that no industries should be allowed to produce more than the amounts needed to maintain the average European standard in Germany. The State Department, as we have seen, insisted that restrictions on living standards were designed only to enable reparations in the form of capital equipment to be made.

The discussion of the subject was confused, and the public has probably never understood the issue.[15] If it were not a subject of international friction it would not be worth while to discuss it. The first point is that the restrictions on the level of industry were designed for the supposed security of the Allies. "Production of metals, chemicals, machinery and other items that are directly necessary to a war economy shall be rigidly controlled and restricted to Germany's approved peace time needs."[16] These needs were defined as the average European standard of living. "Productive capacity not needed for permitted production" was to be removed or destroyed. It was not stated precisely what industries this applied to, but the interpretation accepted by the State Department was presumably that it referred only to the industries mentioned in the preceding sentences—"metals, chemicals, machinery" etc.

[14] In the Potsdam Agreement some of the constructive provisions, notably the provision for economic unity, had been worked out and agreed on the by the European Advisory Commission and were merely taken over and confirmed. Mr. Byrnes does not mention this in his account. See *Speaking Frankly, op.cit.*, p. 85.

[15] It is well discussed by Ratchford and Ross, *op.cit.*, pp. 175-76, but was not fully grasped at higher levels in the U.S. Military Government.

[16] Potsdam Agreement, III, B, 11.

Second, the agreement stated that "primary emphasis shall be given to the development of agriculture and peaceful domestic industries," and, third, that controls should be enforced, among other reasons, to maintain living standards in Germany "not exceeding" the average European standard.

The Russians claimed from the start that any manufacturing plants in the "peaceful industries," as well as those in the war industries, in excess of those needed to produce the average European consumption should be taken as reparation. The U.S. representatives on the Control Council and its committees repudiated this view and held that "peaceful" industries were not bound by the restrictions placed on "metals, chemicals, machinery" etc.

At first sight it might appear that if the proper calculations had been made as to the capacity in the metal, chemical, and machine industries needed to maintain the average European consumption there would be no excess capacity in either peace or war industries. The British seem to have been the only group which attempted to make these calculations, their figure of 9 million tons of steel being the amount estimated as necessary to maintain consumption at the required level. But this was too sensible a proposal to be accepted generally. Actually, the productive capacity in many of the peace industries was not known when the calculations were made. Moreover, the various estimates had been the subject of bargaining and compromise, and many of the final figures were arbitrary.

The disputes between the U.S.S.R. and the West were therefore the outcome of the ambiguities and unworkable criteria in the Potsdam Agreement. They not only raised the question how far the Germans should be allowed to improve their living standards in the future, but also the question whether or not annual deliveries of reparations from immediate production should be made by Germany.

The second question was long a subject of dispute. At Yalta the U.S., U.K., and U.S.S.R. agreed that "reparations in kind" should be made, among other ways, in the form of "annual deliveries of goods from current production for a period to be fixed." At Potsdam the discussion on the subject was inconclusive, but annual deliveries were not ruled out: Mr. Pauley, in a statement made on August 30, 1945, after the Potsdam Conference said, "With respect to the amount of, and time limit on, annual recurring reparations—reparations extracted in the form of current production from year to year

—no decision can be made until the character and amount of removals of industrial capital equipment have been determined by the Allied Control Council and the future economy of Germany is more clearly defined."[17]

Secretary Marshall seems to me to have gone too far when, in opposition to the Russian demand for reparations from current production, he said that "the United States Government considers that the questions of reparations were finally settled at Potsdam."[18] Earlier, however, Secretary Byrnes had made a better, though, I believe, still an inadequate case against the Russian demand when, in his Stuttgart speech, he contended that, "Reparations from current production would be wholly inconsistent with the levels of industry now established under the Potsdam Agreement."[19] In Mr. Byrnes's speech it was not argued that the Potsdam Agreement had disposed finally of reparation questions, but that the Potsdam decisions, together with the subsequent decisions of the Allied Control Council on the appropriate level of industry for Germany, ruled out reparations from current production. But the case was still weak and inconclusive, and if M. Molotov's knowledge of detail had been greater, if his mind had been more subtle, and if he had been less intent on abusing and misrepresenting the Western powers, he might have made a telling reply confined to the merits of the case. It is not clear whether Mr. Byrnes was fully aware of the considerable gap between the output needed to provide the supposed "average European standard" on the one hand and the output which was physically possible even within the limits of the agreement on the level of industry. Probably he had heard of the controversy on the question whether the limits set in the level-of-industry negotiations should be enforced on the peaceful industries as well as on those from which all four countries agreed that reparations should be drawn. Certainly General Draper, the United States' representative on the Economics Directorate in Berlin, persistently argued for the principle that no reparation removals should be made from the plant of the "peaceful industries." But in the end he had to compromise, and the final text of the level-of-industry agreement was ambiguous on the

[17] Department of State Bulletin, September 2, 1945, p. 309.

[18] Statement at London session of Council of Foreign Ministers, December 10, 1947.

[19] Byrnes, *Speaking Frankly, op.cit.*, p. 189. This statement was made in his well-known speech at Stuttgart on September 6, 1946.

point, merely stating that, "Production may exceed the . . . estimates . . . unless otherwise determined by the Control Council."[20] This did not embody the United States position in undiluted form. Thus neither the Potsdam decisions alone nor the Potsdam decisions together with the level-of-industry agreement "finally settled" the reparation question.

No doubt the strongest argument that influenced Washington in practice against reparation from current production was based on the clause of the Potsdam agreement which provided that, "The proceeds of exports from current production and stocks shall be available in the first place for payment for . . . imports."[21] This certainly justified opposition to immediate reparation from the current production of plants which were producing for commercial export and which would not in any case be removed as reparation. But it did not constitute a conclusive case in principle against all reparation from current production.

Looking back on the long-drawn-out negotiations on this subject, it seems clear that the responsibility for the errors and the bitter disputes that stand out in the record cannot be laid wholly on any one country. The truth is that the question of reparation from current production was never adequately studied or considered on its own merits. During my informal talks with U.K. officials in London, I formed the opinion that if there had to be reparation at all it should come from current production. What better method could there be to bring home to the German people their responsibility for the destruction wrought in their name than to require them to replace by hard work a small proportion of the goods which they had wantonly destroyed or stolen? But after August 1944 the chance of a calm and thorough analysis of the subject in Washington disappeared. The last thing the Morgenthau adherents wanted was to see the industrial capacity of Germany brought into operation, even for the benefit of the Allies. The U.S. government, as we have seen, was stampeded into the most ill-advised form of reparation that had yet been devised—that of uprooting factories and factory equipment in Germany and Japan. The Russians, partly for different reasons, were set on the same objective, but they began to realize later that

[20] Plan of Allied Control Council for Reparations and the Level of Postwar German Economy, par. 12 (d).

[21] Potsdam Agreement III, 19.

the benefits to the receiver from this form of reparation were much less than the losses to the giver, and in their own zone they seem to have turned toward a policy of keeping German plants where they were and using them to produce finished reparation goods. They then vigorously revived their demand made at Yalta for reparation from current production in the Western Zones. Their diplomacy was inept, their manners were sometimes boorish, and their aim was transparently selfish. Thus they drew on themselves all the disapproval which enlightened opinion would otherwise have distributed more widely among the Allies.

If an intelligent approach to reparation had been made in the earlier stages, it would have been clearly apprehended that, to the damaged Allied areas, reparation from current production would have brought greater gains than the uprooting of capital equipment, and that it would have avoided the net loss to the productive capacity of Europe as a whole which is an inevitable result of any attempt to transfer the capacity to produce finished goods instead of the finished goods themselves. If the Russians were set on the seizure of factories and their equipment, an attempt should have been made to persuade them to abandon or greatly reduce their demand for this type of reparation in return for agreement on a reasonable program of reparation from current output and especially from the plants which they desired to root up and transfer. It may be that the Soviet Union would have refused such a compromise, but that does not excuse the failure of the Western Allies even to consider the question seriously. Actually, the United States at the outset encouraged the Russians in their choice of the worst form of reparation. Nor can it be seriously maintained that reparation from current production was out of the question even in principle, because of the necessity of earmarking earnings from exports to pay for imports. If capital equipment had not been marked for removal as reparations, it could have been used to produce reparation goods. If financial reforms had been made early and more effective control of the economy had been established, the necessary labor could have been drawn from those who were unproductively employed in an inflationary economy.[22]

[22] The striking rise in production after the currency reform which was belatedly carried out gives some idea of the immense waste of labor in the inflation which had been allowed to develop.

Although the errors of the Western Allies on reparation have been overshadowed by the intransigence of the Soviet Union, in a long view of history they will find their place in the record. The United States and France failed to learn from the previous history of reparation, and both countries repeated old and committed new errors not less serious than those of the past. The failure was both intellectual and moral. It arose out of the assumptions that the chief pitfall to avoid was the imposition of reparations in monetary terms, and that reparation should be a by-product of deindustrialization. The desire to destroy or remove German industries and reduce Germany to the status of a poor country arose out of a sentiment of revenge and a false conception of the means to future security.

Reparation measures were the subject of international agreement, and even if the Soviet Union could be left out of account when policies were changed, on the ground that failure to fulfill her own obligations released the other Allies from theirs, the Western Allies could not be ignored, and their consent was necessary before the burdens imposed on Germany could be lightened. Thus began the process, hardly new in American diplomatic history, of persuading the Allies that the policies into which they had been drawn by the United States should after all be reversed and any benefits that might have accrued to them from those policies should be foregone in the general interest. The process was still in an early stage at the close of the period with which this study deals.

It is fortunate indeed that after the Second World War the United States abandoned isolationism and plunged into the thick of world affairs. But her Allies have discovered that unusual qualities of adjustment and resilience and a well-developed sense of humor are necessary to make the new alliance work.

The next economic error for which a remedy was sought was the separation of Germany into zones of occupation between which, after the war ended, trade had almost ceased to flow. When I visited Germany and Austria in late 1945 and early 1946 I found not only that the arbitrarily created zonal boundaries were almost complete barriers to trade but also that no goods passed between the United States zone of Germany and the United States zone of Austria!

The merging of the three Western Zones of Germany into a West German state with a more or less common economic life was another outstanding effort to undo an error made in the wartime planning for postwar Germany. As we have seen, farsighted persons in both civil and military circles advocated unified Allied military government during the occupation of Germany, but this wise advice was rejected in the Pentagon, partly in a spirit of narrow nationalism and partly out of a mistaken conception of policy toward the Soviet Union.

The difficulty of repairing errors in international affairs is well illustrated in the history of the movement for economic merging of the zones. It would have been easy to continue SHAEF through the occupation; it was difficult to restore economic unity after the break had been made: many months of negotiation were necessary before fusion could begin, and, after it had begun, progress in giving effect to agreed principles was slow in the early stages.

Under more stable conditions the area which Britain controlled had a net export of goods abroad, while the area which the United States controlled had a net import. The Ruhr, however, was dependent on food imports, while Bavaria produced more food than it consumed. Thus the position of the U.K. zone was at its worst during the early postwar period of scarcity but might be expected to improve greatly, both absolutely and in comparison with that of the U.S. zone, as foreign trade revived. The deficit of the British zone seriously damaged the whole financial position of Britain in the early postwar years and thus contributed to recurring financial crises. The British government considered that it was fair in these circumstances to expect the United States to bear more than 50 per cent of the cost of the necessary imports into the combined zones. But Mr. Byrnes rejected Mr. Bevin's modest proposal that the U.S. should bear 60 per cent of the deficit of the combined zones. From his own account of the matter it is clear that he did not grasp the economic issues. He tells us that he "thought it unwise for Britain to be put in the position of a poor relative or a junior partner by contributing less than 50 per cent. . . . It seemed much better to aid Britain in some other way."[23] Actually, if the zones had been combined for economic purposes from the start the U.S., in the early years, would have covered an appreciable proportion of the deficit in the U.K. zone, even if both countries had made equal contributions.

[23] Byrnes, *Speaking Frankly*, *op.cit.*, pp. 196-97.

Fortunately, about the middle of 1946, Mr. Byrnes initiated a movement toward economic unification of the zones. It was a long and slow process, necessitating decisions on a multitude of details. How much easier the postwar economic task would have been if SHAEF had not been dissolved!

A third issue of the greatest importance to both the short- and the long-run welfare of Germany was that of currency reform. In retrospect it seems astonishing and indeed inexcusable that such an indispensable reform should have been so long delayed. The question arises whether, in the United States zone, the delay was connived at by officials in military government who aided and abetted the Morgenthau plan. The chief of the Finance Section in the early period of the occupation had himself been on Mr. Morgenthau's staff in the Treasury. However, another U.S. official, experienced in monetary questions, prepared a memorandum very early in the occupation, pointing out the necessity of an early and far-reaching currency reform, and this memorandum reached General Clay's desk without, however, being acted upon. General Eisenhower and General Clay were men of constructive outlook but they had little understanding of monetary questions and were too preoccupied with other urgent matters to follow all that was done and all that was left undone by their staffs. Moreover, they were gravely handicapped by the directive under which they worked and which forbade participation or assistance by military government in the reconstruction of Germany. Currency reform was essentially a reconstruction question. It was absurd to suppose that it could be undertaken by Germans alone, at least in the status which they occupied until 1948.

Fortunately, however, more constructive forces appeared, and in 1946 a plan for reform was prepared by a group of U.S. officials. Beneficial changes were also made in the personnel of the finance division. There were several causes of the continued delay in the application of reform plans. Great importance was attached in U.S. and U.K. circles to the inclusion of all the zones in any reform. The inevitable Russian procrastination followed. The currency question was entangled in the question of economic unity. It was not likely that a plan acceptable to the West would be acceptable to the East, and for a time the Western authorities hesitated to take the initiative in a step which would seem to close the door to economic unity. This raised a question of principle similar to that which arose in other fields: should measures desirable in themselves be postponed, and how long should they be postponed, in the hope first of placating and then of securing the cooperation of the Soviet Union. I have argued earlier that the tendency in United States circles in the late war and early postwar periods was to lose too much time in this way, without gaining Soviet cooperation in the end. Insofar as the procrastination of the Soviet Union was a cause of delay, this conclusion applies also to currency reform.

The urge to reform promptly may have been weakened by the peculiar adaptations to currency chaos that grew up in Germany after the Second World War and stand in sharp contrast with the inflation after the First World War. The reichsmark was not forced to great depths of depreciation as the mark had been: it was, rather, abandoned as the standard by which exchanges of goods were determined and values set over periods of time. As Mr. Klopstock has pointed out, certain types of goods were used as a medium of exchange and as a means of paying workers and those who rendered professional services, and ". . . the main purpose of business transactions became the protection, improvement and expansion of real asset holdings rather than a monetary profit through supplying goods to consumers."[24]

In addition, the long practice of economic controls in Germany had established habits among the people that aided administrators in the confused conditions of the early postwar years. Orders regarding prices were often obeyed when they could not have been enforced. Conditions were indeed chaotic, but not as chaotic as they would have been if the German population of the early 1920's had been subjected to them instead of the population of the mid-1940's.

But the extent and timing of reforms raise questions of wider scope and deeper content than those concerned merely with currency matters. In the aftermath of a destructive and exhausting war the German people were faced with the problems not only of repairing or rebuilding their industry and commerce but also of reconstructing the social fabric of their economic order. It is easier to make substantial changes at the beginning of social reconstruction than later. Public ownership

[24] F. H. Klopstock, "Monetary Reform in Western Germany," in *Journal of Political Economy* (Chicago), August 1949, p. 278.

of industries whose former owners were guilty of aiding the instigators of war can be established without the burden of compensation. If decisions are postponed and the old fabric is patched up, it becomes much more likely that the previous system will be restored in the end in a slightly modified form than that any new order will emerge. With the passing of the early reforming urge which springs up in the aftermath of war, it becomes more difficult to make fundamental social changes.

Thus the question arises how far the New Colonialism which the occupation established during the critical formative years just after the war was really necessary. As one who does not share the conventional attitude of the times toward colonies in general, I do not use the term colonialism as a term of reproach. Notwithstanding the evils and defects associated with many colonial regimes in the past, it seems probable that the extension of Western European influence over many parts of the world overseas, particularly in Africa, brought great benefits which have far exceeded the injuries which it inflicted. Moreover, the evils were the product of ruder ages and the present generation cannot be held responsible for them, nor can it repair them by simple abdication. Granting that self-government is the proper goal for all colonial areas, the problem is one of timing and the greatest danger at present, as the state of a number of newly independent areas illustrates strikingly, is that a premature independence will be gained by countries with little prospect that they will become and remain viable states able to hold their own in an advancing world.

But the New Colonialism which resulted from the occupation of ex-enemy countries after defeat in war is another matter. These were not undeveloped countries whose peoples were unprepared to stand by themselves in the modern world. They had fallen from grace by running amok in the world of nations and had to be restrained at all costs within their borders in future. But their armed power had been shattered and an unobtrusive Allied force stationed at a convenient point, together with adequate machinery for Allied inspection, would have been enough to prevent rearming. In the past aggressor countries have been defeated and thereafter restrained without prolonged occupation during which the occupying powers have governed them even in domestic affairs.

It can of course be argued that the breakdown of Germany was so widespread that the spontaneous emergence of a new indigenous government was impossible for some time. The force of this argument must be judged by those who were on the spot continuously during the critical period. During the war, however, it was by no means obvious that a complete internal breakdown would occur: possibly it might not have occurred if the Allies had followed President Wilson's tactics and offered weighty inducements to surrender instead of adopting the sterile formula of unconditional surrender.

But even if it were agreed that the immediate or early formation of an indigenous central government was out of the question and that no occupation narrower in scope was practicable, the fact remains that military government by a foreign power in such circumstances is of all methods one of the least likely to increase the prestige of the occupying powers and advance the cause that they wish to serve. The ultimate hope is that future aggression will be prevented by a change in the moral outlook of the German people, bringing with it the conviction that there are nobler missions in life than military conquest and political domination and better ways of living than those based on autocracy and regimentation and upheld by the spy, the bully, and the torturer.

But the wider and more thorough the foreign military occupation, the less likely it is to assist in the growth of the necessary change in outlook. For if it is desired to lead and confirm a people in the path of democracy, the aim will not be achieved by displaying the apparatus of military government before their eyes. If it is desired to demonstrate a better way of life and conduct to a people, the aim will not be achieved by planting in their midst an army made up largely of raw youths, separated by thousands of miles from the restraint of family and neighborhood, subject to new temptations against which nothing in the experience of the majority of them is proof, and consuming liberal rations while the indigenous peoples are desperately short of the basic necessities. In such conditions it is unlikely that, as a whole, the occupying forces will constitute a good example of the best elements in the communities from which they come. When, in addition, account is taken of the decline in the quality of the occupying forces as many of its abler and more experienced members return to peacetime occupations in their own countries, little ground is left for hoping that the prestige of the occupying powers will be as great at the end as it was at the beginning of the occupation. And this conclusion is not substantially altered by pointing to the many men in the occupation forces who have worked with unsparing energy and complete integrity at their tasks and some of whom have continued at their posts when they could have gained materially by going elsewhere. This side of the picture is less spectacular and less known to the indigenous peoples than the other.

The German people have a long and hard path to follow before they will inspire in others confidence that they have turned permanently into the ways of peace. The evil remnants of the old order have not all been extirpated. Nevertheless, it is well that, since the period which this book covers, the apparatus of alien military government has been reduced, an indigenous Western government has been formed and given increasing powers, and the New Colonialism is rapidly fading away. The seeds of reform can grow only from within.

CHAPTER XVIII

Filling One Gap and Creating Another

LORD KEYNES headed a distinguished group of British officials who left London in September 1945 to arrange for the winding up of Lend-Lease, to review and confirm in formal negotiations the results of the earlier informal discussions on the main outlines of commercial, raw material, and cartel policy, and, last and most important, to arrange financial aid to tide over Britain's balance-of-payments difficulties. The amicable nature of the informal preliminary talks in London had made us hopeful of a reasonably quick agreement in Washington.

But weeks and then months passed and the Washington negotiations dragged on in an increasingly unfavorable atmosphere. Sharp words were exchanged and serious divisions were revealed on financial aid to Britain, overshadowing the smooth and agreeable discussions on the other two issues. Lord Keynes presented an exhaustive statement of Britain's financial predicament and its historical origin in her unrivalled war effort. He showed how the loss of overseas assets and the diminution in the power to earn foreign exchange were the result of the early entry of the British people into the war, their resistance to the enemy after their European Allies had fallen and before the United States entered the war, the completeness of their mobilization for war, the curtailment of their exports, and the transference of workers from production for export to production of war goods. The extensive damage to the country from bombing and the running down and lack of replacement of equipment had added to reconstruction needs, and for a time had swollen urgent import requirements. Keynes's exposition was supported by abundant statistics and a careful analysis that laid bare the disturbing facts of Britain's postwar economic position. The conclusion to which all this pointed was that Britain was in urgent need of financial aid to avert disaster but that, having regard to the origin of her difficulties in the contribution made to a common cause, it would be unjust to saddle her with a burden of future debt that would hang over her for many years to come and constitute a source of future Anglo-American friction. Financial assistance should therefore be given as a grant, not a loan.

As we had expected in the embassy, this case, though brilliantly expounded and impressively supported by a wealth of data, had little effect on Washington. Neither the Congress nor the American people nor many American officials had been educated to an understanding of Britain's position and her economic contribution to the war. It had been the conscious or unconscious policy of the Administration and still more of the Press to give more domestic publicity to the role of the United States in the war than to the role of the Allies. This was tactically useful in combating former isolationists masquerading in other guises. But it had unfortunate results in other directions and aided the neo-isolationists in the postwar period. The United States negotiators, therefore, gave little or no attention to the origin of Britain's difficulties, and would consider no remedy other than that of credits to be repaid in the future. Their attitude created widespread disappointment bordering on resentment in Britain.

The friction which arose at the outset over this question of principle was greatly increased when the discussion turned to the size of the loan. Admittedly the difficulties of forecasting were immense, but Lord Keynes presented a carefully reasoned estimate, on which Whitehall had worked for several months, of the amount that would be needed. The United States negotiators countered with a proposal for a credit of substantially less than this amount, based on what they alleged to be domestic political expediency and not on a carefully reasoned estimate of the gap to be filled. Long-drawn-out higgling followed, ending in the time honored but arbitrary compromise of "splitting the difference"! So sharp were the differences and so unwillingly were the compromises made that the whole conference was overshadowed in the public mind by this single issue, and the striking progress made and amicable relations maintained in the discussions on the settlement of Lend-Lease accounts and on commercial policy were obscured in the public mind and failed to offset the impression of disharmony and acerbity left by the discussions on the loan.

Although the members of the United States delegation and their advisers showed a common front in the negotiations, there were disagreements among them in the delegation meetings. Those who were experienced in international affairs were more ready than those whose experience had been mainly in domestic affairs to offer generous terms to Britain. Among the former were William Clayton, Dean Acheson, and Dr. Harry White, and among the latter, Fred Vinson, who had succeeded Mr. Morgenthau as Secretary of the Treasury, and Marriner Eccles, chairman of the board of governors of the Federal Reserve System. Mr. Clayton—and, I believe, Mr. Acheson—advocated a larger loan than that which was given, Mr. Clayton contending that it would be following good banking practice to make the loan large enough to exclude the likelihood of a decline in confidence and a "run on the bank." Dr. White was in favor of an interest-free loan. But Mr. Vinson and Mr. Eccles held that $3,750 million was as much as could be got out of Congress. Mr. Vinson, besides being new and inexperienced in his post, seems to have allowed a personal pique against Lord Keynes to affect his attitude toward questions of substance, just when the times called for far-seeing statesmanship.

The details of the agreements are public property and only the main points will be mentioned here. A "line of credit" of $3,750 million was set up, on which the U.K. could draw up to the end of 1951, and an additional credit of $650 million was given to cover the final settlement of Lend-Lease. On both credits repayments were to be made beginning in 1951 and extending over fifty years. The interest rate was to be 2 per cent on the outstanding amount, but interest payments would be cancelled once and for all in any year in which Britain was faced with balance-of-payments difficulties due to a decline in her current earnings abroad. Then came the most controversial clause of all.[1] A year after the agreement came into force all restrictions on the use of sterling derived from current transactions were to be removed and the holders were to be free to convert it into any other currency, including dollars. Historically this last clause was the culmination of the long agitation in Washington, described earlier, against the "dollar pool"—an agitation carried on in the first place by exporting business interests and supported by officials subjected to pressure from congressmen.

In retrospect it seems surprising that in such a brief time after the

[1] Section 7.

war the convertibility clause in the Loan Agreement should have been adopted. Could it have been seriously believed that in a little over a year after the end of the war the network of world trade would be restored to a point where such a provision could really work successfully? Lord Keynes and his colleagues fought the clause long and hard, but in the end had to give way. On the U.S. side there had been no serious research into the future of international trade: little attention had been given to the illuminating study by the League of Nations Economic Secretariat, published in 1942, which showed the difficulties of establishing and maintaining a multilateral trading system.[2] It would have been reasonable to have adopted a clause providing for the restoration of convertibility of current sterling under specified world economic conditions, and fixing periodical meetings to consider whether those conditions had yet been established. Unfortunately, there was a strong political drive in Washington at the time to set precise and early time limits for the scrapping of economic measures adopted in wartime.

Another unfortunate though much less serious provision of the Loan Agreement was Section 9, which obliged the United Kingdom to accept a share of U.S. imports when limiting the total imports of any product which she had formerly imported to some extent from the U.S. This provision would have been reasonable in ordinary times, but in times of dollar shortage it might force the U.K. to choose between paying out much needed dollars and going without an imported product altogether. It is difficult to determine how far the U.K. was hampered by this clause later. Some useful exceptions to its application were provided.

The negotiations on the settlement of Mutual Aid and on international trade policy stood out in sharp contrast with those on the loan. Unfortunately, the controversies on the loan drew attention away from them and greatly reduced public appreciation in the United Kingdom of the benefits that came from them. The Mutual Aid Settlement, speaking roughly, wiped out all claims for the $16 to $21 million of Lend-Lease goods consumed by the U.K. during the war and prescribed terms of payment identical with those of the loan for the Lend-Lease goods received and consumed by the U.K. after the war and for U.S. military surpluses taken over by the U.K. This stood

[2] League of Nations, *The Network of World Trade*, Geneva, 1942.

in notable contrast with the deplorable terms foisted on the naïve and mild mannered Mr. Baldwin by the U.S. government in 1923, the excuse for which was expressed later by the equally mild and perhaps even more inept President Coolidge in the famous phrase, "Well, they hired the money, didn't they?" In the embassy in London we observed regretfully that the friction over the loan negotiations held back the British people from a full appreciation of this contrast, which in itself was a tribute to the development of the American people in the Roosevelt era.

In London we were gravely disturbed over the effect on British public opinion of the controversies in Washington, and feared trouble in Parliament when the agreements came up for debate. Before the agreements were signed in Washington, Ambassador Winant had been greatly worried over the deterioration in Anglo-American relations as the negotiations dragged on, and had sent for me to take part in drafting with him a message explaining the concern of the British cabinet, expressed to him by Mr. Attlee the day before, and the increasingly unfavorable public attitude toward the United States. In the embassy we had attempted to explain from time to time the attitude of the British people toward the economic losses which they had suffered during the war. But although certain individuals in Washington understood it, the majority did not, and they were taken aback by the British reaction to the loan.

As we had expected, the Washington agreements had a stormy passage in both Houses of Parliament, and the ministers who piloted them through had a difficult and anxious time. If there had been any practicable alternative measure and if the Labor Government had not been backed by a cohesive and well-organized party I doubt whether the Loan Agreement would have been accepted. Here was an object lesson in the errors of those Americans who regretted the victory of the Labor Party and imagined that it would have been better for the United States if Mr. Churchill had been returned with a Conservative majority. The Labor Party had trouble with a tiny majority of its "left" wing. But the whole Conservative Party was a sorry spectacle of confusion, vacillation, and dissension. Ambassador Winant had, with discretion, used his great personal influence in an attempt to persuade responsible Opposition leaders to support or at least not to oppose the agreements. Mr. Eden, Sir John Anderson, and even

Mr. Churchill well understood the necessity of endorsing the agreements, and some of the leaders would have taken their party into the division with the government if they had been able to do so. But a strong revolt broke out among the rank and file, and in a desperate effort to control it the leaders decided on a policy of abstention as a means of diverting conservative members away from the "Noes" in the Commons and the "Not contents" in the Lords. Their lack of control was strikingly brought out when, in the debate, the Conservative leaders both recommended that their followers abstain and themselves abstained, only to find a large section of their followers flouting their advice and voting against the agreements. Ninety negative votes, most of them Conservative, were cast against the Government's 345. This made us anxious regarding the outcome of the debate which was to begin three days later in the House of Lords, where the Conservatives had an overwhelming majority. The Ambassador found that Lord Cranbourne judged it best to urge abstention on Conservatives even though he would have preferred to vote for the agreements himself. But we felt anxious again as the hour for the debate approached: Lord Beaverbrook was agitating among Conservatives for a vote against all the agreements, regardless of the consequences on Britain's financial position. His campaign aroused talk in Labor circles of measures to curb the power of the House of Lords still further than the Parliament Act of 1911 had done.

Meanwhile, Lord Keynes was hurrying back to London. He had been on the other side of the Atlantic when the Commons debate took place, and the Loan and Lend-Lease Agreements had been expounded by Dr, Hugh Dalton, the Chancellor of the Exchequer, in a masterly opening speech, which still reads as an excellent statement of the whole question.[8] But in the House of Lords, Keynes himself could speak, and his presence was urgently needed in view of the weakness of Government representation there. Fortunately he was able to reach England on the first day of debate and to open the adjourned debate the next day in a memorable speech, which, perhaps more than any other single factor, ensured the passage of the resolution and kept down the negative vote to 8. There was an air of uncertainty about the result on the first day: the Labor vote was insignificant in the

[8] Hansard, *Parliamentary Debates,* Vol. 417, No. 58, December 12, 1945, pp. 422-43.

House of Lords, and if many of the Conservative peers had followed the example of the Conservative commoners the Government would have been defeated.

Keynes rose in an unsympathetic House to make the most effective speech of his career. It was a unique position that he had come to occupy. A public servant, brought up in an "academic" tradition, an expert or specialist who had worked on the details of complicated financial measures, he was yet able to sway a political assembly of discordant elements, most of them prejudiced against the measures which he appealed to them to support, but all of them deeply impressed with his sincerity, with the magnitude of his intellect, and with the eloquence and charm of his utterance. Perhaps part of the power of his speech lay in a capacity, which abounds in his writings, to carry his audience in imagination beyond the narrow, immediate "technical" issue to the wider forces which move human societies. His first sentences accomplished this:

"Two days at Westminster are enough to teach one what a vast distance separates us here from the climate of Washington. Much more than the winter waste of the North Atlantic and that somewhat overrated affair, the Gulf Stream, though that is quite enough in itself to fog and dampen everything in transit from one hemisphere to the other. Yet I can well see that no one would easily accept the result of these negotiations with sympathy and understanding unless he could, to some extent at least, appreciate the motives and purposes of the other side. . . . How difficult it is for nations to understand one another, even when they have the advantage of a common language. How differently things appear in Washington than in London, and how easy it is to misunderstand one another's difficulties and the real purpose which lies behind each one's way of solving them. . . ."[4]

The speech was itself a brilliant contribution toward explaining the American attitude to the British people, and it helped to relieve the tension and reduce the friction which had been induced by the negotiations. Once a decision had been reached, no negotiator ever stood more loyally than Keynes did behind the inevitable compromises. He had spoken at times during the negotiations in bitter, sarcastic lan-

[4] Hansard, *Parliamentary Debates*: House of Lords, Fifth Series: CXXXVIII, December 18, 1945, p. 778.

guage which offended some of the more sensitive negotiators. He had most reluctantly accepted, as a matter of necessity and after a last-ditch struggle, some of the provisions finally adopted. Yet, while frankly expressing his regret at some of the decisions, he stood firmly by all of them when he returned, and he allowed no word of recrimination to escape him, nor did he indulge in any of those devices of attacking by indirection into which less scrupulous negotiators, fearful of their prestige, might have been drawn before an audience that would have applauded any manifestation of discontent. He even seems to have underestimated in his speech the risks of the "convertibility clause," although he had carried on a long and bitter struggle against it in the negotiations. Notwithstanding occasional fits of pessimism Keynes's temperament was generally sanguine and he bore no grudges.

This was the last great public act of Lord Keynes. In the following week I left for Germany, and in the spring, just as I was about to discuss with the Ambassador a time for a dinner meeting with Keynes when he came back from the country, the news of his sudden death came. In the intervening period, still fatigued by the long-drawn-out loan negotiations, he had attended the meeting of the International Monetary Fund at Savannah, Georgia, expecting the session to be a quiet one. Unfortunately, it degenerated into another prolonged altercation, this time over what to many of us seemed minor issues, such as the location of the Fund's headquarters and the salaries of its directors. Here Mr. Vinson, still deficient in a sense of humor, continued his personal opposition to Keynes, with whose quick mind he found it difficult to cope in debate on the merits of the issues. It was an unfortunate turn of fate that took Keynes across the Atlantic to this meeting. On the eve of new developments, which, following a deceptive initial spurt toward recovery in Allied countries, were to expose the inadequacy of existing postwar plans and call for bold and constructive imagination, the great architect of so much of the postwar planning frittered away his scanty remaining stock of physical energy on issues that were not even of secondary importance in comparison with the pressing issues of world reconstruction, and on behalf of an institution that was not destined to play any significant role in the next few years.

Keynes's last economic paper appeared shortly after his death[5] and gives some important indirect clues to his outlook on reconstruction. Amid much that is wise, stimulating, and suggestive, it reveals some of the limitations of economists and their methods of analysis. His overoptimistic picture of the near future was based largely on financial statistics showing past tendencies in periods when conditions were very different from what they would be after 1945. He laid stress on the size of the foreign assets held in the United States, particularly the funds of the European Allies which had been blocked during the war, and pointed to the net debtor position (omitting gold holdings) of the United States at the end of 1945. But he did not mention that Western Europe would not receive UNRRA aid and that its import requirements included very large quantities of food as well as raw materials and other producer goods needed to restore its working capital and reequip its industries. His Table VI, showing European dollar holdings, would have appeared much less impressive if it had been compared with figures of import requirements valued in the sharply rising prices which followed the premature abandonment of controls in the United States. Moreover, the Latin American holdings, which at the moment looked impressive, would decline rapidly when wartime shortage of shipping and equipment for civilian needs had passed away and when the pent-up demand for American goods, swollen by inflation, was released with little check from ineffective import controls.

Nor was there any discussion in Keynes's paper of the future effects on the U.K. balance of payments of the breakdown in the system of world multilateral trade and the long and delicate processes of adjustment that would be required in the production and trade of every continent before stable trading relations could be restored between the United States and Great Britain. Surprisingly, Keynes buttressed his optimistic conclusions by paying unexpected tribute, first, to the teachings of the classical economists that, "There are in these matters deep undercurrents at work, natural forces, one can call them, or even the invisible hand, which are operating toward equilibrium"; and, second, to the "magnificent objective approach" of the United States *Proposals for Consideration by an International Conference on Trade*

[5] "The Balance of Payments of the United States," *Economic Journal,* June 1946, pp. 172-87.

and Employment, which he describes as being ". . . expressly directed toward creating a system which allows the classical medicine to do its work."[6]

Keynes made these points in a remarkable paragraph which will be of permanent interest to students of economic thought and, in truth, both of them are relevant and valid in appropriate circumstances. But I should have thought that they were quite out of place in the context in which Keynes put them. Neither of them taken separately nor both taken together could possibly remove, or even appreciably reduce, the pressing postwar international economic difficulties of Britain. The economic times were out of joint and Keynes would have done better to have revived the proposals in the first version of his plan for an International Clearing Union than to have offered the prescription contained in his last article. It was indeed ironical that he who invented the immortal—and devastating—phrase, "In the long run we are all dead," should himself at the last have chosen to eulogize the slow acting "classical medicine" at a time when the international economic order was rapidly moving towards a crisis, and when, if ever, the full implications of his sometimes misapplied phrase should have been driven home with all the wonderful eloquence at his command.

For all that, the passing of Keynes in the spring of 1946 was in its way as great a loss to the economic world as the passing of Roosevelt had been to the world of politics a year earlier. Notwithstanding the vast differences between the characteristics of the two men and the fields in which they worked, they resembled each other in the possession of great personal qualities of constructive leadership, based on rare political insight in the one and economic insight in the other, and on a rare ability in both to persuade their fellow men, which gave each of them a world pre-eminence in his own day and in his own sphere.

As Keynes passes out of the further history of postwar planning we would do well, too, to remember that, like Roosevelt, he lived by faith and not merely by reason. Professor Tugwell has shown the

[6] Keynes's generous tribute to the American contribution to this aspect of postwar planning may be compared with his attitude in 1942. The change may be attributed, not only to the development of Keynes's ideas but also to the closer personal relations between British and American negotiators which had removed earlier misconceptions.

vital role of religious experience in Roosevelt's life.[7] Doubtless Keynes's religion was radically different from Roosevelt's in its intellectual content or formulation. But it was real and vital:[8] the faith that was in him sustained his spirit through many setbacks, and kept him unsparingly dedicated to the causes for which he worked, and to which he sacrificed the limited physical energy that remained to him in the last ten years of his life.

While the loan to Britain and the settlement of Mutual Aid were being negotiated in Washington, London was struggling with more humdrum but not less vital issues of reconstruction and even of mere survival. Throughout the winter and spring the shortages of food and coal were an imminent threat to the very foundations of reconstruction in Europe. The European Coal Organization now filled an indispensable role. The foresight of a very small number of civil servants in London and Washington, and the cooperation of a few leading figures in the American coal industry, staved off disaster by organizing an emergency flow of coal from the United States to be allocated according to need by agreement on the ECO.

On food Washington was less cooperative: the War Food Administration was dominated by men of narrow outlook who dreamily imagined that the prewar world of food "surpluses" had returned. During the winter of 1945-1946 it was difficult to convince leading agricultural officials in Washington of the necessity for further emergency measures to meet the shortage of both foodstuffs and feedstuffs. In the work on food questions in the Economic Committee

[7] R. G. Tugwell, "The Preparation of a President," in *Western Political Quarterly*, June 1948, pp. 150-51.

[8] Two incidents remain vividly in my memory. One evening during the height of the war when the Ambassador and I were dining with the Keyneses in the basement kitchen of their house in Gordon Square, Keynes discussed the new Education Bill which was passing through Parliament. Referring to the provisions in it for undenominational religious teaching which, under the skillful diplomacy of R. N. Butler, Archbishop Temple, and others had been accepted through the country, he said, "Ten years ago I should probably have opposed this. But now I am in favor of it." And he went on to deplore the effects of what he considered to be the decline in the hold of religion and the emptiness that was left when old forms of it were discarded and nothing put in their place. On another such occasion, as we rose from the dinner table Keynes paused a moment, standing at the head of the table, and said, "Some of my friends take a very pessimistic view of the future, but I do not agree. I believe that the world is about to enter on a period of the greatest advances yet made." And his eyes and his voice conveyed to us an intense faith and conviction that unforgettably stamped that moment on my imagination.

for Europe and its food subcommittee, the U.K. representatives were always looking ahead, making studies on future prospects and bringing forward proposals to deal not only with immediate emergencies but also with emergencies expected in the near future. One of their proposals was that an extraction rate (of flour from wheat) of not less than 85 per cent should be accepted by all member countries. This was acceptable to all the European countries but, although I personally agreed with it, as the U.S. representative I could not join the agreement. Sometimes it was said that no useful purpose would be served by U.S. participation in such conservation measures because of the limitations on the quantities that could be transported, both to the eastern seaboard and across the Atlantic. But often this argument was of doubtful validity and its frequent use was unpopular. In 1945-1946 the lukewarm official position that we were obliged to take on the committees on a number of recommendations concerning food was discouraging to the representatives of the countries facing serious shortages.[9] Washington's attitude on food questions at this time was said in some quarters to be one of the reasons for Governor Lehman's decision at the Atlantic City meeting of the Council in March 1946 to resign his position as director of UNRRA. It was particularly on food questions that the Governor there vigorously expressed his dissatisfaction with the U.S. attitude. His resignation was a serious loss to UNRRA and his place was not adequately filled. His integrity, his international loyalty, and his dignified and effective handling of the meetings of the Central Executive Committee had endeared him to the representatives of all countries. His critics have not always appreciated the immense difficulties he had to face, particularly in the earlier stages of UNRRA's history. By the time he left UNRRA it was an effective working organization, carrying out day-to-day operations on a scale never before attempted by any international body.

At this meeting of the UNRRA council the decision was taken not to seek any further contributions for UNRRA. Since the United States was the largest contributor the decision depended on Washington's attitude. Unfortunately, it seemed to have been made already in practice: during the hearings in Congress on the second UNRRA

[9] For an illuminating account of the situation in Washington at this time see Bela Gold, *Wartime Economic Planning in Agriculture* (New York, Columbia University Press), 1949, Chap. XV. This study deserves wide attention.

appropriation the administration spokesmen had been severely heckled by reactionary congressmen and had been pressed back on their last defenses, one of which was that this was the final appropriation of its kind that Congress would be asked to make. This predisposed political circles in Washington to place the most favorable interpretation on reports of economic conditions in Europe.

Having crossed the Atlantic to attend the Council meeting after an interval of sixteen months since my previous visit to the United States, I was struck with the attitude of rather casual and easy optimism about European revival in many Washington circles. This stood in sharp contrast to the attitude on the other side of the Atlantic. An explanation of the difference would be complex, but one general factor that lay behind the contrasting attitudes was the fact of scarcity in the U.K. and Europe and its absence in North America. In Britain and Europe most of the goods that satisfied the basic needs of everyday life were drastically rationed. In addition, the governments were engaged in continual negotiations to decide on the allocation of scarce goods and services among claimant countries. Since most of the products that entered into international trade were abundant in North America and scarce in Europe, the negotiations had very different significance for the two areas.

However, it was not merely differences between the economic environments of Europe and the United States and differences in judgments on the supply situation but also increasing political friction with the Soviet Union which changed the attitude to UNRRA in some political circles in Washington. If there was a possibility that the Soviet Union might become an enemy instead of an Ally in the future, the question arose whether or not it was wise to assist Poland, Yugoslavia, and Czechoslovakia, who were believed to be falling increasingly under Russian domination and whose attitude to the United States was unfriendly if not hostile.

As so often happens in Washington, the question was not examined on its merits. After the summer of 1945 it was confused by rumors and gossip, alleging misuse of UNRRA goods in Eastern Europe. These allegations, beginning in whispers, were later proclaimed from the housetops, and in the end gained wide acceptance in the United States and almost general acceptance in Congress. A complete explanation of this strange spread of a myth cannot be attempted here, but having attended every Council meeting of UNRRA and almost every meeting of the Committee of the Council for Europe from the beginning of the organization to the middle of 1946, and having in the course of my duties to keep in constant touch with UNRRA affairs, I believe that the allegations that UNRRA aid was to a significant extent misused in the Central and Eastern European countries are without foundation—the product of tittle-tattle based on magnification of minor infractions or on fabrications designed to serve political ends. In every area which received UNRRA supplies, including the Ukraine and Byelorussia, UNRRA missions made continuous investigations into the local distribution of supplies. In addition, leading officials of UNRRA made frequent visits to the countries. Every alleged infringement of UNRRA conditions was investigated promptly. Those of us who served as U.S. representatives on UNRRA bodies had no reason to be biased in favor of the U.S.S.R. and the Eastern European countries. A large part of the time I gave to my duties on UNRRA matters in London was consumed in helping to organize the defeat of unacceptable resolutions by the Soviet Union. But, although there is no space in this study to go into details of the allegations made and the results of the investigation into them, it is only fair to record my view that the Eastern and Central European countries and the Ukraine and Byelorussia acted honorably, and that they reasonably fulfilled their engagements with respect to the relief goods which they received from UNRRA. Yet the agitation against UNRRA, fanned by isolationists and other political opponents of the administration, gathered such strength that even among congressmen and others well disposed toward international cooperation it seems to have been widely believed in the end that grave abuses prevailed in UNRRA.[10]

Throughout 1946 the proceeds of the second contribution to UNRRA provided a full and indispensable flow of supplies to the UNRRA countries, and at the end of the year enough remained to

[10] Fortunately, these false impressions are on the way to correction. During the preparation of documents by the staff of a congressional committee examining the European Recovery Program, some congressmen proposed the insertion of statements regarding the alleged abuses and failure of UNRRA, but there were sufficiently well-informed persons on the staff of the committee to persuade the congressmen that such statements were unfounded and should not be inserted. The weakness of UNRRA's public information system contributed also to public misconceptions of UNRRA's achievements.

continue the flow for several months into 1947. The discussions on relief which took place in 1946, therefore, were concerned not with the immediate position in the UNRRA countries but with the position that would arise in the spring or summer of 1947. The question arose, what needs would remain and how should they be met?

The effect of the anti-UNRRA campaign in congressional circles was to discredit in the minds of congressmen the method of meeting international relief needs by international organization. The issue that had been fought out in 1942 and early 1943 was reopened, and this time the supporters of an international approach were defeated by the supporters of a unilateral approach. The turn of the tide was the result of the false or exaggerated stories spread by reactionary congressmen on the supposed abuses of UNRRA relief, together with the frequent repetition of the argument that the United States had no control over the uses to which its supplies were put, although it provided nearly 70 per cent of UNRRA's supplies. On an international body, the critics said, the U.S., having only one among some 50 votes is always outvoted, and its supplies are disposed of in ways of which it does not approve but is powerless to change.

This reasoning seemed plausible to those who had no knowledge of the workings of UNRRA in practice. But it bore no relation to realities. In all the meetings of the Council and of the Committee of the Council for Europe I do not remember any important supply question on which the United States viewpoint was flouted or disregarded. It was important, however, that this result was achieved by persuasion and not by dictation. The doctrine that unless a supply country is given a veto power its supplies will necessarily be used in ways of which it does not approve is based on spurious logic. Actually, the distribution of supplies was made in accordance with general criteria of need agreed on by the countries concerned. Under these conditions there was much less discontent than there would have been if the supply countries had dictated what the distribution should be.

But the deterioration in the relations between the Western Powers and the Soviet Union began in political rather than in relief and reconstruction matters. The Soviet Union has never treated economics in abstraction from politics, even in the smallest degree. In personal discussions with Russian friends in London I soon gave up the habit of prefixing a chain of reasoning with the phrase, "From the economic point of view . . ." Such an approach is unintelligible to Russians brought up in their present social order.[11] But on the American side, also, economic policies seemed to be increasingly entangled in both international and domestic political difficulties throughout 1946.

The subordination of economics to politics in the foreign policy of the Soviet Union had the incidental effect of disclosing to those of us who negotiated with the Russians in London, both informally and on committees, some of the political principles which guided their international policies.[12] The differences which arose with the representatives of the Soviet Union from time to time usually reflected political policies determined at "high levels" in the Kremlin, which even apart from their intrinsic merits and demerits in principle, were often too oversimplified and inflexible to be adapted to technical matters but were yet adhered to with a wooden persistence that ignored difficulties in application and in administration.

Very early we were impressed in London with the clear-cut attitude of the Soviet representatives in personal conversations, and less directly in committees, on the question which countries should shape the postwar world. Unmistakably, Russian policy was that the three Great Powers whose forces had gained the victory should dominate the world, and that the other Allies should play subordinate roles. This conception fitted the circumstances of the war and it was only when the end of the war was in sight that it led to a clash between the U.S.S.R. and the Western Powers. But a second doctrine, which might almost be taken as a corollary of the first, was that after the Big Three the other Allies should be rated in importance, and given a commensurate voice and commensurate material aid, according to the amount and effectiveness of their resistance to the enemy during

[11] In the West the tendency has been in professional economic circles to go too far to the opposite extreme from that of the Russians.

[12] This experience extended, for the writer of this study, from June 1942 to May 1946 in London, and to the spring of 1947 at Lake Success. The press was not admitted to the meetings in London, and the fanfare that proclaimed and wearisomely reiterated, and perhaps in itself aggravated subsequent differences among the wartime Allies, was avoided. Among the numerous popular fallacies on international affairs few have done more harm than the idea that "secret diplomacy" is the villain of the piece. It may be agreed that in most cases the understandings reached in diplomatic negotiations should be made public, but this does not carry with it the corollary that the proceedings which led to the understandings should be held in public or should promptly be made public.

the war. Ironical as it seems today, the Russians rated Yugoslavia at the top of the secondary Allies! The application of these doctrines to UNRRA matters during the war has already been discussed.[13]

These doctrines were often combined with an intense suspicion of the United States and the United Kingdom. Again and again the Russian representatives, either on their own initiative or in support of the Yugoslavs or, later, the Poles, accused UNRRA, which on this matter they regarded as an instrument of the United States, of discriminating against Yugoslavia and Poland and in favor of Greece. Having been obliged to spend many weary hours in committee defending UNRRA against these attacks, I found something ironical in the praise lavished on UNRRA by the Russian representatives in the Assembly at Lake Success in November 1946. When UNRRA was dying the Soviet Union uttered eulogies over it, expressed approval of the principles on which it was based, and argued for its continuance or for the creation of a new international organization based on the same principles.

But until the liquidation of UNRRA was decided on there was little or no change in the attitude of the Soviet Union toward UNRRA. Russian suspicions and Russian accusations that the United States and Britain used UNRRA for their own purposes began in the war years. The postwar period, if it brought any change, brought a change in degree corresponding only to the changed circumstances of Europe. UNRRA greatly increased the extent of its operations after the war, and there was more scope for superficial charges of discrimination in the distribution of aid among the liberated countries. There was a period when port facilities were so inadequate in Yugoslavia that more goods were delivered to Greece than to Yugoslavia. Each month my Russian colleague on the committee in London sat up late at night when the monthly figures of operations were given to members of the committee and, poring over the statistics laboriously, made out a case for alleged discrimination against Yugoslavia, Poland, and sometimes Czechoslovakia. He knew little of the intricacies of procurement, transport, and loading and unloading facilities, and I believe was sincere in his charges, which a superficial interpretation of the statistics might at times appear to support. When he followed up with resolutions criticizing the Director General of UNRRA for

[13] See pp. 160-61.

alleged discrimination, sharp controversies broke out in the committee and it was sometimes difficult to defeat the resolutions. Explanation of the figures required much detailed information from competent operating officials in the countries to which the supplies were being delivered. The representatives of the continental European Allies were reluctant to take vigorous initiative in opposing the Soviet Union, and it was generally necessary for my British colleague and for me to organize the defeat of the resolutions of censure, which to the Russians and Yugoslavs was additional evidence of the undue influence of the United States and Britain on UNRRA policy! But none of these controversies was new in principle after the war.

On some of the broader political issues I believe that a similar conclusion can be reached: the effect of changes in external circumstances on an existing policy has been mistakenly interpreted as a change in policy. As we have seen, the Russians wished to carry over the policy of world control by the Big Three from the time of war to the time of peace and it was impossible for the United States and the United Kingdom either to accept such a role for themselves or to permit the Soviet Union to assume it. It was not the policy of the Soviet Union but that of the Western Allies which changed when peace came.

But the attitude of the U.S. administration on relief matters changed appreciably during 1946 as a by-product of changes in the political outlook. Mr. Byrnes had taken office as Secretary of State with high—and naïve—hopes of settling outstanding differences with the Soviet Union by bargaining and give and take after the manner of senators in the United States Congress. The Potsdam Conference—his first as Secretary of State—was not a success, but it might be said that there he initiated little of the play himself and that President Truman and Edwin Pauley had more influence behind the scenes. Later, however, he had wide scope and quickly ran into difficulties. Although he tenaciously pursued his way in London, at Moscow, at New York, and at Paris, he revised his earlier ideas of negotiating with the Russians; the attitude of East and West to one another hardened and Washington became less willing to associate itself with enterprises that might benefit the Soviet Union and the Eastern and Central European countries which were to an increasing extent becoming her satellites—though the process was as yet far from completion.

The consequence was that, in the course of 1946, the American policy toward international relief was reversed: the principle of international organization of relief on the basis of equality was abandoned after a creditable history, and a haphazard unilateral plan was substituted which was not only slow in coming into operation but also in the end was marred by political discrimination. Since the discussion of this subject was subsequently switched from UNRRA to the United Nations, and relief and reconstruction became increasingly merged in discussions, it will be convenient to carry over the details of subsequent developments into the next chapter.

In the heat of political controversy it has been argued that the West should not have aided Eastern European countries at all, whether through UNRRA or by other means. So easy is it to slip into the attitudes and morals of those against whom it is believed that a righteous "cold war" is being waged. I hold on the contrary that the American, British, and Canadian peoples and others who contributed to UNRRA have reason to be proud of rescuing Eastern Europe from starvation and extreme want after the war. It would be a miserably defeatist as well as a shockingly inhuman attitude to contend that starvation and emaciation should have been allowed to take their course for fear that Eastern Europe might be ranged against the Western World in a hypothetical future war. The Western World would not be worth preserving if its preservation depended upon the denial of the moral values on which the achievements of its civilization have been based.

CHAPTER XIX

The Gathering Crisis

THE gaps in the economic planning which remained at the end of the war were not filled quickly: it was only under the threat of crisis that any of them was filled. But the crisis came earlier in some fields than others. By the end of 1945 a hastily improvised but temporarily effective means of closing the gap in the British balance of payments had been accepted as the alternative to an immediate crisis. For the moment it closed one of the chief gaps left by wartime planning for the postwar period. Unfortunately, it treated the British balance-of-payments difficulties as an isolated problem it itself. Adequate studies were not made, and effective measures were not devised, to deal with the relations between Britain's difficulties and those of other European, of Far Eastern, and of Latin American countries. Any attempt to do this, however, would have exposed to view the second great gap in postwar planning, resulting from the lack of provision for financing and organizing on an international basis the reconstruction of the areas occupied during the war. And that might have meant additional appropriations to be sought from Congress, which seemed for a time to be swinging further to the right in a manner ominously suggestive of the years following the First World War. In addition, there is little evidence that government circles yet understood clearly the extent and significance of the gaps in postwar planning. Wishful thinking combined with inadequate knowledge to postpone action until a sharper emergency arose.

No sooner had the gap in Britain's balance of payments been flimsily closed when another large gap was opened by the decision to undo the wartime planning on relief and abandon all concerted international organization to deal with relief. The new gap would affect not only Eastern Europe but also Austria, Italy, and Greece—all of them areas of great concern to the West and, if anything, even less ready than the countries of Eastern Europe to stand by themselves.

But the opening of the new gap, and the flimsy nature of the covering which had been cast over the old one, were not revealed at once. The crises which were bound to follow because of the inadequacy of the loan to Britain, the premature end of UNRRA, and the failure to provide for Western European reconstruction, were postponed in 1946. Stocks of raw materials could still be drawn on by Britain with the aid of the loan, by Western Europe with the aid of its foreign assets which had been "blocked" during the war, and by Latin America with the aid of dollar credits accumulated in wartime.

But if the crises were postponed there were visible signs to the discerning onlooker that they were impending, and the present chapter, which is concerned particularly with the effects of the gap in planning for reconstruction, will take up the question why so much time was lost and so little was done throughout 1946 to prepare for the gathering economic storms.

Before the war ended, substantial assistance had been given to liberated countries on the European continent. The American, Canadian, and British military authorities had provided relief goods during the military period to the countries which they had liberated in Western and Southern Europe. The total value is said to have amounted to $1,500 million.[1] When the war closed, surplus property sales were an additional source of help.

At the close of the war the masses of people in the European liberated areas as well as in the United Kingdom hoped for a rapid restoration of the economic as well as the political ways of peace. They were ready and anxious to play their part in rebuilding the structure which had been destroyed by German and Italian aggression, though most of them did not wish the new structure to be identical with the old. For some time great progress was made. Except in Germany, iron and steel production showed a large rise, and chemical and engineering production showed a rise still larger. Textiles were slower to rise but were substantially higher at the end of the year. Harvests in 1946 for most European liberated countries were considerably larger than those in 1945. Inland water transport failed to recover rapidly, but the railways filled the gap by carrying more freight with less equipment than before the war.

[1] *Report of Committee of European Economic Cooperation*, II, 11.

In Great Britain the advances were even more striking than those on the European continent, except in coal and textile production. Britain had a more difficult task than the European countries in some respects, for it was vital to her not only to turn back productive factors from war to peace production but also to divert a larger quantity of productive factors than before the war into production for export.

These advances were clear evidence of the vigor of the British and the continental European peoples, but great difficulties remained. The increase in production was uneven—it would have been surprising if it had not been so. Unfortunately, the commodities which had been set back most were among the most important, and on their recovery depended the continued recovery in the production of other commodities and services. Food and fuel production had been seriously affected by the war, and it was not possible to increase agricultural production with the same regularity and assurance as manufacturing production. Restoration of livestock herds, at least of cattle and sheep, is a slow process, and becomes still slower when cereal production has been reduced and when in consequence the area formerly used for animal feeding stuffs must be turned to the production of crops for direct human consumption. But crop production had also fallen sharply, perhaps by one third, and the improvement was only moderate in 1946. Some of the factors used to produce crops had been destroyed, others damaged, others displaced, and others were obtainable from overseas. These losses could not be made good as rapidly as the losses in some manufacturing industries had been made good by the end of 1946. The decline in fuel production was mainly a question of equipment and labor: in the coal mining industry perhaps the restoration of the labor supply was the most important need of all.[2] But coal production involves more strenuous physical labor than many types of manufacturing production require, and it was held back by the low food rations in 1946.

Therefore, notwithstanding the strenuous labors of the British and continental European peoples in 1945 and 1946, much outside help was needed to prevent economic collapse and widespread human suffering. Large imports of food and coal from outside Europe were needed in some areas for the first time in history. But the exporting

[2] Europe depends to a much greater extent than North America on coal as a source of industrial and household fuel.

industries were not yet restored to the point where they could earn enough to offset the cost of the imports. In turning from production data to financial data the situation and prospects of Europe in 1946 appeared less favorable. To close the great gap between imports and exports, loans were needed in addition to UNRRA aid. But loans and UNRRA aid together were insufficient, and assets abroad had to be liquidated on a large scale. Over the whole year nearly equal amounts came from loans and from UNRRA aid, while assets abroad were liquidated to the value of about one-fifth of the total amount supplied in loans and UNRRA aid. The United Kingdom received a part of the U.S. loan and Canadian financial aid, but in turn gave out aid to UNRRA countries and to the most industrialized and therefore the worst hit zone of Germany. The Western European countries raised loans and reduced their gold and dollar holdings, which, unlike Britain's, had not been liquidated in the war. Eastern and Southern and part of Central Europe received UNRRA aid.

Throughout 1946 there was no prospect that any of the countries could be rendered independent of aid from outside Europe for some time to come. Food and raw materials from overseas would be indispensable to subsistence and to recovery of export as well as domestic industries.[8] But Europe's ability to import from overseas markets had greatly declined and there was no chance of its rapid restoration. A large income from investments was lost forever; greatly reduced earnings from rendering international services would take time to restore, and great expansion of export markets after six years of interruption would be difficult even when production was restored.

In these circumstances it seems surprising that throughout 1946 it was assumed in Washington, first, that the need for additional relief had passed except for small amounts that could be given unilaterally to Greece, Italy, and Austria, and, second, that no new measures were needed to deal with reconstruction except an extension of the lending authority of the Export-Import Bank by $1,250 million. In 1946 the State Department gave more attention and assigned more members of its staff to the work on the international trade charter and tariff reduction than to the work on relief and reconstruc-

[8] This was clear even without knowledge of the poor harvests to come in 1947.

tion, although much of the trade charter was applicable only to a "normal" peacetime world in which currencies were freely convertible and a firmly balanced network of multilateral trade had been established.

However, an attempt was made in another quarter in 1946 to draw attention in detail to the economic difficulties of Europe and to the nature of reconstruction needs.

Within the large and complicated structure of councils, commissions, sub-commissions, and committees which was being erected in 1946 in the newly formed organization of the United Nations, a "Temporary Sub-Commission on Economic Reconstruction of Devastated Areas" was set up in June by the Economic and Social Council. Ambassador Winant, after he had arrived in New York, expressed to some of us his concern that so large a part of the economic and social work of the U.N. was being directed to setting up machinery and so small a part to grappling directly with the urgent economic questions of the day—in particular the reconstruction of Europe. By temperament and on principle he disliked international gatherings which became for much of the time mere debating societies. Hence, he strongly supported the idea that a small body should investigate directly the reconstruction needs of Europe, and hoped that concrete recommendations would come from the sub-committee. Unfortunately, political demands raised the membership to twenty countries, with seven observers from other international bodies. Its terms of reference are of interest because of their recognition of the importance of reconstruction problems. The sub-committee was to define the "nature and scope," of these problems, to estimate the progress that had been made, and to advise on the "measures of international cooperation" that might accelerate it. Its operations lasted about six weeks. The meetings were held in London, and working parties made flying visits to the European Allied capitals.

Here was a great opportunity to call to the attention of the world the gravity and magnitude of the task of reconstruction that still remained a year after Germany had surrendered.

Unfortunately, the results of the investigation made little impression. The report itself had to be compiled in haste, and the text had to be agreed on by representatives who held divergent views on many issues. The secretariat of the United Nations was still in the process of formation and had not had time to accumulate data and source materials on contemporary conditions. A few members of the committee, notably the U.S. representative, Dr. Isador Lubin, played an active and constructive part in the preparation of the report. But for the assistance of the secretariats of the Economic Committee for Europe, the European Inland Transport Organization, and the European Coal Organization, the committee would have found great difficulty in preparing any report in such a short time.

But not all the difficulties arose from within the committee and its secretariat. Whatever its shortcomings, the report did provide enough data to show that all was not going well with recovery and that additional aid would be needed. But the committee members were representatives of governments and were obliged to act on instructions. The United States representative seems to have clearly perceived the need of more comprehensive aid from outside Europe, and to have strained the interpretation of his instructions as far as he could. But throughout 1946 Washington was not in a mood to encourage any initiative among its representatives on measures to aid Europe. The fear of Congress was very great, and there was no chance that any measure that would make it necessary to seek additional funds from Congress would be approved in the State Department. Consequently, the report of the sub-commission was not followed up.

When the United Nations Assembly opened in October there was widespread concern among the delegations regarding the economic state of Europe generally and the probable effects of the coming liquidation of UNRRA in particular. Broad discussions of these subjects took place in the Economic Committee of the Assembly. From these discussions, which were at times acrimonious, a central question soon emerged: if UNRRA was to be liquidated when it was acknowledged that recovery in Europe was not complete, what form of international organization, if any, should be set up to complete the work?

The answers to these questions revealed a fundamental difference of view between the United States and most of the European countries. But it was not a difference that could be shown in voting, for the representatives of all the countries realized that, since the greater part of the resources available in the world for relief and reconstruction lay in the United States, it was of little use for the rest of the world to attempt to set up an international body to assist the countries in difficulties unless the United States was prepared to take part in it. The fortunes of war and the distribution of capital and natural resources had placed the United States in the position of an arbiter over proposals for economic assistance to any part of the world. The U.S. delegation was indeed placed in an uncomfortable position. No one could move among the delegates of the other countries without sensing an air of regret and, among some, of disapproval, at the attitude of the United States. It was easy, of course, for highly nationalistic Americans to brush this aside as a manifestation of a growing tendency to expect Uncle Sam to carry the rest of the world on his shoulders. But the members of the U.S. delegation took more statesmanlike attitudes than that, and there was much uneasiness among them over the position which instructions from Washington obliged them to take. As far as economic matters were concerned it would have been better that the meeting of the U.N. Assembly in the autumn of 1946 had never been held.

The official position of the United States at this time was that, "The task of UNRRA is now being brought to a successful conclusion. The job of preventing chaos and starvation in the immediate postwar period and of starting the liberated countries on the road to recovery has been well done. . . . Starvation has been averted in these countries. Great progress has been made on the road to recovery. . . . Long strides have been made towards the resumption of normal industrial and agricultural life. The end of the UNRRA program will find the UNRRA receiving countries with agricultural production within sight of prewar levels, with industrial recovery well under way and with the prospect of substantially increased exports during the coming year." Admitting that "certain countries will still need further help" the statement went on to claim that, "The countries so situated, according to our studies, will be few in number and in comparison with the resources required by UNRRA the amount of assistance involved will be relatively small."[4]

But in order to justify its proposed scheme for dealing with the necessary residual aid on a unilateral basis rather than through a new international organization, the statement, which had just claimed that agricultural production was "within sight of prewar levels," suddenly changed its tune. "Time is of the essence in this matter.

[4] U.S. Delegation to the U.N., Press Release No. 78, November 14, 1946.

You can't postpone hunger, as Mayor LaGuardia has said. By the end of February the UNRRA pipelines will be running dry. The critical period will be in the late winter and early spring . . . we must move and move quickly. The crisis will be over by summer. You don't need a new international organization to do this short-term job."[5] Finally the claim was made that, "We are guided in our approach to this matter by the same principles we followed when we helped to create UNRRA."[6]

This was an ingenuous statement aimed at making the best of a difficult case. But the historian or the political theorist of a future age would be misled if he took it at its face value. It would be more accurate merely to point out that Congress had turned against the idea of an international organization to handle relief, that the administration was afraid to approach Congress for further funds for UNRRA or for any new international body, and finally that, absorbed with other interests, Mr. Byrnes had done little or nothing to examine comprehensively the actual economic prospects of Europe in 1947, not to speak of any longer period. The Assembly set up a "Special Technical Committee on Relief Needs after Termination of UNRRA." A competent U.S. representative sat on this committee which made its report in January 1947. Its findings were that, after UNRRA ended, further financial assistance would be needed by Austria, Greece, Hungary, Italy, Poland, and Yugoslavia. The U.S. representative made a reservation respecting Yugoslav needs on the ground that later information showed that the potato crop was higher than the committee had estimated it to be. But the figures for Poland were not challenged and appeared as the second largest estimate of needs in the list.

In the first half of 1947 residual UNRRA supplies kept the UNRRA countries going. The U.S. administration approached Congress for $350 million to use for residual aid, but more than six months went by before the authorization was granted. The advantages of unilateral action in saving time were not clearly demonstrated. It was fortunate that residual UNRRA supplies lasted as long as they did.

The history of residual aid from the United States shows how completely—for a time—United States policy toward international relief had been reversed by postwar political pressures in Wash-

[5] *ibid.* [6] *ibid.*

ington. Yugoslavia and Poland, although their needs had been certified by the U.N. committee, were refused aid. The rejection of aid to Yugoslavia may have been justified by food conditions in Yugoslavia, but it is difficult to acquit Washington of political motives in refusing aid to Poland. I was in the committee room during the discussions of the special committee at Lake Success and concluded that the Polish representative, with whose work I had already been acquainted in London, was more qualified in agricultural matters than any other representative on the committee and was honest in dealing with the estimates. However, Washington sent three American investigators to Poland who, after a brief visit, came back with the convenient conclusion that Poland needed no aid. Our experience in London during the war had taught us that rapid visits to a country, bringing "eye witness" testimony, were less reliable than appraisal of data by experts experienced in food and agriculture, even when the experts made the estimates outside the country. When the exceptionally critical eye cast upon Polish requirements is compared with the zeal shown in meeting Italian needs, though Poland had been an Ally and Italy for the greater part of the war an enemy, it would be difficult to deny that the growing but at that time far from complete domination of Poland by the Soviet Union played an important role in the one case and the strength of the vote of Italian origin in the United States in the other.

The special pleading that ran through the official explanation of the United States position at the meeting of the Assembly was carried over into a discussion of the International Monetary Fund and the International Bank. From these organizations, it was said ". . . there will be available some fifteen billion dollars for assisting countries in acquiring the foreign exchange necessary for the reconstruction and development of their economic life and for the stabilization of their currencies."[7] This statement sounds impressive: much reconstruction could be done with $15,000 million! But how much of this sum could be used for reconstructing Europe and in what time? The total assets of the Fund and the value of shares subscribed to the Bank have been each in the neighborhood of $8,000 million in the later 1940's. The total sales of currencies by the Fund amounted to $461 million at the end of 1947, and $700 million at the end of 1948. The loan disbursements of the International Bank

[7] *ibid.*

amounted to $300 million in 1947 and to $500 million at the end of 1948. It would be misleading to regard even these sums as freely available to meet any kind of relief or reconstruction need in the receiving countries. Advances by the Fund and by the Bank are designed to meet specific purposes falling within the scope of their charters. The Fund is to assist countries which need only temporary help to restore their balances of payments, and which are likely to be able to repay the advances in a reasonably short period. Thus, for example, Britain was forced to take drastic restrictive measures in 1931, not because its external assets were less than its liabilities but because they were out on longer term and could not be recalled in time to meet a sudden demand for repayment of short-term liabilities. The Fund is admirably designed to meet such contingencies in the future: in such cases it could make advances in full confidence of repayment. But the European countries in 1946 were in no such position as Britain had been in 1931: they needed advances on a scale and for purposes which made early repayment impossible. By no stretching of its terms of reference could the Fund be made to serve an important part of their needs. It was and still is an organization intended to operate in a world which has passed through the rapids of postwar reconstruction into the smoother waters of "normal" peacetime economic conditions. The Articles of Agreement of the Fund state that, "The Fund is not intended to provide facilities for relief or reconstruction or to deal with international indebtedness arising out of the war."[8]

Nor was the International Bank in a position to play a leading role in postwar reconstruction. A substantial part of its funds were to be used for "development" projects. It was required, in making a loan, to pay "due regard to the prospects that the borrower . . . will be in a position to meet its obligations under the loan" and to "act prudently both in the interests of the particular members in whose territories the project is located and of the members as a whole."[9] As we can see from the subsequent operations of the European Recovery Program, the Bank, even if its funds had been large enough, would not have been acting "prudently" in advancing loans to cover the immediate urgent needs of the European countries.

The truth is that, of all the earlier proposals with respect to an international monetary organization, only the original Keynes Plan

[8] Article XIV. Section 1.

[9] Article III, Section 4 (5).

and White Plan were conceived on a scale at all adequate to deal with any significant part of postwar emergency needs for relief and reconstruction. But the Keynes Plan and the earlier drafts of the White Plan were subsequently whittled down to a point where it was believed that they would be acceptable to the U.S. Congress. Both in the size of the resources and in the conditions of their use the final plan was far removed from the earlier proposals, and the Fund and the Bank, instead of being a present help in time of postwar trouble, played, the first a negligible and the second a minor role in the salvaging of economic civilization.

Since the economic difficulties of the European continent were not confined to UNRRA countries, a new approach would have been needed even if UNRRA had continued. The difficulties of Western Europe were rapidly increasing in the later part of 1946 and in early 1947. The initial spurt in manufacturing production, which drew on stocks of raw materials faster than they were replaced, was rapidly slowing down. Considerable financial assistance had been received in loans and in credits on surplus property and Lend-Lease "pipeline" supplies. But exports recovered slowly. Between the middle of 1946 and the middle of 1947 French exports amounted in value to about two-fifths of her imports, Belgian a little less than a half, Norwegian between one-third and one-half, Netherlands about two-fifths. Only the United Kingdom had come close to a balance, with exports roughly four-fifths of imports. These large deficits forced a great liquidation of external assets, for credits and export receipts together were far below what was needed to finance imports. France's losses were particularly heavy: in 1946 her gold reserves dropped by $688 million and her funds in United States banks by $223 million—43 per cent of her external resources. Nor was she in measurable distance of equilibrium at the end of the year: her losses continued in 1947. Belgium and the Netherlands, whose gold reserves remained fairly steady in 1946, began to lose gold heavily in 1947. All these countries also continued to lose deposits in United States banks and short term U.S. Government securities.

These difficulties would have been great enough if import prices had remained stable: they were aggravated by the premature abandonment of controls in the United States, from which, because of the world scarcity, a large proportion of European imports had to be drawn. The initial mistakes had been made by President Truman in the excitement of VJ-Day, but subsequently Congress went much further and, with a reckless disregard of consequences, overruled the administration and cut away all restraints on price rises in the necessities of life. The rise of food prices, in particular, which could have been prevented, not only injured people of low incomes at home but was a serious blow to former Allies who, owing to the effect of the war on European agriculture and later to the disastrous drought and frost in the agricultural year 1946-1947, were forced to buy grain from the United States at any cost. The doctrine of economic laissez-faire, preached by Senator Taft and his colleagues with a spurious logic and a narrowness that was impervious to reasoning, was costly to European as well as to American workers.

The mounting economic difficulties in 1947 were not confined to Europe. The financial positions of many Latin American countries, some of which ended the war as creditors of the United States, rapidly deteriorated. The prices of the exports of Latin American countries had increased more than the prices of their imports, giving them a great advantage in the early postwar years over countries whose exports, like those of the United Kingdom, were mainly of manufactured goods. But this advantage was largely thrown away.

"While the increase in the value of exports slightly exceeded the increase in the value of imports between 1945 and 1946, in 1947 the expansion of imports far exceeded that of exports . . . 14 of the 20 Latin American republics experienced new or greater trade deficits, or smaller surpluses, in the two years 1946-47 as compared with the war years 1944-45."[10]

In 1946 the Latin American countries as a whole balanced their merchandise accounts with the United States: in 1947 their imports exceeded their exports to the United States by $1,000 million. To offset this deficit, they obtained dollars from their exports elsewhere, and most of all from the United Kingdom, which paid $600 million to them during 1946 and 1947. In 1947 their reserves fell heavily. Not only had the United Kingdom to pay much-needed dollars to Latin America in 1947 but in addition some of the South American countries were able to use wartime sterling debts of Britain to buy

[10] D. L. Grove and G. M. Alter, "Latin America's Post War Inflation and Balance of Payments Problem," in *Federal Reserve Bulletin*, November 1948, p. 1345.

out British assets, particularly railway stock. The necessity of food imports also forced Britain and some of the Western European countries into bilateral trade arrangements, notably with Argentina, in which they were obliged to pay extortionate prices for their imports. Argentina not only refused to take part in the work of the International Emergency Food Committee, successor to the Combined Food Board, but also flouted the recommendations of the committee and insisted on taking full advantage of the necessities of the war-torn countries of Europe. It would be difficult to find in the modern age a more cynical disregard of the decencies of international economic intercourse in times of trouble.

We have next to consider how it was that, after the war, Latin America, starting in a far better external financial position than Europe, and continuing to benefit from the existing price relationships between raw materials and fabricated goods, soon lapsed into financial confusion and hindered instead of helping the recovery of Europe.

The economic order in Latin America was ill equipped to deal with the wide and rapid wartime changes which would have strained the resources even of the best governments and most advanced peoples. There would in any case have been great pressure on the financial structures of the countries from the release of pent-up demand for imports, held back by lack of shipping during the war, which were needed to offset depreciation and provide for renewals. But demand for imports did not stop there. Wartime purchases by the Allies on credit were a source of inflation and Washington price policies in financing them had aggravated it. The rise of money incomes led to increased demand, part of which was directed to imported goods. The social system in some of the countries was weighted in favor of small possessing classes, and a wasteful demand for luxury imports and for luxury services abroad intensified the inflation. These unnecessary demands were little checked by formal controls which, in countries where integrity in public life was a rare virtue and administrative machinery and experience were lacking, served more as window dressing than as effective instruments of emergency planning. The absence of effective controls prevented the restrictive selection of imports, such as Britain practiced, which would have mitigated some of the effects of inflation on the external balance of payments. The deterioration in the financial position of Latin America in these years might usefully be examined by those who have inveighed against the United Kingdom controls over imports and the use of foreign exchange.

But balance-of-payments difficulties in the Western Hemisphere extended to the north as well as to the south of the United States. Canada, notwithstanding its high productivity and excellent economic organization, became deeply involved in the economic difficulties of Western Europe, with whose fortunes her own were inseparably linked by the world division of labor which had grown up over several decades, and which was related to the distribution of population and natural resources and the stages of economic development reached in different parts of the world. The ratio of population to land was low in Canada, the supply of capital—aided by past British and contemporary American lending—was high, the contour of the land and the quality of the soil were favorable to extensive mechanical cultivation of grains, and minerals abounded in the vast territories of the north. Canada exported food and raw materials on a great scale and a large proportion of its exports moved across the Atlantic to countries in which population was dense and land scarce, which in consequence depended as overseas sources for part of their indispensable food and raw material supplies and which in more normal times were able to export large quantities of manufactured goods, requiring little land in their production, to offset these imports.

As long as the chief currencies of the world were convertible into one another, this international division of labor worked well for Canada. The net earnings from Canada's trade with Europe could be used to cover the net liabilities incurred in its trade with the United States. But when sterling and dollars ceased to be freely convertible Canada was placed in a quandary. It had either to seek a redirection of its trade or to press the United Kingdom to pay for its products in dollars or convertible sterling. The first course ran counter to the long-run international division of labor that reflected the distribution of population and natural resources, and urgent needs of the people of the United Kingdom in the short as well as long run. Moreover, even if it had been practicable, it would have taken time to put into effect. The second course was likely to upset further the balance of payments of the sterling area with the dollar area, and might even help to provoke a grave financial crisis.

Thus the international economic conditions of 1947 made a sterling crisis unavoidable, not through economic defects within the United Kingdom itself but through the general disorganization of the greater part of the world and notably of continental Europe, the Far East, and Latin America. Europe had made some progress but was still unreconstructed; large parts of the Far East were in a state of chaos; and Latin America had mismanaged its economic affairs. No concerted outside move had been made to assist Western Europe, and only an inadequate move had been made to assist Southern Europe, to reconstruct its halting and limping economic order. Into this gap and into the gap created by the lack of effective controls in Latin America, there flowed in effect a large part of the United States loan to the United Kingdom. The drain on Britain's command of dollars had begun before full sterling convertibility on current transactions had been declared, but it became a torrent when the United Kingdom formally put into effect the convertibility clause of the Anglo-American Loan Agreement of 1945. The deficit for 1946 had been $1,600 million. Early in 1947 an official estimate had placed the probable dollar deficit for the year at $1,400 million. Actually, in the first half of 1947 alone the loss amounted to $1,400 million and the amount available under the loan was fast disappearing.

In view of the comment and criticism which was heard, then and later, over this major crisis in postwar economic history, it is important that the real lesson of 1947 should be dissociated from the irrelevant and often partisan attempts at explanation at the time. It is, of course, true that the inclement winter and the fuel shortage in the early part of 1947 increased the difficulties of reconstruction. But even if these difficulties had not existed the most that can be said is that the crisis might have been postponed for a few months: in the conditions of the time it was bound to come sooner or later. It was the direct consequence of the failure to grasp and make adequate provision for immediate postwar reconstruction, particularly in Europe. The British financial crisis was a symptom of world-wide economic malaise, and its cure was not to be found in Britain alone.[11]

The more we study the crisis of 1947 the more ill-advised the

[11] It was, of course, aggravated by inflationary pressures in the United Kingdom. But this condition was almost world-wide, and the U.K. had done better than most countries in grappling with it. A forced domestic loan in addition to the measures actually adopted might have improved matters.

convertibility clause in the loan agreement of 1945 appears. It is hardly an exaggeration to describe it as the offshoot of pressure from vested interests combined with a narrow doctrinaire view of international economics and a lack of understanding of the structure of international trade. To fix an early and arbitrary date for convertibility in the confused world economic conditions that followed the war, and to imagine that a loan of $3,750 million would safeguard the sterling area, was to carry wishful thinking far beyond the danger point. The inevitable result was to turn the sterling loan into a European reconstruction loan and a means by which Latin American countries could postpone or escape the consequences of economic negligence. For these purposes the loan was inadequate and would have been drained away completely in a few months if sterling convertibility had not been revoked.

Unfortunately, the lesson of the crisis of 1947 was only imperfectly learned. The crisis became a subject of political controversy on both sides of the Atlantic and, as usual, political controversy did more to becloud than to clarify the underlying economic issues. The Conservatives strove to make political capital out of the Labor Government's difficulties. Mr. Churchill had descended from his wartime heights of statesmanship to a far lower political level on which he did not hesitate to misrepresent the achievements and exaggerate the shortcomings of his political opponents. His words gain greater attention on this side of the Atlantic than those of other British statesmen, and in peacetime are too often taken at their face value in the United States. Thus his irrepressible accusations since the crisis of 1947 that the Labor Government "frittered away" the United States loan, though no more than a politician's trick to gain votes from his opponents, have been taken seriously by many Americans and have been turned to Britain's disadvantage by noisy and at times influential anti-British groups. In the United States the Labor Government has had a bad press for the same reasons that President Roosevelt had a bad press during the period of his great reforms. American readers dependent on the press have been drawn off into side issues with little opportunity to trace the world-wide relationships in the setting of which the difficulties of the United Kingdom should be studied. Hence the failure of the attempt at convertibility in 1947 did not long restrain even some sections of political and business opinion from calling for early steps towards a return to sterling convertibility.

Fortunately, however, the administration attitude toward Europe changed markedly in 1947. I am not in a position to trace this change in detail, but Dean Acheson and William Clayton seem to have had much to do with it. Mr. Acheson, from my first direct acquaintance with him in 1941, struck me as having a far better understanding of the economic position and the economic difficulties of the United Kingdom than anyone else at a high level had, and his later work also made him familiar with the economic difficulties of continental Europe. Mr. Clayton, during his visits to Geneva and London at the time of the trade negotiations, was greatly impressed with the short-run difficulties of Britain and Western Europe which prevented them from accepting, or made them hesitate to accept, commitments on commercial policy with which they agreed in principle and which they hoped would be applicable in the long run.

The new Secretary of State, Mr. Marshall, had been long accustomed to working in a large organization whose functions could be exercised efficiently only so long as its central authority was prepared to delegate duties and extensive power to make decisions to trusted subordinates, and normally to accept advice from them on a wide range of matters, confining itself generally to broader questions of policy on which it alone could make the final decisions. Here was a sharp contrast to the methods of Mr. Byrnes, who, following the customs and manners of senators, worked with and took into his confidence only a very small group of officials within the organization, leaving the rest with little knowledge of his intentions and uncertain how far they were expected to go on their own initiative when questions arose that required prompt decisions.

Secretary Marshall had not shrunk from bold decisions when the conditions of the time made them necessary, and he did not do so now when the plan associated with his name began to take form, first in broad, general terms and later, with British and Western European help, as a concrete, detailed scheme, transcending any measures of international aid conceived in the past and bringing new hope to the struggling peoples of a continent which had been the main theater of the most destructive war in history. The development of this large-scale postwar reconstruction scheme, which went far to close the largest gap in postwar planning, lies beyond the period which the present study covers and belongs to a sequel. Later it was extended to cover not only the liberated countries which the Soviet Union could not deter from joining it, but also Germany. Thus it achieved that unified treatment of the task of reconstruction in both Allied and ex-enemy countries which extinguished the last traces of the Morgenthau plan and the notorious directive JCS 1067, and which alone could deal adequately with the common interests of the peoples of that continent which, notwithstanding its recent tribulations, still embodies the greatest achievements of civilization. That this approach did not come earlier is one of the principal criticisms that can be directed against the postwar planning during the war.

CHAPTER XX

The Summing Up

THE diverse threads of discussion in the preceding chapters have now to be drawn together.

The origins of some of the international economic difficulties of the postwar years are to be found in changes that preceded the Second World War. The exceptional combination of circumstances that gave rise to an almost world-wide multilateral trade for about half a century was already breaking up before the war began. The First World War and, even more the Great Depression in the early 1930's, had shaken an inherently delicate structure: the recovery of international trade lagged far behind the recovery of domestic production, and both were slow, painful, and incomplete throughout the decade.

A new calamity then struck this faltering economic order. Between the summers of 1939 and 1945 the intricate structure of social and economic relationships over continental Europe and the Far East, which had determined the growth and the spread of knowledge and skills and the flow of goods and services, and which had established common practices and accommodations among diverse practices, fell apart in a disorderly tangle from which few strands could be extricated unbroken after the war. This disruption of collective human relationships was even more far-reaching than the destruction of property and the defacement of cities and countryside. It is not surprising that convalescence from the demoralizing wartime experiences of the occupied areas has been slow and interrupted by many setbacks. Adolf Hitler went down to crushing military defeat, but not all his works perished with him. His boast that if he fell he would drag down Europe with him should not have been taken lightly.

During the recent war there was greater awareness than during the First World War of the danger that peace would come with the Allies unprepared to deal with the economic aftermath of war. In Britain and Canada the public demanded bold postwar reconstruction measures, but in the United States the forces of reaction were gradually gaining ground and support for bold postwar measures was confined chiefly to government circles. Both in London, where the government was a coalition, and in Washington, where it had to contend with a reactionary opposition, domestic political difficulties affected the course of postwar international economic planning. From time to time the desire to obtain harmony between political parties in the pursuit of a common war aim held back progress on the more controversial issues. Some fields of postwar planning were more affected by them than others, and this contributed to, though it was not the sole cause of, the uneven development of the plans for dealing with different aspects of postwar international economics, and the failure to provide by the end of the war a comprehensive and well-proportioned scheme for winning the peace.

The course of international economic planning during the war revealed a growing separation between plans for the short run and plans for the long run. In the early stages attempts were made to integrate short- and long-run plans. The Hot Springs Food and Agricultural Conference laid down in its field a well-integrated set of economic principles to govern the immediate aftermath of war, the transition period, and long-run development. Similarly the Keynes Plan for an International Clearing Union showed clear recognition of the needs of reconstruction and the dangers of inflation in the early postwar period and proposed to finance relief and reconstruction at least partly through the Union, whose long-term functions would be temporarily curtailed to meet urgent short-term needs in the period of reconstruction. The first version of the White Plan, which was also designed primarily to set up permanent organizations to deal with long-run questions, nevertheless proposed that these organizations should provide large funds for reconstruction. Unfortunately, these farsighted proposals to include provision for the short as well as the long run in the same plans were hurriedly dropped. The short-term functions which Keynes and White first proposed for the international monetary organizations would have required much larger funds than were needed for the long-term functions. Even the earlier amounts proposed for long-term purposes were whittled down through fear of Congress, notwithstanding the protests and misgivings of Britain, and the scope of their use was narrowed. Thus the International Monetary Fund became the most clear-cut case of planning entirely for the long run. It stood at the opposite end of the scale to the relief plans. It could play its part only after a transition period of indefinite duration had ended. Its establishment was a notable achievement, but it was not an example of "putting first things first."

The functions of the International Bank were spread between postwar reconstruction and long-term development. Thus they overlapped two of the categories into which postwar planning has been divided in this study. For about two years after fighting ceased in Europe, the Bank was cited by harassed United States spokesmen, in reply to critics who argued that inadequate provision had been made for meeting the needs of the transition period, as the appropriate body to assist in financing reconstruction. Such arguments were grossly misleading. The total funds which the Bank could command were sufficient to cover only a very small proportion of the total needs for reconstruction, and part of them had to go into long-term development. Moreover, even if the funds had been much larger, the conditions on which loans were to be granted would have made it impracticable to use them for the purposes for which funds were desperately needed in Europe. The Bank made some useful reconstruction loans for limited purposes, but there was never any likelihood that it could meet a considerable part of reconstruction needs and it should, therefore, be classified as primarily an organization to perform a long-run function on a modest scale.

The third organization which was intended to play an important long-run role was the proposed International Trade Organization. As we have seen, the original conception of such an organization came from Britain, not from mossback "Cobdenites," as some British writers suggest, but from economists of modern outlook. Unfortunately, owing to political delays, the planning on trade fell far behind the planning on finance, and when the war ended a long and thorny path remained to be trodden before conferences to establish an International Trade Charter and an International Trade Organization and to reduce tariffs, could be called, and a still longer and thornier one before agreement could be reached.

The later delays can be traced to two causes. The first of these was the insistence at high levels in Washington that the cumbrous mode of reducing tariffs by treaties between pairs of countries, which had been inherited from the prewar period to which it was suited, should be carried over to the postwar period to which it was not suited. This made it inevitable that the negotiations to reduce tariffs would be long-drawn-out. Moreover, it alienated British sympathies and reduced the extent of British cooperation in subsequent negotiations. The second cause of delay was to be found in the decision to introduce into the charter of the proposed International Trade Organization a comprehensive and detailed agreement covering the whole range of commercial policy other than the rates of reduction of tariffs. The subject matter with which an International Trade Organization would be concerned was broader in scope, more complicated in detail, and more controversial in content than the subject matter with which the Fund and the Bank would be concerned. To insist that the establishment of the organization should await detailed agreement on all this was to sacrifice the opportunity to set up the organization before the drive to create new international machinery had spent its force.

I believe, therefore, that the decisions, first, to make no effort to obtain an agreement to reduce tariffs immediately after the war by a simpler method than that of bilateral treaties, and, second, to postpone attempts to set up an International Trade Organization until agreement had been reached on the text of a comprehensive charter, were unfortunate, and that efforts should have been made to obtain congressional approval of a method of reducing tariffs all round in one act to be agreed on at a general conference. If they had failed, the administration would have been no worse off and might even have found it easier to obtain a renewal of the Reciprocal Trade Agreements Act as an alternative to the wider powers. Second, an International Trade Organization might have been set up immediately after the war with brief and simple terms of reference, one of which would have charged it with the responsibility for preparing a code of policy and practices in international trade. I suggest that the adoption without further elaboration of the *Proposals for Expansion of World Trade and Employment* as the charter of the new organization is the most that should have been attempted, and that the decision to go further before setting up the organization was an unnecessary gamble.

Beyond this lay two other even more far-reaching errors in the planning for international trade. First, the short-run difficulties of reviving trade between the liberated areas were not understood and the necessity of a radically different approach to them from that of the Charter was not widely realized. Second, the difficulties of restoring a world multilateral trading system were misconceived. Although economists of modern outlook no longer believed that the reduction of trade barriers alone would restore such a system, most of them did believe that a reduction of trade barriers would do so when combined with the maintenance of full employment. This belief has survived well into the postwar period, with the qualification that, in addition, aid under the Marshall Plan would be necessary up to 1950 or 1951 before a full multilateral system could be established. It is based upon an oversimplified view of international trade and capital movements and an excessive faith in the "price system" as a self-contained instrument of economic change and adjustment. It remains today as a hindrance to an understanding of the conditions of a world multilateral trading order and an unnecessary source of friction between the North Atlantic Allies. However, its significance is greater for the period of recovery after 1946 than for the earlier period, and a detailed analysis of the subsequent developments, as well as the full supporting arguments for this point of view, belong to a study of that period rather than to the present study.

Within its limits, the planning for the long run was carried out thoroughly, and engaged the energies of many of the keenest intellects in London, Ottawa, and Washington. The central idea behind it was to prevent a recurrence of the outstanding economic troubles of the interwar period. A Monetary Fund was to guard against a repetition of the exchange crisis in 1931 and 1932 by providing funds to tide over temporary balance-of-payments difficulties. An International Bank was to guard against the abuses of international lending in the 1920's. An International Trade Organization was to release world trade from the shackles that had been fastened on it after the Great Depression began. Domestic policies aimed at the maintenance of full employment were considered to be conditions of the success of all three organizations, which in turn were considered to be essential to the maintenance of full employment.

At the opposite side of the picture, planning for relief also began early and, in spite of much fumbling and overlapping, was completed in time to establish an effective international organization whose operations far exceeded in scale and variety any international venture hitherto attempted. In the United States the less reputable political elements, which never shrank from deliberate misrepresentation, continually attacked the international character of the organization and in the end succeeded in bringing it prematurely to a close. In the Soviet Union an equally unscrupulous running fire of criticism, based on allegations of favoritism, was maintained against UNRRA until its end approached. In fact, however, the character of the organization was more acceptable than that of any other to the Eastern countries and it is conceivable, although it cannot be proved, that an enlarged UNRRA to cover reconstruction might have brought them within a European recovery program, and staved off the intensification of political hostility between East and West after 1947.

Two important decisions during the planning of relief greatly affected the course of reconstruction. First, the decision that UNRRA assistance should be given only to countries without any external assets to pay for imported supplies made Western Europe ineligible for international relief and hindered the reconstruction of those countries by depleting their assets to meet their needs for consumption goods, especially food. The other outstanding decision was concerned with the relation of relief to reconstruction. Some of the early planners for relief, like the planners for international finance and investment, began with a much broader conception of the scope of their plans than was later accepted. Like the planners for the long run, they were willing to extend, and some of them made concrete proposals for extending, their plans to cover much, if not all, reconstruction as well as relief. But, as with the planners for the long run, so with the planners for relief: the broader proposals were whittled down until they became almost as highly specialized on the shortest of the short runs as the proposals coming from the opposite end had become specialized on the longest of the long runs. The broader plans from each end, which could have been extended into part of the intermediate area that separated them widely, were frustrated by political, financial, and administrative difficulties.

The area that lay between relief measures and long-run measures never received sustained and comprehensive attention. Planning in it was piecemeal and often belated. Frequently events overtook preparations, and expectations were confounded by unforeseen contingencies. By the end of 1946 the neglect of this area in the planning had brought Europe close to economic disaster.

To this record of failure in planning for the period of reconstruction there is one important exception. Two broad types of preparation were needed, the first designed to make the best distribution of scarce goods and services that entered into international exchange in the period of relief and reconstruction, and the second to make provision for the supply from outside the stricken areas of new materials for reconstruction. The first of these needs was well met. The planners successfully applied the lessons learned from experiences in 1919 and the Second World War. By timely and unobtrusive advance planning, initiated mainly by civil servants, remarkable successes were achieved in providing machinery to prevent a competitive scramble for scarce materials and services and to allocate them by agreement to the areas and uses in which they would make the greatest contribution to recovery. Some of the wartime organizations were continued with an extended scope to cover the needs of relief and reconstruction. New organizations were established to serve reconstruction purposes. The combined Food Board was succeeded by the International Emergency Food Council. The Combined Shipping Adjustment Board was succeeded first by the United Maritime Authority and later by the United Maritime Consultative Council. The European Central Inland Transport Organization aided the restoration of transport on railways, roads, and inland waterways and helped to secure the fullest use of existing rolling stock. The European Coal Organization obtained agreement on coal allocations even in the worst period of fuel shortage. The Emergency Economic Committee for Europe obtained agreement on a variety of questions relating to food and feedstuffs, timber, electric power, and other matters. The orderly allocation of food, coal, and shipping according to need and not to the best filled purse and the most experienced purchasing agents, was of immeasurable aid to a continent short of these things.

But the second prerequisite of reconstruction was not met. Neither the organization nor the funds needed for reconstruction were provided on an adequate scale. Thus in the area of planning that lay between relief and long-term measures for improving the economic organization of the world large gaps were left which opened the way for the forces of economic disorder to break through, and on the one side cut off and isolate the long-term measures, rendering them inoperative and leaving them suspended without support on the flanks, while on the other side the provision for relief and rehabilitation was unduly strained and had to be concentrated largely on emergency palliatives.

The failures in planning for reconstruction were many-sided. First, planning to meet the special international economic difficulties of Britain was belated and when measures were hastily devised at the last moment they provided insufficient funds and attached impracticable conditions on their use. Second, planning for external assistance in the reconstruction of the liberated Allied countries was hopelessly inadequate. Third, planning for the reconstruction of ex-enemy countries was rejected outright for Germany and neglected for Japan. Fourth, planning for postwar international trade was confined to the problems of reducing trade barriers: it showed resourcefulness within these limits but for the most part it ignored the short-run problems of reconstructing postwar trade and adopted a somewhat negative approach even to the long-run problems, overestimating the effects of mere reduction of trade barriers and maintenance of full employment.

These errors of omission arose out of widely different causes. Some of them were due to insufficient understanding and foresight even among experts in the fields concerned. Others were due simply to lack of understanding in the higher circles of government, and others again to political fears which prevailed over economic judgments and caused higher circles to shrink from the struggle to obtain legislative sanction for the bold and costly measures which alone could meet the exceptional international needs of the day. Behind these fears lay the hostility of legislative groups sometimes misinformed, sometimes ready to sacrifice the needs of society for the hope of petty local advantage. Behind the legislatures lay public opinion, often believed by politicians to be more hostile to bold measures than it really was, always difficult to ascertain, and sometimes led astray by the demagoguery of groups with vested interests to serve.

The special difficulties of Britain, as we have seen, had been clearly demonstrated by Keynes in Washington in the middle of 1941, and it might have been expected that in the following four years a well-considered plan would have been prepared to deal with them. Yet when the war ended in Europe no Anglo-American discussions had been held on the subject, and when the war ended in the Far East discussions were only just about to begin. Keynes prepared his plan for an International Clearing Union partly as a substitute for the policy of discriminating bilateral bargaining which in his earlier pessimistic mood he had believed to be unavoidable. The first versions of the Keynes and White Plans would have helped in the solution of Britain's special problem, although they would not have provided a complete solution. In the negotiations on Article VII of the Lend-Lease agreement, Britain's special problem was in the minds of those who insisted that in the text strong emphasis should be placed on the necessity of maintaining full employment as well as reducing trade barriers. It was argued, and in 1942 the writer of these lines argued in Whitehall, that such a setting would greatly aid in the solution of Britain's special problem. I believe in retrospect that we carried this argument much too far and exaggerated the extent to which full employment, freer trade, and an international monetary fund would meet Britain's immediate postwar needs. In partial extenuation it might be said that in 1942 there appeared to be some hope of a more ambitious monetary and investment plan than that which was ultimately adopted. Even so, our attitude remained unjustifiably optimistic: we failed to grasp the nature and magnitude of the difficulties that stood in the way of an early restoration of world multilateral trade. In Washington, also, though not among Americans in London, very few officials and, as far as I can ascertain, no congressmen understood the significance and purposes of the sterling area, and some officials and many congressmen were influenced by anti-British sentiment.

Whitehall, for once, was seriously divided. A sharp difference of opinion arose over the question what kind of approach should be made to Washington on the subject. It was agreed that Britain's honorable economic scars would best be healed by grants from the United States, but one group held that in practice it was useless to ask for a grant and that it would be more realistic to seek a loan on very favorable terms. The other group was strongly aroused over the moral aspects of Britain's war-created troubles but some of them failed to distinguish between politically practicable and politically impracticable measures.

The hasty attempt to fill this gap by the loan to Britain in 1945 was a failure. The loan was not wasted, as irresponsible critics have contended, but it was inadequate in amount and, through an astonishingly inept provision for sterling convertibility by the clock, was soon drained off through other gaps in the postwar planning, which had been left by the failure of the planners to provide resources for the reconstruction of liberated areas, and the failure of most of the South American countries to keep their finances in order.

The continental European Allies whose territories had been overrun were left in a different position from that of Britain. Most of them suffered great psychological damage, but some of them suffered less material damage than Britain did: their overseas assets were impounded in London and Washington and restored when free and legitimate governments were reestablished at home. But with the rejection of the earlier monetary proposals and the limitation of UNRRA aid to liberated countries without external assets, they were left at the end of the war without international aid either for relief or for reconstruction. At the same time their domestic production of food and raw materials had fallen and their external assets were rapidly drained by the urgent need of imports, the greater part of which went to meet indispensable consumption needs.

Until at least far on in 1943, the principle seems to have been widely accepted among Washington officials that the immediate consumption needs of Allied countries damaged in the war should be met by grants and that loans should be made only for reconstruction and long-term development. In this way it was hoped that there would be no repetition of the widespread international friction of the interwar period arising out of demands for the repayment of wartime and early postwar loans which could not easily be repaid without considerable changes in the structure of trade and greater willingness in the creditor countries to receive imports. It was recognized that if loans at interest were to be repaid after the war they must be confined to manageable amounts and to uses that would increase the capacity to produce and to export. But in the later stages of the war this principle was quietly and informally abandoned and the scope of grants in the plans was narrowed to the UNRRA contribution. This was a reflection of the characteristically narrow outlook of congressmen and businessmen as the war drew to a close and the hope of "business as usual" returned.

Reconstruction in Allied countries could not be separated in practice from reconstruction in ex-enemy countries. The chief ex-enemy country in Europe and the chief ex-enemy country in Asia had each been the pivot of a network of trading and credit relations which closely affected the countries around them and formed an important part of the world system of multilateral trade. The needs of economic reconstruction could not be circumscribed by national boundaries or by distinctions between those who were Allies and those who were enemies. This was recognized in the earlier planning on Germany by civil servants, but higher circles intervened and a negative policy, originating in the United States and designed to cripple German industries, for a time displaced all policies for reconstruction. It was only after much effort and many disastrous experiences that a constructive policy began slowly to develop. An intrinsically unsound reparation policy, based on the desire to destroy or reduce German and Japanese industries, made matters worse. The failure of ministers in London and their nearest counterparts in Washington to give sustained attention to the subject while there was still time allowed the initiative to pass to the Soviet Union, which wanted reparation first and perhaps deindustrialization second, and to Mr. Morgenthau, who wanted deindustrialization first and reparation second, merely as an instrument of deindustrialization.

The planning for the Far East, though less influenced by fear and animosity, was even more inadequate than the planning for Europe. Immense resources were wasted in an uncritical and clumsily devised effort to raise China out of the chaos into which she had fallen. Washington put its money on the wrong horse. The British appraisal of the position of China was far closer to realities than that of the United States, but was unheeded by Washington, either in the highest circles or elsewhere. The attitude of the United States toward Japan was as naïve at first as its attitude toward China, but in an opposite way. The Japanese Empire was to be dismembered. Formosa was to be returned to China after more than half a century during which her remarkable economic development had been closely intertwined with that of Japan to the benefit of both countries. Korea, although destitute of the makings of political stability, was to become an independent nation. There seems to have been strangely little argument over these decisions, and no attempt to examine the far-reaching economic effects which might be expected to follow these sudden and drastic political changes.

Thus the early promise of postwar planning was not fulfilled. The initial provision for relief through UNRRA was impressive and saved Eastern and Southern Europe from starvation and collapse. The preparations for the long run, so far as they went, were well-conceived and in a reconstructed world would have prevented a recurrence of the economic disasters of the interwar period. But the world had first to be reconstructed, and it was on the means of reconstruction that the planning fell short. By the early part of 1947, recovery had been brought to a standstill and the political as well as the economic order in Europe was in danger.[1] Economic danger signals were being hoisted all over Western Europe as they had already been hoisted over Germany. The new specialized international agencies, creations of long-run planning, were looking on helplessly while cries were heard on all hands for international help of a kind and on a scale which they were powerless to provide. The large and complex structure of the United Nations, with its councils, commissions, sub-commissions, committees, and secretariat—which on paper seemed to cover almost

[1] After the present study was in proof the following passage appeared in an article in the *Contemporary Review* (Sept., 1952, p. 129) by M. Phillips Price, M.P., a distinguished British writer of long experience of Russian and eastern European affairs:

"There was a time directly after the war when Russian foreign policy seemed ready to cooperate with Western Europe at least to the extent of not wanting to force Communism on their zone of Germany. . . . There was certainly a possibility at this time that the Western Slav States like Poland and Czechoslovakia would be left alone to form non-Communist but Russian-friendly governments, and that 'united fronts' would be allowed to function. Russia's stock stood high at this time among some non-Communist parties in Eastern Europe. If that development had been allowed to go on, the prospects of creating a unified Germany on good terms both with the East and the West would have been considerable. But the dream faded. The Soviet elections in February, 1946, removed most non-Communist elements from the Soviet Parliament. The non-Communist generals of the Red Army were retired during the course of 1946, and the decks were cleared for an all-out Communist drive in foreign policy. Even so, the policy did not become clear till 1947, when in the spring of that year Russia rejected the Marshall Aid plan and compelled her Western Slav neighbours to do the same. The deepening economic crisis in Europe, the beginning of the inflationary wave, and the petering out of the American loan before Marshall Aid was offered, made it appear that 'Western Capitalism' was entering upon a period of rapid decline, which would justify the orthodox Communist doctrine of the expansion of World Revolution and the advance of Russia's frontiers and those of her satellites westwards. All that has happened since then over Germany springs from this development of Russian policy early in 1947."

Insofar as this point of view is accepted, the central thesis of the present study goes far to interpret the course of political as well as economic events in the postwar period and to uncover one of the main reasons for the turn for the worse which international relations have taken in the last five or six years. I would be inclined to link the effects of the economic errors which led up to the crisis of 1947 with the effects of the hasty demobilization of the Western armies and the careless talk of some members of the American delegation at Yalta on the probability of early withdrawals of American troops from the occupation forces in Germany.

every economic issue—were floundering without clear sense of direction. The postwar plans framed during the war had been tried. They had great accomplishments to their credit, notably in the relief of Eastern, Central and Southern Europe and the orderly distribution of scarce materials and services. But on the broader issues they had been found wanting.

Then followed a heroic period in international economic history, which lies beyond the scope of the present study. In it the Marshall Plan stands out as the boldest, the most imaginative, and the most successful constructive international measure ever executed. Many failures were belatedly redeemed by the sweep and generosity with which it was applied to Western and Southern Europe after 1947. For the first time the main energies of the governments were given to the task of dealing with immediate reconstruction on a scale related to its magnitude. The new policy placed first things first, subordinated long-run rules of the game to short-run exigencies, and not only returned to the conception, held in Washington up to 1944, that consumer goods should be supplied through grants and not loans but went even further and supplied large quantities of producer goods through grants. Moreover, to the immense credit of the State Department and the Economic Cooperation Administration and in spite of the efforts of recalcitrant congressmen, this large-scale assistance was given without improper interference in the internal affairs of the receiving countries.

The effects were remarkable. Stocks of essential commodities were replenished, "bottlenecks" were cleared, undernourishment was for the most part eliminated, full employment was achieved and maintained in most areas, and hope was renewed among those who had borne the burden and heat of the day during six years of war. The "battle of production" was largely won in Western and Southern Europe in 1948, 1949, and the first half of 1950. Not all difficulties of production were removed, but the rise of production exceeded all expectations and proved that the vigor and capacity of the peoples of Europe and especially of the people of Britain, with their capable Labor Government, were undiminished. At the same time Western Europe, especially Britain, the Scandinavian countries, and the Netherlands, continued to carry through quiet and peaceful internal revolutions, removing many of the undue inequalities and insecurities of the past, proving that totalitarian communism is not only unnecessary but also far less effective than democratic socialism as an instrument for banishing wretchedness and want from modern society, and demonstrating that the welfare state and democracy are not only compatible with, but in the long run are increasingly necessary the one to the other.

Simultaneously, the gradual elimination of the influence of Mr. Morgenthau and Mr. Pauley from policy toward Germany, the modification or removal of many restrictions on industry, the belated removal of straitjackets on exports, the belated reform of the currency, the fusion of the Western Zones (which ought to have been fused from the beginning) and the later application to them of the European Recovery Program, set that part of Germany which had escaped totalitarian shackles on the road to reconstruction and to reunion with the European community. New errors, which lie beyond the scope of this book, have been committed in the process and it would be unwise to assume complacently that Germany has yet shaken off its craving for authority and its insensitiveness to the horrifying misdeeds of its recent past. Political Washington, with characteristic impulsiveness, has been pushed by an irresponsible Congress from one extreme to another, and with characteristic forgetfulness has criticized the Allies who vainly protested against the one for unwillingness to fly suddenly to the other. But much progress has been made.

If, as is sometimes said, the "battle of production" in Europe has been won, the battle of exchange and distribution still hangs in the balance. The error of underestimating the dislocation of the world multilateral trading system, and seeking the reconstruction of trade only through the reduction of trade barriers and the maintenance of full employment, has not yet been fully repaired and will certainly take much longer to repair. To restore the processes of exchange is far more difficult than to rebuild the means of production. Even if this difficulty had been clearly foreseen in detail it is unlikely that a prompt remedy for it could have been devised. It goes deeply into the entire structure of international trade, credit, and economic development, and cannot be resolved by purely financial measures or by the "automatic operation of the price system." If a solution is to be found in a reasonable time a new concerted effort of international planning will be necessary to ensure consistent policies of economic specialization and economic development.

But the unsettled political state of the world will inevitably delay the establishment of a new and viable world multilateral trading system. Even if the armaments race had not been intensified since the middle of 1950, the unstable political conditions in Asia would have hindered the restoration of world trade. And even if serious political friction had ended with the war, the reconstruction of a world-wide trading system permitting free and general convertibility of currencies would have taken much time. It depends as much on "real" as on monetary developments, and no fiscal and financial policies alone can attain it or hold it after it has been attained. It depends as much on the stages and conditions of economic development reached in different areas as on the differences between the natural resources in them. But the diversion of equipment, labor, and materials from production of peacetime goods to production of the means of war, though at first it brought sterling and the dollar nearer to adjustment, will intensify old disharmonies and create new ones in the longer run. The resumption of the rise in the prices of raw materials in comparison with those of manufactured goods, which is partly a reflection of the process of drawing materials away from peacetime uses to military uses, will damage particularly those manufacturing countries in Western Europe which import much of their food and industrial raw materials. The development of the export industries on which Britain in particular, and after her the other Western European countries, must depend for the reestablishment of Europe in a reasonably stable pattern of world trade will be hindered.

Consequently, we would do well to refrain from premature optimism, to observe patience and restraint in international economic matters, and, without sacrificing anything essential to the defense of the Western World, to shape armaments policy in such a way as to avoid unnecessary prejudice to the aim of restoring world trade.[2] And, second, without sacrificing the long-run aim of freer, nondiscriminating trade, we would do well to follow a flexible and not a doctrinaire commercial policy. This implies, not that there should be no rules of the game, as a few British writers seem to imply, but that

[2] The course of stockpiling in the United States had not always conformed to this principle.

exceptions to long-run principles must continue to be made for some time to come.

Since the middle of 1950 the resumption of preparations against the danger of war has raised once more the fundamental issues concerning the comparative weight to be given to the short run and the long run which this study has examined for the war and early postwar years. On the whole it increases the weight which must be given to short-run principles and will force a postponement of the application of long-run principles. The International Monetary Fund, with its recent statement regarding the abandonment of discriminations, and the International Chamber of Commerce, with its doctrinaire approach to the present crisis, wish to continue in a path along which we can go little further until present political difficulties have lessened. As I write these closing lines, there are signs in some quarters of a disposition to return to the economic errors of the peace and to harp unduly on the long run before we have nearly surmounted the difficulties of the short run and, in fact, at a time when these difficulties are more likely to be intensified than to be relieved in the near future.

Before concluding this study something should be said of the more general underlying influences which affected the shape of postwar plans, both their merits and their defects.

First, the question arises how far the plans were a reflection of the state of economic knowledge of the day. It must be admitted at once that in the last resort, the judgment of those at high levels, based often on what was believed to be political expediency, determined the course which was followed. The recommendations of the economists in government were not always followed. Thus the economists were not responsible either for all the economic errors or even for all the economic merits of the peace. They had to work within the limitations of the existing organization of government and even when, as in Britain, that organization was adapted to meet the needs of the times, the preparation and still more the adoption of plans were sometimes delayed unduly. Notwithstanding these limitations, the economist played an immensely greater role in the affairs of state than ever before. An impressive array of economic talent was brought into the service of government in London, Ottawa, and Washington, and the mark of the economist is plainly to be seen in much of the planning and in the international institutions that were proposed and some of which were created to give effect to it. Moreover, the existence of a common stream of Western economic tradition, common economic standards to which appeal might be made, and common experience derived from prewar international mingling in professional and private economic activities, aided official negotiations and still more the informal discussions that preceded them.

The record which has been analyzed in the preceding chapters seems to justify one clear-cut conclusion: the economists were more successful in planning for the long run than in planning for the short run. The Fund, the Bank, and the proposed International Trade Organization were in the main the creation of economists. They reflect, also, the advantages derived from the common background of economic thought in the Western World, particularly in the English-speaking world. But there is much less evidence of outstanding initiative or of important contributions by economists in planning during the war for immediate postwar reconstruction. For the most part, those who carried out such limited and insufficient work as was done in this field were officials who had been previously occupied mainly with wartime supply matters. It may be argued that the economists were not charged to work in this field and that they cannot, therefore, be held responsible for the neglect of it in the planning. But this is hardly a satisfactory explanation, for if the economists had strongly felt the need of greater attention to reconstruction questions they would have striven hard to make their views known through various channels. So far, I have been unable to find much evidence that they did so.

It was not only in the short-term field of reconstruction that weaknesses in present economic fashions revealed themselves: in the long- as well as the short-run view of international trade, postwar issues were oversimplified and postwar plans one-sided, as a direct consequence of the prevailing trends of economic thought and particularly of the insufficiently critical use of the "national income approach" to economics, or, more broadly—to use contemporary jargon—"aggregative economics" or "macro-economics." These approaches to economics abstract drastically from the substance of economic geography. They obscure the variety of human needs and of human wants and of the kinds of goods and methods of production used to satisfy them. As they are concerned primarily with domestic economic accounting, so, naturally, they bypass the complicated structure of the network of world trade and nowhere call for unified appraisal of international economic conditions. The habit of dealing in monetary units, and in percentages derived from them, with large aggregate valuations of heterogeneous data covering widely different goods and services and economic activities, though it has led to improvements in national accounting, is full of dangers where inter-regional and international questions are concerned. Two familiar examples will serve as illustrations of these dangers. The first is the argument widely used in the past that because the money value of American imports and exports of goods constitute only a small percentage of the American national income, the United States was nearly self-sufficient and the loss of its foreign trade would not be a great catastrophe. A second and more recent example is the argument of certain American and British economists that the loss of British foreign investments during the war was not important because the income from them was only a small proportion of the national income. These arguments, which have been used chiefly as instruments of doctrinal controversy, merely obscure the real issues and lead into blind alleys. In such settings the concept of national income is out of place—a hypothetical measure of little significance.

The need of organized international economic knowledge and skill has steadily increased since the First World War broke out. The secretariats of the League of Nations and the International Labor Office laid much of the foundation during the interwar period, and the postwar planners went further during the Second World War. The universities have made important contributions, but it could hardly be expected that they would keep pace with the rapid increase in demand for appropriately trained workers, especially since so many of their best teachers were drawn away into government service during emergencies. Apart from quantitative shortages, there is room for changes in the type of training of those who will enter the international field: present fashions in the study of economics, geography, and history are not suited in all respects to the needs of the international worker. Today most of the academic economists are far more at home in the study of value theory, of the trade cycle, of national income analysis, of statistics and econometrics, than they are in the study of history and geography and the organization, structure and workings of agriculture, mining, manufacturing, industry, transport, and trade. Although these two groups of study impinge on one another, the study of the first group is frequently carried on with only a superficial knowledge of the second. A shortage of staff with a good knowledge of the second group contributed to the delay in the recognition of the needs of reconstruction. My suggestion would be that part of the time given to the exceptionally time-consuming studies of mathematics and statistics would be better given to filling these gaps.[3] On the other hand, the economic geographers and some of the economic historians seem to have developed the opposite vices and have been unduly concerned with classification and description and too frugal in analysis and conceptual schemes. General historians have also at times shown insufficient discrimination in attempting to interpret international events that involve difficult geographical and economic questions.[4] However, the war demonstrated once again the error of assuming that an academic apprenticeship in economics is always an indispensable part of the equipment of a civil servant who is called on to deal with international economic affairs. There were outstanding exceptions in several countries both in the temporary and the permanent civil service. Diversity rather than uniformity of training will best meet the newer needs of governments and international organizations: it should be a diversity that leaves no important gap unfilled in the national and international civil services as a whole.

However well qualified the national and international civil services may be, the organization and allocation of the work on international economic matters raise great difficulties both in national governments and in international organizations. The dangers as well as the advantages of specialization stand out clearly in the present study. During the war, specialization aggravated the artificial separation (which originated partly in political expediency) between planning for relief, planning for reconstruction, and planning for the long run.

[3] This is not to suggest a uniform training for all comers. Doubtless it would be profitable for those who have a special bent for mathematics and statistics to continue to give a large part of their time to these studies, even to the neglect of some of the fields whose importance I have stressed. But this necessitates an opposite emphasis in the training of others who probably constitute a large majority.

[4] Sometimes underestimating but sometimes overestimating economics and geography. However, there are marked advances among modern historians: for instance, Philip Mosely, trained as a general historian, showed excellent economic understanding in the discussions connected with the work of the European advisory commission.

Jurisdictional difficulties sometimes hindered planning and stood in the way of a coordinated advance along the whole front. They were affected by the form as well as the size of the government. In London the existence of the cabinet secretariat and the cabinet committee under the Lord President of the Council diminished these difficulties. In Washington attempts were made under a wholly different structure of government to coordinate the work on postwar matters. The Executive Committee on Economic Foreign Policy achieved more than the other committees that were tried and discarded, but its recommendations on Germany were ignored and its support of a simpler form of reducing tariffs was nullified by the Assistant Secretaries, although in retrospect its judgment must be pronounced correct in both cases.

The structure of international organizations which resulted from the postwar planning likewise created many difficulties of coordination and allocation of functions. It was, however, the outcome of political decisions rather than of a careful appraisal of the respective merits of specialized agencies on the one hand and a single all-embracing international organization on the other. The decision not to revive the League of Nations, nor to establish a successor to it until late in the war, played a large part in the establishment of a network of specialized agencies the relation of whose work to that of the United Nations had subsequently to be determined: it was the only alternative to a standstill along the whole front of postwar international economic organization until near the end of the war.

The growth of population and specialization in economic life and the extension of the economic functions of government are making greater demands on organizing skill than ever before in history. Students of population have usually been too much concerned with the alleged inadequacy of natural resources to meet the needs of increasing populations and too little concerned—it might almost be said wholly unconcerned—with the increased difficulties of social organization which increased numbers create. Today the advocates of political unification of smaller nations would add to these difficulties by superimposing on the natural increase in the size of nations still greater increases through fusion of territories. The contrast which this study has shown between government organization in Washington and that in London and Ottawa will illustrate these difficulties and serve as a warning. Nor are internal conditions in the Soviet Union reassuring as to the prospects of organizing large, diverse continental societies in single states.

The problems of large-scale organizations in government, as in industry, are particularly formidable in the United States. The size of the structure of government and the nature of the Constitution make it even more difficult in Washington than in the other Western capitals to plan evenly over the entire field of international economic matters. Although the machinery for consultation among departments, agencies, and divisions has been extended since the war, it remains cumbersome. The loss of time and the expenditure of energy in the process of reaching agreement within the government is still excessive and continues to deter a number of able persons from entering or continuing in government service. Internal reorganizations since the war have given a greater appearance of "coordination," but the number of persons who have to be consulted before a decision is reached, and the time taken to reach a decision, have increased rather than diminished. No improvement is possible until the number of persons who take part in reaching each decision is reduced. But much depends on the way in which this is done: reduction may lead to a deterioration in the quality of decisions unless consultation is limited mainly to those who have the greatest direct knowledge and experience of the question on which a decision is sought, regardless of their ranking in the bureaucratic hierarchy. Some exceptions, arising out of the relation between rank and responsibility, would have to be made to this principle, but those who are included because of their rank rather than their direct knowledge and experience might well be in a minority. The opposite principle is more often followed, and officials experienced in the subject are frequently left in a small minority. Some of the trouble, which is more often found in Washington than in Whitehall, is a result, or perhaps even a cause, of the chronic tendency to overstaffing in government agencies in Washington. Many officials have their fingers in too many pies.[5] The result of the change here suggested would be that each official would take part in fewer consultations than before but would have more time to con-

[5] In 1943 in a conversation with a leading British Treasury official, I commented on the great burden of work resting on a small number of Treasury officials during the war. He agreed but added, "Still, I would rather be understaffed than overstaffed."

centrate on the subject on which he was competent to form a judgment.

But beyond the defects of organization within the government departments lay much graver and more far-reaching defects in the organization of the government of the United States as a whole. Individual civil servants and statesmen in Washington can act only within a political and social framework the main lines of which were established long ago in a very different world from the present, and which, whether or not it was initially well designed for the conditions of the day, has never been adapted to subsequent changes at home and abroad. However well meaning the intentions, however pure the motives, however accurate the judgment of those who directed the postwar planning in Washington might have been, the plans could have been executed only through a cumbersome political structure which had been devised in a simpler age for a leisurely society seeking to live mainly within itself and avoid "entanglement" with the world outside, and which had gathered later an accretion of vested interests and doctrinal symbols resistent to fundamental change and sheltered under the sanctity of tradition.

The political structure of the United States is less adapted to the prompt and efficient conduct of external affairs than that of any other important country with a democratic form of government. The accredited representatives of the government are placed in an unenviable position both at home and abroad. At home they are individually subjected to irresponsible attacks by the representatives of the legislature; attacks from which the doctrine of collective responsibility of the cabinet protects their counterparts in other leading democratic countries. Abroad they are unable to speak for their government with anything like the degree of authority that lies behind the utterances of the representatives of other democratic countries; their ability to carry out their undertakings is frequently in doubt. The system of government places a premium on obstruction and weights the scales on the side of inertia and reaction. When bold, constructive action is needed, the fate of an administration's proposals is always in doubt: there is no substitute or counterpart to the powerful weapon of a threatened dissolution of the legislature, which under the cabinet system a government can hold over obstructive and recalcitrant groups among the elected representatives. Moreover, the effects of such a system on those who work under it are always discouraging and often demoralizing, deterring many of the ablest individuals in the country from careers in politics or in the government service, and leaving the political field open for those who, however skilled they may be in the art of winning votes and building political machines, have neither the experience nor the understanding nor the integrity which are indispensable to the worthy conduct of public affairs or to the formation of sound judgments concerning the complex international problems on the solution of which world peace and with it the earthly destiny of millions of human beings depend. And to the outside world the system of government in the United States advertises and even exaggerates the divisions and differences within the country, gives to the utterances of the baser types of congressman a weight and significance which they would not have under a cabinet system, and leaves the wondering onlooker in other countries puzzled, bewildered, and often aghast. For a time the emergencies of war subdued the voices of isolationists and reactionaries, and after the war, when they were heard again in less muffled tones, the statesmanlike attitude of Senator Vandenberg restrained their inclination again to destroy the hope of international cooperation, as they had destroyed it in 1919. The world owes an immense debt to the men who, by unsparing work, by their powers of organization and persuasion, and above all by faith in their cause, formulated and carried through the European Recovery Program. But the risks were great, and there is no assurance that in equally difficult situations in the future, men of the same happy combination of qualities will arise to overcome the unnecessary obstacles which a defective system of government places in the way of constructive action.

During the second half of the twentieth century the fate of the world for many generations may well depend on the part played by the United States in international affairs. In these circumstances what political reform could be more important than that which aims at adapting the political structure of the country to the more efficient conduct of international affairs? Those who belittle the chances of fundamental change are taking refuge in a passive fatalism and a counsel of despair. If man can make political constitutions he can also alter them when alteration is imperatively needed to meet changed world conditions and perhaps even to ensure survival. What superstitious sanctity is it that stands in the way of repairing the errors of the constitution-makers who uncritically took over Montesquieu's blundering misinterpretation of the British Constitution in his day? North America itself contains a remarkable demonstration, in Canada, of the practicability of applying the cabinet system to a far-flung country inhabited by peoples of diverse origin and culture. Over nearly all the democratic world outside the United States the cabinet system has established itself in some form or other, and its efficiency has been fully tested and proved under diverse conditions. In its absence democratic government lapses into a confused scramble between factions, without continuity of policy, without dignity or decorum, swayed by unholy combinations of vested interests, a house divided against itself, not by simple party divisions but by a paralyzing conflict between executive and legislative which breeds continuous antagonism within the government of the country and blocks all attempts to achieve national unity in times of crisis.

The political system of the United States is that of an elective monarchy in which the monarch has extensive powers which are viewed with perpetual suspicion and jealousy by the legislature. In Western Europe and the British Commonwealth, under constitutional monarchies the hereditary monarchs have been left without power and, through the cabinet system and the power of dissolution, the executive and the legislature have been successfully integrated.[6] A reverse Point Four program seems to be needed, under which the country that has become the world's greatest industrial innovator at the present time, and is advising a number of other countries on the adoption of new industrial machinery, would itself be ready to introduce new political machinery of demonstrated superiority, and to displace the old, which hinders the efficient conduct of public affairs abroad as well as at home.

But the improvement of the machinery of government, although important and indispensable, would be only a partial remedy for the conditions that led to the economic errors of the peace. Great Britain, with a cabinet system of government, with a genius for the development of democratic institutions that has sowed the seeds of democracy in North America, in parts of Asia, and in Australia, and is now

[6] The shortcomings of French government, so far as they arise out of structural defects, are plainly due to a failure to adopt the practice of immediate dissolution when the cabinet is defeated on an important issue. Hence cabinet succeeds cabinet with infrequent general elections, and an irresponsibility is engendered in the legislature similar to that shown in the U.S. Congress.

sowing them in parts of Africa, nevertheless shares responsibility for some of the economic errors of the peace. The course of planning for postwar Germany shows that the cabinet system is not a panacea for all political ills. It did indeed prevent the gross errors committed in Washington, for no one in the British government had the powers of the President of the United States to approve a statement of policy on Germany by the head of the Treasury and without the consequence or even the knowledge of the Secretary of State. The Prime Minister's irregular action at Quebec was promptly challenged by the Foreign Office. Again, the Chancellor of the Exchequer could not have flown to Washington and urged on Secretary Hull the adoption of an individual policy of his own on postwar Germany or indeed any other important subject. But if the form of government in Britain saved her from the worst blunders of Washington on postwar policy toward Germany, it did not save the British government from sins of omission which in international affairs may at times be as important as sins of commission. As we have seen, the British cabinet, although it had command of far better resources for the making of plans and policies on postwar Germany, drifted inactively and allowed the initiative to pass to Mr. Morgenthau and his active sympathizers in Washington, and to MM. Stalin and Molotov in Moscow, remaining thereafter on the defensive, and able to mitigate only in detail some of the worst features of the plans of Washington and Moscow. It was a sad failure in cabinet leadership.

It does not follow, of course, that improved organization would have done nothing to remedy such failures. Since the outbreak of the First World War the functions of government have greatly increased; each member of the cabinet has been overworked, and it has been impracticable for him to master all the issues arising outside his own department on which the cabinet has had to reach decisions. The cabinet system is not a static institution and there is need of study and experiment to adapt it to the greater demands made upon it.

But the accomplishments and failures in the preparation and execution of plans for the postwar period cannot be explained wholly by taking account of defective organization as well as of faulty economic judgment. Some of the difficulties which the planners faced were not the outcome of mere lack of economic knowledge and insight nor of a mere outmoded structure of government. The acceleration of postwar planning in some fields, its retardation in others, and the uneven development in the different fields both of planning and execution, which led to serious crises in the postwar period, can be traced in part to the characters of individuals who, in the same social setting, were moved by different sentiments, responded to different stimuli, acted from different motives, and sought different ends from those which would have guided other individuals who, but for historical accidents or casual events, might have been in their places. The unique character of the individual goes far to determine the destinies of nations and decide the fate of the world.

To say this is not to revert to a "great man" theory of history. As we have seen, some of the individuals who markedly influenced postwar planning and the execution of plans were far from being great men, and even great men influence history by their smallness as well as by their greatness. Moreover, the opportunities of great men or potentially great men to reach leading positions vary with the nature of the society in which they are placed: recently, for example, mediocrity has seemed to have advantages over greatness in the politics of the United States, just at a time when greatness was most needed. It is the uniqueness of the individual and not necessarily the greatness of particular individuals which, notwithstanding social heritage and material limitations, goes far to determine the course of history in the end. And that, I suggest, will never be exhaustively laid bare, and may not even be penetrated far, by scientific analysis.

Thus morality takes its place along with knowledge and organization as a fundamental determinant of the course of international relations. But its ramifications are extraordinarily complex and cannot be comprehended in simple formulas. Indeed, in international affairs we can rarely make a complete separation between the sheep and the goats. It would even be an oversimplification to state that there are both sheep and goats within each nation and that the category in which the nation as a whole belongs is determined by the preponderance of the one or the other. The fact is that there are characteristics of the sheep and characteristics of the goat—as the shepherd saw them—not only within each nation but also within each individual.[7] Moreover, each individual, however consistently he may have

[7] Doubtless the analogy is unduly flattering to the sheep, unduly disparaging to the goat and uncomplimentary to the human being, but I am provisionally accepting the comparative valuations of the Eastern shepherd!

displayed the characteristics of the sheep in the past, remains subject to the temptation to lapse into the behavior of the goat in the future.

But the individual, so far as he can be judged at all by his fellow men, must be judged according to his lights: morality cannot be separated completely from knowledge and understanding. The present regime in China, for example, seems deplorably ignorant of the outside world. It has misjudged the motives and strength of the West, shown undue subservience to the Soviet Union, and flouted the verdict of the United Nations. But it has also embodied greater personal integrity, public spirit and devotion to duty according to its lights than any Chinese administration has shown for many generations. International conduct cannot, any more than individual conduct in ordinary, everyday life, be represented in black and white. The history of international affairs is full of such paradoxes, and one of the tasks of statesmanship is to take account of them in the formation of foreign policies. The failure to do so in Washington, under pressure from a legislature which throughout history has usually been ready to subordinate the world interests of the nation to opportunities of petty local advantage, has turned the historic friendship of the Chinese for the American people overnight into hostility.

The postwar international economic planning and its application have not produced such spectacular cases as this, but moral conflicts within the individual as well as the community have played an important part in the outcome. As we have seen, the economic errors of the peace were not all due to insufficient knowledge, lack of foresight, and faulty judgment. The planning for postwar Germany took the wrong turn when the desire for revenge and reprisal dominated men who, in different directions, were constructive and generous in their outlook. In other fields of postwar planning there were times when the courage, the integrity, and the persistence of a small number of persons who did not fear unpopularity were more responsible than anything else for constructive achievements, and there were times when excessive caution and fear of disapproval held back those who would otherwise have introduced constructive measures or given bold advice which alone could have met the needs of the time. It is rarely possible to give a documented account of these occasions, but no one who has worked in international affairs will deny their reality and importance in determining the course of events.

Thus improved organization and the use of scientific knowledge in international affairs will not in themselves provide adequate remedies for existing international ills. Bad organization can obstruct achievement, but good organization cannot ensure it: the success even of good organization depends in the end on the characters of the individuals who work within it. Nor can the advance of scientific knowledge and the application of scientific methods to human affairs in themselves create international harmony: on the contrary they enlarge the possibilities of evil as well as the possibilities of good. Ultimately, the course of international affairs, whether political or economic, is determined not only by man's knowledge but also by his moral nature and development. The age-long preoccupation of the human race with morality and religion, notwithstanding all the difficulties and complexities that beset it, has not been misplaced and cannot be replaced successfully by the modern preoccupation with science and material welfare.[8] Man will always be haunted by the presence of moral conflict permeating all human affairs: the conflict is no illusion and cannot be explained away as a result simply of ignorance or of abnormal mental or emotional processes. Advances in knowledge and improvements in organization will mitigate it at those points where it is aggravated by misunderstanding or by defective institutions of government. But the clash of incompatible desires, the conflict of unruly ambitions, the lust for personal gain, and the pursuit of irreconcilable ends will remain as ever-present dangers deeply imbedded in the nature of man and manifesting themselves within each individual as well as in the relations between individuals and between nations. This is not a ground for despair: although man can never secure himself completely against lapses, he is capable of moral development. In the last resort it is on this and not on the advance of scientific knowledge and the improvement of administrative organization that the growth of international justice and the hope of international peace depend.

The constructive achievements of postwar planning had their origin in the spirit of idealism which animated a few individuals who, during the strains and stresses of the war and in the turmoil that followed it, kept unfailingly before them the vision of a better world order to come and strove unsparingly to lay its economic foundations in the im-

[8] To avoid misunderstanding it should be added that this statement is not intended to imply either that morality can be submerged into, or that it can be wholly separated from, religion.

mediate future. Lord Keynes was in some respects their spiritual leader and epitomizes many of their characteristics. They did not work in a spirit of academic detachment but with a sense of mission. They did not win high material rewards and peaceful lives for themselves, nor did they receive general recognition from others. Some of the most distinguished and irreplaceable among them died prematurely through overwork before the fruits of their labors could be gathered. Much of what they did needs to be supplemented and some of it modified in the future. But notwithstanding mistakes, omissions, and political obstacles, their work has led to impressive gains in international economic cooperation. The goal which they sought may take many generations to reach: success in reaching it depends not merely on knowledge and skill but also on the maintenance of that spirit of high endeavor which initiated the original plans in the dark years of war and was reborn in the invention of the European Recovery Program.

Amid the postwar deterioration of international relations and the alarming growth of political reaction in Washington we would do well to recall that the outstanding postwar planners were men of generous outlook and lively imagination who, above all, strove to create truly cooperative international undertakings and not to establish dominion over the world by a Western any more than by an Eastern Great Power or group of Great Powers. The methods used by the Soviet Union to keep its satellites in line, and the efforts of many congressmen in Washington to withhold famine aid from India for political reasons would have been equally abhorrent to them and contrary to their aim of enlarging the sphere of concerted international action, not by the dictation of the few but by the cooperation of the many. In future movements toward a greater degree of unification or common action throughout the world this fundamental clash will continue—between those who would achieve their aim through the domination exercised by a single large state or small group of large states, and those who retain faith in the possibilities of voluntary cooperation among all states, both great and small. Its outcome will determine whether such movements will bring a balance of good or evil to mankind.

Index

GPSR Authorized Representative: Easy Access System Europe - Mustamäe tee 50, 10621 Tallinn, Estonia, gpsr.requests@easproject.com

www.ingramcontent.com/pod-product-compliance
Ingram Content Group UK Ltd.
Pitfield, Milton Keynes, MK11 3LW, UK
UKHW010159180926
475586UK00003B/90
* 9 7 8 0 6 9 1 6 2 7 2 0 5 *